Zahir Bhalloo

Islamic Law in Early Modern Iran

Studies in the History and Culture of the Middle East

Edited by
Stefan Heidemann, Gottfried Hagen, Andreas Kaplony,
Rudi Matthee, and Kristina L. Richardson

Volume 48

Zahir Bhalloo

Islamic Law in Early Modern Iran

Sharīʿa Court Practice in the Sixteenth to Twentieth Centuries

DE GRUYTER

ISBN 978-3-11-123658-2
e-ISBN (PDF) 978-3-11-123973-6
e-ISBN (EPUB) 978-3-11-123993-4
ISSN 2198-0853
DOI https://doi.org/10.1515/9783111239736

Library of Congress Control Number: 2023938345

Bibliographic information published by the Deutsche Nationalbibliothek
The Deutsche Nationalbibliothek lists this publication in the Deutsche Nationalbibliografie; detailed bibliographic data are available on the Internet at http://dnb.dnb.de.

Typesetting: Integra Software Services Pvt. Ltd.
Printing and binding: CPI books GmbH, Leck

MIX
Papier | Fördert gute Waldnutzung
FSC
www.fsc.org
FSC® C083411

www.degruyter.com

Acknowledgements

This study has its origins in my doctoral thesis written far too hastily a decade ago in the Ferdowsi Library at Wadham College, Oxford after I returned from two unforgettable years in Tehran and Damascus. I had the good fortune to discuss my findings at the time with Nobuaki Kondo, Christoph Werner, Hossein Modarressi Tabatabai, and Paolo Sartori who invited me on several occasions to present my work in Vienna. Edmund Herzig played an important role in gently directing the thesis, funded by a Clarendon scholarship and the Soudavar Memorial Foundation, towards its completion. John Gurney introduced me to several people who were pivotal to my stay in Tehran. I would like to mention the late Hossein Mahdavy and his wife Nevine who invited me to their house on several occasions and Ali Mir-Ansari who taught me Persian. Ali, his wife Shahla Khanum, and daughter, Homa, were my adopted family in Tehran. Sayyid Kāẓim Bujnurdī kindly hosted me at the Centre for the Great Islamic Enyclopeadia where I spent time doing research while living in the rooms of the British Institute of Persian Studies (BIPS). My friend Denis Hermann introduced me to Omid Reza'i, whose remarkable work deciphering the minutiae of Persian *sharīʿa* court documents has inspired much of my own research. Our collaboration over the years has helped me better understand some of the secrets of the scribal artisans of these documents. During my stay in Iran, Urs Fruehauf was a splendid travel companion to Gorgan (formerly Astarābād). In Qum, I could not have asked for better guides and hosts than the *sayyidayn*: Sayyid Ṣādiq Ḥusaynī Ishkawarī, director of Majmaʿ-yi Dhakhā'ir-i Islāmī and Sayyid Riḍā Shūshtarī of Zanzibar.

Since the completion of my doctoral thesis, the scope and direction of my research changed from Persian documents to the Indian Ocean and back again. I consider Michel Boivin responsible for the first fortunate *réorientation* which led to three years in Paris at the École des Hautes Études en Sciences Sociales (EHESS) with intermittent fieldwork in Oman working on a project on the Khojas of Muscat. In Paris, I cannot forget Iqbal Surani, who opened my eyes to the *bāṭin* of things, and the kindness of Anne Regourd, Françoise Nalini Delvoye, Sepideh Parsapajouh, Delphine Ortis, Annabelle Collinet, Akil Amiraly and Mamod Meralli-Ballou.

Olly Akkerman rescued me from Paris before it was too late and helped to expand my *Weltanschauung, outre-Rhin,* in Berlin, where a second *réorientation* brought me back to my work on Persian documents, after a post-doctoral fellowship at the Berlin Graduate School of Muslim Cultures and Societies (BGSMCS), Freie Universität Berlin. I am indebted to Konrad Hirschler for his support and guidance during this period and to Abdul Sheriff, Fatma Alloo, Kai Kresse, Ulrike Freitag, Jasmin Mahazi, Raid al-Jamali and Crystal Ennis for ensuring my loyalties

https://doi.org/10.1515/9783111239736-202

remain nevertheless, beyond the *mīms* and *wāws* of the documents, firmly with the Indian Ocean. I have benefitted, at various stages, as this work developed, from the help and guidance of Geoffrey Khan, Christian Müller, Robert Gleave, Nandini Chatterjee, Rudi Mathee, Elke Hartmann, Léon Buskens, Guy Burak, Ismail Warscheid, Annabel Teh Gallop, Nur Sobers-Khan, Said Aljoumani, Kumail Rajani, Elahe Mahbub Farimani, and the anonymous reviewers.

Ingrid Austveg Evans and the editorial expertise of Torsten Wollina, Katrin Hudey, and Anne Stroka at De Gruyter improved my initial text considerably.

I am indebted to Wendy, Moya, Meiske, Heinz, Margarete, Saskia and Oksana for their generosity in Berlin; to Iqbal Akhtar for his close friendship over the years, and to my extended family across the world for their love and support: Sameer, Owais Ali, Farida, Fatma, Mubina, Mustafa, the cats, Nargis, – Ismat, Riyaz, Rehana, Jamila, Mazhar, Niloufer and their respective families –, Jaap, Jen, Quinten, Emma and Luna.

None of this would have been possible without my parents, Salim and Sheila, and my two sisters, Suki and Aleefa. My muse and better half Olly turned my life upside down in the best possible way re-directing me to *ḥaqq*. Our son, Taha Louis gives me hope for the future. I dedicate this work to the memory of my grandparents.

Contents

Note on Transliteration and Dates

This study follows an Arabic system of transliteration based on the one used by the *International Journal of Middle East Studies* (*IJMES*). The following exceptions do not follow the transliteration system: Develū, *bēg*, *bēglerbēgī*, Vafā and Zavārih. Common geographical places names like Tehran, Isfahan, and Shiraz are not transliterated. The silent *h* is not transliterated at the end of the relative pronoun *ki* and Persian words that form the *iḍāfa* with a *hamza*. If the year is cited according to both the Islamic lunar *hijrī* calendar (A.H.) and the common era (C.E.), the *hijrī* year comes first, for example: 1300/1883. The same convention applies if the year is cited according to both the Iranian solar calendar and the common era. In the latter case, the abbreviation sh. (*shamsī*) is added to the year to distinguish it from years cited according to the *hijrī* calendar, which have no abbreviation added, for example: 1300 sh./1921. The abbreviation d. is added before the year to indicate date of death, while r. is used to designate regnal dates.

https://doi.org/10.1515/9783111239736-204

List of Figures and Tables

https://doi.org/10.1515/9783111239736-205

Introduction

Documenting *Sharīʿa* Court Practice in Iran, ca. 1501–1925

This book is about the practice of Islamic law (*sharīʿa*) in early modern Iran (ca. 1501–1925). It seeks to understand who the practitioners of Islamic law were in Iran, how legal documents produced according to Islamic law were validated, annulled, and archived, and how the practitioners of Islamic law intervened in legal disputes. The history of pre-modern Islamic legal practice is usually understood through the lens of Mamluk or Ottoman sources.[1] Paolo Sartori's recent study of the practice of Islamic law in a "marginal" region, Central Asia before the Russian conquest, tries to decentre Mamluk and Ottoman normativity.[2] He argues that rather than conferring normative value on Mamluk and Ottoman Islamic legal practice, it is necessary to first explore practices in specific regions of the Islamic world, such as for example post-Mongol Persianate[3] Central Asia, because "although institutions may appear similar at first, a closer look at the administrative practices, the language, and the legal literature employed suggests that there were fewer similarities than differences".[4] According to Sartori, it is possible to speak of and to describe distinctive "cultures of documentation" of Islamic law.[5] While Sartori's study provides a Sunnī Ḥanafī Persianate example of Islamic legal practice, the present study investigates the practice of Islamic law in a Twelver or Imāmī Shīʿī Persianate setting, in Iran between the sixteenth to twentieth centuries.

The aim is to fill an important lacuna in the existing scholarship. Most studies on the practice of Islamic law so far have been written from the perspective of the four classical Sunnī (Ḥanafī, Mālikī,[6] Shāfiʿī and Ḥanbalī) schools of Islamic law. Few studies have been conducted on Islamic legal practice in Shīʿī (Imāmī or Twelver, Ismāʿīlī and Zaydī) or Ibāḍī contexts. A notable exception in this regard is Brinkley Messick's study of the practice of Zaydī Shīʿī Islamic law in highland

1 See for example Müller 2013 and Aykan 2016.

2 Sartori 2017, 42.

3 Persianate is used in this study to refer to Persian speaking lands or places influenced by the Persian language and culture.

4 Sartori 2017, 43.

5 Sartori and Pickett 2019, 773–778.

6 See the recent work by I. Warscheid which looks at the practice of Mālikī Islamic law in the desert oases of Tuwat, situated today in southwestern Algeria, see Warscheid 2017. For an urban Mālikī perspective from Morrocco, see Buskens 2017.

https://doi.org/10.1515/9783111239736-001

Yemen.[7] Based on ethnographic fieldwork in Ibb, Messick argues that Islamic law can be understood as "a formation of local texts" – the prestige texts of the "library", comprising the legal literature of the *sharīʿa*, and the "archival texts" of day-to-day *sharīʿa* practice (opinions, judgements, instruments), which primarily have links to "the *maḥkama*, the judge's court and its larger surround, which included the private notarial writer".[8] While texts of the library have "cosmopolitan" qualities, possessing a "characteristically non-contextually referential discourse", which "enables them to relocate, to travel", the texts of the "archive" are "contingent" on the time and place they were produced.[9]

Drawing on earlier studies by Sartori, Messick and others which have tried to localise the study of Islamic legal practice within a specific regional context and legal culture of adherents of a particular school of Islamic law, this book has three main lines of enquiry. The first is to investigate how Islamic law was "materialised"[10] in Iran in the form of written artefacts such as legal documents and *sharīʿa* court registers. The aim will be to reconstruct from surviving documentary corpora the Persianate "culture of documentation" of the contingent "archival texts" of Islamic legal practice in Imāmī Shīʿī Iran during the sixteenth to twentieth centuries. This investigation is of interest because while there is a long tradition of studying Islamic legal documents produced in Arabic in various regions of the Muslim world,[11] Islamic legal documents from the Persianate world, which often combine the use of Arabic and Persian, have received relatively little attention. Studies on Islamic legal documents from the Persianate world have focused so far on documents from Ardabīl in Northwest Iran (ca. 12th to 13th centuries),[12] Transcaucasia,[13] medieval Khurāsān (ca. 11th to 13th centuries),[14] and Central Asia (ca. 16th to 20th

7 See Messick 1996 and Messick 2018. See also the recent study on the theory and practice of Zaydi *waqf* law in Yemen by Hovden 2019.

8 Messick 2018, 21.

9 Messick 2018, 26.

10 I use this expression from the title of the European Research Council (ERC) project (2009–20013): "Islamic law materialized: Arabic legal documents (8th to 15th century) (ILM)", see URL: https://cald.irht.cnrs.fr/php/login.php (Accessed 1 April 2023).

11 See for example: Little 1984, 16–49, Gronke 1986, 454–507, Khan 1993; Miura and Sato 2015, 2020, Livingston 2018.

12 Three pre-Mongol New Persian sale contracts (517/1123, 582/1186, 603/1207) and a deed of acknowledgment (*iqrār*) (602/1205) are edited from the corpus of documents from the shrine of Shaykh Ṣafī al-Dīn Ardabīlī (d. 735/1334), in Ardabil, Iran, in Gronke 1982, see Urkunde I, 94–105; Urkunde IV, 142–146; Urkunde VI, 174–182 and Urkunde VII, 192–199.

13 See Aljoumani, Bhalloo and Hirschler 2023.

14 See for example ten pre-Mongol Persian deeds of acknowledgement (*iqrār*s) dated between the years 395–430/1005–1039 in New Persian from Khurāsān edited in Haim 2019a, 2019b; for a

centuries).[15] Not much attention, however, has been paid to the production of Islamic legal documents in Iran following the conversion of Iran to Twelver or Imāmī Shīʿīsm under the Safavids (ca. 1501–1722). Similarly, there is little research on the structure of *sharīʿa* court registers in Iran or Islamic legal opinions (*fatwā*s) comparable to the studies of their Ottoman equivalents.[16]

Nevertheless, from the 1990s onwards, several important editions of Imāmī Shīʿī legal documents and *sharīʿa* court registers, mostly from the Qajar period (ca. 1794–1925), have been published in Iran and Japan.[17] In 1997, Hāshim Rajabazāda and Koichi Haneda co-edited a collection of documents which include land transactions recorded in Qajar *sharīʿa* courts.[18] Subsequent editions of Qajar *sharīʿa* court documents have been published by Hāshim Rajabzāda and Kinji Eura.[19] In 1383sh./2005, Umīd Riḍāʾī (Omid Reza'i) edited a collection of legal rulings (*ḥukm-i sharʿ*) issued by leading Imāmī Shīʿī jurists (*mujtahids*) in the nineteenth century in endowment (*waqf*) disputes in Iran. Subsequently, in 1385 sh./2006–2007, Manṣūra Ittiḥādiyya and Saīʿd Rūḥī edited and analysed two *sharīʿa* court registers belonging to the well-known Qajar era *mujtahid*, Shaykh Faḍlullāh Nūrī.[20] Though such research initially focused on deciphering legal documents and registers as potential sources for reconstructing social, economic, and legal history,[21] attention has now also turned to the formal structure of these documents as written artefacts. In 2008, an important milestone was reached with the publication by Riḍāʾī of a detailed typology and transcription of thirty different types of Qajar-era *sharīʿa*

New Persian settlement contract (473/1080) and a *qāḍī* court record (608/1212) also from pre–Mongol Khurāsān, see Fīrūzbakhsh 1400 sh./2022 and Bhalloo 2023a.

15 For Islamic legal documents in Persian from Central Asia, see for example for Samarqand: Chekovich 1974, Isogai 2003, 3–12, Isogai 2011, 259–282 and for Bukhara: Arends, Khalidov Chekhovich 1979, Bhalloo and Ishkawari 2024a.

16 For a study of the structure of Ottoman *qāḍī* court documents and their register entries, see Milad 1974, 161–243. For a study of the structure of legal opinions (*fatwā*s) issued by Ottoman jurisconsults (*muftī*s) see Heyd 1969, 35–56 and Yaycioğlu 1997.

17 This "documentary" or "archival" turn in the study of the practice of Islamic law in Iran came after earlier research in the 1970s and 1980s on social and economic aspects of the Qajar era carried out by Iranian scholars such as H.F. Farmayan, A. Mahadavi, M. E. Nezam-Mafi (M. Ittiḥādiyya) and others drew attention to the rich collections of archival documents in Persian in Iran, see for example Farmayan 1974, 32–49; Mahdavi 1983, 243–278 and Nezam-Mafi 1989, 51–61.

18 Rajabzāda and Haneda 1997.

19 See Rajabzāda and Eura 1999–2021.

20 20 Ittiḥādiya and Rūḥī 1385 sh./2006–2007.

21 *Waqf* deeds (*waqf-nāmas*) in particular have proven to be an invaluable source for the study of the socioreligious organization of groups such as the Shaykhīs and Niʿmatullāhī Sufis in Qajar Iran, see Hermann and Reza'i 2007, 87–131; Hermann and Reza'i 2008, 293–306 and Hermann 2016, 275–301.

court documents along with important codicological notes relating to sealing practice.[22] Christoph Werner has examined the structure and function of Qajar sale deeds (*bayʿ-nāma*) and settlement contracts (*muṣālaḥa-nāma*).[23] Nobuaki Kondo meanwhile has described the practice of annotation, transcription, and registration of Imāmī Shīʿī legal deeds in Qajar Iran based on a selection of documents, registers, and inventories.[24] In a more recent study, he has examined the structure and function of Qajar era Imāmī Shīʿī conditional sale contracts (*bayʿ-i sharṭ*).[25] Such research is significant because in early modern Iran, unlike in the more centralised Ottoman empire, documentary practices surrounding *sharīʿa* courts were not standardized. Each *sharīʿa* court developed and transmitted its own distinctive scribal and archival practices. In a series of original studies on Islamic legal documents produced in nineteenth-century Tehran,[26] Bushehr,[27] Iranian Kurdistān,[28] and Shiraz,[29] Riḍāʾī has demonstrated that it is possible to speak of the existence of *sharīʿa* courts in different localities in Iran that routinely produced and registered legal deeds based on their distinctive scribal and archival practices. In the absence of centralised recording procedures, each *sharīʿa* court produced documents with different formulae and spatial layout for the main text, judicial attestations, and witness clauses. Each *sharīʿa* court also had its own sealing practice and way of adding registration notes to the document. As a result, it is often possible to identify the existence of a local *sharīʿa* court based on a corpus of legal documents which use the same material supports, textual formulae, spatial layout, registration notes and are sealed by the same scribes or members of a given clerical lineage. An example of this is the corpus of legal documents from the Imāmī Shīʿī *sharīʿa* court of the *shaykh al-islām* family in Neyrīz, a small town in Fārs province. The legal documents issued by this court have sealed judicial attestations belonging to members of the *shaykh al-islām* clerical lineage in Neyrīz over several generations. The Neyrīz corpus also includes documents written on cotton cloth, which suggests that not all Qajar *sharīʿa* courts used paper as a material support for writing legal instruments.[30]

22 Riḍāʾī 2008.
23 Werner 2003, 13–49, Werner 2021, 864–893.
24 Kondo 2014, 561–575.
25 Kondo 2021, 615–639.
26 Riḍāʾī 1385 sh./2007, Riḍāʾī 1386 sh./2007, 44–55.
27 Riḍāʾī 1390 sh./2011, 79–94.
28 Riḍāʾī 1388 sh./2009, 28–47.
29 See chapter 2.
30 Bhalloo and Rezaʾi 2017, 77–106. See also Riḍāʾī 1401 sh./2022.

As the number of such studies of Imāmī Shīʿī legal documentary corpora from Iran increases and more material is edited and published, it will be possible in future to identify new Imāmī Shīʿī *sharīʿa* courts administered by different individuals or clerical lineages. Ultimately, it will be possible, by comparing pre-Safavid, Safavid and post-Safavid practice, to demonstrate ruptures in documentary practice caused by religious and political transitions.[31] The present book based on a combination of hitherto unpublished legal documents and edited sources is intended as a step in this direction. While the bulk of research on Imāmī Shīʿī legal documents has focused on the production of Qajar Iran (ca. 1794–1925), this study aims to provide new perspectives by looking at Imāmī Shīʿī legal corpora from Safavid Iran (ca. 1501–1722) and from the period of transition after the fall of the Safavids during Afghan (ca. 1722–1729), Afshar (ca. 1729–1751), and Zand rule (ca. 1751–1794).[32]

A second line of enquiry in this book is to document who the practitioners of Islamic law were in Iran during the early modern period. "Early modern" refers in this book to the period after the conversion of Iran to Imāmī Shīʿism under the Safavids until the end of Qajar rule (ca. 1501–1925). This period is of interest because unlike Sunnī judicial theory, which stressed the necessity (*ḍarūra*) or public interest (*maṣlaḥa*) of the appointment (*tawliya*) of judges by the *de facto* political power,[33] the Imāmī Shīʿīs from the very beginning considered judicial appointment by any authority other than the Shīʿī Imām or his representative (*nāʾib*) to be illegitimate.[34] While the Imam was present, he or his representative would directly appoint *sharīʿa* judges (*qāḍīs*). During the Imām's occultation (*ghayba*), judicial authority (*wilāyat al-qaḍāʾ*) based on authoritative texts – reports attributed to the sixth Imām Ja'far al-Sādiq (d. 148/765) – was interpreted to have been delegated to Imāmī scholars (*ʿulamāʾ*) who possessed the requisite qualities (*sharāʾiṭ*) for judicial activity (*qaḍāʾ*). Precisely what these qualities were was repeatedly debated by Imāmī writers. The Usūlīs held that the scholar had to be able to extract (*istikhrāj*) his own legal rulings (*ḥukms*) from the sources of the law through exhaustive deductive effort (*ijtihād*). Such scholars were known as *mujtahids*. The term *mujtahid*, which I also translate as jurist throughout this study, refers to this Imāmī Shīʿī Uṣūlī position. The Akhbārī school, a movement

---

31 In the chapter on "Spiral Texts", B. Messick links the transformation of calligraphic practices, spatial organization of text, record-keeping practices and seals in documents to ruptures caused by political transition in Yemen. See Messick 1996, 231–251.

32 Two notable recent exceptions which focus on Safavid legal documents are Sheikh al-Hokamaee 2013, 137–154 and Riḍāʾī 1397 sh./2018, 213–220.

33 See for example Tyan 1943, 177.

34 Calder 1980, 70–73.

which rose to prominence in the eleventh/seventeenth century, placed greater emphasis on the scholar's ability to read, interpret, and transmit the reports (*akhbār*) of the Twelve infallible Shīʿī Imāms.[35] The Akhbārīs, like the earliest Imāmī writers, did not consider it necessary for a *qāḍī* to be a *mujtahid*.[36] Though the Usūlī and Akhbārī positions may have differed on the details of the requisite qualities a scholar had to possess to exercise valid judicial activity, both held that judicial appointment by *de facto* governments was a usurpation of the prerogative of the Imām. Did this Imāmī Shīʿī theoretical position ever affect actual judicial practice in Iran? Most research so far has focused on understanding the Imāmī Shīʿī theoretical position itself and the attempts by Imāmī writers to accommodate this position to the exigencies of a centralised state-sponsored judicial administration.[37] The implications of the Imāmī theoretical position for actual legal practice, however, has received little attention. One of the main concerns of this study will be to assess in each case whether the sources examined emphasize state appointment, or, in line with the Imāmī theoretical ideal, the possession of requisite qualities by scholars when referring to the practitioners of Islamic law in Iran.

A third and final line of enquiry of this book is to investigate how the practitioners of Islamic law in Iran intervened procedurally in the domain of dispute resolution. The working hypothesis is that the Imāmī Uṣūlī emphasis on the ability to carry out *ijtihād* as a *mujtahid* led to a shift in the procedures surrounding *sharīʿa* dispute resolution in Iran. Instead of a centralised system where disputes were settled in the court of the state-appointed *qāḍī* such as in the Ottoman empire, a more decentralised judicial system emerged in Iran involving multiple legal experts recognised as *mujtahid*s who could intervene at various stages of a dispute by certifying judicial claims, issuing legal opinions, or arranging an amicable settlement. As the bulk of the surviving sources for *sharīʿa* court disputes from Iran is relatively recent, this procedural judicial decentralisation is assessed in this book from the perspective of sources from the nineteenth-century Qajar period, when Uṣūlism had become the dominant Imāmī Shīʿī doctrinal position in Iran. Nevertheless, already in the sixteenth century Safavid period, the French traveller Chardin notes that independent scholars could authenticate, alongside state-appointed *qāḍī*s, legal deeds simply because they were perceived to

35 Gleave 2007, 237-238.
36 Calder 1989, 59–60. For a detailed study of the epistemological differences between the Uṣūlī and Akhbārī schools see Gleave 2007, 6–7 and Gleave 2000. On the Uṣūlī-Akhbārī dispute, see also Newman 1992a, 1992b.
37 Calder 1987, 91–105.

be *mujtahids*.[38] This decentralising trend which made it possible for any legal scholar recognised as a *mujtahid* to intervene in the judicial sphere was reinforced in the post-Safavid era by the triumph in the eighteenth century of Uṣūlism over Akhbārism under the influence of the leading Uṣūlī *mujtahid*, Muḥammad Bāqir Bihbahānī (1116–1205/1706–1791).[39] Based on case studies of disputes over property constituted as an Islamic endowment (*waqf*) from nineteenth-century Iran, I argue it is possible to demonstrate that the perceived ability to exercise *ijtihād* as a *mujtahid* had become relevant not only for validating Islamic legal deeds,[40] but also, for issuing a valid legal ruling (Per. *ḥukm-i sharʿ*) in disputes which were adjudicated based on the evaluation of evidence according to the norms of the *sharīʿa*.[41]

Structure and Scope of the Book

This book is divided into six chapters. Each chapter is based on a selection of documentary and narrative sources. The main objective of these chapters is to document the practitioners and practice of Islamic law in Iran in the early modern period. Chapter one is divided into two parts. In the first part, I draw on manuals of administration and decrees of judicial appointment to reconstruct who the practitioners of Islamic law were in Iran during the Safavid period and under subsequent Afghan, Afshār, and Zand rule. The second part of the chapter examines selected legal deeds from Iran during the Safavid and Zand periods. The aim of this analysis is to investigate judicial attestations termed *sijills* which appear on these deeds. These judicial attestations are significant because they shed light on changes in the class of practitioners of Islamic law in early modern Iran. The deeds also have registration notes and registration seals which suggest that they were copied into the archive of the *sharīʿa* court. The diachronic perspective from this chapter sets the stage for chapters two and three, which consist of two synchronic studies focused on the practitioners of two different types of *sharīʿa* courts of the Qajar period, as well as of their scribal and archival practices.

---

38 Chardin 1711, VI, 285–286: ". . . j'ai vu des docteurs éminents en la loi, et des prêtres, qui tendent à parvenir à ce degré qu'on appelle *mouchtehed*, c'est-à-dire ceux qui savent toutes les sciences, lesquels s'attribuaient aussi le pouvoir d'authentiquer des pièces. Leurs actes passaient en justice par respect pour leur personne ou pour leur mémoire. Les juges disaient: C'est un saint homme et doué de grandes lumières, il n'aurait pas voulu faire un faux acte."

39 On Bihbahānī, see H. Algar, "Moḥammad Bāqer Behbahānī", *EIr*, IV/1, 98–99 and Gleave 2013, 415–434.

40 Kondo 2003, 106–128.

41 See chapter 5.

Chapter two examines the corpus of Islamic legal documents produced by a *sharīʿa* court situated in Shiraz, in the southwest Iranian province of Fārs. This *sharīʿa* court belonged to the descendants of Shaykh Aḥmad al-Tammāmī (d. ca. 1130/1717–18), an Arab émigré from Eastern Arabia whose descendants successively occupied the post of *shaykh al-islām* of Fārs. Their house, located in the Sūq al-Ṭayr (Bāzār-i Murgh) quarter of Shiraz, functioned as a *sharīʿa* court for over a century between 1158–1336/1745–1918. The Tammāmī corpus is of outstanding historical significance for understanding the nature of Islamic legal practice in post-Safavid Iran. Moreover, it provides evidence of a different type of archival practice that existed in Iran relating to *sharīʿa* courts alongside the use of registers, which involved preserving summaries on small loose-leaf sheets termed *fard*. Whereas members of the Tammāmī family occupied an official post from the state and received state income, chapter 3 demonstrates the existence of a different type of *sharīʿa* practitioner in Iran whose authority mainly derived from his percieved ability to exercise *ijtihād* as a *mujtahid*. It focuses on the corpus of legal documents and registers from the *sharīʿa* court established by Āqā Sayyid Ṣādiq Ṭabāṭabāʾī Sangalajī (d. 1300/1883) in his house in the Sangalaj quarter of the Qajar capital, Tehran. Though the significance of the documentary corpus from the Tammāmī *shaykh al-islām sharīʿa* court in Shiraz and the *sharīʿa* court of Āqā Sayyid Ṣādiq Ṭabāṭabāʾī Sangalajī in Tehran has already been highlighted in earlier studies,[42] I shed new light on these two *sharīʿa* courts and analyse hitherto unstudied documents from these *sharīʿa* courts.

Chapters four to six are concerned with documenting the practitioners of Islamic law and their intervention in the resolution of civil disputes in early modern Iran. All three case studies presented in chapters four, five, and six concern disputes over religiously endowed property or *waqf* from Qajar Iran. The reason for this particular focus is that *waqf* is one of the few areas of Islamic law where the sources are sufficiently rich to allow a detailed reconstruction of the disputes. The importance of *waqf* disputes for understanding the practice of Islamic law has long been recognised. We can cite for instance the *waqf* disputes examined by Stefan Knost from eighteenth-century Ottoman Aleppo and those examined by David Powers from fourteenth-century Morocco.[43] Christoph Werner and Nobuaki Kondo have also made pioneering contributions by examining several *waqf* disputes from nineteenth-century Qajar Iran.[44] My work differs from this latter scholarship in its focus on documenting the procedural problems of legal rulings

42 I refer to these studies in chapters 2 and 3.
43 Knost 2006, 427–450 and Powers 1990, 229–254.
44 Werner 1999, Kondo 2017.

issued in such *waqf* disputes by the practitioners of Islamic law. These problems, I argue, became relevant in the Imāmī Shīʿī Uṣūlī doctrinal context of Iran in this period.

Chapter four examines the dispute over the validity of the *waqf* of Luṭf ʿAlī Khān Turshīzī (d. 1800–1). This dispute involved some of the preeminent *mujtahids* residing in Qajar Iran and in the Shīʿī shrine cities (*ʿatabāt*) of Ottoman Iraq at the time. It provides important insight into how independent *mujtahids*, who held no official post, were approached by litigants for legal rulings (*ḥukm-i sharʿ*). I use the narrative and documentary sources relating to this dispute to demonstrate the problem of conflicting legal rulings in a decentralised judicial system where multiple *mujtahids* could intervene in a case at different times, either to give a non-binding opinion as a jurisconsult (*muftī*) or a binding judicial certification of a claim as a judge (*qāḍī*). At the same time, I also use this case study to shed light on how the legal rulings of *mujtahids* in actual disputes were incorporated by their students into legal *responsa* collections (*suʾāl wa jawāb*) or resulted in short academic treatises or epistles (*risāla*).

Chapter five examines a different endowment dispute from the Qajar period. I use the corpus of legal and administrative documents belonging to the Dirāzgīsū *sayyids* of Astarābād (Gurgān) in northeastern Iran to reconstruct their litigation against ʿAbbās Khān Qajar, the provincial governor (*bēglerbēgī*) of Astarābād. The *sayyids* claimed that two villages in ʿAbbās Khān's possession were *waqf* lands belonging to a family *waqf* founded by one of their ancestors in the Safavid period. The litigation in the case demonstrates how the validity of a scholar's legal ruling in Iran in this period could be circumvented by one side by their refusal to recognise the scholar's ability to carry out *ijtihād* as a *mujtahid*. Moreover, it demonstrates the problem of determining the binding force of the scholar's legal ruling when it was issued to one side in the absence of the other side. Since the *mujtahid* could act as either a jurisconsult (*muftī*) or a judge (*qāḍī*), it became crucial to evaluate the circumstances of issuance (*kayfiyyat-i ṣudūr*) of the legal ruling in order to determine whether a given legal ruling was issued as: (1) a non-binding legal opinion; (2) a binding judicial certification of a claim based on the evidence of one side, or (3) a binding judicial certification of a claim after the evidence of both sides was reviewed. In some cases, the structure of the text of the legal ruling could help determine its binding force, but in the absence of uniform centralised recording procedures, this was not always the case, as the dispute examined in this chapter will demonstrate.

Finally, chapter six focuses on the revival of a family *waqf* founded in the Safavid era during the nineteenth and early twentieth centuries. The case demonstrates how litigants were able to collect multiple witness testimonies in documents known as *istishhād-nāma* to prove that certain villages and surrounding agricultural lands in the region of Isfahan were *waqf*. These *istishhād-nāmas* would later form the basis of a *mujtahid*'s *ḥukm-i sharʿ* reviving the *waqf*. The first part of the chapter discusses witnessing in claims of *waqf* according to Imāmī Shīʿī law. The second part examines the structure of the *istishhād-nāma*. The third part focuses on how the claimants in the dispute used *istishhād-nāmas* to prove their *waqf* claim. The case studies presented in chapters four, five and six point to the significance of legal practitioners recognised as *mujtahids* in the domain of *waqf* dispute resolution in nineteenth- and twentieth-century Iran. This suggests that an important convergence had occurred by the nineteenth century in Iran between the Imāmī Shīʿī Uṣūlī theoretical ideal of the jurist as judge and actual practice, at least as it relates to cases involving *waqf*. Nevertheless, until further research is carried out on areas of Islamic law besides *waqf*, it is difficult to draw definitive conclusions on the extent to which scholars perceived to be *mujtahids* intervened in dispute resolution in the Qajar period. Evidence from Qajar Tehran, however, suggests that *mujtahids* routinely intervened in different types of civil cases (succession, property disputes, commercial transactions, marital conflicts, maintenance, and custody etc.) and criminal proceedings whenever evidence, in particular witness testimony, had to be evaluated, or when a case required the administration of judicial oaths according to *sharīʿa* norms.[45]

Though this book examines the intervention of the state from the perspective of judicial appointment and the enforcement of the legal rulings of *mujtahids* in disputes, it is not concerned with the dialectical relationship between the justice of the practitioners of Islamic law and the justice of the Safavid, Afghan, Afshar or Qajar political authorities based on customary law (*ʿurf*).[46] It thus does not investigate in depth how justice was sought through petitions to "secular" state officials and their courts dedicated to the redress of grievances (*maẓālim*).[47] Though desirable, this type of study is not the focus of this book. The book is also not about centralising legal reforms and the creation of modern courts of justice in Iran such as the *dīwān-khāna-yi ʿadliyya* from the second half of the ninteenth-century onwards. Instead, this book will aim to identify who the practitioners of Islamic law were in

45 See Kondo 2017, 38–57.

46 On this dialectical relationship in the Qajar period, including references to earlier studies, see Werner 2005, 153–175 and Kondo 22–37. For a similar perspective from the Safavid period, see Abisaab 2018, 1–32.

47 Most research on the institution of *maẓālim* in pre-modern Iran has so far been based on the corpus of approximately two thousand documents, including petitions, reports, answers, and summaries, recorded by the scribes of the Qajar shah, Nāṣir al-Dīn Shāh (r.1848–1896), between 1883–1886, see Nezam-Mafi 1989 and Schneider 2006.

early modern Iran, shed light on some of the scribal and archival practices surrounding their courts, and finally, investigate how they intervened in dispute resolution. What connects the six chapters presented here is the attempt to detect shifts and ruptures in practice related to the Imāmī Shīʿī Uṣūlī doctrinal ideal, which emphasized requisite legal knowledge, not *de facto* state appointment, as the main criterium for exercising judicial power as a *sharīʿa* judge (*ḥākim-i sharʿ*). As the chapters demonstrate, though the pre-Qajar sources confirm the significance of state-appointed *sharīʿa* judges actors and their courts, in the aftermath of the revival of Uṣūlism in the Shīʿī shrine cities of Iraq in the eighteenth century, scholars recognised as jurists (*mujtahids*) became increasingly central to the practice of Islamic law in Iran.[48] This situation has persisted up until the present.

48 On the Uṣūlī revival, see for example Cole 1988, Heern 2011.

Chapter 1
Sharīʿa Courts in Iran before the Qajar Period

Introduction

Research so far on *sharīʿa* courts in Iran has mainly focused on the nineteenth century Qajar period. Little is known about the practitioners of Islamic law and their courts in the Safavid period and under subsequent Afghan, Afshar, and Zand rule. The first part of this chapter draws on Safavid administrative manuals and decrees of judicial appointment to reconstruct who presided over *sharīʿa* courts in Iran before Qajar rule. The second and third parts examine the authentication and registration of legal deeds from the Safavid and Zand periods. The aim is to understand the nature and function of judicial attestations in Arabic which appear on these deeds. These judicial attestations are termed *sijill*s (Ar. *sijill*, pl. *sijillāt*) in model legal formularies (*shurūṭ*) from Safavid Iran. The study of *sijill*s in early modern Persian legal documents is significant because it sheds light on the practitioners of Islamic law involved in validating different types of legal acts. Besides the *sijills*, attention will also be paid to archival traces found on legal deeds. These traces, as we shall see, are of two types: registration notes and registration seals. They suggest that early modern Iranian *sharīʿa* courts, like their Ottoman counterparts, maintained archives.

1 *Sharīʿa* Practitioners and their Courts, ca. 1501–1795

1.1 The Evidence of Safavid Administrative Manuals

The most important sources on the practitioners of Islamic law in Safavid Iran are the three Safavid administrative manuals of *Tadhkira al-Mulūk* (*TM*), *Dastūr al-Mulūk* (*DM*) and *Alqāb wa Mawājib* (*AM*).[1] These manuals were compiled in the turbulent period following the Afghan conquest of Iran and the abdication of the last Safavid shah, Sulṭān Ḥusayn (r. 1694–1722). They were meant as practical guides to the workings of the Safavid state for the new Afghan rulers of Iran. As Vladimir Minorsky has noted, the author of *TM* was "fully versed in the arcana of Safavid chanceries".[2] Since the central Safavid administration had completely broken down

1 See Minorsky 1943 (*TM*), Kondo 2018 (*DM*) and Floor 2008 (*AM*).
2 *TM*, 11.

https://doi.org/10.1515/9783111239736-002

during the siege and famine prior to the fall of its capital, Isfahan, the author uses the past tense for his explanations of the workings of the Safavid state.

According to Nobuaki Kondo, *DM* is a more complete version of the anonymous *TM*. *DM* was compiled by Mīrzā Muḥammad Rafīʿ Anṣārī who was appointed to the office of *muṣtawfī al-mamālik* (Chief Accountant of the Protected Domains) in 1723 and was dismissed in 1728 by the second Afghan ruler Ashraf Shāh (r. 1725–1729). *DM* mentions five officials with notarial and adjudicative functions in the Safavid capital, Isfahan: the *ṣadr-i khāṣṣa*; the *ṣadr-i ʿāmma* also known as the *ṣadr-i mamālik*; the *shaykh al-islām* of Isfahan; the *qāḍī* of Isfahan and the *qāḍī -yi ʿaskar* (military judge).[3] Their respective roles in adjudicating disputes according to Islamic law and notarizing legal deeds is described in *DM* as follows:

> **The *ṣadr-i khāṣṣa* and the *ṣadr-i mamālik*:**
> The *ṣadr-i khāṣṣa,* on Saturdays and on Sundays, and the *ṣadr-i mamālik,* on Wednesdays and Thursdays, would sit with the *dīwān-bēgī* at the Kishik-khāna (Royal Guardhouse) of the ʿĀlī-Qāpū (Royal Palace). Whatever decision (*ḥukm*) the *ṣadr*s would issue on lawsuits, the *dīwān-bēgī* would enforce their *ḥukm*. They (i.e. the two *ṣadr*s) would listen to the claims of people and were occupied with sealing their legal deeds and documents.[4]
>
> **The *shaykh al-islām* of Isfahan:**
> On days other than Friday, he would sit in his own house and would adjudicate the claims of people. He would prescribe good and forbid evil. Divorces were settled in his presence. The handling of the money of orphans and absent individuals was mostly in his hands, though sometimes it was referred to the judges. The legal deeds and documents of people were also sealed by him. Salary: An annual stipend (*waẓīfa*) of 200 Tabrīzī *tūmān*s from the royal treasury (*khizāna-yi ʿāmira*).[5]
>
> **The *qāḍī* of Isfahan:**
> On days other than Friday, he would sit in his own house and adjudicate the claims of people. He would seal legal deeds and documents. The legal ruling (*ḥukm-i sharʿī*) that he would write, would be executed by the political authorities (*ḥukkām-i ʿurf*). The handling of money of orphans and absent individuals was sometimes carried out by him and sometimes by the *shaykh al-islām*. Salary: An annual stipend (*waẓīfa*) of 200 Tabrīzī *tūmān*s from the royal treasury (*khizāna-yi ʿāmira*).[6]

---

3 *DM* also describes one other clerical position, the office of the *mullā-bāshī*, without, however, ascribing any clear adjudicative or notarial duties to it (*DM*, 5). Nevertheless, we know from a legal document from Shiraz, dated Dhū l-Qaʿda 1206/June 1792, that the *mullā-bāshī* was active in notarizing deeds alongside the *qāḍī* and *shaykh al-islām* of Shiraz. See Section 3.

4 *DM*, 7.

5 *DM*, 12.

6 *DM*, 12.

The *qāḍī -yi ʿaskar*:
In previous times, the cases that the *qāḍīs* of Islam adjudicated and settled in each province was carried out by the *qāḍī -yi ʿaskar* during military travels. He would (also) issue decisions (on cases concerning the victorious army) in the Kishik-khāna of the *dīwān-bēgīs*. After the *ṣadrs* were appointed in Isfahan, it was decided that the *dīwān-bēgī* would attend to the *sharīʿa* claims of individuals in the presence of the *ṣadr*. The coming of the *qāḍī -yi ʿaskar* to the Kishik-khāna of the *dīwān-bēgī* was stopped. Towards the end, his (the *qāḍī -yi ʿaskar*'s) role was limited to sealing copies of documents of the personnel of the victorious army such as decrees, annual stipend documents, power of attorney documents and petitions. The *bēglerbegīs* and the governors of the provinces would not accept these documents without his seal. Salary: There was no specific salary assigned to him. He used to take ten dinars from the victorious army.[7]

The following points are important to note from the text of *DM*. The first is an overlap in the function of the *qāḍī* and the *shaykh al-islām*. In fact, the description of their roles is almost identical. They both ran a *sharīʿa* court from their houses in Isfahan. They both received an annual stipend of two hundred *tabrīzī tūmāns* from the royal treasury. They both adjudicated lawsuits and authenticated legal documents. They both administered the money of orphans and absent individuals. The only difference in their respective functions is that the *shaykh al-islām* was active in prescribing good and forbidding evil and in settling divorce cases. According to J. Chardin, however, the *qāḍī*'s jurisdiction also extended to wills, marriages, and divorces.[8] There is thus very little difference in the respective roles of the *qāḍī* and of the *shaykh al-islām*. This is quite different from the Ḥanafī Timurid or Ottoman context, where the *qāḍī* was responsible for adjudicating lawsuits and authenticating legal documents, while the *shaykh al-islām* issued legal opinions as a scholar *muftī* or jurisconsult.

Chardin notes that the judicial power of the *qāḍī* had been progressively reduced in Iran by the creation of the office of the *shaykh al-islām* and the office of the *ṣadr*. The latter office was occupied by two different individuals – the *ṣadr-i khāṣṣa* and *ṣadr-i ʿāmma* or *ṣadr-i mamlik* – based on separate territorial jurisdiction.[9] In fact, *qāḍīs* were subordinate to and appointed by the office of the *ṣadr*, as we shall see from the decrees studied below. The juridical capital of the offices of the *shaykh al-islām* and the *ṣadr* was also increased in the seventeenth century through strategic marriage alliances with the ruling Safavid elite. The judicial competition faced by the office of the *qāḍī* and the *qāḍī -yi ʿaskar* (the latter had jurisdiction during travels and over the military) in Iran from these new offices is clearly visible in the text of *DM*. Like the *shaykh al-islām*, the two *ṣadrs* – the *ṣadr-i khāṣṣa*

7 *DM*, 13. See also *TM*, 43.
8 Chardin 1711, VI, 285–286.
9 Chardin 1711, VI, 255.

and *ṣadr-i ʿāmma* –, also had the power to adjudicate claims and to authenticate legal documents in Isfahan. Each *ṣadr* held court separately twice a week with the *dīwān-bēgī* in the ceremonial public setting of the Kishik-khāna (Royal Guardhouse) of the ʿĀlī Qāpū (Royal Palace).[10] This was, however, previously the role of the *qāḍī-yi ʿaskar* or military judge, whose duties were now reduced to authenticating legal documents related to the military.

While the *qāḍī* of Isfahan, the two *ṣadrs*, the *shaykh al-islām*, and the *qāḍī-yi ʿaskar* were responsible for administering *sharīʿa* justice, the most significant law enforcement agent was the *dīwān-bēgī*. It was the *dīwān-bēgī* who enforced *sharʿī* decisions.[11] The *dīwān-bēgī* and the *dārūgha*, the head of the police (*aḥdāth*), could also adjudicate cases in towns and villages to ensure public order. According to *DM*, if the disputed object was below twelve *tūmāns*, the *dārūgha* would decide, and if it was higher than that, the *dīwān-bēgī* had the right to decide.[12] The *dārūgha*, however, could not intervene in a case once it reached the *dīwān-bēgī*. In addition to the *dārūgha* and the *dīwān-bēgī*, the *muḥtasib* also exercised judicial authority in town by enforcing fair practice in the market and forbidding acts proscribed by the *sharīʿa* such as the consumption of alcohol, prostitution, and gambling. Like the *qāḍī*, the *muḥtasib* was also appointed by the *ṣadr*.[13]

It is clear from the preceding description in *DM* that the *sharīʿa* courts of the Safavid capital, Isfahan, were centered around several appointed judicial actors. In the Safavid capital Isfahan, there were at least three *sharīʿa* courts which adjudicated claims and authenticated legal documents: the *sharīʿa* court of the two *ṣadrs*, the *sharīʿa* court of the *shaykh al-islām* and the *sharīʿa* court of the *qāḍī* of Isfahan. Safavid administrative manuals do not mention jurists or *mujtahids* presiding in this period over independent *sharīʿa* courts. The role of the *ṣadr*, the *shaykh al-islām* and the *qāḍī* as the main *sharīʿa* practitioners in this period is confirmed by Safavid decrees of judicial appointment.

1.2 The Evidence of Decrees of Judicial Appointment

Several decrees of judicial appointment of officials have survived from the Safavid period. They corroborate the evidence of the Safavid administrative manuals by pointing to the significance of the *ṣadr*, the *qāḍī*, and the *shaykh al-islām* as the

---

10 Chardin 1711, VI, 118. The Kishik-khāna or Royal Guardhouse was a special building at the entrance of the ʿĀlī Qāpū or Royal Palace in Isfahan.

11 *DM*, 6–7, 36–38.

12 *DM*, 98.

13 See Riḍāʾī 1392–1393 sh./2014, 43–52.

main practitioners responsible for adjudicating disputes and authenticating legal deeds according to *sharīʿa* norms. The decrees of judicial appointment are in the form of a royal decree or *farmān* when issued by the shah himself and an order termed *mithāl* when issued by the *ṣadr*.[14] After the fall of the Safavids and the breakdown of their judicial system, decrees of judicial appointment are more difficult to find. In what follows, I examine the decrees of judicial appointment from the Safavid period and then discuss a rare decree of judicial appointment from the Zand period.

1.2.1 Two Safavid *Farmān*s of Appointment to the Post of *Ṣadr* dated 957/1550 and 961/1554

The only Safavid decrees of appointment to the post of *ṣadr*, are two *farmāns* of Shāh Ṭahmāsp I dated Ramaḍān 957/1550 and Ramaḍān 961/1554. Both concern the appointment of the theologian ʿAbd al-Razzāq Mīr Sulṭān as *ṣadr-i mamālik* of the provinces of Shīrvān and Shakkī.[15] The text of the two decrees is quite similar. It is an interesting example of two separate *farmāns* issued by the central royal secretariat concerning the same appointment. The only significant difference between the two decrees is that the earlier longer decree dated 957/1550 specifies ʿAbd al-Razzāq's role in promoting the new Twelver Shīʿī religion of the Safavids in the region. The shorter version of the decree dated 961/1554 confirms that ʿAbd al-Razzāq continued to be the holder of this office without sharing it with anyone else (*bi-lā mushārikat*) and that this appointment had not been changed. In addition, his representatives had the power and authority to collect the tax due to the office of the *ṣadr* (*rasm al-ṣadāra*).

From the earlier decree it appears that this tax was deducted from the annual religious alms (*wujūh-i zakāt wa akhmās-i khud*) that the inhabitants of the region had to send to the provincial *ṣadr-i mamālik*. ʿAbd al-Razzāq had the authority to appoint and dismiss all the religious officials of the province, such as *qāḍīs* and *muḥtasibs*. The later decree specifies that he had the authority to appoint and dismiss *quḍāt-i juzʾ wa kull*. The precise meaning of this construction is unclear. H. Busse translates *quḍāt-i juzʾ wa kull* as "low- and high-ranking judges".[16] W. Floor suggests "district judge" for *qāḍī-yi juzʾ* without offering an interpretation for *qāḍī-yi kull*.[17] It is likely, however, that the adjectives *juzʾ* (partial), and *kull* (total or universal), were used to distinguish between judges whose authority to decide cases

14 On the *mithāl* of the Safavid *ṣadr*, see Bhalloo and Rezaʾi 2019.
15 Edition in Busse 1959, 176–177 and Musavi 1977, 124–125.
16 Busse 1959, 176–177.
17 Floor 2000b, 491.

extended across all the lands of the state (*kull-i mamālik*) versus judges whose jurisdiction was limited to a given locality.[18] In both decrees, the governor of the region had to ensure the enforcement of the decree. The decree ends with the formulaic expression that new decrees should not be requested each year. This decree suggests that the appointment of local *qāḍīs* of a provincial region was the responsibility of the *ṣadr*. Moreover, from the evidence of the Safavid administrative manuals discussed earlier and the deeds of sale examined in this chapter, the *ṣadr* himself presided over a court active in authenticating legal deeds and adjudicating disputes according to the *sharīʿa*.

1.2.2 Two Safavid *Farmāns* of Appointment to the Post of *Qāḍī* dated 955/1548 and 1034/1625

A *farmān* of Shāh Tahmāsp I dated Rabīʿ II 955/May 1548 re-appoints Amīr Sayyid Sharīf Bāqī to the post of *qādī al-quḍāt* of Fārs.[19] Amīr Sayyid Sharīf Bāqī is also re-appointed to the office of *kalantar* and *sardār* of Fārs and to the office of *khalīfa al-khulafāʾ* of Fārs. From this decree, it appears that the *qāḍī al-quḍāt* could hold multiple offices, including an administrative one, such as the office of the *kalantar*. According to the decree, the agents (*wukalāʾ*) of Amīr Sayyid Sharīf Bāqī had complete authority in matters pertaining to his office. Since Amīr Sayyid Sharīf Bāqī had decided to reside in the district of Shabānkāra, the decree assigns his brother Khalīlullāh to act on his behalf in Shiraz. Khalīlullāh is described as *nāfidh al-ḥukm* meaning his orders were binding.

Another surviving decree issued by Shāh ʿAbbās I (r. 1579–1629), dated Dhū l-Ḥijja 1034/September-October 1625, confirms the appointment of Qāḍī Muḥammad as *qāḍī* of Gīlān and its region.[20] The decree emphasizes that Qāḍī Muḥammad did not share this office with any other individual (*aḥadī-rā bi-dū sharīk wa sahīm nadānand*) and that he had a monopoly over the adjudication of lawsuits (*wa chūn tanqīh-i murāfaʿāt-i sharʿiyya bi-ū mutaʿliq ast aḥadī dakhl na-namūda wa makhṣūs bi-ū dānand*). Moreover, only local judges (*quḍāt-i juzʾ*) and bailiffs (*mutaqāḍiyan*) that were appointed by him possessed judicial authority. This confirmation of the judicial monopoly of Qāḍī Muḥammad in Gīlān might be purely formulaic as we find similar clauses in other decrees (see below). On the other hand, it is also possible that there was a tendency for other judicial actors in the region to operate independently, either without an appointment or based on a previous appointment. In

18 See Horst 1964, 91.
19 Horst 1961, 301–309.
20 Edition and facsimile in Qāʾim-Maqāmī 1348sh./1969, 26–27.

such circumstances, it was necessary to seek an explicit decree form the shah himself confirming one's authority as the principal judge of a given region.

1.2.3 Two Safavid *Mithāl*s of Appointment to the Post of *Qāḍī* dated 1048/1639 and 1083/1672

Besides direct appointments made by the shah in *farmān*s, the *ṣadr* could also appoint *qāḍī*s through his order known as *mithāl*. A surviving *mithāl* of the central *ṣadr-i mamālik*, Mīrzā Ḥabībullāh, dated Dhū l-Ḥijja 1048/April–May 1639, appoints a certain Ḥājjī Abū Ṭālib as the *qāḍī* of Gīlān and its region.[21] The term used to designate Ḥājjī Abū Ṭālib's position is *aqḍā al-quḍātī*. Derived from Arabic *aqḍā al-quḍāt* (the "most just of judges"), this is transformed into a Persian adjectival construction by the addition of a final *yāʾ*. Similar constructs are used for the office of the *shaykh al-islām* (*shaykh al-islamī*) and the office of *khalīfat al-khulāfāʾ* (*khalīfat al-khulafāʾī*). It is not clear, however, if the construction *aqḍā al-quḍātī* always had the same meaning as the Arabic *qāḍī al-quḍāt* (chief judge) or its Persian equivalent *qāḍī-yi quḍāt*.[22]

The decree is illegible in some parts. It contains the *farmān* of Shāh Ṣafī (r. 1611–1642) on the verso. The document was registered in two archives. It bears the registration remarks of the royal secretariat of the shah on the recto and those of the department of the *ṣadr* (*dīwān al-ṣadāra*) on the verso. According to the *mithāl*, following the death of Ḥājjī Abū Ṭālib's uncle, the former *qāḍī* of Gīlān, Ḥājjī Abū Ṭālib requested the *ṣadr*, Mīrzā Ḥabībullāh, to appoint him to this office. He was appointed to the office (probably through another similar decree), and the present decree was issued to confirm the appointment.

Like the decree appointing ʿAbd al-Razzāq Mīr Sulṭān to the post of *ṣadr*, Ḥājjī Abū Ṭālib is confirmed in this office without partnership (*bi-lā mushārikat*). The inhabitants of Gīlān and its region were to recognise the validity of legal deeds, documents, and writings (*qabālajāt wa asnād wa niwishtijāt*) containing Ḥājjī Abū Ṭālib's seal, judicial attestation, and handwriting (*bi-muhr wa sijill wa khaṭṭ-i sharīʿat-panāh -i mūmā ilayhi muʿtabar dānand*).[23] Moreover, they had to honor and respect him. The remainder of the text has sections which are illegible and difficult to reconstruct. They describe the precise duties of the *qāḍī* of Gīlān. He was responsible for (1) writing legal deeds and judicial attestations (*katb-i ṣukūk wa sijillāt*); (2) presiding

21 Edition and facsimile in Qāʾim-Maqāmī 1348sh./1969, 46–47. See also the *farmān* confirming this appointment probably issued on the verso of the same *mithāl* in Qāʾim-Maqāmī 1348sh./1969, 45.
22 For the use of *qāḍī-yi quḍāt*, see Riḍāʾī 2021, 140.
23 This clause demonstrates how the term *sijill* no longer referred to a document or certificate containing the *ḥukm* of the *qāḍī* in the Safavid era, but came to refer to his written judicial attestation, which, alongside his handwriting (*khaṭṭ*) and personal seal (*muhr*) rendered the legal document valid. See the discussion on the Safavid *sijill* in 2.1.

over contracts and marriages (*īqāʿ-i ʿuqūd wa munakaḥāt*); (3) dividing estates according to the *sharīʿa* (*taqsīm-i mawārīth wa tarakāt*); (4) adjudicating lawsuits and disputes (*qatʿ wa faṣl-i murāfaʿāt wa mushājarāt*); (5) forbidding acts proscribed according to the *sharīʿa*; (6) administering the property of absent and insane individuals (*ḍabt-i amwāl-i ghayb wa-l-ṣufahāʾ wa-l-majānīn*); (7) breaking illicit musical instruments (*kasr-i ālāt-i lahw wa laʿib*); (8) performing divorces before scholars and reliable witnesses in the Friday Mosque and (9) appointing *quḍāt-i juzʾ wa kull* in the region. The decree confirms that no one except Ḥājjī Abū Ṭālib had the right to adjudicate the transactions and financial disputes of the province. The governors and other political authorities had to uphold the authority of Ḥājjī Abū Ṭālib. Finally, new decrees on his appointment should not be requested each year from the central *dīwān al-ṣadāra*, the administrative department of the *ṣadr*, in the Safavid capital.

The formulaic clauses of this *mithāl* of appointment dated Dhū l-Ḥijja 1048/April–May 1639 are also found in another *mithāl* dated Jamādī II 1083/September-October 1672.[24] In the latter *mithāl*, the central *ṣadr-i mamālik*, Abū Ṣāliḥ Muḥammad Muḥsin al-Raḍawī gives Mīrzā Muḥammad Zāhid ʿAbd al-Wahhābī a one-third share in the office of the *qāḍī* of Tabriz and its environs (*yak thulth-i qaḍāʾ wa aqḍā al-quḍātī-yi dār al-salṭana-yi tabrīz wa nawāḥī*). The decree sheds important light on the role played by the central *dīwān al-ṣadāra* in the Safavid capital in dividing the office of *qādī* of a given town or region among members of a single clerical family.

The decree begins with a confirmation from the Chief Accountant of the Endowments of the Protected Domains (*mustawfī-yi mawqūfāt-i mamālik-i maḥrūsa*), that an earlier *mithāl* had been issued by the central *dīwān al-ṣadāra* in the year Pīchī-Īl (Year of the Monkey) 1078, according to the Chinese-Uighur Animal calendar. According to this *mithāl*, one-third of the office of the *qāḍī* of Tabriz and its environs controlled by Mīr Muʿizz al-Dīn Muḥammad ʿAbd al-Wahhābī was transferred to Mīrzā Muḥammad Zāhid ʿAbd al-Wahhābī. In a separate *mithāl*, from the beginning of Tangūz-Īl (Year of the Pig), this one-third was transferred from Mīrzā Muḥammad Zāhid ʿAbd al-Wahhābī to the son of Mīr Muʿizz al-Dīn Muḥammad ʿAbd al-Wahhābī named Mīr Muḥammad Muqīm ʿAbd al-Wahhābī. Based on yet another *mithāl*, from the beginning of Qūy-Īl (Year of the Sheep) 1077, a separate one-third (*thulth-i dīgar*) of the office was assigned to Mīr Muḥammad Fasīḥ b. Mīr Muaḥmmad Hāshim ʿAbd al-Wahhābī. Based on two documents shown to the central *dīwān al-ṣadāra* bearing the endorsements and seals of reliable *sayyids* and scholars of the region to the effect that they were pleased with the conduct of Mīrzā Muḥammad Zāhid ʿAbd al-Wahhābī, the *dīwān al-ṣadāra* issued the present decree in the beginning of Sīchqān-Īl

24 Edition and facsimile in Musavi 1977, 192–195.

(Year of the Rat). The decree transferred one-third of the office previously held by Mīr Muḥammad Fasīḥ b. Mīr Muaḥmmad Hāshim ʿAbd al-Wahhābī to Mīrzā Muḥammad Zāhid ʿAbd al-Wahhābī.

In brief, Mīrzā Muḥammad Zāhid ʿAbd al-Wahhābī and Mīr Muḥammad Muqīm ʿAbd al-Wahhābī now jointly controlled two-thirds of the office in Tabrīz and its environs. It is not clear from the decree if the remaining one-third was also held by another member of the ʿAbd al-Wahhābī clerical lineage. This decree dated 1083/1672 is of significant historical interest because it provides insight into how members of a single clerical lineage could simultaneously hold shares in the office of *qāḍī* in the Safavid period in towns such as Tabriz in the seventeenth century.

1.2.4 A Safavid *Farmān* of Appointment to the Post of *Shaykh al-Islām* dated 1079/1669

In a *farmān* of Shāh Sulaymān (r. 1666–1694) dated 1079/1669, Mīrzā Hidāyat b. Amīr Muḥammad Taqī al-Ḥusaynī is appointed as *shaykh al-islām* of Mashhad in place of Sayyid Tāj al-Dīn al-Khādim al-Mūsawī.[25] The duties of Mīrzā Hidāyat are virtually identical to those described in the decree appointing Ḥājjī Abū Ṭālib to the office of *qāḍī* of Gīlān and its region. The *shaykh al-islām* was to (1) enjoin the masses to obey the *sharīʿa*, while (2) forbidding its proscribed acts. Moreover, he was responsible for (3) collecting alms and ensuring that they were distributed to deserving individuals. He was also in charge of (4) dividing estates according to the *sharīʿa*, (5) presiding over contracts and marriages (6), administering the property of absent and insane individuals and, (7) adjudicating lawsuits and disputes.

There is little to distinguish the duties of *the shaykh al-islām* from those of an ordinary *qāḍī*. This overlap of roles is also confirmed in the description of the function of the *qāḍī* and the *shaykh al-islām* of Isfahan in the Safavid administrative manuals discussed earlier. Like the *qāḍī*, the *shaykh al-islām* had his own *sharīʿa* court and played an important role as a notary. Based on the archive of Safavid documents from the shrine of Imām Riḍā in Mashhad, the *shaykh al-islām* and the *qāḍī* would jointly seal documents containing witness testimonies (*maḥḍar*) or documents determining official weights and measures (*taʿsir-nāmcha*) which were later registered in Safavid fiscal archives or *daftars*.[26]

The overlapping roles of the *qāḍī* and the *shaykh al-islām* also meant that individuals could be appointed to the two offices simultaneously. This can be seen from a Safavid *mithāl* decree dated Muḥarram 1082/1671 appointing Mawlānā

25 Busse 1959, 199–203 and Jahānpūr 1348 sh./1969, 221–264.

26 I am indebted to Elahe Mahbub Farimani for sharing her forthcoming research on the Safavid *maḥḍar* and *taʿsīr-nāmcha* documents in the Āstān-i Quds-i Raḍawī collection.

Muṣṭafā to the office of *qāḍī* and *shaykh al-islām* of the province of Ardalān.[27] This is quite different from the Ottoman empire where the jurisdiction of the *qāḍī* and the *shaykh al-islām* were clearly separate. Based on the biography of the first *shaykh al-islām* of the Safavid capital Qazvin, leading Imāmī Shīʿī scholars were appointed as *shaykh al-islām*. Though these scholars issued legal opinions and wrote legal treatises, they were also involved in areas of judicial activity such as the authentication of legal documents, a role traditionally associated with the *qāḍī*.[28] This continued well after the fall of the Safavid dynasty as the example of the Tammāmī *shaykh al-islāms* in Shiraz (see Chapter 2) and the legal deeds discussed below (see Section 3) demonstrate.

1.2.5 A Zand *Farmān* of Appointment to the Post of *Qāḍī* dated Dhū l-Qaʿda 1183/March 1770

An important *farmān* of Karīm Khān Zand (r.1751–1779) has survived dated Dhū l-Qaʿda 1183/March 1770. It confirms the appointment of Mīrzā Muḥammad Taqī (d. 1222/1807), as *qāḍī* of Tabriz (*qāḍī-yi dār al-saltana-yi tabrīz*) and its surrounding districts.[29] Mīrzā Muḥammad Taqī is assigned a stipend (*dar-wajh-i mawājib-i ū*) of fifty Tabrīzī *tūmāns* and fifty *kharwār* of wheat from the tax revenues of the city (*az bābat-i māliyāt-i dīwānī-yi dār al-saltana-yi tabrīz*). His judgeship (*aqḍā al-quḍātī*), monopoly over the office (*qāḍī bi-l-istiqlāl*), and the validity of documents and judicial attestations bearing his seal were to be recognised by all inhabitants including the governor of Tabriz and his agents. The governor and his agents were responsible for ensuring the *qāḍī* received his stipend regularly each year (*sāl bi-sāl*) from the taxes collected. Receipt of the stipend by the *qāḍī* was to be recorded in a copy of the decree which would be issued as proof (*wa qabḍ- dar-ḍimn-i sawād-i farmān-i muṭʿā bi-jihat-i ḥujjat ṣādir namāyand*). The Zand *farmān* is clearly unambiguous regarding the *qāḍī*'s stipend and the recording of its receipt by the *qāḍī*. This clause is not found in the Safavid decrees of judicial appointment discussed earlier. It is of significant interest that Mīrzā Muḥammad Taqī belonged to the Ṭabāṭabāʾī clerical lineage of Tabriz. This clerical lineage, the descendants of Mīr ʿAbd al-Wahhāb (d. 927/1521), successively held the post of both *qāḍī* and *shaykh al-islām* of Tabriz in the eighteenth

27 Asnād-i Millī, file no. 91, facsimile published in *Faṣl-nāma-yi ārshīw-i millī* year 3, no. 1, Spring 1396sh. /2017, 186.

28 Stewart 1996. For examples of Safavid legal opinions, see Papazian 1968, 496.

29 See Ṭabāṭabāʾī 1349 sh./1970, 497–498. Mīrzā Muḥammad Taqī (d. 1222/1807), was a student of the famous Uṣūlī jurist Muḥammad Bāqir Bihabahānī in Karabala, Iraq and had received a licence (*ijāza*), though it is not clear of which type, from one of his students, Shaykh Muḥammad Mahdī Futūnī, in 1173/1759, before returning to Tabriz, see Werner 2000, 211–212.

and nineteenth centuries.[30] The pattern of clerical lineages in urban centres inheriting a judicial appointment over several generations was not uncommon. Another important example is the clerical lineage of Sayyid Ḥusayn Khātam al-Mujtahidīn (d. 1001/1592–3) whose descendants successively held many important religious and judicial posts during the Safavid and post-Safavid periods, including the post of *shaykh al-islām* of Qazvin.[31] Similarly, the descendants of Muḥammad Bāqir Sabzawarī (d. 1090/1679), successively held the post of *shaykh al-islām* of Isfahan during the eighteenth and nineteenth centuries.[32] The example, presented in this study (Chapter 2) is of the émigré Arab origin Tammāmī clerical lineage of Shiraz, descendants of Shaykh Aḥmad al-Tammāmī (d. ca. 1130/1717–18), who occupied the post of *shaykh al-islām* of Fārs from the eighteenth to nineteenth centuries.

2 Scribal and Archival Practices of Safavid Legal Documents

The most significant rupture in the scribal practice of Islamic legal documents in Persian after the Mongol Ilkhanid period is in the way they were validated. The earliest known pre-Mongol Islamic Persian legal documents from eleventh century Khurāsān were authenticated through Arabic witness clauses at the bottom of the document alone.[33] From the twelfth to thirteenth centuries a separate Arabic judicial attestation of the *qāḍī* is visible in Persian legal documents in addition to the witness clauses.[34] This judicial attestation of the *qāḍī* should be distinguished from the pious formula the *qāḍī* used as his personal signature generally termed *ʿalāma* in the western parts of the Islamic world and *tawqīʿ* in the eastern Islamic lands.[35] The *qāḍī*'s judicial attestation in Arabic, his *tawqīʿ*, and the accompanying witness clauses all had an authenticating function.[36]

By the fourteenth-century Mongol Ilkhanid period in Iran, the top left-hand corner of Persian legal documents had become a clearly demarcated space for writing the *qāḍī's* Arabic judicial attestation and his *tawqīʿ*, while witness clauses

30 Werner 2000, 207–268.
31 Jaʿfariyān 1382 sh./2003, 122–194.
32 Mahdawī 1371 sh./1992.
33 See Haim, 2019 415–446.
34 M. Gronke terms these judicial attestations Legaliserungsvermerk, see Gronke 1982, 62–64. In the eleventh century such attestations began with a *yaqūlu* deposition clause by the *qāḍī*, see the verso of a Central Asian *waqf* deed dated 458/1066 in Khadr 1967, 320.
35 The formula *al-ḥukm li-llāh al-ʿaliyy al-kabīr* is used as a *tawqīʿ* by a *qāḍī* in a thirteenth century court record from Khurāsān dated 608/1212, see Bhalloo 2023a.
36 See Bhalloo 2023a.

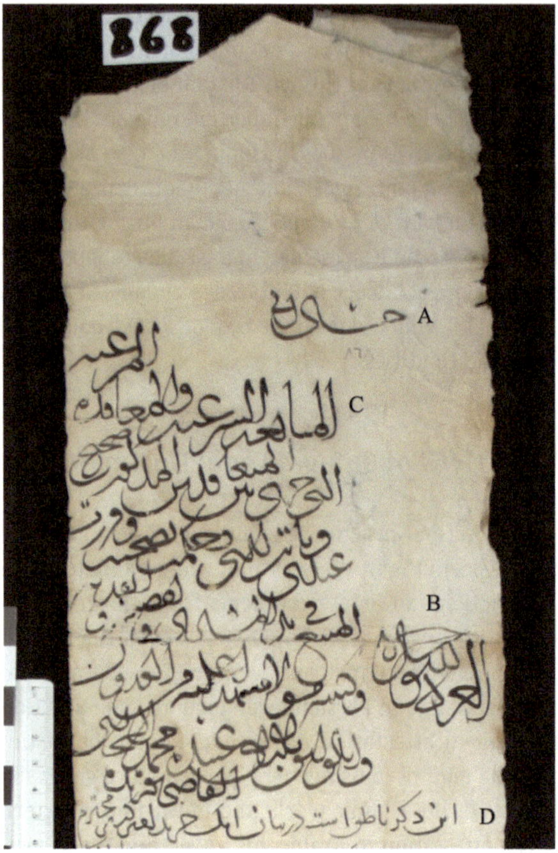

Figure 1: The *qāḍī*'s seven-line Arabic judicial attestation on the top-left corner of a Persian deed of sale dated 700/1301 © Document no. 868, Islamic Museum, al-Ḥaram al-Sharīf, Jerusalem.[37]

were written at the bottom of the document after the main text.[38] In a Persian sale deed dated 30 Ramaḍān 700/8 September 1301, for example, the first line of the main text in Persian (see Figure 1D) is preceded by a seven-line judicial attestation in Arabic by the *qāḍī* Muḥammad al-Bukhārī (C).[39] In the attestation, the

37 I am indebted to C. Müller for providing me an image of this document.

38 The spatial significance of the top left-hand corner for recording notarial attestations is already visible in tenth and eleventh century Fatimid legal documents, see for example document no. 14 in Gaubert and Mouton 2014, 83.

39 On this deed, Haram #868 in the documentary corpus from al-Ḥaram al-Sharīf in Jerusalem, see Little 1984, 383.

qāḍī confirms the sale (as recorded in the deed) between the two parties (the buyer and the seller) had occurred correctly before him and that he had issued a decision (*ḥukm*) on its validity. The attestation contains two pious formulas used by the *qādī* as *tawqī*'s, *ḥasbī rabbī* (My Lord is Sufficent) (A) and *al-ʿizza li l-lāh waḥdahu* (Glory belongs to God alone) (B).

In contrast, however, to the usual Mongol Ilkhanid practice of a single judicial attestation by the *qāḍī* on the top-left hand corner of the deed,[40] in the post-Mongol period, it was common for several judicial actors to write attestations sealed using round black ink seals.[41] The top-left hand corner of the document was also no longer as significant for writing the judicial attestation. Judicial attestations began to be recorded and sealed on different parts of the document. This spatial decentering of the *qāḍī's* position on legal deeds is confirmed by the sources examined in the first part of this chapter which point to the overlapping notarial and adjudicative functions of the post of *qāḍī*, the *ṣadr*, and the *shaykh al-islām* in early modern Iran.

2.1 The Practice of Writing a *Sijill* on Safavid Legal Documents

During the twelfth and early thirteenth centuries in Transoxiana *sijill* referred to a document containing a witnessed record of court proceedings before the *qāḍī* along with his decision or *ḥukm.*[42] In Safavid practice, however, we know from the evidence of legal formularies (*shurūṭ*), that *sijill* was used to refer to the

40 *Waqf* deeds are a notable exception and are already authenticated in Iran by multiple judicial attestations in the fourteenth century. See for example the authentication of the endowment deed of Rashīd al-Dīn dated 709/1309 (Hoffmann 2000, 349–371) and the Kujūjī endowment deed dated 782/1380 (Werner et al. 2013, 38–44).

41 This is already visible in fifteenth-century deeds from the Turkmen Qarāqūyūnlū and Aqqūyūnlū period, for example the *waqf* deed of the village Vagarshapat (Uch Kilisiya) dated 832/1428, see Papazian 1968, 57–65, 253–62, 416–26, 515–22. On the use of ink as a sealing medium in the Islamic world and the method of applying seal impressions onto documents, see Gallop and Porter 2012, 101. Round black ink seal impressions were used by *qāḍīs* and *muftīs* to seal Central Asian Islamic legal documents well into the modern period, see Bhalloo and Ishkawari 2024a.

42 Hallaq 1998, 420. In thirteenth century Iran, a sale deed from Ardabīl dated 606/1209 authenticated by the issuance of a *ḥukm* by the *qāḍī* is referred to by one of the witnesses as a *sijill* (*yashhadu ʿalā al-sijill al-ʿālī aʿlāhu l-llāh*), see Gronke 1982, Urkunde IX, 241. In fourteenth century Mamluk practice, the term *sijill* was used to describe rolls which transcribed a series of related legal proceedings along with the testimonies of witnesses and the issuance of a *ḥukm* by the *qāḍī* validitating these legal acts. For an example of a Mamluk *sijill* roll from Aleppo see Sabghini 2014. A shift in terminology occurs in the Ottoman period when *sijill* is used to refer to the equisized codex registers kept by the *qāḍī*. For a detailed discussion of these transformations see Bhalloo 2024b. For the use of the term *sijill* in an administrative context in the Islamic world, see for example Fatimid decrees known as *sijill manshūr* in Stern 1964, 85.

formulaic attestations in Arabic on legal deeds in which the judge confirmed the validity of the occurrence of the legal act before him as it was recorded in the document.[43] In some Safavid cases, such judicial attestations also specify the issuance of a *ḥukm* by the judge on the validity of the contract as in the Ilkhanid Mongol Persian sale deed (700/1301) mentioned earlier.

Safavid legal deeds usually contain multiple Arabic judicial attestations (*sijill*s) by various appointed judicial actors such as the *qāḍī*, *ṣadr* and *shaykh al-islām*.[44] The *sijill* was thus no longer associated with the activity of the *qāḍī* alone. This made it difficult to distinguish the hierarchy of judges that added their *sijill*s onto legal documents. According to Qawām Muḥammad Shīrāzī, who served as deputy to successive *qāḍī al-quḍāt* of Safavid Fārs, this resulted in the practice of writing an *ʿuriḍa* clause (*ʿuriḍa niwishtan*) around the *sijill* of the highest-ranking judge.[45] *ʿUriḍa* is derived from the passive verbal form of the Arabic root *ʿ- r-ḍ* meaning to present something. From the few Safavid legal documents that have come to light so far containing an *ʿuriḍa* clause, it becomes clear that the complete *ʿuriḍa* formula is *ʿuriḍa ʿarḍuhu*: his presentation was, reviewed, submitted to a critical examination (by the judge).[46] In a sale deed dated Dhū l-Qaʿda 999/August 1591 in which the village of Kafshgarān on the outskirts of Qum is sold by the wife of the Safavid shah Ṭahmāsp I, the verb *ʿuriḍa* (see Figure 2A) is written above the noun *ʿarḍuhu* (Figure 2B). The

43 See the formulas for different types of *sijill*s depending on the type of legal document in the Safavid legal formulary entitled *Dastūr* of Qawām Muḥammad Shīrāzī completed in Shiraz in Dhū l-Ḥijja 1050/April 1641: Riḍāʾī 2021, 115–139. This Safavid understanding of the term *sijill* as the written judicial attestation of the judge on the deed can be compared to the *imzā-i kadī* or *ibāre-i tasdik* of Ottoman judges that appear at the top of Ottoman legal deeds (*hüccet*), see Gökbilgin 1979, 111–112, İpşirli 1988, 178. These types of judicial attestations are termed *ʿunwān al-ṣukūk* and *imḍāʾ* by al-Bursāwī (d. 982/1574), see Veselý 2011, 252, footnote 7–8. See for example an Ottoman deed of sale dated 877/1472-73 with a single judicial attestation in Arabic on the top left-hand corner in Tak 2019, 148. I am indebted to Tomoki Okawara for drawing my attention to this document.

44 As in the case of Safavid legal deeds, it was not uncommon for Ottoman *hüccets* to contain judicial attestations written by more than one judge, see Kotzageorgis 2014.

45 Riḍāʾī 2021, 156. Qawām Muḥammad Shīrāzī, according to his own admission, was appointed to act as deputy *qāḍī* (*bi-niyābat-i qaḍā*) at the *sharīʿa* court in Shiraz of five successive Safavid *qāḍī-yi quḍāt* (Ar. *qāḍī al-quḍāt*) of Fārs. He was first granted permission to act on behalf of the earliest known Safavid *qāḍī-yi quḍāt* of Fārs, Muḥibb al-Dīn Ḥabībullah Sharīfī (see Rezaʾi 2022), at his *sharīʿa* court, towards the end of the career of the latter. He assumed the same function under four subsequent *qāḍī-yi quḍāt* of Fars: the philosopher Amīr Ghiyāth al-Dīn Manṣūr Dashtakī and later his son Amīr Sharaf al-Dīn ʿAlī Dashtakī, and then Mīr Sharaf al-Dīn Bāqī Sharīfī and his son Amīr Ṣadr al-Dīn Muḥammad Thānī Sharīfī. Qawām Muḥammad Shīrāzī does not mention holding any function at the *sharīʿa* court of Amīr Amīn al-Dīn Shāh Muḥammad Abū Turāb Injū, the *qāḍī-yi quḍāt* of Fārs when he completed his legal formulary in 1050/1641, see Riḍāʾī 2021, 151–155.

46 Ṭabāṭabāʾī 1352 sh./1973, 991–996.

main judicial attestation is written inside the descending crescent of the letter *ḍāḍ* of the verb *ʿuriḍa*. The addition of a black line above this descending crescent encloses the main text of the principal *sijill* inside the letter *ḍāḍ* (Figure 2C). The name of the *ṣadr-i khāṣṣa*, Abū l-Wulā Injū (Figure 2D) along with his seal (Figure 2E) appears directly below the *ʿuriḍa ʿarḍuhu* clause.[47]

Figure 2: The *ʿuriḍa ʿarḍuhu* clause around the principal *sijill* on the top-right hand corner of a Safavid sale deed dated Dhū l-Qaʿda 999/August 1591. © Document no. 4042f, Kitāb-khāna-yi Markazī wa Markaz-i Asnād-i Dānishgāh-i Tihrān, Tehran.

2.2 *Sijills* on a Safavid Sale Deed from Qazvin dated 989/1581

In general, most surviving Safavid legal documents contain multiple *sijills* without an *ʿuriḍa ʿarḍuhu* clause. An example is a sale deed measuring 93.2 x 22 cm from the Safavid capital Qazvin (1555–1598) dated Rabīʿ I 989/May 1581.[48] The deed records the sale of land on the outskirts of Qazvin by the Safavid shah Muḥammad Khudābanda (r. 1578–1587) to a woman from the Safavid royal family, Shahrbānū Khānum, wife of Mīrzā Salmān Wazīr. The sale deed contains the *sijills* of two judicial actors: the *ṣadr-i khāṣṣa*, Abū l-Wulā Injū, and the *ṣadr-i ʿāmma* or *ṣadr-i mamālik*,

47 Document no. 4042f, University of Tehran Library. I am indebted to U. Riḍāʾī for providing me an image of this document. On the use of the verb *ʿuriḍa* in the formulae of Ottoman judicial attestations, see Veselý 2011.

48 Document no. 997/49, Sāzmān-i Asnād wa Kitāb-khāna-yi Millī-yi Jumhūrī-yi Islāmī-yi Īrān, Tehran. Edition in Ishrāqī 1376 sh./1997, 5–9. I am indebted to Ali Mir-Ansari for providing me an image of this document.

Figure 3: Section of a Safavid sale deed roll (*ṭūmār*) measuring 93.2 × 22 cm from Qazvin dated 989/1581. The *sijill*s and round black ink seals of the *ṣadr-i mamālik* (A) and the *ṣadr-i khāṣṣa* (B) are visible on the right-hand margin of the document perpendicular to the main text. © Document no. 997/49, NLAI, Tehran.

Shams al-Dīn Tāj al-Ḥusaynī. Their *sijill*s appear on the right-hand margin of the document perpendicular to the lines of the main text (see Figure 3A and B). In this instance, the *ṣadr-i khāṣṣa*, has written the longer *sijill* (A) extending over nine lines of the main text of the document probably reflecting his higher status and the fact that this document was produced and archived at his *sharīʿa* court (see below).

In contrast, the *sijill* of the *ṣadr-i mamālik*, is shorter, far more compact and squeezed together (B). Both *ṣadrs* use the same pious formula as their signature (*tawqīʿ*). In this case, the Arabic pronoun *hū* used to refer to God is repeated twice to give the formula: *huwa hū* (He is God). Like the *ḥasbala*, this formula appears to have become associated in the Safavid Iranian context with judicial authority. The next segment of the *sijill* of the *ṣadr-i mamālik* begins with a pious invocation (*khuṭba*) in praise of God, the Prophet, and his family. The conjunction *wa-baʿd* (and then) introduces the third segment of the *sijill* where the *ṣadr-i mamālik* confirms the shah has acknowledged the legal content of the document, namely the sale carried out on his behalf by his legal representative (*wakīl*) and the transfer and receipt of the purchase sum and object of sale by the buyer from the seller. In the fourth segment, the *ṣadr-i mamālik* renders the content of the legal contract binding and confirms being a witness to it using the formula: *fa-alzamtu bi-maḍmūnihi wa-faḥwāhi wa-ashhadtu ʿala maknūnihi wa-muḥtawāhi.*[49] This is followed by the name of the *ṣadr-i mamlik*, which appears after the clause *ḥarrarahu* (he wrote it).

The *sijill* of the *ṣadr-i khāṣṣa* begins with the pious formula, *huwa hū*, followed by a long pious invocation (*khuṭba*) in praise of God, the Prophet, and his family. This is followed by an attestation confirming the shah has acknowledged the particulars of sale. The *ṣadr-i khāṣṣa* also renders the contract binding and acts as a witness using the following formula: *fa-aṣghaytuhu wa-shahadtuhu ʿalayhi wa-anfadhtuhu wa-amḍaytuhu.*[50] The use of first person past-tense verbs here was to ensure that the *sijill* text was understood rhetorically as an origination (*inshāʾ*) whose binding force was inherent in itself and not an assertion or report (*khabar*) which could be accepted or rejected.[51] The *sijill* ends with a clause in which the *ṣadr-i khāṣṣa* prays for the continued existence of the victorious Safavid state (*dāʿiyan li l-dawla al-abadiyya al-qāhira*). This is followed by the name of the *ṣadr-i khāṣṣa.*

It is likely that the main text and the *sijill*s were written by at least two or more different scribes before being sealed by the parties involved. The *ṣadr-i khāṣṣa* and the *ṣadr-i mamālik* affixed their round black ink seals onto the document before the text of their *sijill* was copied next to it. The text of the *sijill* thus runs over the impression made by the seal. This was common practice to circumvent forgery. The inscription (*sajʿ-i muhr*) in *naskh* on the round black ink seal of

49 I made it (the document's) content binding and I am a witness to its hidden aspects and (clear) details.
50 I listend carefully (to the shah's acknowledgement of sale), I am a witness to it, and I made it (the sale) binding and effective.
51 See Jackson 1996, 170–177.

the *ṣadr-i mamālik* is *ḥasbī allāh ʿabduhu shams al-dīn muḥammad al-husaynī 989*. The diameter of the seal is 2.5 cm. The pious formula *hasbī allāh* used by the *ṣadr-i mamālik* for this seal is different from *huwa hū* used in the text of his *sijill*. The seal inscription also includes the name of the *ṣadr* and the year in which the seal was made, 989/1581. The seal was thus made in the same year as the document. The round black ink seal of the *ṣadr-i khāṣṣa* is slightly larger with a diameter of 3 cm. The inscription in *naskh* on the seal is: *huwa l-ḥaqq abū l-wulā shāh maḥmūd al-ḥasanī al-ḥusaynī 979*. Once again, a different pious formula from the one used in the *sijill* is used for the seal inscription. In addition to the *sijill*s and seals of the *ṣadr-i khāṣṣa* and the *ṣadr-i mamālik*, the document also contains the witness clauses of seven witnesses including the shah himself each of which are sealed.

2.3 Registration and Archiving of Safavid Legal Documents

Besides its main text, *sijill*s and witness clauses, the Qazvin sale deed roll dated 989/1581 also contains a registration seal and accompanying registration note. These appear on the right-hand margin of line 37 (see Figure 4).

The registration seal has a rectangular base with an ornamental triangular shape or "hat" at the top (*muhr-i kulāh-dār*). The base measures 3 cm x 1.5 cm and the height of the hat is 2 cm. The inscription of the seal in *nastaʿlīq* is: *huwa l-walī thubita fī jarīdat al-maḥkama al-ʿiliyya al-nājiyya al-injuwiyya wa-l-māmalik al-maḥrūsa wa-l-ʿasākir al-manṣūra* (He is the Guardian. It has been registered (or established) in the *jarīda* of the exalted Injuwiyya *sharīʿa* court of the protected domains and victorious army).[52] We shall return to the meaning of *jarīda* later (see below). The use of the adjective *injuwiyya*, derived from Injū is an indication the *sharīʿa* court in question belonged to the *ṣadr-i khāṣṣa*, Abū l-Wulā Injū. It is interesting to note that the *ṣadr-i khāṣṣa* uses different pious formulae for the registration seal of his *sharīʿa* court (*huwa l-walī*), the text of his *sijill* (*huwa hū*) and for the inscription of the personal round black ink seal he used to seal his *sijill* (*huwa l-ḥaqq*).

Above the registration seal of the Injuwiyya *sharīʿa* court is the registration note in Arabic *thubita fī l-taʾrīkh* – it has been registered (or established) on the date (of its writing) (Figure 5C). Directly below the registration seal is a smaller round black ink seal belonging to one of the witnesses of the documents, the legal representative (*wakīl*) of the shah, Jābir b. Maḥmūd Anṣārī. It has the following

52 See Riḍāʾī 1397 sh./2018, 213–220.

inscription in *naskh*: *jābir b. maḥmūd 972.*[53] The small round black ink seal of Jābir b. Maḥmūd Anṣārī (Figure 5D), the registration seal of the Injuwiyya *sharīʿa* court of the *ṣadr-i khāṣṣa* Abū l-Wulā Injū (Figure 5E), and the large round ink seal (Figure 5F) of the *ṣadr-i mamālik*, Shams al-Dīn Tāj al-Ḥusaynī, are affixed over the bottom and top edge of two sheets of paper glued to each other on the verso (see Figure 5). The notes and seal impressions were thus divided across two sheets probably to circumvent forgery.

Figure 4: Detail of the registration seal of the *sharīʿa* court of the *ṣadr-i khāṣṣa*, Abū l-Wulā Injū and the registration note *thubita fī l-taʾrīkh* on the Qazvin sale deed roll dated 989/1581. © Document no. 997/49, NLAI, Tehran.

At least two other sale deeds, one relating to the sale of land in Astarābād (992/1584) and the other in Hamadān (995/1587), were also probably produced and registered in the same *sharīʿa* court of the *ṣadr-i khāṣṣa*, Abū l-Wulā Injū, in the Safavid capital Qazvin. The Astarābād deed concerns sale of land by the Safavid shah Muḥammad Khudābanda.[54] It has an almost identical *sharīʿa* court registration seal including the

53 Riḍāʾī 1397 sh./2018, 213–220.
54 Edited with facsimile in Dhabīḥī and Sutūda 1354 sh./1975, VI, 621.

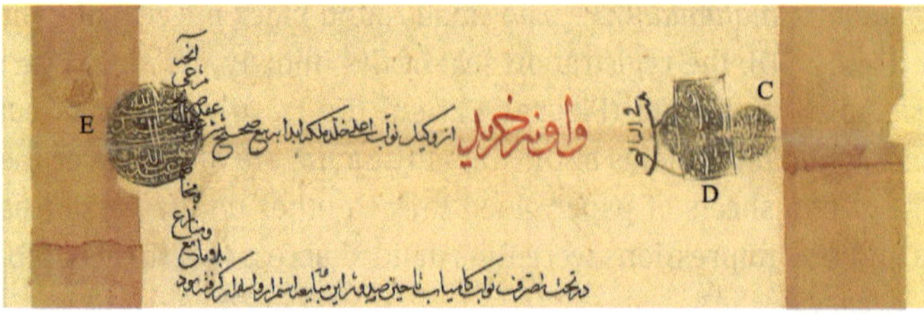

Figure 5: Line 37 of the sale deed roll from Qazvin dated 989/1581 © Document no. 997/49, NLAI, Tehran.

registration note *thubita fi l-taʾrīkh* as the Qazvin sale deed (989/1581). However, the registration seal is affixed below the last line of the deed and not on the right-hand margin as in the Qazvin sale deed (989/1581). The Hamadān deed (995/1587) records the sale of land in Hamadān by a Safavid official to a local tribal leader in Hamadān.[55] It states explicitly that the Safavid official appeared in the *dīwān al-ṣadāra al-ʿiliyya al-ʿāliyya al-manṣūriyya al-injuwiyya* to authorize the sale. It is possible therefore that the Injuwiyya *sharīʿa* court described in the Qazvin sale deed (989/1581) referred to the *dīwān al-ṣadāra*. The evidence from the administrative manuals from late Safavid Isfahan, as we have seen, however, suggest that the *ṣadr* also presided over a *sharīʿa* court along with the *dīwān-bēgī* in the Royal Guardhouse (Kishikkhāna) of the Royal Palace. The Hamadān sale deed (995/1587) also contains a registration seal. It is affixed, as in the Qazvin sale deed (989/1581), on the right-hand margin of the document where two sheets of paper are glued together (see Figure 6). The Hamadān registration seal, however, is different from the one used in the Qazvin (989/1581) and Astarābād (992/1584) sale deeds. The shape is identical, but the inscription is in *naskh* not *nastaʿlīq* script. In addition, the registration note *thubita fi l-taʾrīkh* is missing above the registration seal.

These sale deeds suggest that the Injuwiyya *sharīʿa* court of the *ṣadr-i khāṣṣa* in the Safavid capital Qazvin used at least two different registration seals between the years 1581–1587. The only other document discovered so far from Safavid Iran which suggests that Safavid *sharīʿa* courts actively registered documents concerns the sale of land within the Zoroastrian community in Yazd. The document contains the text of a sale deed dated Jamādī I 950/August 1543 on the recto (see Figure 7). The verso is used to record a related deed of acknowledgement (*iqrār*) dated Jamādī II 959/June 1552 (see Figure 8).[56] The document was authenticated by two *sayyids*:

55 Edited with facsimile in Bīgdilī 1367 sh./1988, 24, 245.

56 Document nos. 146370/1 and 146370/2, Markaz-i Asnād wa Maṭbūʿāt-i Astān-i Quds-i Raḍawī. I am indebted to Zahra Talaee and Elahe Mahbub-Farimani for the images of this document.

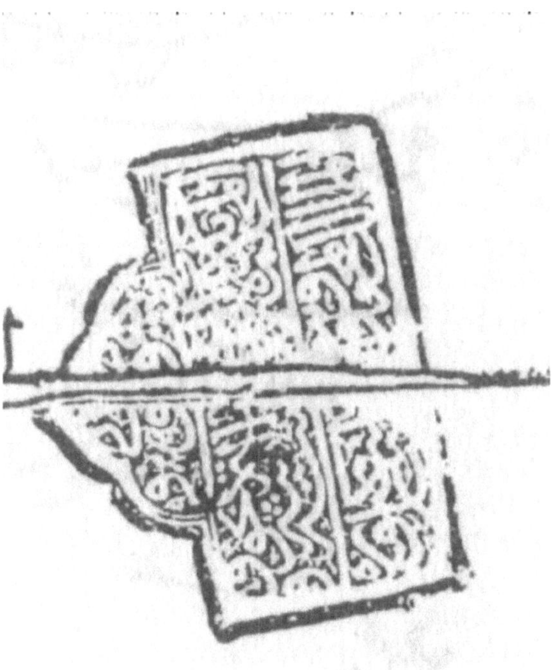

Figure 6: Detail of the second registration seal with the inscription in *naskh* of the *sharīʿa* court of the *ṣadr-i khāṣṣa*, Abū l-Wulā Injū, in the Safavid capital Qazvin.[57]

Maqṣūd ʿAlī Ṭabāṭabāʾī and Zayn al-ʿĀbidīn Ḥusaynī. The former wrote and sealed the *sijill* on the right-hand margin of the sale deed. The latter has affixed his seal between the first and second lines of the sale deed and the *iqrār*. To prevent falsification, it was common practice to affix the seal on to the blank sheet before text was recorded above it.

Unlike the Safavid sale deeds discussed above, the Yazd legal document contains no registration seal. It contains two marginal registration notes. These registration notes are recorded in the form of a calligraphic signature (*ṭughrāʾ*). The first registration note relating to the sale deed on the recto is visible on the right hand-margin of the verso (Figure 8A). A second registration note, relating to the *iqrār* deed on the verso, appears on the verso between lines 6 and 7 (Figure 8B). This inter-linear registration note is sealed using a small round black ink seal. The two registration notes have the following text: *uthbita fī jarīdat al-maḥkama al-ʿiliyya al-*

57 Dhabīḥī and Sutūda 1354 sh./1975, VI, 621.

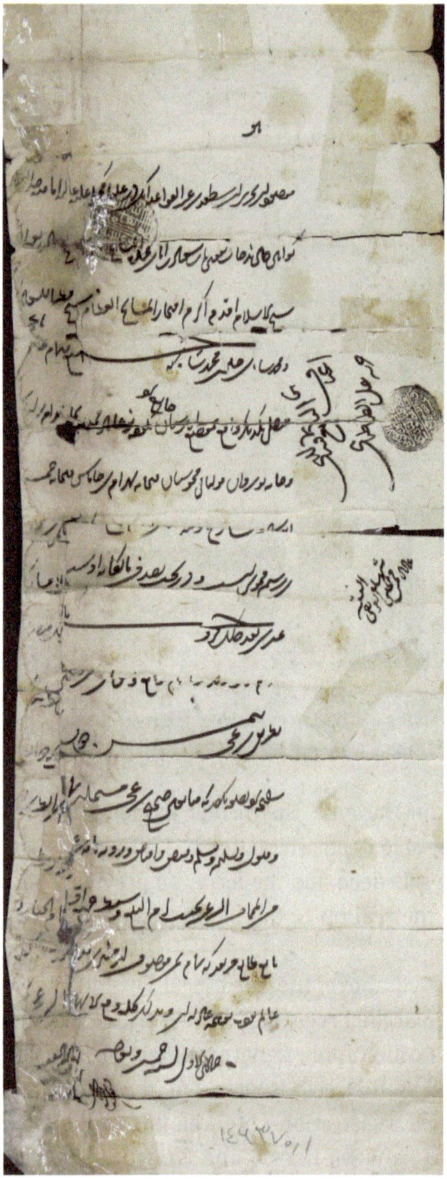

Figure 7: Recto: A sale deed dated 950/1543 from the Imāmiyya *sharīʿa* court in Yazd with multiple horizontal fold lines measuring 41 cm x 14.5 cm © Document no. 146370/1, Markaz-i Asnād wa Maṭbūʿāt-i Astān-i Quds-i Raḍawī, Mashhad, Iran.

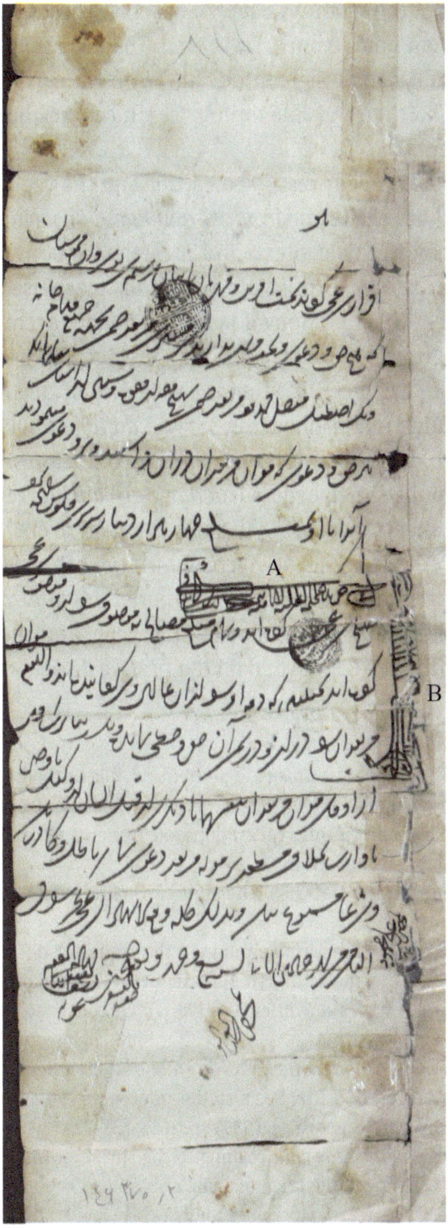

Figure 8: Verso of the sale deed from the Imāmiyya *sharīʿa* court in Yazd containing a deed of acknowledgement (*iqrār*) dated 959/1552 with two registration notes, one inter-linear in the centre (A) and the other (B) on the right-hand margin. © Document no. 146370/2, Markaz-i Asnād wa Maṭbūʿāt-i Āstān-i Quds-i Raḍawī, Mashhad, Iran.

imāmiyya (it was registered in the *jarīda* of the Imāmiyya *sharīʿa* court).[58] These are the earliest known *sharīʿa* court registration notes from Safavid Iran. The use of *uthbita* registration notes in the form of a calligraphic signature is known from earlier bureaucratic practice. Such registration notes are visible on fourteenth-century administrative decrees from Ilkhanid Mongol Iran.[59]

The registration seals on the Safavid sale deeds discussed earlier and the registration notes on the Yazd legal document use the term *jarīdat al-maḥkama* or *jarīda* of the *sharīʿa* court. What did *jarīda* mean in this context? Did it refer to a bound codex register or to loose sheets of paper?[60] The term *jarīda* and *daftar* were used inter-changeably in Iran since at least the Ilkhanid Mongol period to denote archival registries or repositories.[61] These registries did not necessarily involve the use of registers in the form of a bound book or codex. Based on the evidence of documents preserved in the shrine of Imām Riḍā in Mashhad, the Safavid *daftar-i tawjīhāt*, which registered state expenditure, for example, consists of a collection of copies of receipts (*barāt, qabḍ*) and administrative orders (*raqam, parwāncha*) recorded in full or as summaries on loose sheets measuring 19 cm x 13 cm or 18 cm × 13 cm and in some cases 13 cm × 11 cm.[62] These sheets are termed *fard* (pl. *afrād*) in Persian. The Safavid *daftar-i tawjīhāt* thus consisted of a collection of archival *fard* sheets.[63] The title of the *daftar* to which a *fard* sheet belonged, the year, and the number of *fard* sheets contained in a *daftar* were indicated on the first *fard* sheet.[64]

58 Riḍāʾī reads *thubita* (Riḍāʾī 1397 sh./2018, 217) however, in this case an *alif* is visible at the beginning and it could also be read *uthbita* based on similar *uthbita* registration notes known from Ilkhanid Mongol decrees, see footnote 109. The last part of this registration note remains undeciphered. Riḍāʾī suggests *thubita fī l-taʾrīkh* though this is uncertain.

59 See for example four inter-linear registration notes between line 1 and 2 in Urkunde XIX, plate 74, in Herrmann 2004.

60 According to Abu Naṣr al-Samarqandī (d.ca. 1155), the *jarīda* contained the copies of documents kept by the *qāḍī* for a given year, while the the Ottoman Ḥanafī jurist Ibn Nujaym (d.969–70/1563) uses *jarīda al-ḥisāb* to refer to the *qāḍī*'s *dīwān* or archive which consisted of sheets of paper (*al-kharāʾiṭ*), see Hallaq 1998, 428, footnote 76.

61 See the registration notes *uthbita fī l-jarīda* and *bar daftar thabt karda shud* used in a decree from Ardabīl dated 725/1327 in Hermann and Doerfer 1975, 319. See also the references to *jarīda* and *daftar* in *inshāʾ* manuals in Maḥbūb Farīmānī and Khusrawbēgī 1395 sh./2016, 228–229.

62 Eighteen thousand archival *fard* papers of the *daftar-i tawjīhāt* relating to the shrine of Imām Riḍā in Mashhad have survived dating from the begining of the reign of Shāh ʿAbbās I (r. 1588–1629) to the end of the Safavid period. For the structure of these *fard* papers, see Khusrawbēgī and Maḥbūb 1394 sh./2016, 43. For an example of a copy (*sawād*) of an original Safavid *parwāncha* decree and its registered summary in a *fard* paper, see Shahīdī 1397sh./2019, 256–258.

63 Khusrawbēgī and Maḥbūb 1394 sh./2016, 39. The relationship of archival *fard* sheets to fiscal rolls termed *ṭūmār-i nasaq* requires further research.

64 Khusrawbēgī and Maḥbūb 1394 sh./2016, 39.

In some cases, the *fard* sheets were numbered. Though there is no evidence so far of archival *fard* sheets from a Safavid *sharīʿa* court *jarīda*, *fard* sheets from the nineteenth century are known from the *sharīʿa* court of the *shaykh al-islām* Tammāmī family in Shiraz as we shall see in Chapter 2. Based on this, it is reasonable to assume that Safavid *sharīʿa* courts maintained *jarāʾid* which consisted of similar archival *fard* sheets that either summarized or recorded legal documents in full in the same accounting *siyāq* script of the *fard* sheets that have survived from various Safavid fiscal *daftars*. Registration notes and registration seals which confirmed the entry of a legal document into the *jarīda* of the *sharīʿa* court, referred therefore to its copying onto an archival *fard* sheet.

At this stage of research, however, it is not clear how such *fard* sheets were organized, folded, and held together, in various archival *daftar* repositories (*daftar-i tawjīhat, daftar-i awrācha, daftar-i mawqūfāt* etc.). There is some evidence to suggest that *fard* sheets were folded in half to form four sides along the lines of Fatimid archival bifolia or Mamluk bifolio *daftar* sheets.[65] *Fard* sheets from premodern Iran, however, do not show traces of archival holes. They were not, as in Fatimid and Mamluk practice, pierced then held together with a string threaded through the centre of the paper (tacketing) to form stacks or bundles of sheets (*iḍbāra*).[66] According to the Safavid *siyāq* manual of Kirmānī written in 951/1544–4, *fard* sheets were preserved in bags (Per. *kīsa*).[67] It is possible that such sheets were simply folded inside the bag without tacketing. The use of archival bags in Ilkhanid Mongol Iran is known from a rare fourteenth century archival list preserved in the Ḥaram al-Sharīf documentary corpus.[68] Based on this list, we know that inventories of documents preserved in archival bags were also produced.

65 On Mamluk bifolio *daftar* sheets see for example Little 1984, 333–374, Livingston 2018, 139, 213–215, and in particular, Aljoumani and Hirschler 2023, 110–116. For an example of a *fard* sheet folded in half see Chapter 2.

66 See Rustow 2020, 341–342. For an example of a Mamluk bifolio *daftar* sheet where the string is still visible in the archival holes see Aljoumani and Hirscler 2023, plates I.8a-I.8c. For similar tacketing of flat sheets from the fourteenth century Ḥaram al-Sharīf corpus, see Livingston 2018, 144–145.

67 See Kirmānī 1398 sh./2019. I am indebted to Elahe Maḥbūb Farīmānī for this reference. For the use of archival bags to store fiscal documents in early modern Europe, see the archival bags hanging in the office of the tax collector in the painting by Pieter Brueghel the Younger, Paying the Tax (The Tax Collector), ca. 1615.

68 See Bhalloo and Watabe 2024c forthcoming.

3 *Sijills* on a Legal Document from the Zand Period, 1198–1206/1784–1792

From the preceding analysis of administrative manuals, decrees of judicial appointment and *sijills* on legal deeds, it has become clear that the two *ṣadrs* (the *ṣadr-i khāṣṣa* and the *ṣadr-i mamālik*), the *shaykh al-islām* and the *qāḍī* were the main appointed *sharīʿa* practitioners of the Safavid period. The chaotic period of transition after the fall of the Safavid dynasty from 1722 onwards led to a breakdown of the Safavid system of judicial administration in Iran. The precise extent and nature of this breakdown is not clear. In the Safavid period, according to the decrees of appointment examined earlier, the shah and the *ṣadr* were directly involved in appointing judges. Did centralised judicial appointment occur in the post-Safavid period? The Zand decree of appointment examined earlier dated Dhū l-Qaʿda 1183/ March 1770 suggests it did.

Nevertheless, two important changes appear to have occurred. The first is the decline and eventual eclipse of the office of the *ṣadr* and his department, the *dīwān al-ṣadāra*. The *dīwān al-ṣadāra* played a key role in the centralisation of the judiciary and the administration of endowments in the Safavid period. The Safavid deed of sale from Qazvin discussed above suggests, moreover, that the *dīwān al-ṣadāra* in Qazvin also functioned as a *sharīʿa* court where Islamic legal deeds were produced and registered. The *ṣadr* was actively involved in judicially certifying such documents. In the post-Safavid period, however, the *ṣadr* is no longer identified as a significant practitioner of Islamic law in Iran. The *sijills* of documents from the post-Safavid period point, on the one hand, to the continued significance of the *qāḍī* and the *shaykh al-islām*, and, on the other, to the importance of a new actor, the *mullā-bāshī*, a post created in the late Safavid period.

To get a sense of these changes in the administration of *sharīʿa* courts in Iran after the fall of the Safavids, I will examine the *sijills* that appear on a legal document from the Zand period. The document is in the form of a vertical roll (*ṭūmār*) measuring 100 cm x 19.7 cm.[69] The roll is made up of three sheets of blue paper glued to each other. Each of the three sheets of the roll were produced in Shiraz in 1206/1792, a year after Āqā Muḥammad Khān Qājār captured the city.[70] The first sheet contains an original deed recording a divorce dated 24 Dhū l-Ḥijja 1206/13 August 1792. The middle sheet contains a certified copy of a deed granting powers of attorney (*wikāla*) dated 25 Shawwāl 1206/16 June 1792. The third and final sheet contains a copy of a marriage

69 The Arabic term *ṭūmār* was used in Persian to refer to deeds issued on rolls made up of multiple sheets of paper. The term itself dervises from the Greek *tomarion* which referred to sections constituting one sixth of a papyrus roll, see Khan 1993, 17.

70 Document no. 1393.310–2292, Kitāb-khāna wa mūza-yi millī-yi malik, Tehran.

deed written in the form of a settlement contract (*muṣālaḥa-nāma*) dated 22 Shaʿbān 1189/11 July 1784. The latter two documents are copies (*sawād*) made of two original (*aṣl*) deeds produced in Isfahan that were annexed to the original deed of divorce produced in Shiraz. This is clear because the copyists transcribe the *sijill*s of Islamic legal practitioners holding judicial positions in Isfahan that appeared in the respective original deeds. The deed of divorce dated 24 Dhū l-Ḥijja 1206/13 August 1792, however, appears to be an original produced in Shiraz itself as it contains no transcribed *sijill*s and has two original *sijills* of practitioners from Shiraz. These *sijill*s appear on the top left-hand corner of the document. The *sijill* on the left is of the *mullā bāshī*, Muḥammad Ḥusayn, while the *sijill* on the right is of the *qāḍī* of Shiraz, also described as the *qāḍī* of Fārs (*qāḍī-yi fārs*), Zayn al-ʿĀbidīn ʿAlawī (see Figure 9A and B). The *sijill* of the *mullā-bāshī* starts with an *ʿuriḍa* clause. The formula used is *ʿuriḍa maḍmūn dhālika ṣarīḥan*: its contents (i.e., of the document) were clearly examined. As we have seen from earlier Safavid practice the *ʿuriḍa* clause marked the principal *sijill* and highest-ranking judicial actor on the sheet.

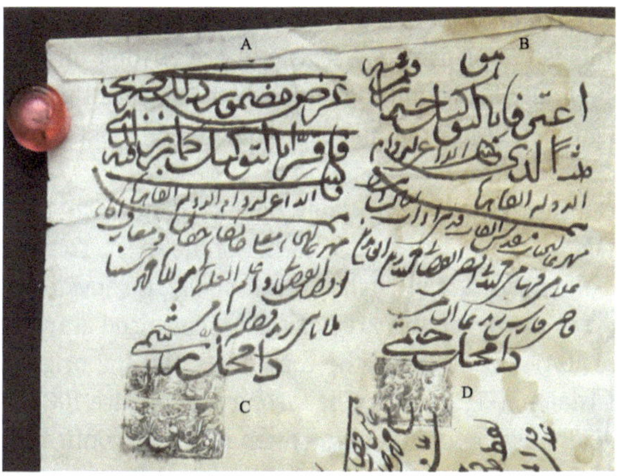

Figure 9: Top left-hand corner of an original (*aṣl*) deed of divorce produced in Shiraz in Dhū l-Qaʿda 1206/June 1792 containing the *sijill* of the *mullā-bāshī* (A) and the *sijill* of the *qāḍī* (B) © Document no. 1393.310–2292, Kitāb-khāna wa Mūza-yi Millī-yi Malik, Tehran.

Both the *mullā bāshī* and the *qāḍī* have affixed square seals below their respective *sijills*. The inscription in *nastaʿlīq* on the square seal of the *mullā bāshī* is *ufawiḍḍu amrī ilā l-lāh, ʿabuduhu muḥammad ḥusayn* (Figure 9C). The inscription on the *qāḍī*'s seal also in *nastaʿlīq* is *ibn zayn al-ʿabidīn al-ʿalawī* (Figure 9D). The use of round black ink seals by judicial officials commonly found in legal documents from the Turkmen, Timurid and Safavid periods thus almost completely disappears in post-

Safavid legal documents.[71] It is tempting to interpret this material shift, as a clear sign of the breakdown of a state appointed system of Islamic legal practitioners in Iran. In this case, however, it is likely that both the *mullā-bāshi* and the *qāḍī* were certifying deeds as appointed judicial actors on behalf of the state. Their *sijills* both end with the self-referential clause: *al-dāʿī li-dawwām al-dawla al-qāhira* (the one who calls for the continuation of the victorious state). This clause was also used by appointed practitioners on legal documents from the Safavid period as we have seen in the case of the *sijill* of the *ṣadr-i khāṣṣa* in the sale deed from Qazvin. It is also used by the *qāḍī* and *shaykh al-islām* in eighteenth-century sale deeds from Tabriz.[72] This self-referential clause appears right after the words *wa-kataba* which is written in a stylized manner with the *wāw* extending into the *kāf* of *kataba* and the *bāʾ* stretched across the length of the *sijill*. Similarly, the *lām* of the word *maḥall* in the clause *maḥall-i muhr* (place of the seal of) which follows the self-referential clause is also stretched. It marks the beginning of a new segment where the scribe describes the names and titles of the *mullā bāshī* and the *qāḍī*. This is followed by the third and final segment where the scribe has written in large bold *naskh* letters the formula *dhā maḥall rashmī* for the *mullā bāshī* and *dhā maḥall khatmī* for the *qāḍī*. These two formulas signify "this is the place of my seal" and are written directly over the respective seals of the *mullā bāshī* and the *qāḍī*, which suggests that the *mullā bāshī* and *qāḍī* first affixed their seals on to the paper before the scribe wrote these formulas.

The copy of the deed granting powers of attorney dated 25 Shawwāl 1206/ 16 June 1792 also contains two *sijills* on the top left-hand corner of the sheet. The first *sijill* is a transcription of the *sijill* of the *qāḍī* of Isfahan (*aqḍā al-quḍātī shaykh muḥammad qāḍī-yi dār al-salṭana-yi iṣfahān*) that appeared on the original deed granting powers of attorney (see Figure 10A). The scribe of the copy notes that the original *sijill* was sealed by the *qāḍī* of Isfahan (Figure 10B). The second *sijill* (Figure 10C), in contrast, is not a transcribed *sijill*. It is an original *sijill* written in Shiraz confirming that the deed granting powers of attorney was identical to its original (*dhā muṭābiq li-aṣlihi al-muʿtabar*). It is not clear to whom this second *sijill* belonged as it is sealed by both the *mullā-bāshi* (Figure 10D) and the *qāḍī* of Shiraz (Figure 10E). Both the transcribed *sijill* of the *qāḍī* of Isfahan and the original *sijill* certifiying the validity of the copy of the deed granting powers of attorney produced in Shiraz simply end with the clause *wa kataba al-dāʿī*. In the Safavid period, as we have seen in the *sijills*

71 There are some exceptions, however, see for example the round seals of the *sijills* on the recto and verso of the deed of sale (1207/1793), measuring 34 cm x 20 cm concerning the transfer of a farm known as Basit in the village of Nahand, Document no. 14142A81, WWQI, Amir Hossein Nikpour Collection.

72 See Document nos. 11 and 12 in Werner 2000, 346–354.

Figure 10: Copy produced in Shiraz of an original deed granting powers of attorney from Isfahan dated Shawwāl 1206/May 1792 © Document no. 1393.310-2292, Kitāb-khāna wa Mūza-yi Millī-yi Malik, Tehran.

of the sale deed from Qazvin, it was common for judicial actors to mention their names at the end of their respective *sijill*s. This helped to circumvent any confusion about who wrote a given *sijill* in later transcriptions made of the deed.

The third sheet is the earliest document in the roll. It is a copy of the original marriage deed produced in Isfahan. It contains the transcription of two *sijill*s which appeared in the original deed. These transcribed *sijill*s are useful as the copyist in some cases describes the function held by the person who wrote the original *sijill*. The first *sijill* on the original marriage deed was sealed by the *qāḍī* of Isfahan, Shaykh Muḥammad (*qāḍī-yi dār al-salṭana-yi iṣfahān*) on the right (see Figure 11A) and the *shaykh al-islām* of Isfahan, Mīrzā Murtaḍā (*shaykh al-islām-i dār al-salṭana-yi iṣfahān*) on the left (Figure 11B). The latter Mīrzā Murtaḍā (d. 1226/1809), was a descendant of the well-known Uṣūlī jurist Muḥammad Bāqir al-Sabzawarī (d. 1090/1679), whose descendants held the post of *shaykh al-islām* of Isfahan under Zand and Qājār rule.[73] This practice of joint judicial certification by the *qāḍī* and *shaykh al-islām* of the town is also attested in deeds from Tabriz, such as in a sale deed dated 1186/1772 and 1197/1783.[74] Such deeds either contained one *sijill* sealed by both the *qāḍī* and the *shaykh al-islām*, or two separate *sijills* belonging to and sealed by the *qāḍī* and *shaykh al-islām* respectively. In the case of the marriage deed it is not clear whether the *sijill* sealed by both the *qāḍī* and the *shaykh al-islām* belonged to the *qāḍī* or to the *shaykh al-islām*.

73 Mahdawī 1371 sh./1992.
74 See Document nos. 11 and 12 in Werner 2000, 346–354.

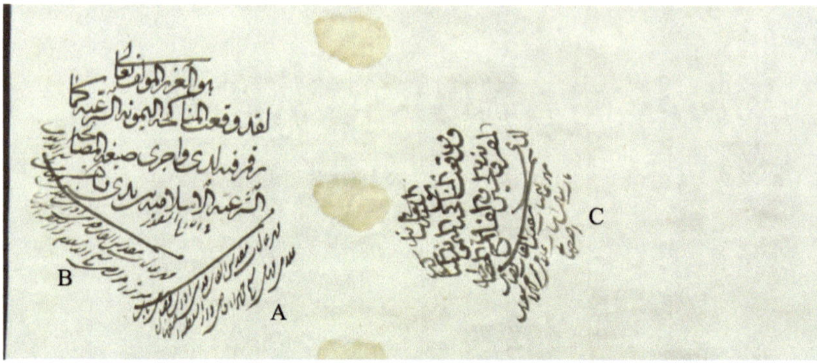

Figure 11: Top-left hand corner of a copy (*sawād*) produced in Shiraz in 1206/1792 of an original marriage deed from Isfahan dated 1198/1784. © Document no. 1393.310-2292, Kitāb-khāna wa Mūza-yi Millī-yi Malik, Tehran.

The Iṣfahan marriage deed, however, also contained a second *sijill* belonging to a certain Mīr Muḥammad Ismāʿīl Iṣfahānī (Figure 11C). The scribe producing the copy of the deed in Shiraz, however, does not ascribe an official post to him. It was not uncommon for independent scholars to add their *sijill*s to legal deeds. As in the case of the Safavid era, independent Imāmī scholars were able to intervene in notarizing legal documents without holding a judicial post in Iran based on their perceived legal knowledge. An example of this in the post-Safavid period is the judicial certification of the Safavid *waqf* deed of Amīr Faḍlullāh Shahristānī (d. after 963/1556) dated 7 Ramaḍān 963/25 July 1556. Among the scholars that judicially certified the validity of the *waqf* deed is the leading *mujtahid* in Karbala, Iraq, at the time, Muḥammad Bāqir Bihbahānī (1116–1205/1706–1791).[75] It is also not surprising to find the *sijill* of the *qāḍī* and *shaykh al-islām* of Isfahan recorded on the top left-hand corner of the sheet. As we have noted earlier the top left-hand corner of legal deeds, since at least the fourteenth century Ilkhanid Mongol period, was reserved for the judicial attestation of appointed *sharīʿa* practitioners. In this case, the scribe probably reproduced the spatial organization of the *sijill*s in the original deed. Mīr Muḥammad Ismāʿīl Iṣfahānī's *sijill* is thus written separately at a right angle to the *sijill* sealed by the *qāḍī* and *shaykh al-islām*. What is surprising is that the copy of the marriage deed has not been certified by the *mullā-bāshī* and the *qāḍī* of Shiraz like the copy of the deed granting of powers of attorney. It is possible that the certification appearing on the latter document sufficed for both copies.

75 Khusrawī 1384 sh./2005, 64.

Conclusion

This chapter has attempted to reconstruct who the practitioners of Islamic law in early modern Iran were from three different sources: Safavid administrative manuals, decrees of judicial appointment, and judicial attestations termed *sijill*s appearing on legal documents from the Safavid and post-Safavid periods. I have tried to demonstrate that the study of *sijill*s in legal deeds is key to understanding shifts in the class of practitioners of Islamic law in Iran. The *sijill*s we have examined corroborate the evidence of the Safavid administrative manuals and decrees of judicial appointment. They suggest that Imāmī scholars who held the post of *ṣadr*, *qāḍī* and *shaykh al-islām* were responsible for authenticating legal deeds in the Safavid period. In the post-Safavid period, the *sijill* of the *mullā-bāshī* is briefly significant on some deeds, but it is mainly the *sijill*s of the *qāḍī* and *shaykh al-islām* that dominate the legal paperwork of Iranian towns during the post-Safavid period of transition under Afghan, Afshar and Zand rule. Nevertheless, we can already begin to detect the presence of the *sijill*s of Imāmī scholars on legal deeds who do not appear to hold a clear official state position but whose authority is based on their legal knowledge. This practice, as we have noted, is mentioned by Chardin as early as the seventeenth century Safavid period.

Following the revival of the Imāmī Shīʿī Uṣūlī school of jurisprudence in the eighteenth century, it is the juristic ability of Imāmī Shīʿī scholars that becomes central to the exercise of judicial power in Iran. Scholars that received state stipends as the *shaykh al-islām* or *qāḍī* of a town continued to add their *sijill*s onto legal documents as we shall see in Chapter 2, the validity of a legal document, however, could now also be challenged on the basis that it did not contain the *sijill* of a recognised *mujtahid* or jurist.[76] It is scholars recognised as *mujtahid*s that would, as Chapters 3 to 6 demonstrate, come to monopolize the practice of Islamic law in the Qajar period, both in terms of validating, annulling and registering legal documents, and in issuing legal rulings according to the *sharīʿa* in civil and criminal proceedings.[77]

In addition to *sijills*, I have also demonstrated in this chapter the significance of registration notes and registration seals in legal deeds from the Safavid period. These registration notes and registration seals provide evidence of the existence of different *sharīʿa* courts in this period termed *maḥkama*. Each *maḥkama* had a specific name ascribed to it such as for example Injuwiyya in Qazvin or Imāmiyya in Yazd. Safavid model legal formularies (*shurūṭ*) confirm that there were specific nam-

76 See for example Kondo 2003, 116.

77 On the role of *mujtahid*s in criminal cases in Qajar Tehran, see Kondo 2017, 30–31.

ing practices to describe individual *sharīʿa* courts in this period (*taʿrīf-i maḥkama*).[78] Moreover, the registration notes and registration seals on legal documents clearly suggest that these *sharīʿa* courts copied original documents in a *jarīda* type archive composed of loose sheets termed *fard*. This is quite different from the practice of Ottoman *sharīʿa* courts which used equisized bound codex registers termed *sijill* for archival purposes. In early modern Iran, however, as we have seen, the term *sijill* did not refer to a scroll certificate or book but to a written formula, more precisely to the Arabic judicial attestation of Imāmī scholars on legal documents. Regrettably no exemplars of archival *fard* papers from a Safavid *sharīʿa* court *jarīda* has come to light so far. The earliest examples of such archival *sharīʿa* court *fard* papers are from the nineteenth century *sharīʿa* court of the *shaykh al-islām* Tammāmī family in Shiraz examined in Chapter 2. In contrast, there are many surviving archival *fard* sheets related to Safavid fiscal administration.[79] As more research is conducted on these fiscal archival *fard* sheets, we will have a better understanding of how documents, including those relating to judicial administration, were archived in early modern Iran. In the examples cited above, little more is known about the life cycle, circulation, and preservation of the original legal documents after they were authenticated and registered in the *sharīʿa* courts. It is likely these documents were kept by the parties involved in the transactions. They were preserved for centuries in household family archives before ending up in modern collections and archival institutions in Iran.

78 See Riḍāʾī 2021, 144–145.
79 Farīmānī and Khusrawbēgī 1395 sh./2016.

Chapter 2
The *Sharīʿa* Court of the Tammāmī *Shaykh al-Islām*s in Shiraz

Introduction

The previous chapter focused on the practitioners of Islamic law in early modern Iran and the scribal and archival practices of their *sharīʿa* courts from the Safavid era to the rise of the Qajars. This chapter and the next will continue this investigation from the perspective of two Qajar era *sharīʿa* courts, one based in Shiraz and the other in Tehran.

According to A. Sepis, writing in 1844, the private houses of *mujtahids*, *shaykh al-islāms*, *qāḍī*s, and *pīsh-namāzes* were the *sharīʿa* courts where all civil proceedings and cases relating to marriage, divorce, succession, and contracts were judged in Qajar Iran.[1] The *mullā-bāshī*, whose *sijill* appears on the Zand legal document examined in Chapter 1, is not mentioned by Sepis as a significant judicial actor in the nineteenth century. Sepis also does not refer to the *imām-jumʿa* or prayer leader of the Friday Mosque (*masjid-i jāmiʿ*).[2] Nevertheless, as we shall see in the case study in Chapter 5, there is evidence to suggest that the scholar who occupied the post of *imām-jumʿa* in Iranian towns in the nineteenth century played an active role in authenticating legal deeds and adjudicating claims according to the *sharīʿa*.

1 Sepis 1844, 97–114.

2 The emergence of the *imām-jumʿa* as a judicial actor probably occurred before the Qajar period, when this post came to be occupied by individuals who were also appointed simultaneously to the post of *shaykh al-islām* and *qāḍī*. For example, in 1151/1738–39, Mīrzā Muḥammad Raḥīm b. Muḥammad Jaʿfar Sabzawarī (d. 1181/1768), a descendant of Muḥammad Bāqir Sabzawarī, was appointed by Nādir Shāh Afshār (r. 1736–1747) to the post of *qāḍī of* Isfahan. He was subsequently appointed to the post of *shaykh al-islām* of Isfahan and *imām-jumʿa* of the Masjid-i Jāmiʿ (Friday Mosque) in Isfahan, see Muṣliḥ al-Dīn Mahdawī 1371 sh./1992. The *imām-jumʿa*'s in the nineteenth century appear to be mainly involved in the adjudication of claims (*murāfaʿa*) according to the *sharīʿa* and notarizing legal documents. In Tabriz, for example, the *imām-jumʿa* of Tabriz, Mīrzā Luṭf ʿAlī (d.1262/1845), plays a prominent role in the adjudication of the dispute over the Zahīriyya endowment, see Werner 1999. The *imām-jumʿa* of Tehran, Ḥājjī Mīrzā Yaḥyā Imām-jumʿa Khūʾī (d.1364/1945), is known to have routinely validated legal transactions and recorded them in registers now deposited in the library of the University of Tehran. On these registers see Susan Asili, "From Home to Notary: Women's Economic Life in the Late Qajar Period", unpublished paper presented on March 6, 2023, at The Institute for Advanced Studies on Asia, University of Tokyo, Tokyo.

https://doi.org/10.1515/9783111239736-003

Sepis also distinguishes *mujtahid*s from scholars that held other posts. This distinction in the nineteenth century can be quite artificial, as it gives the impression that scholars that occupied the posts of *qāḍī, shaykh al-islām, imām-jumʿa* or *pīsh-namāz* were not recognised in their local communities as *mujtahid*s able to carry out *ijtihād*.[3] Holding an official post and being recognised locally as a *mujtahid* were not mutually exclusive. Whether an Imāmī scholar was recognised as a *mujtahid* by his contemporaries must be determined on a case-by-case basis. Even if no contemporary evidence exists, the silence of the sources does not confirm that the scholar in question was not considered a *mujtahid*. There is a tendency, however, in the Qajar sources for certain scholars, especially those that studied for long periods with leading *mujtahids* in Iran and Iraq, to be described by their contemporaries as *mujtahids*. The practice of scholars obtaining authorizations or licences (*ijāzas*) from the leading *mujtahids* confirming their ability to carry out *ijtihād*, confirms the dominance of the Imāmī Uṣūlī doctrinal position in Iran in this period.[4] The intervention of independent scholars recognised as *mujtahid*s in authenticating documents or adjudicating legal disputes in Iran does not, however, exclude the survival well into the nineteenth century of *sharīʿa* courts that were linked to an official judicial post which had been occupied successively by memebers of the same clerical lineage.

One such clerical lineage presiding over probably the most important *sharīʿa* court in Shiraz was the Tammāmī clerical lineage that had for generations occupied the post of *shaykh al-islām* of Fārs. In what follows, I introduce the corpus of legal and administrative documents which mention members of the Tammāmī *shaykh al-islām* clerical lineage and their *sharīʿa* court in Shiraz. Next, I investigate the origins and settlement in Shiraz of the Tammāmī *shaykh al-islām* clerical lineage. This is followed by a reconstruction of the biographies of members of the lineage that occupied the post of *shaykh al-islām* of Fārs. In the fourth part, I focus on the scribal and archival procedures of the Tammāmī *shaykh al-islām sharīʿa* court. I conclude the chapter by assessing the extent to which the Tammāmī *shaykh al-islām* clerical lineage and its *sharīʿa* court was affected by the dominant Imāmī Uṣūlī doctrinal position, which stressed the importance of the ability to carry out *ijtihād* for valid judicial practice.

---

3 Not much is known about the post of *pīsh-namāz* or prayer leader. Individuals who held this position are sometimes involved in the adjudication of claims according to the *sharīʿa*, for example in the dispute over the village of Amīrzakariya, see Abe 2016.

4 On the two types of *ijāza*s, the *ijāza* of *riwāya* or Imāmi Shīʿī *ḥadith* transmission, and the *ijāza* of *ijtihād* (juristic ability) transmitted by Imāmī Shīʿī scholars, see Kondo 2009.

1 The Tammāmī Corpus

The exact number of legal and administrative documents related to members of the Tammāmī clerical lineage is not known. This is because what I term here "the Tammāmī corpus" is scattered across several collections, most of which have not been catalogued. Even for the catalogued collections of documents from Shiraz it is often difficult to determine whether a given document belongs to the Tammāmī corpus. Nevertheless, the judicial attestations (*sijills*), seals, registration notes, and layout (as we shall see below) of legal deeds can help establish whether a given document was issued by the Tammāmī *shaykh al-islām sharī'a* court. In the case of administrative decrees relating to the Tammāmī *shaykh al-islāms*, it is of course much easier to identify a Tammāmī connection, since these documents often explicitly mention the Tammāmī *shaykh al-islams* as, for example, recipients of a state stipend.

The two main collections which contain Tammāmī legal and administrative documents are the Bādkūba-ī and Kāẓimaynī collections. The Bādkūba-ī collection originally belonged to a certain Mr. Bādkūba-ī in Shiraz. His documents were kept in a small chest (*ṣandūqcha*) that was bought in 1384 sh./2005 by the Idāra-yi Kull-i Awqāf wa Umūr-i Khayriyya of Fārs from Mr. Bādkūba-ī. In 1386 sh./2007, the Bādkūba-ī collection was transferred to the Sāzmān-i Awqāf wa Umūr-i Khayriyya in Tehran, where it remains to this day.[5] The exact content and number of Tammāmī documents in the Bādkūba-ī collection is not known, as the collection has not yet been catalogued.[6] The Kāẓimaynī collection of around a thousand Qajar legal and administrative documents from Fārs, including a number of Tammāmī documents, belonged to another private collector, Mīrzā Muḥammad Kāẓimaynī. His collection was given as a gift to the museum of the shrine of Imām-zāda Ja'far in Yazd. The Kāẓimaynī collection has been catalogued.[7] A selection of facsimiles from this collection have also been published.[8] Besides the Bādkāba-ī and Kāẓimaynī collections, Tammāmī documents can also be found in the Sāzmān-i Awqāf wa Umūr-i Khayriyya in Tehran in the files relating to the province of Fārs.[9] There are also a number of Tammāmī documents held in the Madrasa-yi Imām-i 'Asr in Shiraz,[10] in the National

5 Riḍā'ī, 1388 sh./2009, footnote 2, 49.

6 For a list of some of these documents, see Riḍā'ī 1390 sh./2012, 93.

7 A preliminary checklist was published by S. J.H. Ishkawarī, see Ishkawarī 1387 sh./2007. A second catalogue (which covers most but not all documents) was produced by U. Riḍā'ī, see Riḍā'ī 1387 sh./2008.

8 For the first set of facsimiles, see Ishkawarī 1383 sh./2005.

9 Riḍā'ī 1390 sh./2012, 92–93.

10 This collection was digitized recently in Shiraz by Sayyid Ṣādiq Ḥusaynī Ishkawarī.

Library and Archives of Iran (NLAI),[11] and in the Majlis Library in Tehran.[12] It is quite likely that there are Tammāmī documents in the archive of the shrine of Imām Riḍā in Mashhad (Āstān-i Quds-i Raḍawī) and in the provincial *waqf* archive of Fārs in Shiraz. Besides these institutional collections, there are Tammāmī documents which remain in private hands in Shiraz. These documents belong to the descendants of individuals who referred to the Tammāmī *sharīʿa* court in the late eighteenth and nineteenth centuries.[13] The number of these Tammāmī documents in private collections probably exceeds the number held in the institutional collections mentioned so far. Some of these Tammāmī documents belonging to different families have recently been made available on the digital archive Women's World in Qajar Iran (WWQI) at Harvard University.[14]

In what follows, I refer to only a small corpus of around twenty legal and administrative Tammāmī documents selected from these collections. It is likely that we will be able to offer a far more detailed study of the judicial activities of this important clerical lineage based on a much larger corpus of Tammāmī documents in the future, as more are identified and become available. Some of the Tammāmī documents I cite have been discussed previously by Riḍāʾī, as I indicate in the text and in the footnotes. Two Tammāmī documents, however, are presented and analysed here for the first time. In addition to the Tammāmī documents themselves, I also draw on narrative sources, in particular the nineteenth-century historical and geographical work on the region of Fārs, *Fārs-nāma-yi Nāṣirī*, compiled by Mīrzā Ḥasan Fasāʾī (1237–1316/1821–1898) in 1304/1887.[15] Finally, I also highlight a hitherto unexplored source for the history of this clerical lineage: manuscripts owned by the Tammāmī family.

11 See the settlement deeds (*musālaḥa-nāma*) dated 1223/1808 and 1231/1816 in Shahristānī 1381 sh./2002, 63–64.

12 Riḍāʾī 1398 sh./2019, 231–234, 236, 252.

13 A small collection of Tammāmī documents in private hands belongs, for example, to Muhandis Muḥammad Bāqir Shaykh al-Islām in Shiraz, see Riḍāʾī 1390 sh./2012, 94.

14 URL: http://www.qajarwomen.org/en/index.html (Accessed 1 April 2023). See for example the roll relating to the estate of the *imām-jumʿa* of Fārs, Shaykh Abū Turāb discussed in this chapter.

15 On Fasāʾī and his chronicle, see H. Busse et al., "Fārs-nāma-ye Nāserī" *EIr*, IX, fasc. 4, 374–378. All references to the *Fārs-nāma-yi Nāṣirī* are from Fasāʾī 1382 sh./2004.

2 Origins and Settlement of the Tammāmi Clerical Lineage in Shiraz

2.1 Baḥrānī Arab Émigré Akhbārī Scholars in Shiraz: Al-Karzakānī and his Students

Research on the emigration of foreign Imāmī or Twelver Shīʿī scholars to Iran in the Safavid period has until now focused on the migration of Arab scholars from the region of Jabal ʿĀmil in southern Lebanon.[16] Another wave of migration which has received comparatively little attention occurred in the seventeenth century from Bahrain and Eastern Arabia to Shiraz. Scholars from these areas usually have the *nisba* al-Baḥrānī in the sources. Among the Baḥrānī scholars that migrated to Shiraz from Bahrain in the seventeenth century was Shaykh Ṣāliḥ b. ʿAbd al-Karīm b. Ḥasan b. Ṣāliḥ al-Karzakānī al-Baḥrānī (d. 1098/1687) from the village of Karzakān in Bahrain.[17]

We do not know precisely when al-Karzakānī migrated to Shiraz, but he probably arrived either during or before the reign of Shah Sulaymān (r. 1666–1694), as the latter is said to have appointed al-Karzakānī to the post of *qāḍī al-quḍāt* of Fārs.[18] From the legal formulary of Qawām Muḥammad Shīrāzī we know the names of the successive *qāḍī al-quḍāt* of Fārs in the Safavid period until 1050/1641, when the post was occupied by Amīr Amīn al-Dīn Shāh Muḥammad Abū Turāb Injū.[19] Al-Karzakanī must have been appointed to the post at some point after this date and before his death in 1098/1687.

Al-Karzakānī, described as a traditionist (*muḥaddith*), belonged, like many Baḥrānī scholars of his time, to the Akhbārī school of Imāmī Shīʿī jurisprudence.[20] In the Safavid period, Shiraz was a major Akhbārī centre for the study of *ḥadith*, and al-Karzakānī probably taught at the famous Madrasa-yi Manṣūriyya along with other Baḥrānī *ḥadīth* scholars. One of al-Karzakānī's most important students was Sayyid Niʿmatullāh al-Jazāʾirī (1640–1701), a well-known Akhbārī scholar who studied at the Madrasa-yi Manṣūriyya before it was destroyed by a fire in ca. 1070/1659–1660.[21] A lesser-known student of al-Karzakānī who is relevant for us here is a certain Shaykh Aḥmad b. ʿAlī b. Muḥammad al-ʿAmirī al-Jazāʾirī al-Tammāmī. On 10 Ṣafar 1094/8 February 1683, Shaykh Aḥmad al-Tammāmī finished copying the *ḥadīth*

16 See for example Abisaab 1994, 103–122.
17 Ishkawarī 1382 sh./2003, 482.
18 Ishkawarī 1382 sh./2003, 489.
19 Riḍāʾī 2021, 20–21.
20 On Akhbārism and Akhbārī scholarship, see Gleave 2007.
21 On al-Jazāʾirī's life and works, see Rizvi 2010, 228; Ishkawarī 1382 sh./2003, 485, 517.

compilation *Rijāl al-Wasīṭ* of Muḥammad b. ʿAlī b. Ibrāhīm al-Mīrzā al-Astarābādī (d. 1028/1619). Al-Karzakānī wrote an authorization (*ijāza)* to transmit Imāmī Shīʿī *ḥadith*s for Shaykh Aḥmad al-Tammāmī next to the title of the manuscript on 2 Rabīʿ I 1094/1 March 1683.[22]

Shaykh Aḥmad al-Tammāmī was thus part of the Baḥrānī Akhbārī milieu of scholars of mid- to late-seventeenth century Shiraz, led among others by individuals such as al-Karzakānī. What is not clear is whether Shaykh Aḥmad al-Tammāmī was the first Tammāmī to settle in Shiraz. According to Fasāʾī, the origins of members of the Tammāmī clerical lineage was the Tammāmī Arab tribe (*tāʾifa-yi tammāmī*) of the oasis towns of al-Qaṭīf and al-Aḥsāʾ on the eastern coast of Arabia.[23] Fasāʾī suggests that the first Tammāmī to settle in Shiraz was Shaykh Aḥmad's father Shaykh ʿAlī b. Muḥammad al-Tammāmī.[24] Fasāʾī bases this claim on a narrative source, *Ṭayf al-Khayāl*, completed in 1116/1704–5. Its author, Muḥammad Muʾmin al-Jazāʾirī al-Shīrazī, who was born and lived in Shiraz between 1074–1098/1664–1687, notes with pride that he studied Arabic syntax, grammar, rhetoric, and jurisprudence under Shaykh ʿAlī b. Muḥammad al-Tammāmī.[25]

The only other reference to a Shaykh ʿAlī al-Tammāmī in the sources appears in a multi-text manuscript (*majmūʿa*) compiled by Ṣāliḥ b. Jārallāh al-Ṣaymarī and copied by his student in 1111/1699.[26] One of the texts of the manuscript is a poem lamenting the departure of the month of Ramaḍān, written in part by three individuals, Shaykh Ṣāliḥ b. ʿAbd al-Karīm al-Baḥrānī (al-Karzakānī), Shaykh ʿAlī al-Tammāmī, and the copyist's teacher, Shaykh Ṣāliḥ b. Jārallāh al-Ṣaymarī.[27] Āqā Buzurg Tihrānī suggests that Shaykh ʿAlī al-Tammāmī died after 1058/1648–9.[28] Since we know, however, that Shaykh ʿAlī al-Tammāmī taught Muḥammad Muʾmin al-Jazāʾirī al-Shīrazī, his death must have occurred after the latter's birth in 1074/1664. Shaykh ʿAlī al-Tammamī was not alive in 1111/1699 when the multi-text manuscript of Ṣāliḥ b. Jārallāh al-Ṣaymarī was copied, as he is referred to as *al-marḥūm shaykh ʿalī al-tammāmī*. According to Fasāʾī, Shaykh ʿAlī's son Shaykh Aḥmad died around 1130/1717–18.[29]

---

22 Tihrānī and Munzawī 1372 sh./1993, VI, 42–43; Ishkawarī 1382 sh./2003, 523.

23 Fasāʾī 1382 sh./2004, 54.

24 Fasāʾī 1382 sh./2004, 54. Unlike Fasāʾī, Āqā Buzurg, refers to Shaykh Aḥmad as Shaykh Aḥmad b. Muḥammad al-Tammāmī and not Shaykh Aḥmad b. ʿAlī b. Muḥammad al-Tammāmī. This is repeated, following him, in all other secondary sources. Āqā Buruzg also, however, separately mentions the existence of a Shaykh ʿAlī al-Tammāmī, a contemporary of Shaykh Ṣāliḥ b. "Abd al-Karīm al-Baḥrānī (al-Karzakānī), see Tihrānī (1403/1982–3), 402.

25 Barkat 1397 sh./2019, 11–19.

26 Tihrānī and Munzawi, 1372 sh./1993, VI, 374.

27 Tihrānī and Munzawi, 1372 sh./1993, VI, 374.

28 Tihrānī and Munzawi, 1372 sh./1993, VI, 509.

29 Fasāʾī 1382 sh./2004, 54.

2.2 The Post of *Shaykh al-Islām* of Fārs before the Tammāmī Clerical Lineage

Though the Tammāmīs were, according to Fasāʾī, active in notarizing legal documents in Shiraz from the end of Safavid rule, that is from the first half of the eighteenth-century, it was only in the Afsharid period (1736–1796) that the family rose to prominence and was able to secure an official post. During the reign of the last Safavid shah, Sulṭān Ḥusayn, the post of *shaykh al-islām* of Fārs was occupied by Mīrzā Muḥammad Mahdī Nassāba, a member of the important Nassāba *sayyid* clerical lineage which traced its descent from the Prophet.[30] In 1136/1724 during the Afghan conquest of Iran, the *shaykh al-islām*, Mīrzā Muḥammad Mahdī Nassāba, was killed. According to Fasāʾī, the new Afghan rulers appointed a certain Shaykh Muḥammad Amīn as *shaykh al-islām* of Fārs.[31] It was after Shaykh Muḥammad Amīn's death that the first member of the Tammāmī clerical lineage, Shaykh Aḥmad al-Tammāmī's son, Shaykh Muḥammad al-Tammāmī, was appointed *shaykh al-islām* of Fārs by Nādir Shāh Afshār (r. 1736–1747).[32] Shaykh Muḥammad al-Tammāmī's appointment marked the beginning of a period of over a century where the post of *shaykh al-islām* of Fārs became hereditary within the Tammāmī clerical lineage in Shiraz (see Figure 12).

3 Reconstruction of the Tammāmī *Shaykh al-Islām* Clerical Lineage

3.1 Shaykh Muḥammad b. Shaykh Aḥmad

There is little reason to doubt Fasāʾī on the appointment of Shaykh Muḥammad al-Tammāmī as *shaykh al-islām* of Fārs by Nādir Shāh Afshār. The earliest dated documents of the Tammāmī corpus, three legal rolls, were clearly produced in a *sharīʿa* court presided over by Shaykh Muḥammad al-Tammāmī in Shiraz under Afshār rule. The three rolls date from Shaʿban 1152–Jamadi II 1160/November 1739–June 1747.[33] Shaykh Muḥammad's rectangular seal, which appears on two of these rolls, has the following inscription (*sajʿ-i muhr*) in *nastaʿlīq*: *fawwaḍtu amrī ilā l-llāh al-*

30 We know this based on a later note on one of the *sijills* of the *waqf* deed of Khwāja Husām al-Dīn Afshār Nāʾib al-Mulk, dated 1119/1707–8, see Riḍāʾī 1390 sh./2012, 50.

31 Fasāʾī 1382 sh./2004, 54.

32 Fasāʾī 1382 sh./2004, 54.

33 Riḍāʾī 1387 sh./2008, 17; roll 1 (document nos. 2, 3, 4). The second roll (Hājar Khātūn) and the third roll (Shaykh Ṣāliḥ b. Qāsim Khalafābadī) are not listed in the catalogue.

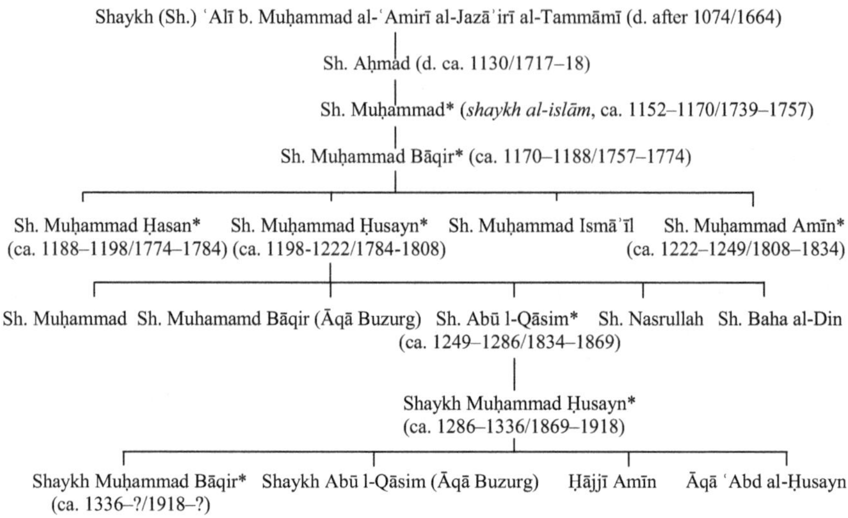

Figure 12: The Tammāmī *shaykh al-islām*s are marked with an asterisk* with approximate period of activity as *shaykh al-islām* of Shiraz/Fārs indicated in brackets.

aḥad al-ṣamad wa-anā ibn aḥmad al-imāmī al-tammāmī. This reading is confirmed by Fasāʾī, who notes that he had in his possession a document endorsing his grandfather's right to the post of the administrator of the endowment of the Madrasa-yi Manṣūriyya in Shiraz, sealed by Shaykh Muḥammad al-Tammāmī. In Fasāʾī's own transcription of Shaykh Muḥammad's seal, he also includes the date the seal was made: 1130/1717–18.[34]

In addition to the three rolls and Fasāʾī's document, there are at least seventeen manuscripts of Imāmī Shīʿī works owned by Shaykh Muḥammad which have survived. These manuscripts were constituted by Shaykh Muḥammad as an endowment and they contain a *waqf* deed sealed by him.[35] Regrettably, I have not been able to consult any of these manuscripts. Based on these manuscripts, it is likely that the Tammāmī family owned an important library of books. In addition to Shaykh Muḥammad's manuscripts, there are also several manuscripts known which contain the seals of other members of this lineage (see Section 3.8 below). Not much more is known about Shaykh Muḥammad. Fasāʾī suggests he died

34 Fasāʾī 1382 sh./2004, 54.

35 I have arrived at this figure based on a search of the occurrence of al-Tammāmī in *al-Dharīʿa*. See for example MS no. 774, containing the well-known Shīʿī legal text, *Man lā yaḥḍuruhu al-faqīh.* On the first folio it has the seal of Shaykh Muḥammad al-Tammāmī including the text of a *waqf* deed, see Ishkawarī 1380 sh./2001, 434.

around 1170/1756–7.[36] Besides Fasāʾī's mention of his appointment as *shaykh al-islām* of Fārs, there is no explicit reference in the Tammāmī documents to him holding this office.

3.2 Shaykh Muḥammad Bāqir b. Shaykh Muḥammad

Shaykh Muḥammad's son, Shaykh Muḥammad Bāqir, became the next *shaykh al-islām* of Fārs. The earliest document containing his seal is one of the three rolls dated 8 Jamādī II 1160/17 June 1747.[37] This roll also contains the seal of Shaykh Muḥammad Bāqir's father, Shaykh Muḥammad. It is another example of father and son taking part in sealing documents produced in their *sharīʿa* court. Fasāʾī notes that the document issued to his grandfather was also sealed by Shaykh Muḥammad and his son Shaykh Muḥammad Bāqir. There are, so far, at least three other Tammāmī documents known to contain the seal of Shaykh Muḥammad Bāqir. The first is an original *waqf* deed dated 21 Jamādī II 1171/31 January 1758, which contains the *sijill* and seal of Shaykh Muḥammad Bāqir along with eight other individuals.[38] The second is a copy (*sawād*) of a settlement contract (*muṣālaḥa-nāma*), dated 29 Jamādī II 1175/25 January 1762, which was produced under his supervision and contains his *sijill* and seal.[39] The third document is an original question-and-answer ruling by Shaykh Muḥammad Bāqir dated Dhū l-Qaʿda 1176/June 1763.[40] In these documents, Shaykh Muḥammad Bāqir is described as *shaykh al-islamī muḥammad bāqirā tammāmī shaykh al-islām-i ulkā-yi fārs.*

Fasāʾī transcribes Shaykh Muḥammad Bāqir's seal as follows: *fawwaḍtu amrī ilā l-lāh al-ṣamad al-tammāmī al-imāmī bāqir b. muḥammad sana 1137.*[41] The date this seal was made is 1137/1724–5. Fasāʾī also records a second seal used by Shaykh Muḥammad Bāqir, whose transcription according to him was uncertain, as follows: *ufawwiḍu amrī ilā l-llāh al-aḥad al-ṣamad muḥammad bāqir al-tammāmī al-imāmī ibn aḥmad sana 1161.*[42] The date this seal was made is 1161/1748. Neither of these seals recorded by Fasāʾī is, however, visible in the Tammāmī documents at our disposal. Instead, a different seal appears. It is square in shape and contains

36 Fasāʾī 1382 sh./2004, 54.
37 Hājar Khātūn roll, Mirza Muḥammad Kāẓimaynī Collection, Yazd.
38 *Waqf* deed of Ḥājjī Maḥmūd Tājir b. Ḥājjī Muḥammad ʿAlī, file no. 90, Fārs Province, Sazmān-i Awqāf wa Umūr-i Khayriyya, Tehran.
39 Riḍāʾī 1397 sh./2018, 102–103.
40 Riḍāʾī 1397 sh./2018, 102–103.
41 Fasāʾī 1382 sh./2004, 54.
42 Fasāʾī 1382 sh./2004, 54.

the following inscription in *nastaʿlīq*: *lā ilāha illā allāh al-malik al-ḥaqq al-mubīn ʿabduhu muḥammad bāqir al-tammāmī.*[43] Fasāʾī suggests that Shaykh Muḥammad Bāqir died around 1197–1198/1782–4.[44] This, however, is inaccurate. In a settlement contract dated 14 Rajab 1188/20 September 1774, Shaykh Muḥammad Bāqir is already referred to as the "former deceased *shaykh al-islām* of Fārs" (*marḥimat wa ghufrān-panāh jannat wa riḍwān-ārām-gāh shaykh muḥammad bāqirā al-tammāmī shaykh al-islām-i sābiq-i fārs tāba tharāhu*).[45]

3.3 Shaykh Muḥammad Ḥasan b. Shaykh Muḥamamad Bāqir

The settlement contract dated 14 Rajab 1188/20 September 1774 sheds considerable light on Shaykh Muḥammad Bāqir's family.[46] It was drawn up to divide Shaykh Muḥammad Bāqir's estate, including the house he owned in the Sūq al-Ṭayr/Bāzār-i Murgh (Bird Market) quarter of Shiraz, among his heirs following his death. According to the document, Shaykh Muḥammad Bāqir had two wives, from whom he had four sons and four daughters. The names of the daughters are not mentioned in the document. The four sons are: Shaykh Muḥammad Ḥasan, Shaykh Muḥammad Ḥusayn, Shaykh Muḥammad Ismāʿīl from one wife, and Shaykh Muḥammad Amīn from the other wife. Shaykh Muḥammad Ḥasan is referred to in the document as *ʿalī-jinab qudsī alqāb . . . shaykh al-islāmī-yi muʿaẓẓam ilayh.* Moreover, his rectangular seal, with the inscription *fawwaḍtu amrī ilā l-llāh al-aʿlā wa-anā ibn muḥammad al-tammāmī ḥasan* in *nastaʿlīq,* also appears affixed at the bottom of the document directly over the date, thus closing the main text of the document. This suggests that at the time the document was produced, Shaykh Muḥammad Ḥasan presided over the Tammāmī *sharīʿa* court as the *shaykh al-islām* of Fārs, as opposed to his brother Shaykh Muḥammad Ḥusayn, as suggested by Fasāʾī.[47]

It is interesting to note that this contract also contains the *sijill* and seal of Zayn al-ʿAbidīn al-ʿAlawī, the *qāḍī* of Shiraz whom we encountered in the previous chapter. The document also contains the *sijill*s and seals of other members of the Tammāmī clerical lineage about whom we know nothing but who were clearly involved in notarizing legal documents produced in the *sharīʿa* court of the *shaykh al-islām* in late

43 Riḍāʾī 1397 sh./2018, 103.
44 Riḍāʾī 1397 sh./2018, 55.
45 Riḍāʾī 1387 sh./2008, 17; document no. 5. This document has been edited in Riḍāʾī 1390 sh./2012, 105–108.
46 Riḍāʾī 1397 sh./2018, 105–108.
47 Fasāʾī 1382 sh./2004, 55.

eighteenth-century Shiraz, such as Muḥammad Sadiq b. ʿAbd al-Ghanī al-Tammāmī (see also below on Shaykh Muḥammad Ṣāliḥ al-Tammāmī).

3.4 Shaykh Muḥammad Ḥusayn b. Shaykh Muḥammad Bāqir

We do not know precisely when Shaykh Muḥammad Ḥasan died. The *waqf* deed of Ḥājj Abū Ṭalib Ḥammāmī b. Raḥīm Iṣfahānī dated Rabīʿ I 1198/24 January 1784, however, provides clues to the transmission of the post of *shaykh al-islām* within the Tammāmī clerical lineage.[48] The top of the document contains a double *sijill*. The *sijill* and seal of the *qāḍī* of Shiraz, Zayn al-ʿĀbidīn al-ʿAlawī, appears on the right, while the *sijill* and seal of the *shaykh al-islām*, Shaykh Muḥammad Ḥasan's brother, Shaykh Muḥammad Ḥusayn, is on the left. The rectangular seal of Shaykh Muḥammad Ḥusayn has the following inscription in *nastaʿlīq*: *lā ilāha illā allah al-malik al-ḥaqq al-mubīn ḥusayn ibn muḥammad bāqir al-tammāmī*. So far only one other document, a deed of gift (*hiba-nāma*) dated 18 Dhū l-Ḥijja 1210/24 June 1796, also contains the *sijill* and rectangular seal of Shaykh Muḥammad Ḥusayn.[49] We know, however, from a *waqf* deed dated 15 Shawwal 1220/6 January 1806 held in a private collection that Shaykh Muḥammad Ḥusayn also had another seal, oval in shape, which carried the following inscription in *nastaʿlīq*: *ʿabduhu muḥammad ḥusayn*.[50] Based on these documents, it is clear that Shaykh Muḥammad Ḥusayn was the *shaykh al-islām* of Fārs during the period of transition from Zand to Qājār rule.

Three decrees issued by the first Qajar ruler, Āqā Muḥammad Khān Qājār (r. 1789–1797), dated Dhū l-Ḥijja 1206/August 1792, Shawwal 1209/May 1795 and Ramaḍān 1210/March 1796, confirm this.[51] According to the decree dated 1206/1795, the shah granted an annual state stipend (*mustamarrī-yi sāliyāna*) in the form of a *tuyūl* to Shaykh Muḥammad Ḥusayn as the *shaykh al-islām* of Shiraz. The properties assigned in the *tuyūl* were all located on the outskirts (*ḥawma*) of Shiraz. They included the village (*qarya*) of Shamsābād-i Māhūrīn, which belonged to crown land (*khāliṣa-yi dīwānī*), two orchards (*basāṭīn*) called Aṣīlābād and Amīr Qawām al-Dīn, a garden known as Bāghcha-yi Āqā, and the Manṣūrī mill (*ṭaḥūna-yi manṣūrī-yi arbabī-yi ʿalī-jināb mushārun ilayh*), belonging to Shaykh Muḥammad

48 Document no. 18, Fārs province, Sāzman-i Awqāf wa Umūr-i Khayriyya, Tehran; for an image of this double *sijill*, see Riḍāʾī 1397 sh./2018, 105.

49 Mīrzā Muḥammad Kāzimaynī Collection, Yazd, document no. 002/390.

50 For an image of this seal, see Riḍāʾī 1397 sh./2018, 15.

51 See Ishkawarī, 1383 sh./2005: facsimiles nos. 18 and 34. The decrees dated Dhū l-Ḥijja 1206/August 1792 and Ramaḍān 1210/March 1796 have been edited in Riḍāʾī 1390 sh./2012, 109–113.

Ḥusayn. The state stipend was composed of the income generated by the village of Shamsābād-i Māhūrīn, which in 1206/1792 amounted to 25 Tabrīzī *tūmāns* in cash and 15 *mann* of grain in kind, in addition to a tax exemption on the taxes (*kharāj*) collected from the orchards, the garden, and the mill. Since the taxes collected are not specified in the decree, it is difficult to estimate the exact total revenue of the state stipend. From the decree dated three years later, 1209/1795, it is clear, however, that the *shaykh al-islām* had been able to increase the income generated by the village now listed as 60 Tabrīzī *tūmāns* in cash and 60 *kharwār* grain in kind. These three decrees constitute the earliest evidence of the state-derived stipend of the Tammāmī *shaykh al-islāms*.

In addition to this state stipend, the other major source of revenue of the Tammāmī *shaykh al-islāms* was from the administration (*tawliya*) of endowments (*mawqūfāt*). No less than seven *waqf* deeds between 1220–1323/1806–1905 mention the Tammāmī *shaykh al-islāms* as administrators (*mutawallīs*) entitled to the administrator's salary (*ḥaqq al-tawliya*), which varied anywhere between one-twelfth to half of the revenues of the *waqf* after all expenses were paid.[52] The earliest *waqf* deed is dated 15 Shawwal 1220/6 January 1806.[53] The founder, Mihr ʿAlī Khān Qājār, constitutes 4 out of 6 *dāng*[54] of the village of Ābāda located in Fārs, in addition to all other lands and water rights attached to the village as *waqf*. The administration of the *waqf* is assigned to Shaykh Muḥammad Ḥusayn, and after his death to his brother Shaykh Muḥammad Amīn (see below), and after him to the eldest male descendant of Shaykh Muḥammad Ḥusayn, and so on. It is beyond the scope of this study to examine in detail the assignment of revenues of this *waqf*. After all expenses of the *waqf* were paid, one-tenth of its revenues belonged to the administrator as his salary (*ḥaqq al-tawliya*). The remaining nine-tenths of the *waqf*'s revenues were to be divided into four equal parts. Three parts were to pay for feasts during mourning ceremonies for the martyrdom of al-Ḥusayn, held during the months of Muḥarram and Ṣafar. The last part was to pay for the pilgrimage expenses of *sayyids* (descendants of the Prophet) and the poor of Shiraz to the shrine cities of Iraq in order that they pray for the founder.

What is significant here is that the *waqf* deed itself was clearly prepared in the *sharīʿa* court of Shaykh Muḥammad Ḥusayn. His *sharīʿa* court is described in the document as follows: *ʿuliyā maḥkama-yi muḥkama-yi ʿiliyya-yi ʿalīyya-yi nāmiyya-yi sāmiyya-yi muḥammadiyya-yi ḥusayniyya-yi islāmiyya-yi tammāmiyya bi-*

52 For a list of these *waqf* deeds, see table 2–5 in Riḍāʾī 1390 sh./2012, 102.
53 This *waqf* deed has been edited in Riḍāʾī 1390 sh./2012, 114–120.
54 *dāng* refers to one-sixth part of any real estate, see Lambton 1969, 426.

dār al-ʿilm-i shīrāz.[55] The use of such clauses with descriptive adjectives, including adjectivizing the name of the *shaykh al-islām (muḥamadiyya-yi ḥusayniyya)* to name a *sharīʿa* court, is a practice that goes back to the Safavid period and possibly even earlier. Qawām Muḥammad Shīrāzī terms this referential naming practice *taʿrīf-i maḥkama* (literally: description of the court) in his legal formulary.[56] We will see in the second part of this chapter how the *taʿrīf-i maḥkama* is also a key element of the registration notes that appear on the *sharīʿa* court documents produced by the Tammāmī *shaykh al-islām sharīʿa* court.

3.5 Shaykh Muḥammad Amīn b. Shaykh Muḥammad Bāqir

According to Fasāʾī, Shaykh Muḥammad Ḥusayn died around 1225–1226/1810–12.[57] However, this must have occurred some years earlier. In a settlement contract dated 26 Dhū l-Qaʿda 1222/25 January 1808, four male heirs of Shaykh Muḥammad Ḥusayn transfer their respective shares from his estate to the fifth male heir, Shaykh Abū l-Qāsim, who would later become *shaykh al-islām* (see below).[58] This settlement contract, which contains the *sijill* and seal of Shaykh Muḥammad Amīn is significant because it is also the earliest document of the Tamāmmī corpus which has a registration note confirming its registration in the *shaykh al-islām sharīʿa* court. It is not clear why Tammāmī documents from the period of Shaykh Muḥammad Amīn suddenly begin to include a registration note. According to Dīwān-Bēgī Shīrāzī, Shaykh Muḥammad Amīn began in the middle of his tenure as *shaykh al-islām* to carefully register transactions due to the extensive falsification of documents in Shiraz at the time.[59] From the evidence of the settlement contract, it appears that the use of a special stylized registration note was an innovation that was introduced as soon as Shaykh Muḥammad Amīn became *shaykh al-islām*. The absence of registration notes in documents produced by the *shaykh al-islām sharīʿa* court prior to Shaykh Muḥammad Amīn does not mean that some form of archiving did not occur. It is likely that documents were registered, but this was not explicitly recorded in the documents themselves.

Besides the internal Tammāmī family settlement contract dated 26 Dhu l-Qada 1222/25 January 1808, there are at least seven documents containing the *sijill* and

55 Riḍāʾī 1390 sh./2012, 115.
56 Riḍāʾī 2021, 143–157.
57 Fasāʾī 1382 sh./2004, 55.
58 This document has not been catalogued. Mīrzā Muḥammad Kāẓimaynī Collection, Yazd, digital image nos. 6993 and 6994.
59 Riḍāʾī 1397 sh./2018, 107.

seal of Shaykh Muḥammad Amīn with a registration note that the document was registered in the *shaykh al-islām sharīʿa* court. These seven documents are: (1) a settlement contract dated 27 Jamādī I 1223/21 July 1808;[60] (2) a settlement contract dated Dhū l-Qaʿda 1223/December 1808–January 1809;[61] (3) the *waqf* deed dated Rajab 1223/August-September 1808 of Muḥammad Riḍā Khān b. Ḥājjī Muḥammad Ḥasan Sawād-Kūhī;[62] (4) a settlement contract dated 2 Jamādi I 1228/3 May 1813 concerning a herbal shop in Shiraz between the two sons of Faḍlullāh, Abū Turāb and Fath ʿAlī, and Ḥājj ʿAlī Riḍā b. ʿAbd al-Riḍā;[63] (5) a sale deed dated 18 Rajab 1229/6 July 1814 concerning Mīrzā Aḥmad's house at the Maydān-i Shāh in Shiraz;[64] (6) the *waqf* deed of Ḥasan ʿAlī Mīrzā Farmān-farmā (1203–1251) dated 8 Shawwal 1223/27 November 1808;[65] and (7) a document dated Rajab 1243/April confirming Mīrzā Abū ʿAlī Qassām b. Mīrzā Muḥamamd Hāshim (on him see Section 4.2.4), the "registrar" of the *shaykh al-islām sharīʿa* court, as the administrator (*mutawallī*) of the endowment of his ancestors in the Bayḍā district of Fārs province.[66]

Though we know these documents were registered in the *shaykh al-islām sharīʿa* court, it is not always clear if they were also produced in the *shaykh al-islām sharīʿa* court. The fact that Shaykh Muḥammad Amīn's *sijill* does not appear to be the most prominent *sijill* on some of these documents suggests that the document was probably produced in other *sharīʿa* courts of Shiraz. The document was later taken to the *shaykh al-islām sharīʿa* court, at which point the *sijill* and seal of the *shaykh al-islām* and the registration note of the *shaykh al-islām sharīʿa* court were added.[67] The settlement contract drawn up on 27 Jamādī I 1223/21 July 1808 was, for example, registered almost ten months later, on 8 Rabi II 1224/23 May 1809, in the *shaykh al-islām sharīʿa* court. Similarly, the *waqf* deed of Muḥammad Riḍā Khān Sawād-Kūhī was written on Rajab 1223/August-September

60 Riḍāʾī 1397 sh./2018, 108.
61 Shahristānī, *Jilwa-ha-yi hunar*: 64.
62 File no. 15, Fārs province, Sāzman-i Awqāf wa Umūr-i Khayriyya, Tehran.
63 WWQI, document no. 15161A112.
64 Shahristānī 1381 sh./2002, 63.
65 This document has been edited and published with a facsimile, see Riḍāʾī 1385 sh./2006, 77–94.
66 Riḍāʾī 1385 sh./2006, 81.
67 This could also occur in the case of a copy. An original sale deed dated 16 Rabīʿ II 1234/12 February 1819 was produced in the presence of a certain Mullā ʿAbdullāh and contains his *sijill*. Its copy was authenticated and registered later in the *shaykh al-islām sharīʿa* court and contains the *sijill*s of Shaykh Muḥammad Amīn and his son Shaykh Abū l-Qāsim, see *Fihrist-i Majmūʿa*: 236. See also the example of a copy of deed of acknowledgement of debt dated 2 Ṣafar 1228/4 February 1813 and an additional note written by Shaykh Muḥammad Amīn produced in the *shaykh al-islām sharīʿa* court, 252.

1808, but the *sijill* of Shaykh Muḥammad Amīn was only added to the document around ten months later, on 8 Jamādī II 1224/21 July 1809.

The only exceptions are the *waqf* deed of Ḥasan ʿAlī Mīrzā Farmān-farmā, dated 8 Shawwal 1223/27 November 1808, and the document related to Mīrzā Abū ʿAlī Qassām b. Mīrzā Muḥamamd Hāshim, registrar of the *shaykh al-islām sharīʿa* court, dated Rajab 1234/April 1819. In both cases, we can be quite sure that the documents were produced and registered in the *sharīʿa* court of the *shaykh al-islām* itself. The *waqf* deed of Ḥasan ʿAlī Mīrzā Farmān-farmā contains a double *sijill* at the top of the document. On the right is the *sijill* and seal of Ḥājjī ʿAlī Akbar Nawwāb (1187–1263), known as Basmal. On the left is the *sijill* and seal of Shaykh Muḥammad Amīn. Besides the spatial importance given to the *sijill* of Shaykh Muḥammad Amīn, the seal that is directly above the start of the main text of the document has the inscription *lā ilāha illa allāh al-malik al-ḥaqq al-mubīn abūdhu ʿalī naqī*. Based on other Tammāmī documents we know that this seal belonged to a scribe of the *shaykh al-islām sharīʿa* court, and it is likely that he produced this deed. The document confirming the rights of Mīrzā Abū ʿAlī Qassām b. Mīrzā Muḥamamd Hāshim, registrar of the *shaykh al-islām sharīʿa* court, was issued by Shaykh Muḥammad Amīn also most likely also produced in the *shaykh al-islām* court itself.

As we shall see below in documents produced during the period of Shaykh Muḥammad Amīn's successor, Shaykh Abū l-Qāsim b. Shaykh Muḥammad Ḥusayn, a new set of textual practices allow us to immediately identify the production of a document by one of the scribes of the *shaykh al-islām sharīʿa* court (see Section 4.3).

From the documents discussed above, we know that Shaykh Muḥammad Amīn used a single rectangular seal measuring 1.9 cm x 1.6 cm with the following inscription in *nastaʿlīq*: "*lā ilāha illā allāh al-malik al-ḥaqq al-mubīn ibn muḥammad bāqir, muḥammad amīn . . . 12 . . .*"[68] The *nisba* al-Tammāmī does not appear on this seal. Riḍāʾī suggests this is perhaps because the seal cutter could not fit this in, or Shaykh Muḥammad Amīn, unlike his predecessors and successors, preferred not to emphasize the Arab origins of his lineage.[69] As in the case of Shaykh Muḥammad Ḥusayn, two administrative decrees have survived relating to Shaykh Muḥammad Amīn. These decrees were issued by Fatḥ ʿAlī Shāh (r.1797–1834). They are dated Jamādī II 1234/March–April 1819 and Ramaḍān 1234/June-July 1819. The decree dated Jamādī II 1234/March–April 1819 assigns in the form of a *tuyūl* taxes from a village named Shaykh ʿAlī Chūpān as an annual stipend to Shaykh Muḥammad Amīn.[70] The tax

68 Riḍāʾī 1397 sh./2018, 108.

69 Riḍāʾī 1397 sh./2018, 111.

70 Ishkawarī 1383 sh./2005, document no. 34. On *tuyūl* assignments, the holders of which (*tuyūl-dār*) enjoyed the temporary right to collect government taxes from a certain area for their own benefit, see Lambton 1969, 101–102, and, for the Qajar era *tuyūl*, 139–140. See also for comparison

revenues amounted to 125 *tūmān*s in cash and 75 *kharwār* of grain in kind. In the decree dated Ramaḍān 1234/June-July 1819, an additional 25 *tūmān*s in cash and 71 *kharwār* and 25 *mann* of grain in kind of taxes collected from the outskirts of Shiraz are also assigned to Shaykh Muḥammad Amīn in the *tuyūl*. Shaykh Muḥammad Amīn's total state-derived income was thus clearly higher than that of his predecessor, Shaykh Muḥammad Ḥusayn.

Like his predecessor, Shaykh Muḥammad Amīn also derived income from his role as the administrator of various endowments. We know that prior to Rajab 1249/November-December 1833, the *shaykh al-islām* of Fārs was appointed by the central government in Tehran as administrator of endowments in the districts of Qīr and Kāzirūn in Fārs province (see below).[71] In some cases, as we have seen above, *waqf* deeds specified, in case of an extinction of descendants in the lineage of the founder, that the administration of the *waqf* should be assigned to the *shaykh al-islām*. This happened, for example, in the case of a field (*mazraʿa*) located on the outskirts of Shiraz that was constituted as an endowment at the start of Muḥarram 1222/March 1808 by Ḥājjī Mīrzā Muḥammad Riḍā b. Mīrzā Muḥammad Shafīʿ.[72]

3.6 Shaykh Abū l-Qāsim b. Shaykh Muḥammad Ḥusayn

The next *shaykh al-islām* of Fārs, Shaykh Muḥammad Amīn's nephew, Shaykh Abū l-Qāsim, was born in Shiraz in 1211/1796–7, according to Fasāʾī.[73] In around 1223/1808–9, Shaykh Abū l-Qāsim married the daughter of Ḥājj ʿAlī Akbar Nawwāb (1187–1263), who, as we have seen, had endorsed the *waqf*-deed of Ḥasan ʿAlī Mirza Farmān-farmā along with Shaykh Muḥammad Amīn.[74] According to Fasāʾī, Shaykh Muḥammad Amīn died around 1248/1833 or 1249/1834.[75] This is confirmed by a rental contract dated 26 Dhū l-Ḥijja 1249/6 May 1834, in which Shaykh Abū l-Qāsim is described as: "*shaykh abū l-qāsimā shaykh al-islām*".[76] The production of this rental contract appears to be one of Shaykh Abū l-Qāsim's first acts as *shaykh al-islām*. In the contract, he hires a carpenter for a period of five months to carry out repairs to the glasswork and joinery of the interior of his house and the façade

the *tuyūl*s assigned to the Ṭabāṭabāʾī clerical lineage in Tabriz, in Werner 2000, 244–250. On *kharwār* and *mann* weights for grain, see Floor 2008, 88 and 93–101.

71 Ishkawarī 1383 sh./2005, document no. 14.

72 File no. 164, Fārs province, Sāzmān-i Awqāf wa Umūr-i Khayriyya, Tehran.

73 Fasāʾī 1382 sh./2004, 55.

74 Riḍāʾī 1385 sh./2006, 80; Riḍāʾī 1390 sh./2012, 80.

75 Fasāʾī 1382 sh./2004, 55.

76 Document no. 002/6, Mīrzā Muḥammad Kāẓimaynī collection, Yazd.

facing Mecca. We know that the house which was also the site of the *shaykh al-islām sharīʿa* court was located in the Suq al-Ṭayr/Bāzār-i Murgh (Bird Market) quarter of Shiraz. On 20 Jamādī I 1254/11 August 1838, Shaykh Abū l-Qāsim renovated and expanded the house further.[77] The house, however, was destroyed in an earthquake in Shiraz on 25 Rajab 1269/4 May 1853 and had to be rebuilt again. It was used briefly as a school before the Islamic revolution in Iran in 1979, after which it was demolished to make way for a parking lot.

Two decrees, one by Fatḥ ʿAlī Shāh dated Rajab 1249/November-December 1833 and one by Muḥammad Shāh (r. 1834–1848) dated Rabi I 1253/June-July 1837, enable us to reconstruct the sources of Shaykh Abū l-Qāsim's revenues.[78] According to the decree by Fatḥ ʿAlī Shah, the stipendiary tax assignments and administration of endowed lands of the districts of Qīr and Kāzirūn awarded to Shaykh Abū l-Qāsim's father, Shaykh Muḥammad Ḥusayn, and his uncle, Shaykh Muḥammad Amīn, were now allocated to Shaykh Abū l-Qāsim. This decree suggests that the member of the Tammāmī clerical lineage who became *shaykh al-islām* inherited all state-assigned revenues and privileges from his predecessors. In the decree by Muḥammad Shāh dated Rabīʿ I 1253/June–July 1837, Shaykh Abū l-Qāsim is awarded an additional annual stipend of 89 *tūmāns* from the taxes of the district of Kuhgīlūye. In a separate decree by Muḥammad Shāh, also dated Rabīʿ I 1253/June–July 1837, Shaykh Abū l-Qāsim is instructed to ensure that 55 *tūmāns* from the endowed lands of the districts of Qīr and Kāzirūn are spent in accordance with the clauses of the endowment.

The latter decree might suggest inappropriate use of *waqf* revenue by Shaykh Abū l-Qāsim, who was clearly a significant administrator of multiple endowments both in Shiraz and Fārs province. Regrettably, we are only partially able to reconstruct the role of Shaykh Abū l-Qāsim as an administrator of local endowments from the surviving sources. We know that Shaykh Abū l-Qāsim was appointed as administrator of the endowments constituted by several prominent women. Māh-Bīgam (Ṣadr al-Ḥājiyya), daughter of Ḥājj Muḥammad Ḥusayn Ṣadr (d. 1239) and her daughter, Hājiyya Nurī Jān Khānum, each constituted half of the same village and a field in the district of Kirbāl as an endowment at the beginning of Dhū l-Qaʿda 1258/December 1842 and on 18 Rajab 1261/23 July 1845, respectively.[79] They assigned half of the revenues of their endowment after all expenses were paid to Shaykh Abū l-Qāsim as the endowment's administrator. Similarly, Zulaykha Khānum (Ḥājiyya Wazīra), wife of Shukrullāh Khān Nūrī, constituted on 9 Ramaḍān 1261/11 September 1845 several fields in the district of Murūdasht, Kirbāl, and

77 Riḍāʾī 1397 sh./2018, 110.
78 Ishkawarī 1383 sh./2005, document no. 109.
79 Riḍāʾī 1390 sh./2012, 80–81.

Qaṣr al-Dasht as an endowment.[80] Her endowment deed was drawn up in the presence of Shaykh Abū Turāb, the *imām-jumʿa* of Shiraz (on him see below) and the *pīsh-namāz* Ḥājjī Mullā Muḥammad. She allocates one-fifth of the endowments revenues after all expenses were paid to Shaykh Abū l-Qāsim's salary as administrator.

From the preceding, it is clear that Shaykh Abū l-Qāsim had managed to secure a considerable amount of revenue both from the state and from his role as the administrator of pious endowments in Shiraz, which he had inherited from his father and his uncle. It was, however, his influence in the socio-legal affairs of Shiraz through the *shaykh al-islām sharīʿa* court that facilitated the marriage of his son, Shaykh Muḥammad Ḥusayn (see below), to a daughter of the powerful Shiraz notable Hajjī Mīrzā ʿAlī Akbar Qawām al-Mulk (1203–1282/1789–1865).[81] The alliance between the two families was sealed through an impressive endowment constituted by Ḥājjī Mīrzā ʿAlī Akbar Qawām al-Mulk at the *shaykh al-islām sharīʿa* court on 12 Jamadi II 1272/19 February 1856. The *waqf* deed dated 12 Jamādī II 1272/19 February 1856 contains a series of successive marginal notes dated 9 Dhū l-Ḥijja 1273/ 31 July 1857, 14 Ṣafar 1274/4 October 1857, 7 Rabīʿ I 1276/4 October 1859 and 25 Dhū l-Qaʿda 1277/4 June 1861, through which Ḥājjī Mīrzā ʿAlī Akbar Qawām al-Mulk added additional properties to the original endowment.[82]

A total of twenty villages were endowed, either in full or in part. These villages included nine from the district (*bulūk*) of Arsanjān; four from the district of Kavār; three from the district of Kirbāl; three from the district of Khafr and one from the outskirts of Shiraz. Besides the twenty villages (*qarya*), the properties of the endowment also included twelve fields (*mazraʿa*) and several mills in these districts. Ḥājji Mīrzā ʿAlī Akbar Qawām al-Mulk appointed his son-in-law, Shaykh Muḥammad Ḥusayn, as the supervisor of the endowment, with a right to the supervisor's salary after all expenses were paid. In the *waqf* deed, which contains the *sijill* and seal of Shaykh Abū l-Qāsim, his son Shaykh Muhamamd Ḥusayn is referred to as the *shaykh al-islām-i mamlikat-i fārs*. Shaykh Abū l-Qāsim was clearly preparing Shaykh Muḥammad Ḥusayn for his role as future *shaykh al-islām*.

Shaykh Abū l-Qāsim had already constituted on 12 Ramadan 1274/26 April 1858 a section of his house as an endowment for the performance of mourning ceremonies in commemoration of the martyrdom of al-Ḥusayn.[83] On 17 Ramadan 1274/ 1 May 1858, two adjoining fields of land Shaykh Abū l-Qāsim owned in the district of Kavār were added to the endowment to cover the expenses of the Ḥusayniyya. Shaykh Abū l-Qāsim's son was appointed administrator of the endowment. Shaykh

---

80 Riḍāʾī 1390 sh./2012, 80–81.
81 Riḍāʾī 1390 sh./2012, 82.
82 File no. 119, Fārs province, Sāzman-i Awqāf wa Umūr-i Khayriyya, Tehran.
83 Riḍāʾī, 1397 sh./2018, 111.

Abū l-Qāsim's house now thus comprised both the *shaykh al-islām sharīʿa* court and a functioning Ḥusayniyya. This was clearly a useful strategy for attracting clients to a space which had a dual legal and religious function.

According to Fasāʾī, in Muḥarram 1285/April–May 1868, Shaykh Abū l-Qāsim left Shiraz for the *ḥajj* pilgrimage to Mecca. After completing the *ḥajj*, he went to Medina to visit the graves of the Prophet and his family. Shaykh Abū l-Qāsim died in Medina in Muḥarram 1286/April–May 1869 and was buried in the Baqīʿ cemetery.[84] From the documents which contain Shaykh Abū l-Qāsim's *sijill* and seal, we know that he used at least two different seals during his lifetime. The first is a rectangular seal made in in 1241/1825–6, measuring 2 cm x 1.5 cm, with the following inscription in *nastaʿlīq*: *lā ilāha illā l-lāh al-malik al-ḥaqq al-mubīn ibn muḥammad ḥusayn abū l-qāsim al-tammāmī 1241.*[85] The second seal, made in 1260/1844–5, is oval and has the following inscription in *nastaʿlīq*: *ibn muḥammad ḥusayn abū l-qāsim al-tammāmī 1260.*[86]

3.7 Shaykh Muḥammad Ḥusayn b. Shaykh Abū l-Qāsim

With the death of Shaykh Abū l-Qāsim, his only son, Shaykh Muḥammad Ḥusayn, became *shaykh al-islām* of Fārs. As we have seen, he had not only married into one of Shiraz's prominent political families, but he had also inherited a considerable amount of revenues both in the form of state stipends and from the administration of endowments from his father. Though the total amount from *waqf* revenue which Shaykh Muḥammad Ḥusayn received is not known, in Dhū l-Ḥijja 1282/April–May 1866 the annual sate stipend allocated to his father was calculated at 250 Tabrīzī *tūmān*s in cash and 150 *kharwār* of grain in kind.[87] Two decrees, the first by Jalāl al-Dawla, dated Shaʿbān 1303/May–June 1886, and the second by Ihtishām al-Dawla, dated Shawwāl 1305/June-July 1888, suggest that Shaykh Muḥammad Ḥusayn received at this time an annual cash stipend that amounted to 515 *tūmān*s and 5,000 *dīnār*s from the taxes collected from Shaykh ʿAlī Chūpān, Māʾīn, Isfadrān-Nārak, the fields of Khālidābād, Khayrābād and Aḥmadābād, and from land in Arsanjān.[88]

Not surprisingly perhaps, Shaykh Muḥammad Ḥusayn had time for artistic pursuits with such a stipend. Besides presiding over the *shaykh al-islām sharīʿa* court, he wrote poetry under the nom de plume Ṣafā-yi Shīrāzī. However, the period of Shaykh Muḥammad Ḥusayn is also the era where the *shaykh al-islām*

84 Fasāʾī 1382 sh./2004, 55.
85 Riḍāʾī, 1397 sh./2018, 110.
86 Riḍāʾī 1397 sh./2018, 111.
87 Riḍāʾī 1390 sh./2012, 62.
88 Riḍāʾī 1390 sh./2012, 102; Ishkawarī 1383 sh./2005, document no. 26.

sharīʿa court begins to face competition from the emergence of new *sharīʿa* courts in Shiraz. These new *sharīʿa* courts (see below) adopt the same scribal and archival techniques used by the older *shaykh al-islām sharīʿa* court, in particular, the practice of deeds produced under Shaykh Muḥammad Amīn and Shaykh Abū l-Qāsim. The fact that new *sharīʿa* courts adopt the scribal and archival norms of the *shaykh al-islām sharīʿa* court is a good indicator of the political patronage and religious prestige that the *shaykh al-islām sharīʿa* court had come to acquire in Shiraz during the preceding decades.

We know from surviving documents that Shaykh Muḥammad Ḥusayn had already begun to seal documents during the period of his father Shaykh Abū l-Qāsim as early as 8 Shawwāl 1271/24 June 1855. Shaykh Muḥammad Ḥusayn used two seals for his *sijill*s, though the dates they were made are uncertain. A rectangular seal measuring 1.9 cm x 1.7 cm has the following inscription in *nastaʿlīq*: *al-wāthiq bi-llāh al-ghanī ʿabduhu ibn abū l-qāsim, muḥammad ḥusayn al-tammāmī.*[89] A second seal, also rectangular in shape, has the inscription in *nastaʿlīq*: *ufawwiḍu amrī ila l-lāh muḥammad ḥusayn b. abū l-qāsim.*[90]

3.8 Shaykh Muḥammad Bāqir b. Shaykh Muḥammad Ḥusayn

Shaykh Muḥammad Ḥusayn's death occurred in 1336/1918.[91] A document entitled "Copy of the Guardianship of the Manuscripts in the Attic facing Mecca left behind by the deceased *ḥājjī shaykh al-islām*, may God illuminate his grave, dated Jamādī I 1337/February–March 1919" divides Shaykh Muḥammad Ḥusayn's collection of eighty manuscripts, with an estimated total value of 1,200 *tūmān*s, among his four sons and four daughters according to the Islamic law of inheritance.[92] The document was drawn up by Shaykh Muḥammad Ḥusayn's eldest son, Shaykh Muḥammad Bāqir, who like his father was also a poet and wrote poetry using the nom de plume Vafā. Shaykh Muḥammad Bāqir is referred to in documents of this period (see below) as the *shaykh al-islām* of Fārs (*shaykh al-islām-i mamlikat-i fārs*). Though we know Shaykh Muḥammad Bāqir and his younger brother, Shaykh Abū l-Qāsim (Āqā Buzurg), played an active part in notarizing documents of the *shaykh al-islām sharīʿa* court during and after the lifetime of their father, Shaykh Muḥammad Ḥusayn, it is

89 Riḍāʾī 1390 sh./2012, 102: Ishkawarī, 1383 sh./2005, document no. 30.
90 Riḍāʾī 1397 sh./2018, 112–113.
91 Riḍāʾī 1397 sh./2018, 112–113.
92 For an edition of this document entitled *ṣūrat-i qayyimat-i kutub-i khaṭṭī dar bālā-khāna-yi rū bi qibla-yi mukhallafa-yi marḥimat wa ghufrān-panāh jannat-ārāmgāh ḥājjī shaykh al-islām tāba tharāhu bi-tārīkh-i shahr-i jamādi l-awwal 1337,* see Riḍāʾī 1394 sh./2015, 815–822.

likely that the term *shaykh al-islām-i mamlikat-i fārs* was by the early twentieth century used mainly as an honorific and no longer designated the exercise of an actual official post linked to a state stipend. Shaykh Muḥammad Bāqir and his brother Shaykh Abū l-Qāsim are the last known members of the Tammāmī clerical lineage who presided over the *shaykh al-islām sharīʿa* court in Shiraz and authenticated legal documents during the final years of Qajar rule.

4 Scribal and Archival Practice of the Tammāmī *Shaykh al-Islām Sharīʿa* Court

In the preceding sections I have used surviving legal and administrative documents to reconstruct the biographies of members of the Tammāmī clerical lineage that occupied the post of *shaykh al-islām* of Fārs and presided over the *shaykh al-islām sharīʿa* court in Shiraz from the mid-eighteenth to the early twentieth centuries. In what follows, I will examine the scribal and archival practice of the *shaykh al-islām sharīʿa* court. The legal documents of the Tammāmī corpus are either on single sheets of paper or on multiple sheets which are glued together to form a roll (*tūmār*) (see Figure 13).

The earliest three multiple sheet legal rolls record court proceedings during the period of Shaykh Muḥammad b. Shaykh Aḥmad and his son Shaykh Muḥammad Bāqir b. Shakyh Muḥammad. These eighteenth-century rolls are unique. New sheets of paper were glued to create a rotulus which recorded different stages of legal proceedings relating to a given case in the *shaykh al-islām sharīʿa* court. These rolls also record witness testiomines and the rulings issued by the *shaykh al-islām* at each stage of the proceedings.

There are no comparable examples of such rolls from the nineteenth and twentieth centuries from the *shaykh al-islām sharīʿa* court. The surviving multiple sheet rolls of the nineteenth and twentieth centuries from the *shaykh al-islām sharīʿa* court consist mainly of deeds of sale, endowment, or settlement, including their copies. In some cases, several such complete deeds are glued together to form a roll. This is still not identical to the eighteenth-century rolls, which allows us to reconstruct step by step different stages of legal action in a case as it occured in the *shaykh al-islām sharīʿa* court.

In the first part, I will look at one of these eighteenth-century multiple sheet rolls produced during the period of Shaykh Muḥammad b. Shaykh Aḥmad relating to the estate of the deceased Raʾīs ʿAlī Akbar. In the second part, I investigate the production, authentication, copying, archiving, and annulling of deeds produced by the *shaykh al-islām sharīʿa* court in the nineteenth and early twentieth centuries.

Figure 13: Bottom of a multiple sheet sale deed roll (*ṭūmār*) from Shiraz dated 8 Muḥarram 1289/ 18 March 1872 © Document no. 106, Madrasa-yi Imām-i ʿAsr, Shiraz.[93]

I will focus first on a conditional sale deed produced on a single sheet of paper. I will then examine a nineteenth-century multiple sheet roll dividing an estate and

93 I am indebted to Sayyid Ṣādiq Ḥusaynī Ishkawarī for kindly providing me with an image of this document from the uncatalogued Madrasa-yi Imām-i ʿAsr collection in Shiraz. The document number refers to the number assigned to the image in the digital archive held at the Majmaʿ-yi Dhakhāʾir-i Islāmī in Qum.

its copy. Finally, I will discuss the archival loose-leaf sheets of paper known as *fard* produced and kept by the *shaykh al-islām sharī'a* court.

4.1 An Eighteenth-Century Multiple Sheet Legal Roll: The Estate of Ra'īs 'Alī Akbar

The earliest documents produced by the *shaykh al-islām sharī'a* court that have survived are three rolls (*ṭūmār*) recording legal proceedings from the mid-eighteenth century. One of these rolls, which I examine here, has been edited and published with facsimiles by Riḍā'ī.[94]

The roll is 98.5 cm long. It is composed of five pieces of paper of varying dimensions: 14 cm x 12 cm, 24.5 cm x 13.5 cm, 14 cm x 14 cm, 24 cm x 14 cm and 22 cm x 14.5 cm. The scribe has glued the bottom verso edge of one paper to the top recto edge of another to extend the length of the document with new papers. The presence of horizontal fold lines on the papers suggests that the document was preserved by rolling and then pressing. There is also, however, a vertical fold line running through the centre of the papers. This vertical folding has resulted in a significant tear visible on most of the papers. The tear shows signs of recent repair using tape stuck to the middle of the verso of the first, second, and third papers to keep the document together. To circumvent forgery, the document contains seals affixed to the overlapping sheet joints where the papers are glued to each other. Since only half a seal is visible at the top edge of the fifth paper, it is certain that a sixth paper, which formed part of the original document, is missing.

The five surviving papers record around six months of court proceedings relating to the estate of a certain deceased Ra'īs 'Alī Akbar of Shiraz that took place before Shaykh Muḥammad between Sha'bān 1158–Ṣafar 1159/September 1745–March 1746. The papers are attached in such a way that the earliest proceedings are found on the paper at the bottom of the roll, while the most recent proceedings are recorded on the paper at the top of the roll. Except for the second paper, where the verso is blank, the scribe first filled the recto of each paper followed by the verso before adding an additional paper to the roll.

In what follows, I summarise the contents of the five papers and reconstruct the codicological production of the roll. The first paper contains a petition by Ṣāliḥa, daughter of the deceased Ra'īs 'Alī Akbar.[95] According to the petition, Ṣāliḥa

94 See Riḍā'ī 1391 sh./2012, 391–408.
95 Riḍā'ī 1391 sh./2012, edition: 395–396; bottom half of image no. 1: 402.

asserts that following the death of her father, she, her sister Zaynab, and their stepmother were his only legal heirs. Ṣāliḥa and Zaynab were children from Raʾīs ʿAlī Akbar's first wife, who pre-deceased her husband, while their stepmother, Raʾīs ʿAlī Akbar's second wife, was a woman named Badr Jahān Khānum. Raʾīs ʿAlī Akbar had left behind his house in the Bāl-kaft quarter of Shiraz to his heirs. Most of this house was either in ruins or on the verge of collapse, and neither of his heirs could restore it. Ṣāliḥa asked the *shaykh al-islām sharīʿa* court to have the house inspected and valued so that it could be sold. Shaykh Muḥammad's sealed ruling, dated 22 Shaʿbān 1158/19 September 1745, is written in the form of a "spiral text" starting on the bottom right-hand margin of the paper. The ruling begins with the pious invocation *hū* (He is). Shaykh Muḥammad instructs five individuals, a certain Mīrzā Muḥamamd Zakī *qassām-i manāzil*, Ḥājjī Muḥammad Ṭāhir, Ḥājjī Muḥammad Raḥīm ʿAṭṭār, Āqā Muḥammad Ṣādiq, the *kadkhudā* of the Bāl-kaft quarter, and Raʾīs Muḥammad Mahdī, an inhabitant of the said quarter, to conduct a comprehensive set of investigations. They were to investigate the legal ownership of the property, who the legal heirs were, whether the house was indeed on the verge of collapse, whether it was in the best interest of the minors involved to sell the house, and what the estimated sale price should be. These details were to be recorded in writing, sealed by all five individuals, and submitted to Shaykh Muḥammad for review. In addition, these details were to be conveyed orally to him.

On the verso of the first paper, precisely as Shaykh Muḥammad had ordered, we find the text of the report of the five individuals.[96] According to the report, Mīrzā Muḥammad Zakī, Ḥājjī Muḥammad Ṭāhir, Ḥājjī Muḥamamd Raḥīm ʿAṭṭār, Āqā ʿAlī (Ḥājjī Muḥammad Ṭāhir's brother), Āqā Zayn al-Dīn ʿAṭṭār, and a certain Shaykh Muḥammad Amīn, carried out the investigations ordered by the *shaykh al-islām*. They confirmed that the legal heirs of the deceased Raʾīs ʿAlī Akbar were his second permanent wife (i.e., not via a temporary marriage) and two daughters who were minors. They had inspected Raʾīs ʿAlī Akbar's house, its adjoining land, including a stable and a store, and confirmed that the house was in a decrepit state and that it was in the best interests of the minors for it to be sold. They had estimated the value of the house at 20 *tūmān*s and put it on the market for sale. The text of this report is sealed by seven of the eight mentioned individuals directly below the last line.

As we have seen, the legal action recorded in the first paper was carried out at the request of Ṣāliḥa, daughter of Raʾīs ʿAlī Akbar, who was a minor. It is likely that she was represented by a proxy or legal guardian in the *sharīʿa* court. The second paper glued on top of the first paper also contains a petition on the

96 Riḍāʾī 1391 sh./2012, edition: 396; image no. 2: 403. On spiral texts, see Messick 1996, 231–251.

recto.[97] The petition is by the proxy (*wakīl*) of Badr Jahān Khānum, second wife of the deceased Raʾīs ʿAlī Akbar. After confirming who the legal heirs of Raʾīs ʿAlī Akbar were, Badr Jahān Khānum's *wakīl* claims that Raʾīs ʿAlī Akbar still owed Badr Jahan Khānum 600 *nādirīs* out of a sum of 800 *nādirīs*, that is the equivalent of 400 Tabrīzī *tūmāns* in cash, in lieu of her dowry. The *wakīl* asked the court if he could present witnesses in support of the claim. On the bottom right-hand margin of the paper, Shaykh Muḥammad, or probably his scribe, has written a brief note: "He is. It is true" (*hū; ṣaḥḥa*). The witnesses can give their testimonies (*shuhūdī ki bāshad iqāmat namāyand*). Eight witness depositions follow directly after this note. The depositions are written one after the other as a spiral text around the petition of the *wakīl*. Each deposition is preceded by the name of the witness. Witness one, two, three, four, seven and eight are men, while witness five and six are women. The names of the male and female witnesses are written in the form of a cipher with some letters extended. For example, in the case of the name of the first witness, the *alif* and *qāf* of *āqā* are extended. In other cases, such as witness three the letter *tāʾ* of *ʿālī-ḥadrat* is extended. The names of the women begin with the word *musammāt* (the woman called so and so), of which the final *alif* has been extended and the initial *sīn* shortened, making it exceedingly difficult to read. Such scribal shorthand conventions were probably routinely used by the scribes of the *shaykh al-islām sharīʿa* court to write documents quickly. The practice of extending some letters, however, also helped to organise each witness deposition text block and separate it from the next.

In the case of witness one and four, the scribe has also recorded the text of the oral testimony itself, which is preceded by the clause: *shahādat dād ki* (he testified that . . .). For the remaining witnesses whose oral testimony is not recorded (for example witness two, three and five), the scribe simply mentions the name of the witness, followed by the clause *bi-dastūr shahādat dād* (he testified upon the order, presumably of the *shaykh al-islām*) or *bi-dastūr* in short. The testimonies of the two women contain a different clause which suggests their testimony was based on the report of another person and not on first-hand knowledge of the facts they had acquired themselves. In this case, the scribe has used the clause *shahādat-i khud taḥmīl bar fulān namūd* (she testified based on the report of so and so). The scribe records the names of each of the male individuals the female witnesses based their reported witness testimony upon. The scribe also notes that these secondary male witnesses testified independently in court (*wa mūmā ilayhim adā-yi shahādat namūdand ayḍan*). Witness one, two, three and four have affixed their seal below their respective depositions. Two of the secondary male witnesses mentioned have also affixed their seals below the depositions of the female witnesses. The depositions by

97 Riḍāʾī 1391 sh./2012, edition: 397; top half of image no. 1 and bottom half of image no. 3: 404.

the male witnesses all contain the word *ṣaḥḥa* (it is valid) recorded above the extended letter that precedes the name of the witness. The depositions of the two women, however, do not contain the *ṣaḥḥa* remark, perhaps because their testimonies were not based on personal knowledge but hearsay evidence.

The verso of paper two is blank.[98] The reasons for this are not entirely clear, but it might be explained by the fact that the next sequence of proceedings involved a ruling by Shaykh Muḥammad. It was probably considered "spatially" inappropriate to write the ruling of the *shaykh al-islām* on the verso of the document. The ruling therefore appears on the recto of a new piece of paper, paper three, which is glued above paper two.[99] The ruling, dated Ramaḍān 1158/September–October 1745, is written diagonally across the document and begins with the pious invocation *huwa ḥasbī* (He is sufficient for me). Shaykh Muḥammad notes that based on the witness testimonies and his study of the marriage contract in the handwriting of the deceased *qāḍī*, Zayn al-ʿAbidīn, and other investigations, it had become clear that a permanent marriage had indeed occurred between Badr Jahān Khānum and the deceased Raʾīs ʿAlī Akbar. Moreover, the latter owed Badr Jahan Khānum forty Tabrīzī *tūmāns* in cash in lieu of her dowry, of which he had paid her only ten Tabrīzī *tūmāns*. He therefore still owed her the sum of thirty Tabrīzī *tūmāns*. Accordingly, Shaykh Muḥammad ruled that she was entitled to thirty *tūmāns* from the estate of her deceased husband after she declared her claim orally upon the instruction (*bi-talqīn*) of Mullā Abū l-Ḥasan Qārī and in the presence of Mīrzā ʿIzz al-Dīn Masʿūd Mūsawī, the *pīsh-namāz*. Shaykh Muḥammad's rectangular seal with the inscription: *fawwaḍtu amrī ila l-lāh al-aḥad al-ṣamad wa-anā ibn aḥmad al-tammāmī al-imāmī muḥammad* is affixed below the ruling.

The verso of paper three contains a confirmatory note that Badr Jahān Khānum had on 21 Ramaḍān 1158/17 October 1745 stated her legal claim orally after being prompted to do so by Mullā Abū l-Ḥasan Qārī in the presence of the witnesses listed on the margins.[100] The main text is sealed by Mullā Abū l-Ḥasan Qārī. From the bottom right-hand margin upwards, the names of four witnesses who were present are listed, each of whom has affixed their seal below their name. These witnesses on the verso of paper three, along with the witnesses appearing on the verso of paper two, were present in the *shaykh al-islām sharīʿa* court when these papers were being produced. We know this because the seals of these witnesses were affixed to the paper before the scribe copied the text of their testimony or their name above it. The next sequence of proceedings in the

98 Riḍāʾī 1391 sh./2012, bottom half of image no. 4: 405.

99 Riḍāʾī 1391 sh./2012, edition: 398; top half of image no. 3: 404.

100 Riḍāʾī 1391 sh./2012, edition: 398–399; top half of image no. 4: 405.

case appears on the recto of paper four, which is glued above paper three.[101] Once again, we have a petition, this time by Badr Jahān Khānum herself, without a proxy, and a ruling by Shaykh Muḥammad. In the petition, Badr Jahān Khānum reiterates her claim to thirty *tūmān*s owed to her in lieu of her dowry from her deceased husband's estate and confirms that she made the oral declaration of her legal claim as the *shaykh al-islām* had ordered. She notes that based on "the seperate glued writing on the verso of the writing annexed below" (*bi-mawjib-i niwishta-yi ʿalāḥida-yi mawṣūla dar taht-i niwishta-yi mulaṣṣaqa-yi dhayl*), i.e., the verso of paper one, the value of the house of her deceased husband was estimated at and put on the market for twenty *tūmān*s. The house had, however, attracted no buyer. Badr Jahān Khānum asked if she could take possession of the house in lieu of the debt owed to her by her deceased husband. The ruling of Shaykh Muḥammad, which begins with a different pious invocation, *bismillāh khayr al-asmā'* (in the name of God the best of names), confirms Badr Jahān Khānum's legal right to take possession of her deceased husband's house. The ruling is dated 12 Dhū l-Qaʿda 1158/6 December 1745.

On the verso of paper four is a confirmatory note dated two days later, on 14 Dhū l-Qaʿda 1158/8 December 1745, confirming that Badr Jahān Khānum had taken possession of her deceased husband's house and that this property was transferred to her private ownership.[102] The bottom edge of the verso of paper five is glued to the top edge of the recto of paper four. The recto of paper five contains a note by Shaykh Muḥammad which orders, based on the request of Badr Jahān Khānum, a revaluation of the house of the deceased Ra'īs ʿAlī Akbar.[103] The note is sealed by Shaykh Muḥammad and is dated 10 Ṣafar 1159/4 March 1746. The verso of paper five contains the new estimate of the value of the house.[104] Due to neglect and rainfall, the house was now valued at fourteen *tūmān*s, that is six *tūmān*s lower than the previous valuation. The new valuation is also more detailed than the first one, with the different components of the house, grounds, stable, and store valued separately under stylized headings entitled *darb*, of which the letter *bā'* is extended to organise the text. The evaluation ends with the generic note *bayāḍa shud* (left blank), written over the blank space to prevent any fraudulent additions. An illegible seal is affixed on the bottom right-hand corner.

The paper trail concerning the fate of the house of deceased Ra'īs ʿAlī Akbar, who is described in the roll as a "farmer" (*zārʿī*), ends here. From the preceding, it is clear that the initial claim of the two children of Ra'īs ʿAlī Akbar, Ṣāliḥa and Zaynab,

101 Riḍā'ī 1391 sh./2012, edition: 399; image no. 5: 406.
102 Riḍā'ī 1391 sh./2012, edition: 400; image no. 6: 407.
103 Riḍā'ī 1391 sh./2012, edition: 400; bottom half of image no. 5: 406.
104 Riḍā'ī 1391 sh./2012, edition: 400–401; bottom half of image no. 6: 407.

to their father's house, based on the Islamic law of inheritance, was overruled due to the outstanding debt claim of the wife of Ra'īs 'Alī Akbar, Badr Jahān Khānum. As we have mentioned, a sixth paper was attached to the roll which is now lost. The scribe or scribes that produced the papers of the roll did so in successive stages over a period of almost half a year. It is possible that the roll was given to Badr Jahān Khānum at the end of the proceedings. More than one original copy of the roll could also have been produced, one of which was preserved in the *shaykh al-islām sharī'a* court and the other given to Badr Jahān Khānum. As we shall see below, it was common practice to make several original copies of deeds, in which case this was noted on the document. Since this is not recorded on the roll, it is possible that only a copy of the roll and not a duplicate original was preserved in the *shaykh al-islām sharī'a* court.[105]

4.2 A Nineteenth-Century Single-Sheet Legal Document: The Conditional Sale Deed of Ḥājjī Imām-Qulī b. 'Alī Muḥammad Bēg Nūrī

The evolution of the scribal and archival techniques used in the *shaykh al-islām sharī'a* court and its relationship to other *sharī'a* courts in Shiraz is complex and beyond the scope of this chapter. What is certain is that the scribes who worked in the *shaykh al-islām* court in the eighteenth and nineteenth centuries derived their practice from the *shaykh al-islām sharī'a* courts of the Safavid period. This Safavid practice was itself heir to the practice of preceding periods, most notably the Ilkhanid Mongol period. I will present in this section some of the documentary practices of the *shaykh al-islām sharī'a* court relating to legal deeds as they had crystallized in the mid-nineteenth century under the direction of Shaykh Abū l-Qāsim al-Tammāmī. These distinctive documentary practices make the production of the *shaykh al-islām sharī'a* court instantly recognisable.

Moreover, as we shall see in the following part relating to multiple sheet documents, the addition of certain graphic marks allows us to confirm without doubt the *sijill* of Shaykh Abū l-Qāsim and his successors. The documentary norms of the Tammāmī *shaykh al-islām sharī'a* court in the early nineteenth century prior to Shaykh Abū l-Qāsim were less strict. It is thus difficult to establish whether a given document was produced in the *shaykh al-islām sharī'a* court itself or whether it was produced in a different *sharī'a* court but taken to the

105 The roll relating to Shaykh Ṣāliḥ b. Qāsim Khalafābādī is an example of a copy of an original roll produced in the Tammāmī *shaykh al-islam* sharī'a court in the mid-eighteenth century. This roll preserved in the Mīrzā Muḥammad Kaẓimaynī collection in Yazd has not been catalogued.

shaykh al-islām for the addition of the *shaykh al-islām*'s *sijill* and registration in the *shaykh al-islām sharīʿa* court archive.

By the time of Shaykh Abū l-Qāsim, we can, however, identify four key elements of all deeds produced by the *shaykh al-islām sharīʿa* court: (1) the main text and witness clauses; (2) the *sijill* and seal of the *shaykh al-islām* (3) the seals of scribes of the *shaykh al-islām sharīʿa* court and (4) the registration note and seal of the registrar of the *shaykh al-islām sharīʿa* court. Each of these elements had a precisely designated place on the sheet of paper. In what follows we will examine how these elements come together in the conditional sale (*bayʿ-i sharṭ*) deed of Ḥājjī Imām-Qulī b. ʿAlī Muḥammad Bēg Nūrī, dated 15 Jamādī II 1276/9 January 1860.[106] This deed is written on a single sheet of paper (see Figure 14). A conditional sale contract (*bayʿ-i sharṭ*) was a type of sale which included the right of recession if a stipulated condition was met by the seller (the original owner).[107] In this case, the original owner and seller, Ḥājjī Imām-Qulī b. ʿAlī Muḥammad Bēg Nūrī, sold a field (*mazraʿa*) on the outskirts of Shiraz to a certain Mīrzā Muḥammad ʿAlī and his sister Farrukh Sulṭān, who were both the children of Ḥājjī Muḥammad Ibrāhīm ʿAllāf Shīrāzī.

4.2.1 Main Text and Witness Clauses

The main text (*matn*) is composed of thirteen lines in Persian. It begins with the introductory clause "the summary of the contents of this righteous deed is" (*khulāsa-yi mufād īn kitāb-i ṣawāb ān ki)* (see Figure 14D). Several types of introductory clauses were used by the scribes of the *shaykh al-islām* court. In some cases, the scribes begin with the clause *wa-baʿd* (and then) and leave a blank space before writing the introductory clause.[108] In this example, however, the *wa-baʿd* clause is missing. The main text ends with the date the document was written: 15 Jamādī II 1276/9 January 1860. The entire block of main text is written on the bottom left-hand corner of the sheet, thus creating two large empty spaces on the top and on the right-hand side of the sheet. An additional marginal note was added subsequently to the main text of the document. This marginal note which begins with the clause *sharḥ-i ḥāshiya ān ki* runs vertically from top to bottom at a right angle to the main text (Figure 14K).

On the bottom right-hand margin is a list of names of three witnesses written at a hundred and thirty-five-degree angle to the main text. The witness list has

106 Document no. 69, Madrasa-yi Imām-i ʿAsr collection in Shiraz. For an edition of this document see the appendix. Regrettably, its dimensions were not measured when the collection was digitized.

107 For a detailed study of this type of sale contract in nineteenth-century Qajar Iran, see Kondo 2021.

108 See for example document nos. 47 and 49, Madrasa-yi Imām-i ʿAsr collection, Shiraz.

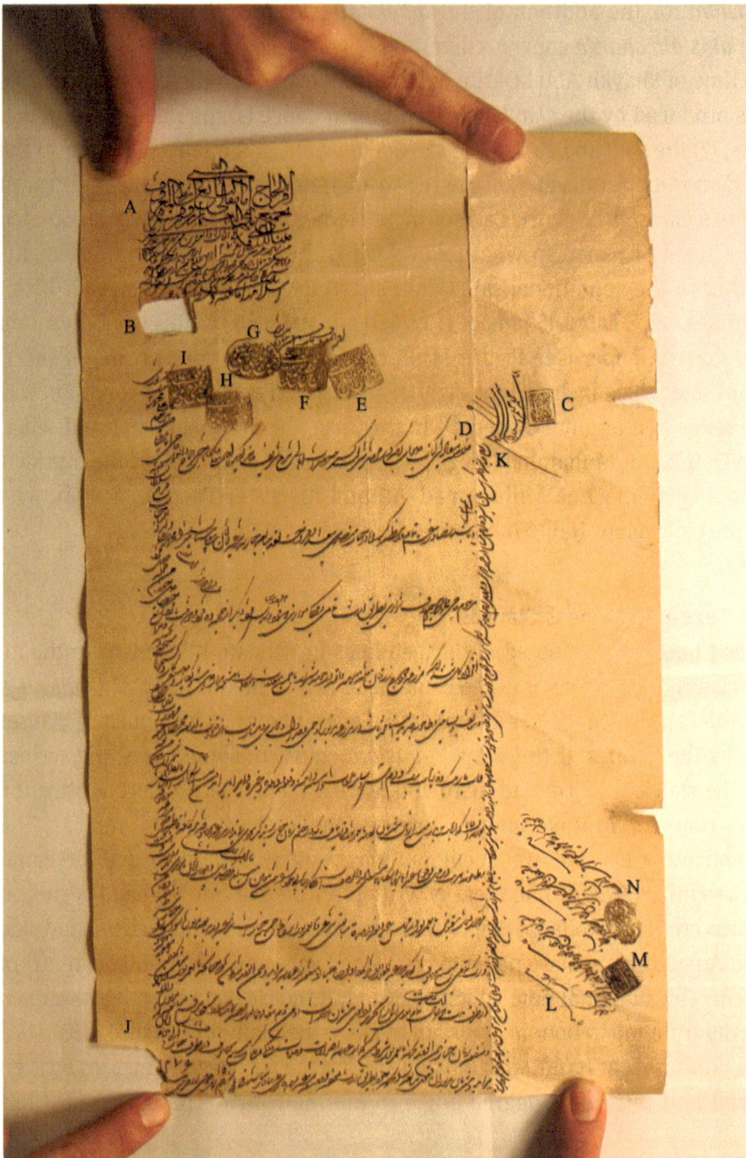

Figure 14: The conditional sale deed of Ḥājjī Imām-Qulī b. ʿAlī Muḥammad Bēg Nūrī dated 15 Jamādī II 1276/9 January 1860 produced in the Tammāmī *shaykh al-islām sharīʿa* court of Shiraz © Document no. 69, Madrasa-yi Imām-i ʿAsr collection, Shiraz.

the Arabic heading, *shāhid ʿalā dhālika* (witness to it) (Figure 14L). The name of each witness is separated from each other using the honorific *ʿalī-ḥaḍrat* of which the letter *tāʾ* is extended. We encountered this practice of separating witness names using extended letters in the legal roll relating to the estate of the deceased Raʾīs ʿAlī Akbar (see 2.1. above). However, in this case there is no *saḥḥa* (it is true) written above the extended *tāʾ*. Two of the three witnesses have affixed their seal next to their names (Figure 14M, N).

What is not clear is at what stage the scribe added the witness names to the bottom right-hand margin of the document. There are examples of incomplete deeds where the *sijill* of the *shaykh al-islām* and main text are completed, but the witness list section has not yet been filled in.[109] This suggests that the addition of the names of witnesses and sealing of this section of the deed took place towards the end of the production of the document.

4.2.2 *Sijill* and Seal of the *Shaykh al-Islām*

As discussed in Chapter 1, the word *sijill* was used from at least the Safavid period if not earlier in Iran to refer to the judicial attestation written in Arabic by judges confirming the validity of a legal act that had occurred before them. Along with witnesses and seals, the *sijill* had an authenticating function. It made documents drawn up by scribes legally valid as evidence. Spatially, from the Ilkhanid Mongol period onwards, the top-left hand corner of documents became the preferred space for writing the *qāḍī*'s *sijill*. This practice is still clearly visible in the Qajar conditional sale deed of Ḥājjiī Imām-Qulī b. ʿAlī Muḥammad Bēg Nurī (Figure 15A). The *sijill* of the *shaykh al-islām* on the top-left corner of this deed can be divided into six parts. It begins with the pious invocation *ḥasbī allāh* (God is sufficient for me) (Figure 15A). This is followed by the authenticating clause confirming that the well-known (*al-maʿrūf*) Ḥājjī Imām-Qulī, the conditional seller (*al-bāyʿi al-shāriṭ*), acknowledged (as accurate), before the *shaykh al-islām*, all that came to his knowledge of what was mentioned and written in the text (of the document) (*aqarra al-ḥājj imam-qulī al-bāyʿi al-shāriṭ al-maʿrūf bi-jamīʿ mā numiya ilayhi hasbamā zubira wa-ruqima fīhi matnan ladayya)* (Figure 15B). The next segment contains the date after the clause *wa-katabahu al-dāʿī*: and he (i.e., the *shaykh al-islām*) wrote it (i.e., the *sijill*) (Figure 15C). It is quite likely, however, that the *sijill* was written by a professional scribe and only sealed by the *shaykh al-islām*. This *wa-katabahu al-dāʿī* clause is therefore not to be taken literally. The letter *wāw* is joined to the letter *kāf* of *kataba* and the letter *bāʾ* is extended to divide the *sijill* into two parts. The date is written below the extended *bāʾ of wa-katabahu*: *fī l-thālīth wa l-ʿishrīn*

109 See for example document no.58, Madrasa-yi Imām-i ʿAsr collection, Shiraz.

min shahr jamādī al-ākhār min shuhūr ʿarabiyya muṭābiq sana 1276. In this case the *sijill* of the *shaykh al-islām* is dated 23 Jamādī II 1276/17 January 1860, it was thus written eight days after the main text had been copied by the scribe. This seems plausible as there are examples of deeds where the *sijill* has still not yet been recorded on the top-left corner of the document.[110]

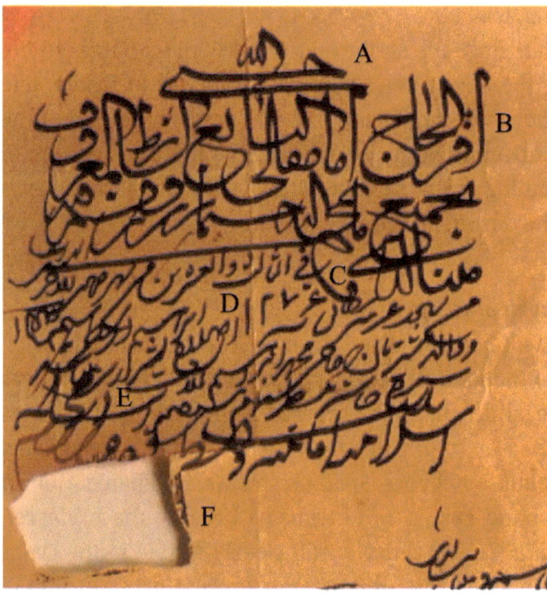

Figure 15: The *sijill* of Shaykh Abū l-Qāsim al-Tammāmī (d. 1286/1869) dated 23 Jamādī II 1276/ 17 January 1860. © Document no. 69, Madrasa-yi Imām-i ʿAsr collection, Shiraz.

The segment immediately after the date is a correction note in Persian by the *shaykh al-islām*. According to the correction note, the scribe was to add Ibrāhīm missing on the third line of the main text in the name of the father of the two buyers: Ḥājji Muḥammad Ibrāhīm ʿAllāf Shīrāzī (*iṣlāh-i ibrāhīm dar satr-i siyum wa wālid-i mushtariyān ḥājjī muḥammad ibrāhīm ʿallāf shīrazī*) (Figure 15D). If one examines the third line of the main text, the scribe does add the name Ibrāhīm in accordance with the *shaykh al-islām*'s correction. There is also a correction note for the marginal text.

The insertion of such correction notes in the text of the *sijill* is unique. We find no other comparable example among the *sijill*s of other clerics in Iran in the nineteenth and early twentieth centuries. Such correction notes might be an innovation

110 See for example document no. 120, Madrasa-yi Imām-i ʿAsr collection, Shiraz.

of the *shaykh al-islām sharīʿa* court under Shaykh Abū l-Qāsim. On the other hand, it is also possible that this practice was transmitted from earlier *sharīʿa* courts that preceded the *shaykh al-islām sharīʿa* court in Shiraz and whose production has not yet come to light. It is beyond the scope of this chapter to examine the range and function of such correction notes added to the *sijill* of the *shaykh al-islām*. The correction notes, however, confirm that the *shaykh al-islām*'s *sijill* was recorded onto the document after the main text and marginal notes of the deed were copied by the scribe.

The final segment of the *sijill* is the clause: "it (i.e. the deed) should be registered and recorded in the Imāmī *shaykh al-islām sharīʿa* court" (*dar mahkama-yi islāmiyya-yi imāmiyya thabt wa ḍabt namāyand)* (Figure 15E). The *namāyand* part of the verb is torn from the image but is clearly visible in other documents. In Chapter 1, we already discussed how adjectives were used by scribes to describe a particular *sharīʿa* court in the Safavid period. In this case, *islāmiyya* is clearly a reference to the *shaykh al-islām sharī*ʿa court. The fact that this "archival" clause orders the archiving of the document confirms, moreover, that documents produced in the *shaykh al-islām* court were only archived after the *sijill* of the *shakyh al-islam* had been added to the main text of the document.

As we have already noted, it was customary for the seal to be affixed over the text of the *sijill*. This is clearly visible in the *sijill*s of the *shaykh al-islām* and his son in the multiple sheet roll examined below. In the case of the conditional sale deed of Ḥājjī Imām-Qulī b. ʿAlī Muḥammad Beg Nūrī, however, the seal of the *shaykh al-islām* has been removed from the document (Figure 14B, Figure 15F). The letter *ḥāʾ* from *al-ḥaqq* can still just be made out in the hole where the seal was removed. We know this word formed part of the inscription of Shaykh Abū l-Qāsim's rectangular seal: *lā ilāha illa allāh al-malik al-ḥaqq al-mubīn ibn muḥammad ḥusayn, abū l-qāsim al-tammāmī 1241.*

The other seal removed from the document is the seal that was affixed at the end of the main text right after the date (Figure 14J). Based on the practice of other surviving deeds, it is unlikely that this seal belonged to the *shaykh al-islām*. It was probably a seal used by one of the scribes of the *shaykh al-islām sharīʿa* court. The removal of seals from a document (*lāsha kardan/muhr kishīdan*) made the document null and void. In this case, it suggests the seller (the original owner) was able to repossess the object of sale within the time frame stipulated in the conditional sale deed. The deed was therefore annulled.[111]

111 It is also possible, however, that the annulment occurred in the cooling off period, usually three days, where the contract could be cancelled by one or other party unilaterally, see Kondo 2021, 620. On the practice of removing seals from Islamic legal deeds in order to make them invalid, see Rezai 2008, 23–24. For a Morrocan example, where the signatures of professional witnesses are removed from the document, see Buskens 2017, 195.

4.2.3 Seals of the Scribes

Below the *sijill* of the *shaykh al-islām,* there are five seals visible in the space above the first line of the main text (see Figure 14E–I). The inscriptions of the seals are as follows: (E) *lā ilāha illā allāh al-malik al-ḥaqq al-mubīn ʿabduhu ʿabd al-jawād;* (F) *lā ilāha illā allāh al-malik al-ḥaqq al-mubīn ʿabduhu asadullāh ibn muḥammad ʿalī;* (G)*ʿabduhu al-rājī muḥammad riḍā al-ḥusayni;* (H) *lā ilāha illā allāh al-malik al-ḥaqq al-mubīn ʿabduhu muḥammad al-ḥusaynī* and (I) *muḥammad ʿalī ibn muḥammad mahdī al-tammāmī.* Copies of deeds produced in the *shaykh al-islām sharīʿa* court allow us to identify the owners of some of these seals. Seal F belonged to Shaykh Asadullāh; seal H belonged to Mīrzā Muḥammad-i Muḥarrir and seal I belonged to Shaykh Muḥammad ʿAlī b. Muḥammad Mahdī al-Tammāmī. It is likely that seal G belonged to Muḥammad Ridā Kirbālī.[112] In this case, Shaykh Asadullāh has also written a small *sijill* above his seal: *aqārra al-maʿrūf bi-mā ruqima fīhi matnan wa hāmishan ladayya* (the well-known person acknowledged as it is written in the text and margins before me). This is significant because it suggests that some of the "scribes" working in the *shaykh al-islām sharīʿa* court possessed enough legal authority to write *sijill*s as notaries.

According to Riḍāʾī, the order and place where such seals were affixed depended on the number of years of experience the scribe had acquired in the *shaykh al-islām sharīʿa* court.[113] In general, the more experienced the scribe was, the closer his seal was to the right-hand margin of the document and to the seal of the registrar (see below). In other words, it appears that the relative experience of the scribe decreased from the right to the left of the document. In addition to this rule, precedence among the scribes was also determined by the relative proximity of their seal to the first line of the main text. Seals appearing above the first line of the main text had precedence over those appearing below it. In addition, seals which appeared directly above or below the first line of main text belonged to more experienced scribes than seals affixed much higher above the first line of the main text. Based on this, it is possible to suggest that the seal of the most experienced scribe in the case of the deed of Ḥājjī Imām-Qulī is seal H, belonging to Mīrzā Muḥammad-i Muḥarrir (Mīrzā Muḥammad, the scribe) as it is the closest to the first line of the main text. Based on the occurrence of this seal in the Tammāmī corpus, this appears to be accurate, as Mīrzā Muḥammad-i Muḥarrir worked for the *shaykh al-islām sharīʿa* court for almost forty-four years from ca. 1249–1293/1833–1877.[114] The precise logic of the order and spatial arrangement of the seals on each deed,

---

112 On the appearance of these scribes in other deeds produced by the Tammāmī *shaykh al-islām sharīʿa* court, see Riḍāʾī 1386 sh./2008, 26–38.

113 Riḍāʾī 1386 sh./2008, 26–38 and Riḍāʾī 1388 sh./2009, 56–60.

114 Riḍāʾī 1388 sh./2009, 56.

however, was probably only known to the group of scribes themselves, as it functioned as an effective way of preventing forgery.

4.2.4 Registration Note and Seal of the Registrar

The last addition to the deed of Ḥājjī Imām-Qulī was the note and seal of the registrar of the *shaykh al-islām sharīʿa* court. The registration note and seal were affixed on the right-hand margin of the document at a right angle to the first line of the main text (Figure 14C). In some cases, this registration note and seal can also appear on the left-hand margin of the document or on the verso of the document.[115] From surviving original documents and copies, we know the registrar of the *shaykh al-islām sharīʿa* court was referred to by the following terms: *thabt-dār-i maḥkama, sar-rishta -dār-i maḥkama* and *thubbāt-i maḥkama.*[116] The earliest deed which contains a registration note suggesting the document was registered in the *shaykh al-islām sharīʿa* court dates from the period of Shaykh Muḥammad Amīn. It is a settlement deed relating to the inheritance of the former *shaykh al-islām*, Shaykh Muḥammad Ḥusayn. It is dated 26 Dhū l-Qaʿda 1222/25 January 1808.[117] The registration note appears above the square seal of the registrar. It reads as follows: *thabt-i maḥkama-yi muḥkama-yi ʿiliyya-yi ʿaliyya-yi islāmiyya shud* (it was registered in the exalted *shaykh al-islām sharīʿa* court).

The final *tāʾ* of *thabt* without dots is extended above the seal. Above the *thabt*, the *shīn* of *shud* is extended. The slanting stroke at the top of the two *kāfs* of *maḥkama* and *muḥkama* is written above the extended *shīn* along with a *dhamma* vowel probably belonging to *shud*. The three dots of the *shīn* of *shud* are initially visible but are omitted in later registration notes. The remainder of the registration note (*maḥkama-yi muḥkama-yi ʿiliyya-yi ʿaliyya-yi islāmiyya*) is written sandwiched in between the extended *tāʾ* of *thabt* and the *shīn* of *shud*. In this case there is an additional *thabt shud* written above the first *thabt shud* (see Figure 16B-2).

An early example of the *thabt shud* registration note is also visible on a settlement deed dated 2 Jamādī I 1228/3 May 1813[118] (see Figure 16A). The square seal of the registrar on this note has the following inscription in *naskh*: *ibn muḥammad hāshim, sayyid ʿalī al-ḥusaynī.* From surviving deeds, we know that Sayyid ʿAlī b. Muḥammad Hāshim al-Ḥusaynī was the registrar of the *shaykh al-islām sharīʿa* court for around thirty-four years from 26 Dhū l-Qaʿda 1222–12 Muḥarram 1256/25

115 Document nos. 115 and 94, Madrasa-yi Imām-i ʿAsr collection, Shiraz.
116 Riḍāʾī 1388 sh./2009, 52; Riḍāʾī 1385 sh./2006, 81.
117 Mīrzā Muḥammad Kāẓimaynī collection, Yazd, image # 6993.
118 WWQI, document no. 15161A112, Meisam Ahmadi Kafshani collection.

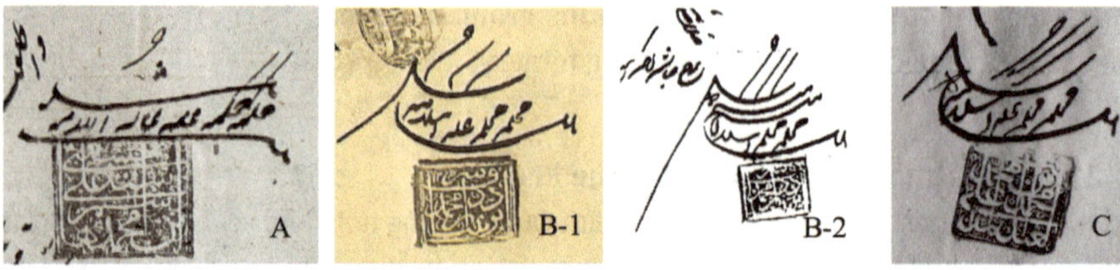

Figure 16: Registration notes and seals of three registrars of the Tammāmī *shaykh al-islām sharīʿa* court.

January 1808–16 March 1840.[119] He is the same person as Mīrzā Abū ʿAlī Qassām b. Mīrzā Muḥammad Hāshim (also known as Mīrzā Bābā), whom Shaykh Muḥammad Amīn confirmed as the administrator of an endowment in the district of Bayḍā, Fārs province, in a document dated Rajab 1243/April 1819. This document describes Mīrzā Abū ʿAlī Qassām b. Mīrzā Muḥammad Hāshim as the expert (registrar) of the *shaykh al-islām sharīʿa* court of Fārs and Shiraz" (*sar-rishta-dār-i maḥkama-yi muḥkama-yi islāmiyya-yi mamlikat-i fārs wa khiṭṭa-yi shīrāz*).[120]

Sayyid ʿAlī also introduced his son, named Muḥammad, to the *shaykh al-islām sharīʿa* court. The latter used a similar seal to his father's, square in shape with the inscription in *naskh, al-ʿabd al-mudhnib muḥammad b. sayyid ʿalī al-ḥusaynī.*[121] This seal is found among the seals of scribes on deeds produced by the court.[122] It does not appear, however, in the position of the registrar's seal and note. This suggests that Sayyid ʿAlī's son did not inherit the position of registrar of the *shaykh al-islām sharīʿa* court from his father. Instead, the position went to an outsider, a new arrival, a certain Ḥājjī Mīrzā Muḥammad Thabt-Dār (literally the "registrar") whose seal has the following inscription in *naskh*: *dārad sharaf bar anbiyāʾ muḥammad 1250* (see Figure 16B-1).[123]

Based on deeds containing this seal, Ḥājjī Mīrzā Muḥammad Thabt-Dār worked as the registrar of the *shaykh al-islām sharīʿa* court for around forty-seven years from 14 Jamādi II 1263–12 Dhū l-Qaʿda 1310/30 May 1847–28 May 1893.[124] It is also Ḥājjī Mīrzā Muḥammad Thabt-Dār's registration note and seal that we find on the deed of Ḥājjī Imām-Qulī (see Figure 14C, Figure 16B-2). However, for reasons that are not entirely clear, in this case, as we have noted earlier, he has added an additional

119 Riḍāʾī 1388 sh./2009, 52.
120 Riḍāʾī 1388 sh./2009, 81.
121 Riḍāʾī 1388 sh./2009, 52.
122 Riḍāʾī 1388 sh./2009, 173, image nos. 3 and 4.
123 Riḍāʾī 1388 sh./2009, 53.
124 Riḍāʾī 1388 sh./2009, 55.

thabt shud note above the first *thabt shud* of the registration note (Figure 16B-2). This is different from his usual registration note and seal (Figure 16B-1). It is possible that the document was archived twice, or alternatively, that Ḥājjī Mīrzā Muḥammad Thabt-Dār wanted to bring the note closer to the first line of the main text.

The number of deeds that the *shaykh al-islām sharī'a* court registered during the period of Ḥājjī Mīrzā Muḥammad Thabt-Dār must have been considerable, because we find the appearance of the seal and registration note of another registrar, named Muḥammad 'Alī, who was probably Ḥājjī Mīrzā Muḥammad Thabt-Dār's assistant. Unlike Ḥājjī Mīrzā Muḥammad Thabt-Dār, who used only one seal throughout his professional career, the assistant registrar used at least three different seals with the following inscriptions in *naskh*: *rabbī najji'nī bi-muḥammad wa 'alī*; *al-'abd al-mudhnib muḥammad 'alī ibn muḥammad* (Figure 14C); *al-'abd al-mudhnib al-ḍa'īf muḥammad 'alī al-sharīf 1301.*[125] In contrast to the registration note of Sayyid 'Alī al-Ḥusaynī, we find the adjectives *'iliyya* and *'aliyya* used in a more random fashion in the registration notes by Ḥājjī Mīrzā Muḥammad Thabt-Dār and his assistant. In the case of the deed of Ḥājjī Imām-Qulī, both adjectives are omitted.

The addition of the registration note and seal of the registrar onto the document upon the order of the *shaykh al-islām* as recorded in his *sijill* was only one part of the archival process of the document. On several Tammāmī single-sheet deeds, we find an additional registration note summarizing in a single line the content of the document and its date. This additional registration note was written on the right-hand margin at the edge of the sheet (see Figure 13A). The precise placement of the note was no doubt intentional and related to the way the sheet was folded. On the deed of Ḥājjī Imām-Qulī, however, this type of registration note has not been added to the sheet, which might suggest that the deed in question is not an original archival copy preserved in the *shaykh al-islām sharī'a* court but is rather the original copy that was given to the buyer or the seller, in this case Ḥājjī Imām-Qulī.

It is important to distinguish here between two types of copies of an original document produced by the *shaykh al-islām sharī'a* court. One type of copying involved transcribing an original document to produce a transcript (*sawād/rū-niwisht*) (as we shall see below). In this case, the scribe simply copied verbatim the main text and the text of the *sijill*s of the original document, while mentioning the names of the individuals who had affixed seals in the original. Witness clauses in the original were often not transcribed in the copy. In contrast, an identical original (*nuskha-yi hamsang*) or duplicate was a twin reproduction of the original document including its main text, *sijill*s, seals, and witness clauses. In

125 Riḍā'ī 1388 sh./2009, 54.

what follows, I will briefly examine the production of a multiple sheet legal roll and its transcript (*sawād*) in the Tammāmī *shaykh al-islām sharīʿa* court.

4.3 A Nineteenth-Century Multiple Sheet Legal Roll and its Transcript: Dividing the Estate of Shaykh Abū Turāb (d. ca. 1283/1867)

A multiple sheet roll which divides the estate of the *imām-juʿma* of Fārs, Shaykh Abū Turāb (d. ca. 1283/1867), among his descendants was prepared at the *shaykh al-islām sharīʿa* court in Shiraz.[126] The main text is dated Friday 8 Dhū l-Qaʿda 1283/14 March 1867. The roll is made up of four sheets of paper of varying dimensions. The bottom verso edge of each sheet is glued to the recto edge of the next sheet. The paper is of Italian provenance from Pontremoli, Tuscany. The watermark (Figure 17) is clearly visible on the left-hand margin of the second sheet of paper written at an angle of two hundred and seventy degrees to the lines of the main text.

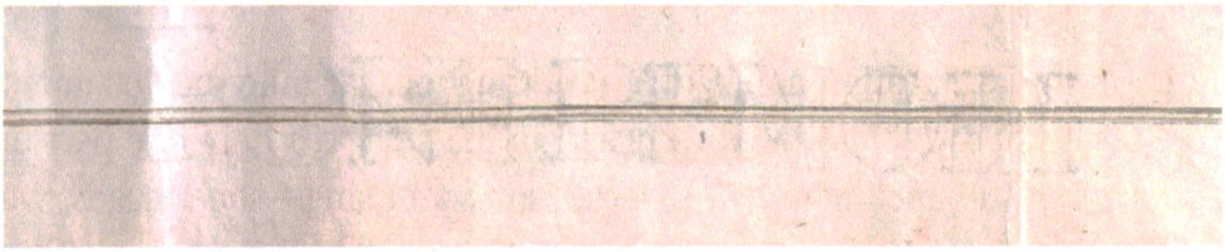

Figure 17: Pontremoli watermark on the second sheet of the Shaykh Abū Turāb roll.

In contrast to the deed of Ḥājjī Imām-Qulī, the content of Shaykh Abū Turāb's roll is organised within schematic ruled lines. At the top of the first sheet is the pious invocation *huwa l-mālik bi-l istiḥqāq* (God is the real owner of all lands) (Figure 18A). This was a common pious invocation used to begin deeds relating to the purchase or transfer of land. Below the pious invocation is a prayer (*khuṭba*) in praise of God, the Prophet, and his family (Figure 18B).

Directly below the *khuṭba* is the *sijill* of Shaykh Abū l-Qāsim on the left (Figure 18C) and the *sijill* of his son Shaykh Muḥammad Ḥusayn on the right (Figure 18D). The *sijill* of Shaykh Abū l-Qāsim begins with the pious invocation *ḥasbī allāh* (God is sufficient for me). The next segment confirms that the five male heirs of the deceased *imam-jumʿa* of Fārs, Shaykh Yaḥyā, the new *imām-jumʿa*, Shaykh Zayn al-ʿĀbidīn, Shaykh Majd al-Dīn and Mullā ʿAlī Akbar, acknowledged what was written in the document from beginning to end. The *wa-kataba*

126 WWQI, document no. 14130A3, Banu Badr al-Shariʿah ʿAlavi (Imami) Collection. Regrettably, the dimensions of this roll are not listed on the WWQI website.

al-dāʿī clause, written almost as a single line, introduces the next segment of the *sijill* which contains a note by the *shaykh al-islām*, Shaykh Abū l-Qāsim. According to the note, the female heirs of Shaykh Abū Turāb testified as witnesses to the validity of the content of the deed, and this was recorded in the margins. The note also confirms that the word *al-maʿrufīn*, which was incorrectly written by the scribe after the names of the male heirs in the *sijill*, probably in a draft copy, was now correct (*iṣlāḥ-i lafẓ-i maʿrufīn dar sijill ṣaḥīḥ ast*). This correction clause is followed by the archival clause: “the deed should be registered and recorded in the *shaykh al-islām sharīʿa* court” (*dar maḥhkama-yi islāmiyya-yi imāmiyya-yi ithnā ʿashariyya thabt wa ḍabt namāyand*).

The date the *sijill* was written is not mentioned in the *sijill* of Shaykh Abū l-Qāsim. It appears, however, in the *sijill* of Shaykh Muḥammad Ḥusayn (Figure 18D), which is dated 5 Dhū l-Ḥijja 1283/10 April 1867, almost a month after the deed was first drawn up. Shaykh Muḥammad Ḥusayn’s *sijill* is much simpler than his father’s. It simply confirms as valid and authentic all that was recorded in the document. Shaykh Abū l-Qāsim has affixed his seal with the inscription *lā ilāha illa allāh al-malik al-ḥaqq al-mubīn ibn muḥammad ḥusayn abū l-qāsim al-tammāmī 1241* twice below his *sijill*. Shaykh Muḥammad Ḥusayn, however, has only affixed his seal with the inscription *al-wāthiq bi-llāh al-ghanī ʿabūdhu ibn abī l-qāsim, muḥammad ḥusayn al-tammāmī* once below his *sijill*. It was not uncommon for a single *sijill* to have more than one seal. What is unusual here, however, are the *ṣaḥḥa* notes (it is valid) that appear in the form of ciphers close to the seal in the *sijill* of Shaykh Abū l-Qāsim and Shaykh Muḥammad Ḥusayn respectively. The *ṣaḥḥa* note of Shaykh Abū l-Qāsim has a prominent extended letter *ḥāʾ* that almost forms a round circle (Figure 18C; Figure 19A). In the case of Shaykh Muḥammad Ḥusayn’s *ṣaḥḥa* note, the letter *ḥāʾ* is extended vertically downwards to form an l shape (Figure 18D; Figure 19B).[127] These graphic ciphers formed out of *ṣaḥḥa* allow one to identify without reading a single seal or *sijill* the production of the document in the *shaykh al-islām sharīʿa* court.

It is not clear precisely when these ciphers began to be added to the *sijill* of the *shaykh al-islām*. It appears, however, to be a development that occured during the period of Shaykh Abū l-Qāsim. One reason could be the emergence of several new rival *sharīʿa* courts in Shiraz in this period (see below), which came to adopt the same scribal and archival techniques as the *shaykh al-islām sharīʿa* court. The *ṣaḥḥa* cipher was thus used as an unmistakable sign of a document produced in the *shaykh al-islām sharīʿa* court. If the *shaykh al-islām* added his *sijill* to a document produced in another *sharīʿa* court, the *ṣaḥḥa* note is absent from his *sijill*. The *ṣaḥḥa* cipher also appears at the top of archival pieces of paper known as

127 An alternative reading for this note is *thubita*: it has been registered (established).

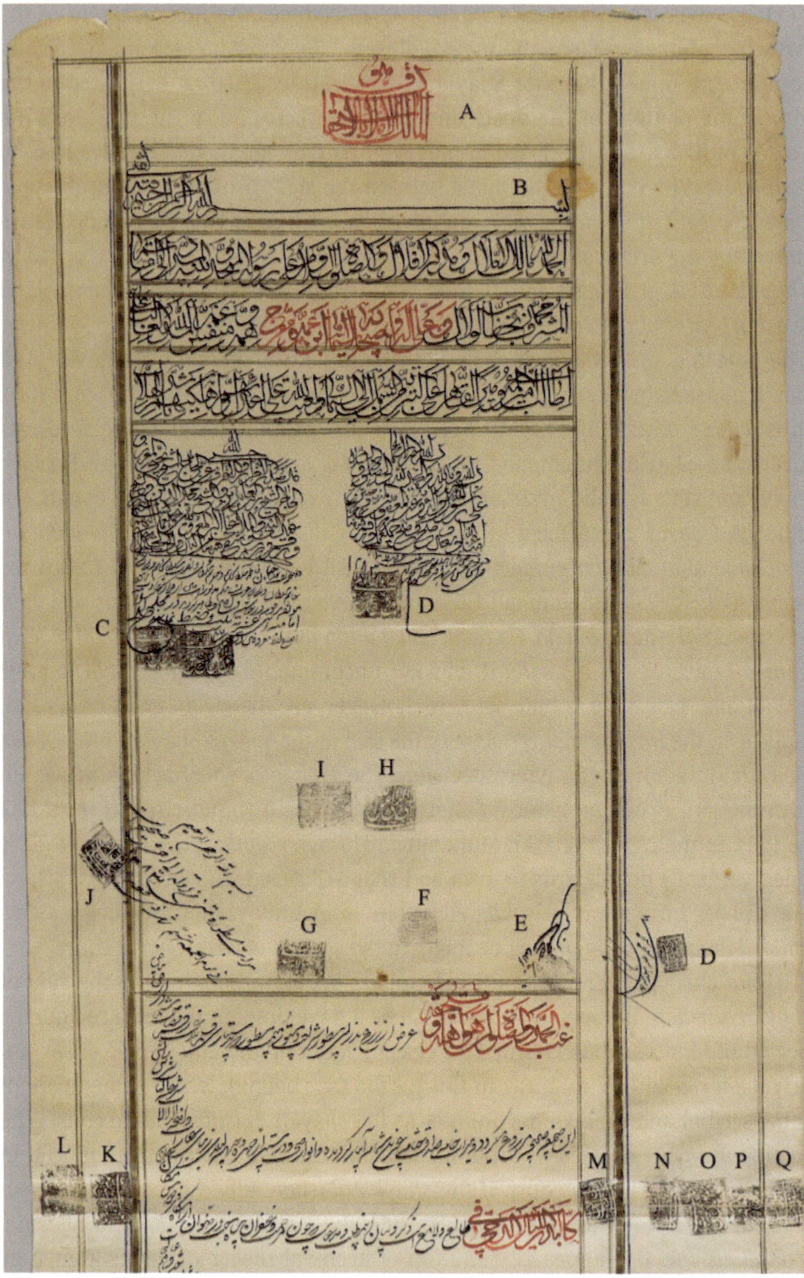

Figure 18: Detail of the first sheet of the Shaykh Abū Turāb roll. © Document no. 14130A3, WWQI, Banu Badr al-Shariʿah ʿAlavi (Imami) Collection.

A 

Figure 19: The *ṣaḥḥa* note next to the seal on the *sijill*s of Shaykh Abū l-Qāsim (A) and Shaykh Muḥammad Ḥusayn (B).

fard used by the Tammāmī *shaykh al-islam sharīʿa* court (see Section 2.3) and was also added, as we have seen, to witness clauses, including the present deed.

Directly below the *sijill*s of Shaykh Abū l-Qāsim and Shaykh Muḥammad Ḥusayn are a number of seals above the first line of the main text (Figure 18E–I). We have already encountered such seals belonging to the scribes of the *shaykh al-islām sharīʿa* court in the example of Ḥājji Imām-Qulī's deed. Based on the copy and other deeds, some of these can be identified. Seal F with the inscription *ʿabduhu asadullāh al-ḥusayni* belonged to Ḥājji Mullā Asadullāh. Seal H has the inscription *al-rājī ilā allāh ʿabūdhu yūsuf,* while seal I has *ʿabduhu muḥammad ḥusayn al-ḥasanī al-ḥusaynī al-injuwī.* Seal E, which is almost illegible, is affixed directly below the note specifiying the number of identical originals of the deed that were produced by the *shaykh al-islām sharīʿa* court: *al-kitāb ʿalā khamsa nusakh* (the document has five orignals). The seal on the left-hand margin next to the first line of the main text is the seal of the registrar, Mīrzā Muḥamamd Thabt-Dār, with the inscription: *dārad sharaf bar anbiyāʾ muḥammad 1250* (Figure 18D). On the right-hand margin is a note which is sealed by Shaykh Yaḥyā, the new *imām-jumʿa* of Fārs, confirming the content of the deed (Figure 18J). This note and seal were added to the document on the same date as the main text, that is, Friday 8 Dhū l-Qaʿda 1283/14 March 1867.

On the glue joint between the first and second sheet of the roll, Shaykh Abū l-Qāsim (Figure 18K) and Shaykh Muḥammad Ḥusayn (Figure 18L) have affixed their seals on the left-hand side, while on the right-hand side are the seals of Shaykh Yaḥyā (Figure 18M) and three other individuals (Figure 18N–Q). This is repeated on the glue joint between the second and third sheet of paper and the third and fourth sheet. On 6 Jamādī I 1338/27 January 1920, fifty-three years after the original deed dividing Shaykh Abū Turāb's estate was first produced in the *shaykh al-islām sharīʿa* court, a transcript of the roll, probably at the request of one of the heirs, was produced in the same *sharīʿa* court. Unlike the original roll, it is composed of three sheets of paper. Far less elaborate, it has no ruled lines and does not use red ink to highlight certain words, clauses, and pious invocations. The transcript carefully reproduces the main text and *sijill*s of the original roll. Seals are reproduced with the clause *maḥall-i muhr-i* (place of the seal of). In some cases, the name of the owner of the seal is mentioned, for example: place of the seal of the deceased Shaykh Yaḥyā. The two *sijill*s of Shaykh Abū l-Qāsim and Shaykh Muḥammad Ḥusayn appearing in the original are also copied in the transcript. In addition, two new *sijill*s are added onto the top right-hand margin of the copy, both of which have correction notes. The first *sijill* is sealed by *al-wāthiq bi-llāh al-ghanī* and the second by the last member of the Tammāmī clerical lineage, referred to as *shaykh al-islām-i mamlikat-i fārs*, Shaykh Muḥammad Bāqir b. Shaykh Muḥammad Ḥusayn (see Figure 20). Both these new *sijill*s confirm that the transcript is identical to its original. The witness clauses that appeared at the bottom right-hand corner of the original are not reproduced in the transcript. The registration notes in the original are reproduced in the transcript. There are also new sealed registration notes added to the transcript suggesting the copy was registered in the *shaykh al-islām sharīʿa* court.

4.4 The *Fard* Archive of the *Shaykh al-Islām Sharīʿa* Court

In the preceding sections, we examined the scribal practices of a single-sheet deed and a multiple sheet legal roll, along with its transcript produced in the *shaykh al-islām sharīʿa* court. We noted the presence of the registration note and seal of the registrar of the *sharīʿa* court on the right-hand margin of these documents. Further, we distinguished between the types of documents the *sharīʿa* court produced: an original (*aṣl*), an identical original (*nuskha-yi hamsang*) or a transcript (*sawād/rū-niwisht*). While part of the archival practice of the *sharīʿa* court no doubt involved preserving original duplicates and transcripts of deeds, there was also a different kind of archival practice which involved summarizing documents onto small pieces of paper known as *fard* (pl. *afrād*). We have already mentioned the significance of *fard* loose leaf sheets for archival practice in early modern Iran in Chapter 1. In what follows we will investigate these *fard* papers more closely to shed light on what exactly was meant by the registration notes of the *shaykh al-islām sharīʿa* court.

According to Dihkhudā, the term *fard* (pl. *afrād*) referred to pieces of paper used by government accountants (*mustawfiyān*) to record revenues and expenses of a region or for a specific purpose which were stacked one under the other.[128]

128 See Dihkhudā, *Lughhat-nāma*: "*fard, waraqa-ī bi-miqdār-i nisf-i qatʿ-i khishtī ki mustawfiyān bar ān jamʿ wa kharj-i wilāyatī ya iyālatī ya kharj-i khāṣṣī ra mī-niwsihta zīr-i ham dasta mī-karda-and.*" See URL: https://www.parsi.wiki/fa/wiki/336556 (Accessed online 1 May 2023). The term *qaṭʿ-i khishtī*

Figure 20: The original (*aṣl*) (left) and transcript (*sawād*) (right) of the Shaykh Abū Turāb roll produced in the Tammāmī *shaykh al-islām sharīʿa* court. © Document no. 14130A3, WWQI, Banu Badr al-Shariʿah ʿAlavi (Imami) Collection.

The use of *fard* papers in Iran for archival purposes can be traced at least to the Safavid period. The earliest Safavid *fard* papers that have come to light so far in Iran are from the shrine of Shaykh Ṣafī al-Dīn in Ardabil and the shrine of Imām al-Riḍā in Mashhad.[129] It is likely that the use of *fard* papers originated in a bureaucratic fiscal milieu to record accounts before its use in a judicial context. The earliest judicial examples of *fard* papers known from Iran so far are from the Tammāmī *shaykh al-islām sharīʿa* court in Shiraz, though as we have demonstrated in Chapter 1 there is evidence to suggest that Safavid *sharīʿa* courts also maintained *fard* archives termed *jarīda*. The exact number of surviving *fard* papers from the Tammāmī *shaykh al-islām sharīʿa* court is not known. Only five *fard* papers have been examined so far, of which four have been edited and published along with facsimiles.[130] These five *fard* papers, however, are of significant interest because they shed light on the archival practice of the *shaykh al-islām sharīʿa* court. We shall discuss each of them in turn.

The first *fard* paper measures 22.4 cm x 11.5 cm (see Figure 21).[131] A vertical fold line is visible in the middle. The paper contains summaries of twenty-two acknowledgements of debt. The first acknowledgement on the recto is dated 1 Muḥarram 1274/22 August 1857, and the last acknowledgement appearing on the verso is dated 29 Muḥarram 1274/19 September 1856. This might be unintentional, or perhaps each paper was used to record debts for the duration of an Islamic lunar month. The scribe of the *fard* uses the accounting shorthand script known as *siyāq*. Most words appear as ciphers. At the top right-hand corner of the recto leaf is the note *fard-i tamassukāt bi-lā wathīqa* (*fard* paper relating to debt acknowledgements without a deed) (Figure 21A).[132] At the centre of the recto leaf are the words: *thabt*

usually refers to square shaped sheets or books of equal dimensions. *Fard* papers were half of this, and, therefore, rectangular in shape.

129 For Ardabil, see Ḥukamāʾī 1387sh/2008; for Mashhad, see Farīmānī Maḥbūb and Khūsrawbēgī 1395 sh. /2017, 221–251. There is evidence from the Qajar period to suggest that *fard* papers were stacked between wooden planks. It is possible that such planks were pierced with holes through which strings were used to tie the stack of *fard* papers between the wooden planks forming a bundle. See for example the wooden planks of the Qajar era *daftar-i tawjīh* measuring 22 cm x 12 cm x 2 cm dated Qūy-Īl 1312 (1283/1866–1867) preserved in NLAI, file. no. 2476. (Personal communication with U. Riḍāʾī).

130 Riḍāʾī 1388 sh./2009, edition: 76–105, facsimiles nos. 174–183.

131 Riḍāʾī 1388 sh./2009, edition: 76–83; facsimiles nos. 4–1 and 4–2.

132 The term *tamassuk* (pl. *tamassukāt*) refers to small pieces of paper used to record legal documents such as an obligation of payment of a debt, see Dihkhudā, *Lughhat-nāma*: "*tamassuk, niwishta-i ki bi-kasī dahand tā hingām-i giriftan-i zar-i qarḍ ya chīzi dīgar az kasī tā way ʿinda al-ṭalab agar inkār kunad ān dīgarī rā hamān niwishta bāshad barāya ithbāt-i daʿwā-yi khud; niwishta wa sanad wa ḥujjat-i maktūb-i dayn; tarda wa dastāwīz wa sanad wa ḥujjat.*" See URL: https://www.parsi.wiki/fa/wiki/192514 (Accessed online 1 May 2023).

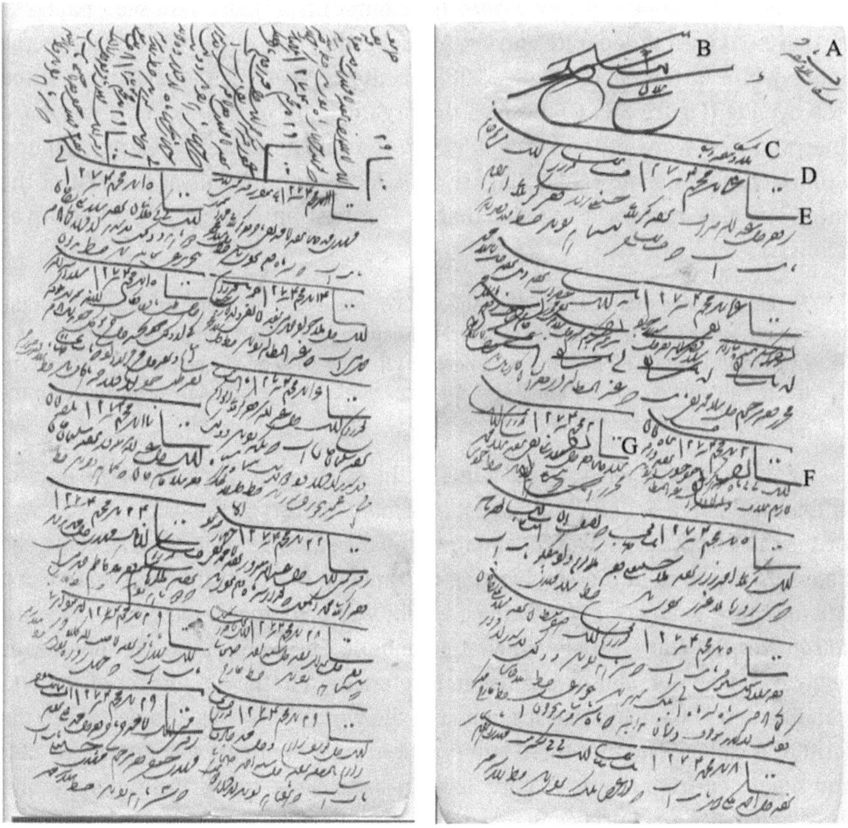

Figure 21: Recto (right) and verso (left) of a *fard* paper measuring 22.4 cm x 11. 5 cm from the Tammāmī *shaykh al-islām sharīʿa* court.[133]

shud, ṣaḥḥa . . . numra-yi chihil īlan-īl (it was registered, it is correct . . . number 40, Year of the Snake) (Figure 21B). The year is mentioned according to the Chinese-Uighur Animal Era. Below this is the clause *tamassukāt bi-lā wathīqa wa-ghayrihi* (Figure 21C), suggesting that the first mention of this clause in the note on the top-right corner of the leaf was probably for quick archival reference. The expression *bi-lā wathīqa* might suggest that the summaries were simply recorded in the *fard* archive and that the *sharīʿa* court did not preserve an identical original or copy of the deed given to the creditor and the debtor.

133 I am indebted to Omid Rezaʾi for providing me with an image of this document in the Bād-kūba-ī collection in the Sāzmān-i Awqāf wa Umūr-i Khayriyya, Tehran published in Riḍāʾī 1387 sh./2008.

The entries appear below a *dafʿa* horizontal line (Figure 21D, see Chapter 3, section 2.6.1) used to separate entries. A single entry was either written across the entire width of the paper (Figure 20E), or alternatively two entries were fitted side by side (Figure 21F, G). Besides the organization of the entries under *dafʿa* lines, the first word of the entry *bi-tārīkh* (on this date) is written as a cipher, with only the letter *tāʾ* visible (Figure 21E). Most of the words of the rest of the entry are also written using shorthand. The first entry (Figure 21E) reads as follows:

> At the beginning of Muḥarram 1274/August 1857, twenty-five *tūmān*s cash according to the current value from the property of Maryam Khānum, wife of Ḥājjī ʿAbdallāh Ṣarrāf, is owed by Karbalāʾī Ḥasan ʿAlī Bazzāz son of Karbalāʾī Ibrāhīm. It is established that he is to return the twenty-five *tūmān*s within a period of six months. It (the original document) is in the handwriting of Mīrzā Faḍlullāh.[134]

Each entry ends by specifying the name of the scribe who wrote the original deed, in this case Mīrzā Faḍlullāh (*khaṭṭ-i mīrzā faḍlullāh ast*). If the original deed was written by a scribe who was not employed by the *shaykh al-islām sharīʿa* court, the clause used is: it is in the handwriting of someone from outside the *sharīʿa* court (*khatt-i khārij az maḥkama ast*). Once a debt was paid, the scribe wrote the word *ikhrāj* over the entry, usually above the amount. The word *ikhrāj* literally means removed, taken out, and by extension, it refers here to the annulment of the outstanding debt. Like the numerical amount, the word *ikhrāj* was also written in the form of a cipher. The first three letters *i-kh-ra* were written together (Figure 22A) and separated from the *ā-j* (Figure 22B). In some cases, the scribe omits the first three letters *i-kh-ra* entirely and one only finds the *ā-j*.

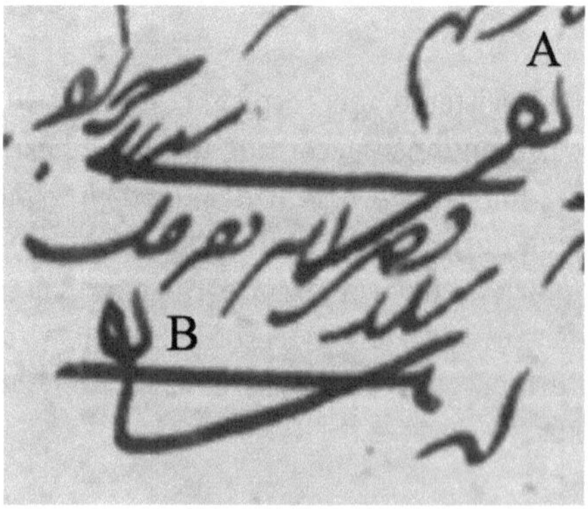

Figure 22: The word *ikhrāj* (removed) written over a debt payment on a *fard* paper from the Tammāmī *shaykh al-islām sharīʿa* court.

134 Riḍāʾī 1388 sh./2009, edition: 76.

It is clear, therefore, that the *fard* papers, at least those relating to the payments of debt, were consulted regularly. The survival of a petition containing the ruling of the *shaykh al-islām* dated 22 Shawwāl 1309/20 May 1892 suggests that the *fard* papers relating to Shiraz were systematically organized according to its eleven quarters during the nineteenth century. The petition contains the following note: "it was compared with the previously archived transactions relating to the quarter of Maydān-i Shāh for the year 1291/March 1874–January 1875" (*ba thabt-i sābiq ki muʿāmalāt-i maḥalla-yi maydān-i shāh dar sana-yi 1291 bāshad muqābala shud*).[135]

Besides being arranged according to the quarters for the town of Shiraz, the *fard* archive of the *shaykh al-islām sharīʿa* court also included a section for the outskirts (*ḥawma*) of Shiraz and other districts (*bulūk*) of the province of Fārs. We know this because the second, third, and fourth *fard* papers that have been edited so far relate to the outskirts of Shiraz, while the fifth paper concerns the district of Fasā. In contrast to the first *fard* paper, the second, third, and fourth paper relating to the outskirts of Shiraz record summaries of deeds of settlement (*muṣālaha*), rent (*ijāra*), definitive sale (*bayʿ-i qaṭʿī*) and conditional sale (*bayʿ-i sharṭ*). The second paper contains summaries of twelve deeds dated 17 Rabīʿ II 1274–1 Jamādī I 1274/5 December 1857–17 January 1858.[136] The third paper contains summaries of nine deeds dated 2 Jamādī I 1274–29 Jamādī II 1274/19 December 1857–15 January 1858.[137] The fourth paper has summaries of ten deeds dated 12 Jamādī I 1274–9 Jamādī II 1274/29 December 1857–25 Janaury 1858.[138] On the top right-hand corner of the leaf, instead of the note *fard-i tamassukāt bi-lā wathīqa* is the note *fard-i ḥawma*. The deeds are summarized using sub-headings, "buyer" (*mushtarī*); "seller" (*bāyiʿ*); "object of sale" (*mabīʿ*). We also find next to entries which contain the cipher *ikhrāj*, an additional note on the right-hand margin: "according to the order of the *shaykh al-islām* it was annulled" (*hasb al-amr-i sharīʿatmadar ikhrāj shud*).[139] The annulling of deeds at the *shaykh al-islām sharīʿa* court thus involved not only the removal of the seal (*lāsha kardan/muhr kishīdan*) of the *shaykh al-islām* from his *sijill*, as we have seen in the case of the deed of Ḥājjī Imām-Qulī, but also recording this on the corresponding entry in the *fard* archive. An additional third step, not visible in the deed of Ḥājjī Imām-Qulī, was to write the word *ikhrāj* over the seal and registration note of the registrar on the original deed.

135 Riḍāʾī 1388 sh./2009, 71.
136 Riḍāʾī 1388 sh./2009, edition: 84–90; facsimile nos. 4-3 and 4-4.
137 Riḍāʾī 1388 sh./2009, edition: 91–98; facsimile nos. 4-5 and 4-6.
138 Riḍāʾī 1388 sh./2009, edition: 99–105; facsimile nos. 4-7 and 4-8.
139 Riḍāʾī 1388 sh./2009, 75; see facsimiles nos. 4a, 4b, 182–183.

The fifth and final *fard* paper examined so far from the *shaykh al-islām sharīʿa* court relates to the district of Fasā.[140] The entries of this *fard* are dated 6 Dhū l-Ḥijja 1321/23 February 1904. It differs from the previous four *fard* papers through its larger size, measuring 70 cm x 11 cm. It has at least four horizontal fold lines. This horizontal folding was probably meant to reduce the size of the sheet so that it could be preserved with the smaller *fard* papers.

Conclusion

There can be little doubt that the Tammāmī clerical lineage was heir to the practice of the new Imāmī *sharīʿa* courts of Shiraz following the conversion of Iran to Imāmī Shiʿism during the Safavid period. The Tammāmī documents thus provide us with a glimpse of documentary practices that were probably used by the *shaykh al-islām sharīʿa* court of Shiraz during the Safavid period. The Tammāmī example demonstrates the significance of two types of *sharīʿa* court practitioners besides the *shaykh al-islām*: professional scribes (*muḥarrir*) and registrars (*thubbāt*/*thabt-dār*/*sar-rishta-dār-i maḥkama*). Many of these scribes and registrars belonged to local notable *sayyid* lineages in Shiraz descended from the Prophet, such as the Sharīfī and the Injū *sayyids*. During the Safavid period, these lineages had produced individuals who had occupied the post of *qāḍī-yi quḍāt* of Fārs. In the post-Safavid era, such local *sayyid* lineages carefully transmitted their scribal and archival savoir faire from father to son while collaborating over several decades with new influential clerical lineages such as the Tammāmī *shaykh al-islām*s.

The Tammāmī clerical lineage was not the only clerical family to employ scribes or run a *sharīʿa* court from their house in Shiraz. In Chapter 1, we identified the existence of another *sharīʿa* court where the *mullā-bāshī*, Muḥammad Ḥusayn, and the *qāḍī* of Shiraz, Zayn al-ʿĀbidīn al-ʿAlawī, were active in notarizing legal documents during the Zand period. As we saw, their *sijill*s appear on the divorce deed produced in Shiraz dated Dhū l-Qaʿda 1206/1792. Based on this document, it is possible to suggest that there was at least one other major *sharīʿa* court in Shiraz alongside the Tammāmī *shaykh al-islām sharīʿa* court during Zand rule. In contrast to the Tammāmī *shaykh al-islām sharīʿa* court, the *sharīʿa* court of the *qāḍī*/*mullā-bāshī* in Shiraz made use of an *ʿuriḍa sijill*, beginning with the clause *ʿuriḍa ʿala l-maḍmūn ṣarīḥan* (the contents were clearly examined). As we have seen in Chapter 1, the practice of writing an *ʿuriḍa*-type *sijill* can be traced to the

140 Riḍāʾī 1388 sh./2009, 72–73.

Figure 23: The *'urida sijill* on the top-left hand corner of a sale deed form Isfahan during the Zand period, dated Jamādī II 1207/January 1793 © Document no. 1393.21.02294, Malik Libray and Museum, Tehran.

Safavid period. Surviving sale deeds from Isfahan demonstrate that the *'urida sijill* continued to be used until the end of the Zand period.[141] (see Figure 23).

The practice of writing an *'urida sijill*, however, clearly belonged to a different *sharī'a* scribal tradition than the *ḥasbala sijills* of the Tammāmī *shaykh al-islām sharī'a* court, which usually begin with the pious formula *ḥasbī allāh* (God is sufficient for me). These two ways of writing *sijills* must have once existed together in Shiraz during the Zand period. Their form made it immediately clear whether a document was issued by or authenticated by the *qāḍī/mullā-bāshī sharī'a* court or the Tammāmī *shaykh al-islām sharī'a* court. It is, however, the *ḥasbala sijill* used in the Tammāmī *shaykh al-islām sharī'a* court which came to dominate the notarial practice of Shiraz during the Qajar period. One reason for this was probably the relative longevity of the Tammāmī *shaykh al-islām sharī'a* court compared to the *qāḍī/mullā bāshī sharī'a* court of Shiraz.

By the mid-nineteenth century, at least one other *sharī'a* court was also archiving documents in Shiraz: the *sharī'a* court of the *imam-jum'a* of Fārs. From around 1296/1879 to the first half of the twentieth century, this number had increased to ten. New *sharī'a* courts emerged in Shiraz which adopted the scribal and archival practice of the Tammāmī *shaykh al-islām sharī'a* court. These *sharī'a* courts include: (1) the *maḥkama-yi niẓāmiyya* of Shaykh Ḥusayn 'Arab Nāẓim al-Shar'iyya; (2) the *maḥkama-yi ṭāhiriyya* of Muḥammad Ṭahir; (3) the *mahkama-yi murtaḍawī* of Shaykh Murtaḍā; (4) the *maḥkama-yi ja'fariyya* of Muḥammad Ja'far Mūsawī; (5) the *mahkama-yi muḥammadiya*; (6) the *mahkama-yi hujjat al-islām*; (7) the *sharī'a* court of Ahmad b. Muḥammad 'Alī; (8) the *sharī'a* court of Muḥammad Bāqir; (9) the

141 Document no. 1393.21.02294, Kitāb-khāna wa mūza-yi millī-yi malik, Tehran. The deed measures 31.7 x 20.3 cm.

sharīʿa court of Abū Tālīb Ḥusaynī and (10) the *sharīʿa* court of Muḥammad Jaʿfar.[142] The documents produced by each of these *sharīʿa* courts use *ḥasbala sijills*, include sealed registration notes, and organize the main text and witness clauses according to the practice of the *shaykh al-islām sharīʿa* court. The transmission of such documentary practices between *sharīʿa* courts was no doubt related to the movement of scribes between these courts in Shiraz. Nevertheless, we are still at an early stage of research in understanding the relationship between the Tammāmī *shaykh al-islām* sharīʿa court and new *sharīʿa* courts that emerged in Shiraz during the nineteenth and twentieth centuries.

What is certain at this stage of research is that the scribal and archival practice of the Tammami *shaykh al-islām sharīʿa* court, such as its judicial attestations, its registration notes, and its use of *fard* papers, can all be traced to the Safavid period. The picture that emerges therefore is of continuity rather than rupture in the case of the Tammāmī *shaykh al-islām sharīʿa* court. In terms of religious change, the origins of the Tammāmī clerical lineage, as we have seen, are linked to the Akhbārī milieu of Shiraz in the seventeenth century. This milieu emerged following the influx of Baḥrānī scholars from Eastern Arabia and Bahrain to Shiraz. In the mid-eighteenth century, however, it was the Uṣūlī school of Imāmī Shīʿī jurisprudence that witnessed an important revival in the shrine cities of Iraq under *mujtahid*s such as Muḥammad Bāqir Bihbahānī. Henceforth, being perceived as a trained Uṣūlī *mujtahid* became increasingly significant for engaging in valid judicial activity in Iran. Did the Tammāmīs therefore reinvent themselves at any point as Uṣūlīs despite their Akhbārī origins?

In the nineteenth century, Fasāʾī refers to Shaykh Abū l-Qāsim as a *faqīh-i nāfdih al-aḥkām,* a jurist whose rulings were valid and enforceable. Similarly, according to Fasāʾī, Shaykh Abū l-Qāsim's son, Shaykh Muḥammad Ḥusayn, was also *nāfidh al-aḥkām* after he studied under two *mujtahids* (*mujtahidān*), Ḥājji Shaykh Mahdī Kajurī and Ākhund Mullā Muḥammad ʿAlī Maḥallatī. This suggests that Shaykh Abū l-Qāsim and his son Shaykh Muḥammad Ḥusayn were recognised locally as *mujtahids,* since a similar expression *mujtahid-i nāfidh al-ḥukm* is used in Qajar sources to refer to the judicial authority of *mujtahid*s (see Chapter 5). Nevertheless, Shaykh Abū l-Qāsim and Shaykh Muḥammad Ḥusayn certainly did not belong to the top tier of Usūlī *mujtahid*s in Iran at the time, such as Mīrzā-yi Qummī, Sayyid Muḥammad Bāqir Shaftī or Mullā Aḥmad Narāqī. The judicial authority of the Tammāmī *shaykh al-islām*s did not derive from their legal scholarship. Instead, it was based upon: (1) the historic presence of their *sharīʿa* court in

142 Riḍāʾī 1388 sh./2009, 51. For examples of deeds produced by these *sharīʿa* courts, see Riḍāʾī 1398 sh./2019, 33–42; 356–364.

Shiraz which had long acted as an important archive for legal transactions; (2) the expert documentary practice of the scribes of their *sharīʿa* court; (3) the role of the *shaykh al-islām*s as administrators of prestigious religious endowments, and (4) their influential social connections through marriage with the political elite of Shiraz.

While the early Safavid *shaykh al-islām*s were notable Imāmī Shīʿī scholars who issued legal opinions, by the nineteenth century the main judicial activity of the *shaykh al-islām* was to notarize legal documents. Most surviving documents of the Tammāmī corpus are deeds notarized by the Tammāmī *shaykh al-islām*s. The usage of the term *shaykh al-islām* in the late Safavid and post-Safavid Iranian context is therefore clearly different from its use in the Ottoman world to refer to the chief *muftī*. In Iran, from the mid-eighteenth century onwards, the role of *muftī* was the prerogative of scholars who could carry out *ijtihād* as a *mujtahid*. After he had received sufficient legal training in Iran or Iraq under a small number of leading Uṣūlī *mujtahid*s, any scholar could aspire to be recognised locally as a *mujtahid*. The scholar's perceived ability to carry out *ijtihād* as a *mujtahid* gave him the authority not only to issue legal opinions in cases, but also to judicially certify claims in a dispute. Some of these scholars could also decide to preside over a local *sharīʿa* court and actively register legal documents without being appointed to an official post by the state. The rise of new *sharīʿa* courts presided over by independent scholars recognised as *mujtahid*s who exercised judicial authority without state appointment represents a significant shift from state-sponsored *sharīʿa* courts associated with an official post, such as the *sharīʿa* court of the Tammāmī *shaykh al-islām* s. This shift was made possible by the dominance of Uṣūlism in Iran in the nineteenth century and ultimately by the conversion of Iran to Imāmī Shiʿism under the Safavids. The next chapter focuses on the *sharīʿa* court of one such independent scholar who was judicially active in Tehran in the mid-nineteenth century and recognised as a *mujtahid*, Āqā Sayyid Ṣādiq Ṭabāṭabāʾī Sangalajī (d. 1300/1883).

Chapter 3
The *Sharīʿa* Court of Āqā Sayyid Ṣādiq Ṭabāṭabāʾī Sangalajī in Tehran

Introduction

The Tammāmī *shaykh al-islām sharīʿa* court which flourished in Shiraz between the mid-eighteenth to early twentieth centuries examined in the previous chapter gives us a sense of the practice of the *shaykh al-islām sharīʿa* courts of Safavid Iran. It was a *sharīʿa* court which was historically linked to an official judicial post, the post of the *shaykh al-islām* of Fārs. Though the post was eventually reduced to a mere honorific title during the tenure of the last Tammāmī *shaykh al-islāms*, the *sharīʿa* court's judicial authority continued to derive from its historic presence in the *shaykh al-islām*'s house located in the Bāzār-i Murgh/Sūq al-Ṭayr (Bird Market) quarter of Shiraz. This authority, as we have seen, was materially expressed through the *sharīʿa* court's distinctive scribal and archival practices.

This chapter presents a different type of *sharīʿa* court in Iran in the nineteenth century which had no link to an official judicial post. This type of *sharīʿa* court was presided over by independent scholars whose ability to exercise judicial power as practitioners of Islamic law derived, in accordance with the dominant Imāmī Uṣūlī legal doctrine, from their perceived ability to carry out *ijtihād* as jurists (*mujtahids*). As an example, we will investigate the *sharīʿa* court in Tehran of Āqā Sayyid Ṣādiq Ṭabāṭabāʾī (d.1300/1883), a scholar who was recognised as a *mujtahid* by his contemporaries.

The first part reconstructs the trajectory of Āqā Sayyid Ṣādiq Ṭabāṭabāʾī and his *sharīʿa* court based on surviving documentary and narrative sources. The second part examines the scribal and archival practices of Āqā Sayyid Ṣādiq Ṭabāṭabāʾī's *sharīʿa* court. This analysis will focus on: (1) Āqā Sayyid Ṣādiq Ṭabāṭabāʾī's *sijill*, his judicial attestation in Arabic on legal documents, (2) the issuance of Sangalajī's legal ruling (*ḥukm-i sharʿ*) and his ratification (*imḍāʾ*) of the rulings of other scholars, and (3) the recording practices of the entries in the two surviving registers from his *sharīʿa* court. The chapter concludes by comparing the documentary culture of Āqā Sayyid Ṣādiq Ṭabāṭabāʾī's *sharīʿa* court with other *sharīʿa* courts in Tehran and the Tammāmī *shaykh al-islām sharīʿa* court of Shiraz.

https://doi.org/10.1515/9783111239736-004

1 Āqā Sayyid Ṣādiq Ṭabāṭabāʾī Sangalajī and his *Sharīʿa* Court

Biographical information about Āqā Sayyid Ṣādiq Ṭabāṭabāʾī Hamadānī (d. 1300/1883) (see Figure 24), as he is called by the contemporary Qajar chronicler, Iʿtimād al-Salṭana (d. 1313/1896), is scarce. The *nisba* Hamadānī suggests that Āqā Sayyid Ṣādiq Ṭabāṭabāʾī traced his origins to Hamadān, located approximately 360 kilometers southwest of the Qajar capital, Tehran. From the inscriptions on his seals, we know that his father's name was Muḥammad Mahdī Ṭabāṭabāʾī. His mother was the daughter of a leading Uṣūlī *mujtahid* in Karbala, Iraq, Sayyid Muḥammad ʿAlī Ṭabāṭabāʾī (1180–1242/1766–1826), known as Mujāhid.[1] There is no evidence to suggest that Āqā Sayyid Ṣādiq Ṭabāṭabāʾī's father or grandfather had occupied any kind of official judicial post. Āqā Sayyid Ṣādiq Ṭabāṭabāʾī was not heir to a local family-run *sharīʿa* court like the Tammāmī *shaykh al-islām sharīʿa* court in Shiraz. Āqā Sayyid Ṣādiq Ṭabāṭabāʾī studied in Karbala, Iraq under the leading Uṣūlī *mujtahid*, Muḥammad Ḥusayn Hāʾirī Iṣfahānī (d. 1254/1838–9), known as Ṣāḥib Fuṣūl, after his famous work on the principles of Islamic jurisprudence (*uṣūl al-fiqh*), entitled *al-Fuṣūl al-gharwiyya fi l-uṣūl al-fiqhiyya*. Āqā Sayyid Ṣādiq Ṭabāṭabāʾī wrote a commentary in Arabic on this treatise by his teacher.[2] When Āqā Sayyid Ṣādiq Ṭabāṭabāʾī returned to Iran in around 1845, he settled in the quarter of Sangalaj in Tehran.[3] He lived in Galūbandak street in Sangalaj, was the prayer leader of the Friday Mosque, and taught at the Chālḥiṣar madrasa in Sangalaj.[4] He is thus sometimes known by the *nisba* Sangalajī.[5] In what follows I refer to him as Sangalajī. He is also, however, often referred to simply as Āqā Sayyid Ṣādiq in the Qajar sources.

When exactly Sangalajī presided over a *sharīʿa* court at his house in Sangalaj and began to actively register legal documents is not known. Two registers from his *sharīʿa* court have survived. The first register contains summaries of documents which date from 5 Shʿabān 1284–1 Ṣafar 1286/2 December 1867–13 May 1869.[6] The second one has documents dated between 7 Jamādī II 1291–12 Jamādī I 1294/22 July 1874–25 May 1877. In addition to the documents recorded in these two registers, at least nine *waqf* deeds, four settlement contracts, one rental contract, and one sale

---

1 Riḍāʾī 1385 sh./2006, 58.

2 This commentary is entitled *Ḥāshiya al-fuṣūl fī ʿilm al-uṣūl*, see MS no. 31992, Kitāb-khāna wa markaz-i asnād-i majlis-i shūrā-yi islāmī.

3 Kondo 2017, 43.

4 Kondo 2017, 43.

5 This *nisba* is particularly associated with his son.

6 MS no. 296/23845, NLAI. A partial facsimile of the first register was published by Riḍāʾī 1387 sh./2008.

Figure 24: A Qajar-era portrait of Āqā Sayyid Ṣadiq Ṭabāṭabāʾī Sangalajī (d. 1300/1883).[7]

deed containing Sangalajī's judicial attestation in Arabic (*sijill)* have survived.[8] Seven legal rulings (*hukm-i sharʿ*) by Sangalajī issued on single-sheet documents are also known.[9] More recently, a legal ruling issued by Sangalajī in the question-and-answer style and a ruling by another cleric which contains a ratification (*imḍā-yi ḥukm*) by

7 The original painting is preserved in the Golestan Palace in Tehran.

8 For a list of these deeds preserved in the Sāzmān-i Awqāf wa Umūr-i Khayriyya in Tehran and their file references, see Riḍāʾī 1385 sh./2007, 59. See also Rajabzāda and Eura 2020, 180–181. It is likely that many more deeds authenticated by Sangalajī exist in private collections.

9 The first four rulings, dated Muḥarram 1286/April-May 1869, Jamādī I 1286/August 1869, 8 Jamādī II 1292/12 July 1875, and 19 Rabīʿ I 1299/8 February 1882, are preserved in the Sāzmān-i Awqāf wa Umūr-i Khayriyya, Tehran, see Riḍāʾī, 1385 sh./2007, 59. The fifth, dated Dhū al-Ḥijja 1281/April 1865, is held in NLAI, MS no. 67032/692. For an edition and facsimile of the ruling dated Jamādī I 1286/August 1869, see Riḍāʾī 2008, 189–190. Two further legal rulings dated 20 Rabīʿ I 1277/6 October 1860 (document no. 91) and 24 Ṣafar 1280/10 August 1863 (document no. 102) are edited and published with facsimiles in Ṭabāṭabāʾī 1361 sh./1982, 317–318, 340–341.

Sangalajī have also come to light (see below). It is likely that there are many more similar documents, which, along with the documents recorded in Sangalajī's two surviving *sharīʿa* court registers, constitute what I term here the Sangalajī corpus.

The earliest document from the Sangalajī corpus which sheds light on Sangalajī's judicial activities in Tehran is the *waqf* deed of the Qajar prince ʿAlī Mīrzā Ẓill al-Sulṭān (1210–1271/1796–1855) (see the discussion in 2.2). The *waqf* deed is dated 5 Dhū l-Ḥijja 1246/17 May 1831.[10] The deed constitutes a garden and two pieces of land outside Darwāza-yi Dawlat in Tehran as *waqf*. The administration of the *waqf* was assigned to the founder during his lifetime and after his death to a certain Shaykh Jaʿfar and his lineal male descendants. The deed contains six *sijills* validating the *waqf*. Between 1277–1278/1861–1862, four clerics, including Sangalajī, wrote a reply to a question sealed by a certain *ʿabduhu abū l-qāsim* on the margins of the *waqf* deed. From the question and replies, it appears that an attempt had been made in the 1860s to usurp the *waqf* by raising doubts about the authenticity of its main *sijill*. Sangalajī's reply confirming the authenticity of this *sijill* in response to the question of *ʿabduhu abū l-qāsim* is dated 17 Dhū l-Qaʿda 1277/27 May 1861. It is sealed by Sangalajī using an oval seal with the following inscription in *nastaʿlīq*: *muḥammad ṣādiq al-ḥusaynī al-ṭabāṭabāʾī*.[11]

On the verso of the *waqf* deed, exactly where Sangalajī's reply appears on the recto, is the registration note, "it was registered" (*thabt shud*), below which is a square seal with the following inscription in *naskh*: *muḥammad ḥusayn*. This registration note (see the discussion in 2.3. below) suggests that the *waqf* deed, including *ʿabduhu abū l-qāsim*'s question and Sangalaji's reply, were entered into the *sharīʿa* court registers maintained by Sangalajī. Based on this, it is possible to conclude that by 1861 Sangalajī was presiding over a *sharīʿa* court in his house in Sangalaj, Tehran, and was actively registering legal documents. Regrettably, the registers for the years 1861–1866 from Sangalajī's *sharīʿa* court have not survived. As noted above, the earliest surviving register contains records dating from 1867. Since the earliest known legal deeds which contain Sangalajī's *sijill* dated 1272/1856 and 1274/1857–1858 do not contain a sealed registration note, it is likely that Sangalajī only began to maintain a register from the 1860s onwards.[12]

10 For an edition of this document, see Riḍāʾī 1385 sh./2007, 63–67.

11 It is not clear if this is the same seal as the earliest known seal belonging to Sangalaji, which is oval and has the following inscription in *nastaʿlīq*: *muḥammad ṣādiq al-ḥusaynī al-ṭabāṭabāʾī 1245/1829–1830*, see Riḍāʾī 1385 sh./2007, footnote 17.

12 See the two *waqf* deeds dated 12 Shawwal 1272/16 June 1856 and 1274/1857–1858 mentioned in Riḍāʾī 1385 sh./2007, footnote 17. The only exception to have come to light so far is a recently edited settlement contract measuring 44 cm x 32 cm dated 7 Jamādī I 1274/24 December 1857 which contains Sangalaji's *sijill* (Rajabzāda and Eura 2020, 180–181). The deed contains a registration note *thabt shud*

In a pattern that is familiar from other *sharī'a* courts in Iran in the nineteenth century, such as the *sharī'a* court of Sayyid Ismā'īl Bihbahānī in Tehran (d. 1295/1878) or that of the *shaykh al-islām* families of Neyrīz, Shiraz, Isfahan, and Zanjān, Sangalajī's son, Sayyid Muḥammad Ṭabātabā'ī Sangalajī (1257–1339/1842–1921), inherited his father's *sharī'a* court after the latter's death in 1300/1883. Sayyid Muḥammad Ṭabātabā'ī, however, is more well known as one of the leaders of the Constitutional Revolution in Iran (1905–1911). Not much is known about his judicial activities. On 16 Jamādī I 1312/15 November 1894, he ratified a legal ruling (*ḥukm-i shar'*) issued over a decade earlier in 1298/1880–1881.[13] Sayyid Muḥammad Ṭabātabā'ī also appears to have continued the archival practice of his father's *sharī'a* court and maintained his own registers for some time. At least one register which has not yet been examined, belonging to Sayyid Muḥammad Ṭabātabā'ī, has survived. It contains entries dated between 1325–1326/1907–1908.[14] In addition, we know from surviving documents that between 1312–1315/1894–1897, at least two different registrars, 'Alī Akbar and Nūrullāh, worked for Sayyid Muḥammad Ṭabātabā'ī. The former, 'Alī Akbar, had also worked for Sangalajī.[15]

In contrast to the practice of Sanglajī's *sijill*, which he wrote at the top left-hand corner of documents (examined below), his son preferred to write his *sijill* in the interlinear space between the first and second line of the main text. Whereas Sangalajī used *naskh* script for his *sijill*, his son used *shikasta nasta'līq*. The pious formulas that began their respective *sijill*s are also different. Sangalajī used *bismihi ta'āla*: in His (God's) exalted name, while his son preferred *bismillāh al-raḥmān al-raḥīm*: in the name of God, the compassionate, the merciful. Though such differences in the way the *sijill* was written may seem minor, they were, along with seal impressions, crucial to identifying the authenticity of legal documents produced in the courts of *sharī'a* practitioners in Iran in this period.

---

on the recto sealed by a certain *najaf 'alī 1271*. As Sangalajī's *sijill* is the main *sijill* on the deed, it is likely that the *'ālī-maḥkama-yi dār al-khilāfa-yi tihrān* mentioned in the contract refers to Sanaglajī's *sharī'a* court. If Najaf 'Alī worked for Sangalajī then it would suggest that Sangalajī already maintained registers prior to the 1860s. Later, however, the seal of Sangalajī's registrar and the latter's registration note appear exclusively on the verso of documents, behind Sangalajī's *sijill* on the recto.

13 Riḍā'ī 1385 sh./2007, 62.

14 MS no. 7486, Kitab-khāna-yi markazī wa markaz-i asnād-i dānishgāh-i tihrān.

15 Riḍā'ī 1385 sh./2007, 62.

2 Scribal and Archival Practices of Sangalajī's *Sharīʿa* Court

2.1 Sangalajī's *Sijill*

As Chapter 1 demonstrates, the term *sijill* in Iran had by the Safavid period come to refer to the judicial attestations in Arabic which *sharīʿa* practitioners wrote on different types of legal contracts and declarations. These attestations certified the validity of the legal act as recorded in the document. Chapter 2 discussed the *sijill* of the Tammāmī *shaykh al-islām* of Shiraz on a conditional sale deed. Using Sangalajī's *sijill* as an example, this section analyses the relationship between the written *sijill* and verbally expressed formulae known as *ṣīgha* (pl. *ṣiyagh*) necessary for the validity of different types of legal contracts and declarations. The *sijill*, as I will demonstrate, functioned in practice as a formal written attestation that the *ṣīgha* formula had been verbally expressed by an individual or parties – depending on the type of legal act – before the judge.

Model formulae for writing *sijill*s for different types of legal acts were recorded in Imāmī Shīʿī notarial manuals (*shurūṭ*) from the Safavid period onwards. The verbally expressed *ṣīgha* formulae, however, were recorded in a different type of Imāmī legal genre known as *Ṣiyagh al-ʿuqūd wa-l-īqāʿāt* (verbal formulae for bilateral contracts and unilateral declarations) that flourished in Iran from at least the Safavid period onwards.[16] The discussion that follows is based on the *Ṣiyagh al-ʿuqūd wa-l-īqāʿāt* treatise in Persian of a recognised *mujtahid* active in Qajar Iran, Mullā ʿAlī al-Qazwīnī al-Zanjānī (1209–1290/1795–1873).[17]

According to Zanjānī, there were two categories of verbally expressed formulae (*ṣīgha*). Those relating to bilateral contracts or *ʿaqd* (pl. *ʿuqūd*) involving two parties with an offer (*ījāb*) made by one side and an acceptance (*qabūl*) by another side, such as a contract of sale or marriage, and those relating to unilateral declarations of single individuals called *īqāʿ* (pl. *īqāʿāt*), such as a declaration of divorce. It is beyond the scope of this analysis to discuss in more detail the distinction Imāmī jurists made between different types of *ʿuqūd* and *īqāʿāt*.[18] What is

16 al-Zanjānī, 1372 sh./1993.

17 al-Zanjānī 1372 sh./1993, 35.

18 *Ṣiyagh al-ʿuqūd wa-līqāʿāt* treatises like Zanjānī's distinguish in detail different types of *ʿuqūd* and *īqāʿāt*. Zanjānī divides *ʿuqūd* into two types: *ʿaqd-i lāzim*, bilateral contracts that could not be annulled separately by one side, such as a sale contract, and *ʿaqd-i jāʾiz*, those that could be revoked separately by one side, such as an offer of a gift. There was also a difference in *ʿuqūd* depending on whether acceptance (*qabūl*) by the other side had to occur immediately (*fawran*) after the offer was made or whether a delay (*tarāḥī*) was possible. In contrast, the *iqāʿāt* were binding as soon as they were pronounced by one side, such as a declaration of divorce or the declaration of issuance of a legal ruling (*ḥukm*). For an important study on the significance of

of interest here is that each type of *ʿaqd* or *īqāʿ* had a distinctive formula that had to be verbally expressed by one side in the case of an *īqāʿ*, or by both sides, in the case of an *ʿaqd*, for the act to be legally valid.

As an example, we will investigate here the verbal formula for constituting an endowment (*waqf*), which was considered an *īqāʿ*. In the case of a school (*madrasa*) constituted as a *waqf* for public usage, Zanjānī gives as an example the following Arabic formula, which was to be recited by the founder: *waqaftu hādhihi l-madrasa ʿalā ṭullāb al-ʿulūm wa-fawwaḍtu tawliyatahu ilā zaydin wa-thawābihi ilā l-walidayn qurbatan ilā l-llāh* (I have endowed this school for students, and I have assigned its administration to Zayd and its divine reward to [my] two parents, seeking nearness to God).[19] This verbal formula fulfilled the requirements according to Zanjānī for founding a valid public endowment. It included: a declaration by the founder (*wāqif*) constructed in the Arabic past tense (*waqaftu*) of his intention to create a pious endowment, seeking nearness to God, and it specified the property to be endowed (*madrasa*), its beneficiaries (students), and its administrator (*mutawallī*), in this case Zayd.

Zanjānī, like most Imāmī Shīʿī jurists, did not consider it necessary for the verbally expressed *ṣīgha* formula to be recited in Arabic. If the founder could not recite the *ṣīgha* of *waqf* in Arabic, he could either recite it in its Persian translation, or better still, appoint as a precaution an authorized proxy (*wakīl*) who could recite the formula in Arabic on his behalf. The practice of appointing one or more *wakīls* to recite the verbal Arabic formulae for marriage, on behalf of the female party or both parties if they are non-Arabic speakers, is still common practice throughout the Islamic world today. If someone was mute, he was also permitted to express his intention through a clearly understood sign. The recitation of a verbal formula in Arabic by the founder or his authorized proxy was only, however, the first part of the legal act of founding an endowment according to Imāmī Shīʿī law. The second part involved the release, transfer, or delivery (*iqbāḍ*) of the endowed property by the founder and its receipt (*qabḍ*) by the administrator (*mutawallī*). This was known as *al-qabḍ wa-l-iqbāḍ*, a practice examined in more detail in Chapter 4.

In theory, it was only after the recitation of the *ṣīgha* and transfer of property had occurred that a *sijill* which attested to the founding of the *waqf* could be recorded onto the *waqf* deed. As an example, we will look at the *sijill* of Sanglajī dated Ṣafar 1275/September 1858 on a *waqf* deed dated 1274/1857–1858 (see Figure 25). The

verbally expressed formuale by the parties to a sale and its relationship to written sale contracts in Islamic law, see Rāġib 1997.

19 al-Zanjānī 1372 sh./1993, 35, 398.

Figure 25: *Sijill* of Sangalajī dated Ṣafar 1275/ September–October 1858 on a *waqf* deed dated 1274/1857–1858.[21]

waqf was founded jointly by two individuals and the *sijill* of Sanglaji on the deed reads as follows:

> In the name of God, the Exalted. The *waqf* of the two successful founders was constituted (*qad waqʿa al-waqf*) according to what is mentioned (in the deed) along with its stated stipulations. The legal transfer and receipt of endowed property (*wa-qad ḥaṣala al-qabḍ wa-l-iqbāḍ al-sharʿiayn*) occurred in the month of Ṣafar 1275/September–October 1858.[20]

The writing of the *sijill* on the *waqf* deed, which occurred in this case some months after the deed was drawn up, was the final act in the entire legal process. In Sangalajī's *sijill*, the *wa-qad ḥaṣala al-qabḍ wa-l-iqbāḍ* clause confirmed that the transfer of property by the founders of the endowment to the administrator had taken place. The *qad waqʿa al-waqf* (the *waqf* was constituted) clause, meanwhile, confirmed that the necessary verbal formula for founding the *waqf*, which began with the Arabic verbal past-tense *waqfatu* (I constituted the endowment) was declared by the two founders before Sangalajī. In other *sijill*s, the occurrence of the verbally expressed formula (*ṣīgha*) of *waqf* is explicitly recorded in the written *sijill* (see below). Alternatively, it was indicated in the main text of the deed itself. For example, the conditional sale contract of Ḥājjī Imām-Qulī examined in the previous chapter ends with the generic clause: the customary legal formula was recited in Arabic and Persian (*wa ṣīgha-yi sharʿiyya-yi ʿurfiyya jārī-yi ʿarabī wa fārsī shud*).

20 The *sijill* reads: *bismihi taʿāla qad waqʿa al-waqf al-masfūr min al-wāqifayn al-muwaffaqayn ʿalā l-jihat al-mazbūra wa-l-shurūṭ al-masṭura wa-qad ḥaṣala al-qabḍ wa-l-iqbāḍ al-sharʿiyayn fī shahr ṣafar al-muẓaffar sana 1275.* The image of this *sijill* is from Riḍāʾī 1385 sh./2007, 58.

2.2 The *Waqf* Deed of Ẓill al-Sulṭān, 1246/1831

Based on the preceding analysis of the relationship between the verbally expressed formula (*ṣīgha*) of constituting a *waqf* and the written *sijill* recorded on the *waqf* deed, it is now possible to understand the meaning of the text of the main *sijill* on the *waqf* deed of the Qajar prince ʿAlī Mīrzā Ẓill al-Sulṭān mentioned earlier and the confirmation of its authenticity by Sangalajī. The main *sijill* on the original *waqf* deed of Ẓill al-Sulṭān was written by another Imāmī scholar, Shaykh Ibrāhīm al-Jazāʾirī. The text of his *sijill* explicitly refers to the recitation of the verbal formula (*ṣīgha*) as follows:

> The matter occurred before me as it is written and mentioned (in the document), Ibrāhīm al-Jazāʾirī, in need of the forgiveness of his generous Lord. The verbal formula of constitution of the *waqf* (*wa-qad jarat ṣīghat al-waqf*) was performed through authorized proxy on behalf of the said minister (i.e. the founder of the *waqf*) (*wikālatan ʿan jināb al-wazīr al-marqūm*).[22]

Ẓill al-Sulṭān thus most likely appointed Shaykh Ibrāhīm al-Jazāʾirī as his authorized proxy (*wakīl*) to recite the verbal formula in Arabic constituting the *waqf* on his behalf, and this was recorded in Shaykh Ibrahim al-Jazāʾirī's written *sijill* on the *waqf* deed. This is confirmed in Sangalajī's reply to the question by *ʿabduhu abū l-qāsim* that appears on the margins of the *waqf* deed. In his reply, Sangalajī refers to the recitation of the verbal formula of constitution of the *waqf* by Shaykh Ibrāhīm al-Jazāʾirī as the authorized proxy to prove the validity of the *waqf*:

> In His (God's) exalted name. The above *sijill* and handwriting (*sijill wa khaṭṭ*), based on what has now become evident to me, is that of the deceased Shaykh Ibrāhīm al-Jazāʾirī, may God exalt his rank. Based on what he has written, he himself performed the recitation of the verbal formula of constitution of the *waqf* (*ṣīgha-yi waqf khud-i ān marḥūm jārī namūda-and*). It is evident that a *waqf* constituted by someone like him or in his presence is to be judged as valid. Written by the miserable wretch (Sangalajī) on 17 Dhū l-Qaʿda 1277/27 May 1861.[23]

In addition to referring to the recitation of the verbal formula of the constitution of the *waqf*, Sangalajī also confirms that he recognised Shaykh Ibrāhīm Jazāʾirī's

---

22 See the edition in Riḍāʾī 1385 sh./2007, 65: "*al-amr kamā suṭira wa-zubira ladayya al-rājī ʿafwu rabbihi l-karīm al-jazāʾirī ibrāhīm, wa-qad jarat ṣīghat al-waqf wikālatan ʿan jināb al-wazīr al-marqūm.*"

23 Riḍāʾī 1385 sh./2007, 66: "*bismihi taʿāla; sijill wa khaṭṭ-i fawq az qarārī ki dar īn tārīkh bar īn aqall al-ḥājj maʿlūm shuda ast az marḥūm maghfūr mabrūr al-fāḍil al-ʿālim al-kāmil . . . al-ʿallāma al-fahhāma al-taqī al-zakī al-ṣafī al-shaykh ibrāhīm al-jazāʾirī aʿlā allāhu maqāmahu wa muqtaḍā-yi ānchih marqūm namūda-and ṣīgha-yi waqf-rā khud-i ān marḥūm jārī namūda-and wa maʿlūm ast ki waqf-i ṣādir wa wāqiʿ khuṣūṣan az mithl-i īshan yā dar maḥḍar-i īshan maḥkum bi-ṣiḥḥat ast, ḥarrarahu al-aqall fī 17 dhī l-qaʿda al-ḥarām 1277.*"

"*sijill* and handwriting" (*sijill wa khaṭṭ*). This construction refers not only to the handwriting of Shaykh Ibrāhīm Jazāʾirī, but also to the formal aspects of his *sijill*. In the decentralised judicial context of Iran under Qajar rule, *sharīʿa* practitioners such as Sangalajī possessed the necessary codicological expertise to recognise the *sijill*s of their contemporaries and thereby confirm the authenticity of legal documents. This was possible based on the unique practice of each scholar in writing his *sijill* in terms of the choice of formulas he used, the script, spatial layout, calligraphic form, and other features such as codes. It is thus impossible, for example, to confuse Sangalajī's *sijill* with the equally distinctive *sijill* of his son, or of the Tammāmī *shaykh al-islām*s of Shiraz discussed in the previous chapter.

2.3 Spatial Relationship between Sangalajī's *Sijill* and the Registration note and Seal of the Registrar of his *Sharīʿa* Court

It was common practice in nineteenth-century Tehran for clerics to write their *sijill*s themselves. In contrast, the main text (*matn*) of legal documents was often written by a scribe (*muḥarrir*). In other words, surviving legal documents from Tehran contain autograph *sijill*s. Riḍāʾī has identified the *sijill*s of over a hundred Imāmī scholars that were judicially active in Tehran during the Qajar period.[24] The prevalence of autograph *sijill*s, however, does not exclude the possibility that a given *sijill* was written by a scribe depending on the individual practice of the cleric in question. In the case of Sangalajī, an entry in one of his surviving *sharīʿa* court registers confirms that he would write his *sijill* onto original legal documents himself (on this entry see below). Depending on the type of legal document, the formula he used for the *sijill* was different.

For legal documents containing the text of Sangalajī's legal ruling (*ḥukm-i sharʿ*), he would write the *sijill* on the top-left hand corner of the document. This is clearly visible in a legal ruling (*ḥukm-i sharʿ*) dated Dhū al-Ḥijja 1281/April 1865. The main text of the ruling written by the scribe is in Persian in *shikasta-nastaʿlīq* script. Sangalajī's *sjill* is in Arabic, in *naskh* script using almost no dots (*iʿjām*) to distinguish various consonants that have the same form, such as the letters *rāʾ* and *zāʾ* (Figure 26). The *sijill* begins with the pious invocation *bismihi taʿāla* written in the form of a cipher floating above the rest of the text of the *sijill*. Below this is the clause: *al-amr kamā suṭira wa-zubira* (the matter is as it is written and recorded). The next segment contains the date the *sijill* was written: *ḥurrira fī*

24 See Riḍāʾī 1382 sh./2004, 60–91. Compare this with autograph judicial attestations which Velkov terms "signatures-formules" on Ottoman legal deeds (*hüccets*), see Velkov 1992.

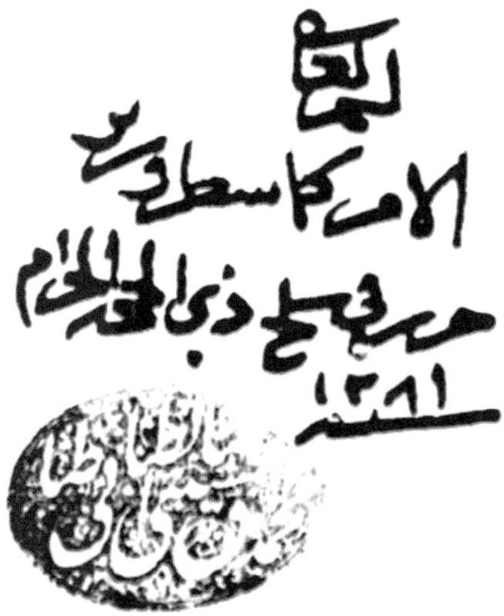

Figure 26: Sangalajī's *sijill* and seal on the recto of a legal ruling (*ḥukm-i shar'*) issued in Dhū al-Ḥijja 1281/April 1865. © MS no. 67032/692, NLAI, Tehran.

Figure 27: Registration note and seal of the registrar *muḥammad bāqir ibn ḥusayn* on the verso of a legal ruling (*ḥukm-i shar'*) by Sangalajī issued in Dhū al-Ḥijja 1281/April 1865. © MS no. 67032/692, NLAI, Tehran.

silkh dhī l-ḥijja al-ḥarām sana 1281 (written at the beginning of Dhū l-Ḥijja 1281/1865). Directly under the *sijill*, Sangalajī has affixed his oval seal with the following inscription in *nastaʿlīq*: *muḥammad ṣādiq al-ḥusaynī al-ṭabāṭabāʾī*.[25]

25 Based on other legal documents, Sangalajī used at least three identical oval seals which were made at different dates in 1245/1829–1830, 1285/1868–1869 and 1286/1869–1870.

Meanwhile, precisely where Sangalajī's *sijill* and seal appear spatially on the recto of the sheet, a registrar from Sangalajī's *sharīʿa* court has written the registration note "it (i.e. the document) has been registered" (*thabt shud*), also in *naskh* without dots, on the verso of the paper (Figure 27). What this meant was that the text of the document and its *sijill* appearing on the recto of the sheet had been entered into Sangalajī's *sharīʿa* court register. Below the registration note, the registrar has affixed his own square seal, which has the following inscription in *naskh: muḥammad bāqir ibn ḥusayn.*

Based on other surviving single-sheet documents of the Sangalajī corpus dated between 1277–1299/1861–1882, at least ten individuals copied original documents into the register-archive maintained by Sangalajī's *sharīʿa* court. After the original document was copied into the register, as we have seen above, the registrar would add the registration note *thabt shud* (it was registered) on the verso of the original document where Sangalajī's *sijill* appeared on the recto. The seal of the registrar appeared affixed below the registration note. The inscriptions of ten known seals of registrars working for Sangalajī and the dates of the documents in which their seals appear are as follows: (1) *muḥammad ḥusayn* (1246/1831; 1277/1861); (2) *muḥammad bāqir ibn ḥusayn* (1281/1864); (3) *ʿabduhu muḥammad bāqir ibn muḥammad ḥusayn* (1283/1884); (4) *al-ʿabd al-mudhnib muḥammad* (1286/1869; 1287/1870); (5) *al-ʿabd al-mudhnib muḥammad kāẓim* (1286/1869); (6) *huwa l-ʿaliyyu l-ʿaẓīm* (1287/1870); (7) *huwa l-ʿaliyyu l-akbar* (1288/1871–1872; 1299/1882); (8) *ʿabduhu al-rājī ʿisā bin ʿabbas al-ṭabāṭabāʾī* (1290/1873); (9) *kāẓim al-raḍawī* (1290/1873); and (10) *ʿabduhu ḥaydar ʿalī* (1298/1881).[26]

Unlike in the case of the Tammāmī *shaykh al-islām sharīʿa* court, therefore, there is little evidence to suggest a monopoly over several decades by one individual of the position of registrar in Sangalajī's *sharīʿa* court. The archival practice of Sangalajī's *sharīʿa* court, which spatially linked Sangaljī's *sijill* on the recto to the registration note and seal of the registrar on the verso of the document, is also different from the practice of the Tammāmī *shaykh al-islām sharīʿa* court in Shiraz examined in the previous chapter. In Tehran, the *sharīʿa* court of at least one other *mujtahid*, Sayyid Ismāʿīl Bihbāhānī (d. 1295/1878), followed an identical archival practice to that of Sangalajī's *sharīʿa* court.

As the *sijill* on the recto of the sheet was the most important part of the document since it confirmed the validity of the transaction or ruling recorded in the document, linking it spatially to the registration note and seal of the registrar on the verso made sense. It reinforced the percieved authority of the document. The registration note and seal of the registrar left a visible archival trace informing readers of the document that, along with the *sijill* it contained by Sangalajī, it was "archived" somewhere and could be retrieved in case of future disputes.

26 Riḍāʾī 1385 sh./2007, 59.

2.4 *Sijill*s with Ciphers

The archival practice of Sangalajī's *sharīʿa* court, however, did not prevent attempts to discredit Sangalajī's judicial authority during his lifetime. A statement by the Qajar chronicler Iʿtimād al-Salṭana suggests that some sort of plot had been hatched against Sangalajī in Tehran. Iʿtimād al-Salṭana notes:

> A group of unscrupulous devils had gathered around the door of [Sangalajī's] court. They would take bribes from the litigants and through various evil suggestions would find ways of weakening the binding force of the rulings of that great leader of Islām [Sangalajī].[27]

Though Iʿtimād al-Salṭana does not explicitly refer to an attempt at forging Mujtahid-i Sangalajī's *sijill*, from 1286/1869 if not earlier, Sangalajī began to add a series of coded letters and numbers at the end of his *sijill*. These coded letters and numbers are clearly visible at the bottom of a *sijill* dated 13 Muḥarram 1286/25 April 1869 on a sale deed dated 6 Muḥarram 1286/18 April 1869[28] (Figure 28). These coded letters and numbers are also found in some of the entries in his two surviving registers.

Figure 28: A *sijill* of Sangalajī ending in a series of coded letters and numbers after the date 13 Muḥarram 1286/25 April 1869.[29]

27 Riḍāʾī 1385 sh./2007, 61: *jamīʿ az shayāṭīn bar dar-i maḥkama-yi way gard āmada būdand az mutarāfiʿīn rishwa mīsitadand wa bi-anwāʿ-i wasāwas wa laṭāʾif dar-i istiḥkām-i aḥkām-i ān raʾīs-i islām rakhna afkandand.*

28 The text of the *sijill* reads: *bisimihi taʿāla; iʿtarafa al-bāyiʿ al-mazbūr bi-mā zubira min al-mubāyaʿa wa-qabūl al-thaman wa-isqāṭ al-khiyārāt wa-l-ilzām kamā zubira fi l-hāmish ladayya fī 13 muḥarram al-ḥaram 1286 l-m-6-4-d-m-?-y——————————w-y-9-4-m-n-4.*

29 File no. 002/6–3, Sāzmān-i Awqāf wa Umūr-i Khayriyya, Tehran, published in Riḍāʾī 1385 sh./2007, 60.

As Sangalajī's *sharīʿa* court in Tehran was the place where the transactions of land and property of some of the most powerful men and women in Qajar Iran took place, it is not surprising that Sangalajī took such precautions with his *sijill*. At least one contemporary of Sangalajī, who was also recognised as a *mujtahid* and presided over a *sharīʿa* court, also used coded letters for his *sijills*. This was Shaykh Faḍlullāh Nūrī (d.1909). The *sijill* of Shaykh Faḍlullāh Nūrī dated 4 Safar 1304/2 November 1886 on a deed of acknowledgement (see Figure 29) dated 24 Muḥarram 1304/23 October 1886, for example, reads as follows:

> In the name of God, the Beneficent, the Compassionate. Sayyid Hashim acknowledged that he knew what was in the document. Written on 4 Safar 1304/2 November 1886, before me, the miserable wretch, Faḍlullāh al-Nūrī.[30]

This is followed by a sequence of coded letters: *th-kh-r-ṭ-u-b-ṭ-w*. Shaykh Faḍlullāh Nūrī's rectangular seal appears affixed at the bottom left-hand corner of his *sijill*. It has the following inscription in *nastaʿlīq*: *dhālika faḍlullāh yuʿṭīhi man yashāʾ*. As in the case of the *sijill* of Sangalajī, the *sijill* of Shaykh Faḍlullāh Nūrī is in

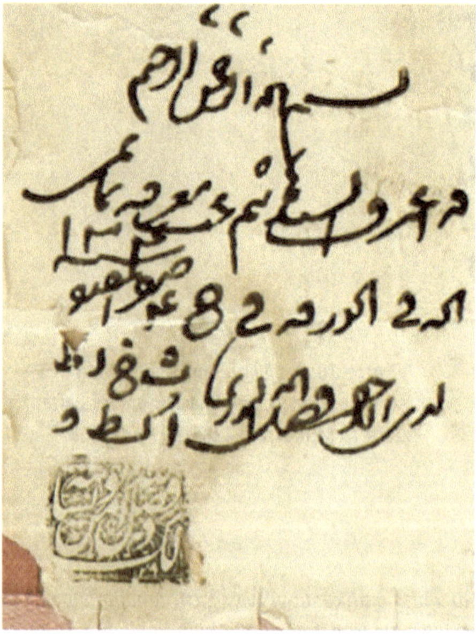

Figure 29: *Sijill* of Shaykh Faḍlullāh Nūrī (d. 1909) with coded letters dated 4 Ṣafar 1304/ 2 November 1886 and his seal on a deed of acknowledgement (*iqrār*) from Tehran dated 24 Muḥarram 1304/23 October 1886 © Document no. 1258A4, WWQI, Tehran Notary 25 Museum, ʿAbd al-ʿAlī Sulṭānī Muṭlaq Collection, Tehran.

30 Document no. 1258A4, WWQI, Tehran Notary 25 Museum, ʿAbd al-ʿAlī Sulṭānī Muṭlaq Collection. The deed measures 35 cm × 21.5 cm. The text of the *sijill* reads as follows: *bismillāh al-raḥmān al-raḥīm qad iʿtarafa al-sayyid hāshim ghabba maʿrifatihi bi-mā numiya ilayhi fi l-waraqa fī yawm? 4 ṣafar al-muẓaffar sana 1304 ladayya al-aḥqar faḍlullāh al-nūrī th-kh-r-ṭ-u-b-ṭ-w.*

Arabic, uses *naskh* script, and has almost no dots to distinguish consonants that have the same form in Arabic. This practice was not accidental. It meant the *sijill* could only be read by someone with a sufficient knowledge of Arabic, such as, in the context of Persian-speaking Iran, the *sharīʿa* practitioners themselves.

Like Sanglajī, Shaykh Faḍlullāh Nūrī also recorded legal documents he ratified or issued in a *sharīʿa* court register (see the conclusion below), though we find no evidence of archival traces, such as a registration note or seal of a registrar on documents which contain his *sijill* or legal ruling.

2.5 Recording Practices of Sangalajī's Legal Ruling and his Ratification

The preceding sections focused on Sangalajī's *sijill* and its relationship to archival traces found in legal documents judicially certified by him. In what follows, I examine recording practices relating to Sangalaji's legal ruling (*ḥukm-i sharʿ*) and his ratification (*imḍā-yi ḥukm*) of the legal ruling of other scholars. This analysis is intended as an introduction to how legal rulings according to the *sharīʿa* were issued and ratified by Imāmī scholars in Iran in the nineteenth century.

2.5.1 A Legal Ruling of Sangalajī dated 1290/1874

An example of a legal ruling issued by Sangalajī in the question-and-answer style (*suʾāl wa-jawāb*) is recorded on a sheet of paper containing three horizontal and six vertical fold lines.[31] There are some signs of repair of tears on the paper using sellotape. The verso has not been photographed. It is therefore not possible to see the registrar's note and seal on the verso of the document where Sangalajī's answer is recorded on the recto. Sangalajī's seven-line answer appears on the top-left corner of the sheet. It is written at an angle of one hundred and forty degrees to the text of the question in the same black *naskh* script used by Sangalajī to write his *sijill*s (Figure 30A). The answer is sealed by Sangalajī using his oval seal with the inscription in *nastaʿlīq*: *muḥammad ṣādiq b. muḥammad mahdī al-ḥusaynī al-ṭabāṭabāʾī 1286* (Figure 30B). The seal was clearly affixed to the sheet before either the question or the answer was recorded by the scribe, since letters from the question and answer are written over the seal. This probably suggests that the document was prepared in Sangalajī's *sharīʿa* court itself and all elements were recorded onto the sheet within a short space of time.

31 Document no. 1258A17, WWQI, Tehran Notary 25 Museum, ʿAbd al-ʿAlī Sulṭānī Muṭlaq Collection, Tehran. Regrettably, the dimensions are not listed on the WWQI website.

The question itself has no date, but Sangalajī's answer is dated 2 Dhū l-Ḥijja 1290/21 January 1874. The text of the question begins with the introductory clause: *ḥujjat al-islamā qiblat al-anāmā* (Figure 30C). The evocative *alif* is used after the honorifics *ḥujjat al-islām* and *qiblat al-anām* (the direction to which the masses turn for guidance). The question thus begins by addressing Sangalajī as follows: *O Proof of Islam! O Guide of the People!* It was customary to leave a gap after writing this clause (Figure 30D) and before starting the main text of the question. Unlike Sangalaji's answer in *naskh* script, the twelve lines of the question are written in *nastaʿlīq* script. The first eight lines of the question are recorded on the bottom left-hand corner of the sheet while the last four lines continue onto the bottom right-hand margin forming a "spiral text" (Figure 30E). This way of writing texts in a spiral was common throughout the Islamic world and is well known for example in the Yemeni context.[32] I will translate here the main text of the question:

> [Question (*suʾāl*), lines 1–12]:
>
> *O Proof of Islam! O Guide of the People!* Concerning the village of Dih-i Naw in the district of Ghār, a question (*suʾāl*) has been asked of the Ḥujjat al-Islām (Proof of Islam). This village was originally the property of Nawwāb Akbar Mīrzā, and after that it was transferred to the deceased Fakhr al-Dawla, and after that it appears in your excellency's registers (*dar thabt-i jināb ʿālī*), where you have recorded: "On 3 Jamādī I 1283/13 September 1866, the deceased Fakhr al-Dawla transferred it (i.e. the village of Dih-i Naw) to Khurshīd Khānum". Your excellency knows that acknowledgements are (often) recorded on deeds (*iqrār-i rasm al-qabāla*) only to be later invalidated. Many such sales and transactions are drafted as deeds but, for one reason or another, do not occur and only the deed of proxy (*qabāla-yi wikāla*) remains (valid), or they (i.e. the parties) annul the transaction document by tearing (its seals), but do not return to the (*sharīʿa* court) register (*du-bāra bi-thabt rujūʿ namī-kunad*) to annul its registration. It (the transaction) remains recorded in the register (*thabt dar daftar mī-mānd*) and becomes a source of difficulty for people.
>
> Secondly, the proof of ownership is possession (*sanad-i mālik taṣarruf ast*), therefore please investigate whether from 1283/1866 until now or before this date, at any point, even for one day or a single hour, Khurshīd Khānum held possession of the said property. No one has seen or heard of her possession of the place. For a long time until now it has a different female owner and possessor. In the said circumstances, what is the ruling (*ḥukm*) of your excellency, Proof of Islam? Please write down whatever is the ruling of God (*ḥukm-i khudāwandī*) so that action takes place in accordance with it."

The question sheds interesting light on the problem of registration of legal acts in the *sharīʿa* court. Individuals could register, for example, in the *sharīʿa* court, a unilateral acknowledgement of a transfer of property, which in practice does not take place or is annulled after it takes place but is not cancelled (*ikhrāj*) in the *sharīʿa*

32 See Messick 1996, 231–250.

court register. In this case, the petitioner suggests that the acknowledgement of the deceased Fakhr al-Dawla concerning the transfer of the village of Dih-i Naw to Khurshīd Khānum remained a "paper" acknowledgement (*iqrār-i rasm al-qabāla*). The transfer did not take place in practice despite its registration in Sanagalī's *sharī'a* court. After complaining about the problem created by legal transactions registered in *sharī'a* courts which do not end up occurring in practice, the questioner also advances the argument that actual possession was stronger than a claim based purely on an acknowledgement. There was no evidence to suggest that Khurshid Khāanum had ever possessed the village. The question ends with a formulaic request clause asking Sangalajī to write his *ḥukm* on the paper so that it could be acted upon.

In his short answer, written on the top left-hand corner of the sheet, Sangalajī dismisses the questioner's attempt to cast doubt on the legal validity of the acknowledgement of the deceased Fakhr al-Dawla recorded in his register. After the pious formula *bismihi ta'āla* (in the name of the Exalted), which Sangalajī used to begin all his writing in legal documents, the answer starts with the adverb *balī*, meaning "yes" in Persian. This *balī* is found at the beginning of all such rulings by Sangalajī framed as answers to questions. It is also reproduced in his registers and helps to identify entries containing question-and-answer rulings. It is likely that it was used as a short affirmative reply, agreeing to the request by the questioner for a ruling. After the *balī*, Sangalajī's answer consists of five lines. The last line of the reply contains the date the answer was written on and Sangalajī's seal. In contrast to the question written in *shikasta-nasta'līq* script by the scribe, Sangalajī's answer, which he wrote himself, is in *naskh*. We shall see how these two scripts, *naskh* and *shikasta nasta'līq*, are reproduced in the entries of Sangalajī's registers to distinguish what he himself wrote on the actual document from the text of his scribes.

> [Answer (*jawāb*), lines 1–7]:
>
> In the name of the Exalted (*bismihi ta'āla*). Yes (*balī*). This acknowledgement (by Fakhr al-Dawla) occurred without doubt. The acknowledgement cannot simply be qualified legally as a "paper" acknowledgement (*iqrār-i rasm al-qabāla*). In order for it to be invalidated, legal proceedings (*tarāfu'*) must take place before a judge who is permitted to judge (*ḥākim-i shar'-i jā'iz al-ḥukūma*). Written on 2 Dhū l-Ḥijja 1290/21 January 1874. Seal: *muḥammad sadiq ibn muḥammad mahdī al-ḥusaynī al-ṭabāṭabā'ī 1286.*

The use of the term *ḥukm* (ruling) in short and the Persian construction *ḥukm-i khudāwandī* (ruling of God) by the questioner to refer to Sangalajī's answer is significant. In other examples, the Arabic construction *ḥukmullāh* is used instead.[33]

33 See for example document no. 49 in Riḍā'ī 1383 sh./2005, 198–200.

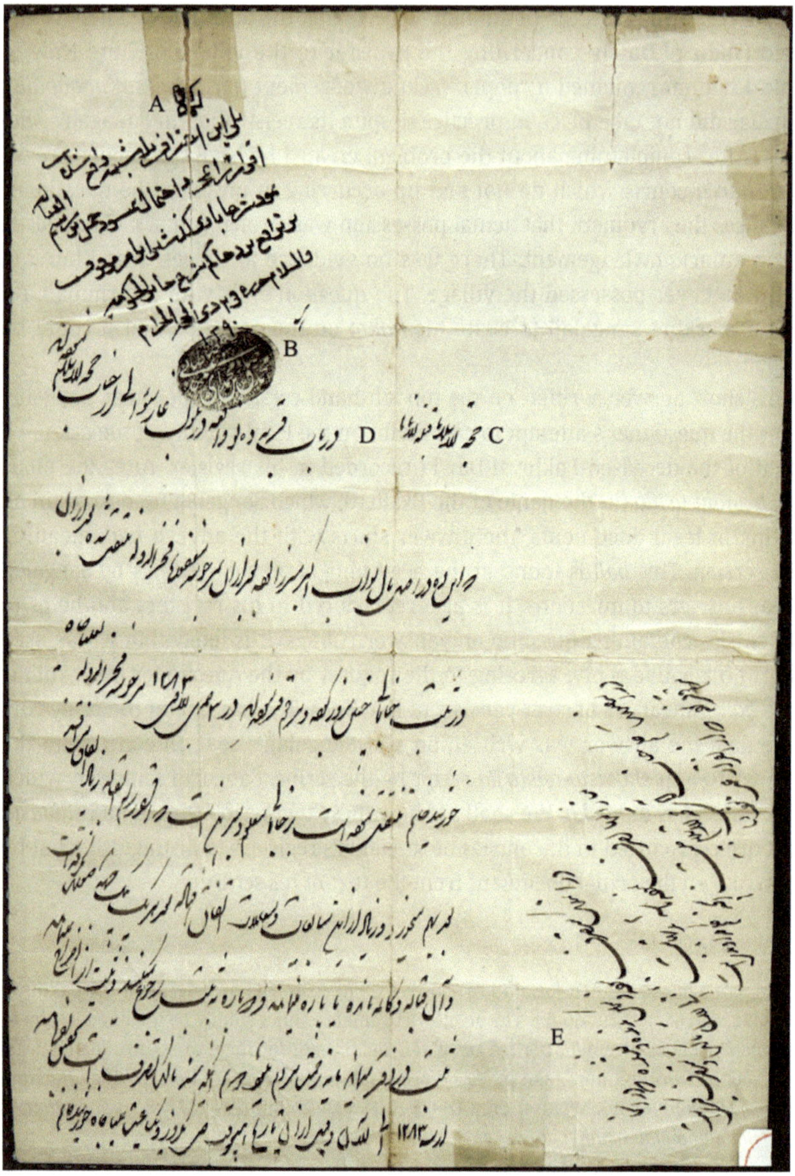

Figure 30: A legal ruling (*ḥukm-i sharʿ*) of Sangalajī dated 2 Dhū l-Ḥijja 1290/21 January 1874 issued as an answer to a question. © Document no. 1258A17, WWQI, Tehran Notary 25 Museum, ʿAbd al-ʿAlī Sulṭānī Muṭlaq Collection, Tehran.

Such terms provide us with clues to how such legal writings by *mujtahids* such as Sangalajī were perceived. It was the *mujtahid*'s duty to infer the correct ruling of God in accordance with the *sharī'a* in each case.

In the example above there is no indication that Sangalajī was acting as a judge. Instead, he gives his opinion on the circumstances of the case. He dismisses the attempt made by the questioner to persuade him to declare the transfer of possession of the village to Khurshīd Khānum illegal. Neither the question nor the answer, however, provide more details on the exact circumstances in which the questioner sought Sangalajī's opinion on the case. Saganaljī notes in his answer that any claim in the case to the contrary had to be adjudicated via a lawsuit before "someone who was permitted to act as a judge". In accordance with the dominant Uṣūlī doctrine of the period, this meant an Imāmī scholar who could carry out *ijtihād* as a *mujtahid*. Sangalajī's legal ruling here, therefore, is not a binding judicial decision. Instead, it is only his non-binding legal opinion on the facts of the case as presented to him by the questioner.

2.5.2 Sangalajī's Ratification of a Legal Ruling dated 1296/1879

Like the first document containing Sangalajī's legal ruling or *ḥukm-i shar'*, the second document which contains a legal ruling he ratified shows signs of folding.[34] Three horizontal and three vertical fold lines are visible on the sheet of paper which measures 34 x 22 cm. The document can be divided into the following segments. The first segment records the ruling of a certain Ḥājj Mullā Muḥammad Kāẓim in an internal family land dispute. It begins at the top of the sheet with the pious invocation *bismillāh khayr al-asmā'* (in the name of God, the best of names) (Figure 31A). The remaining twelve lines of the main text are in *shikasta-nasta'līq* script written in the form of a block on the bottom left-hand corner of the sheet. The twelve lines are introduced by the clause *makhfī wa masṭūr namānad*: let it not remain hidden (Figure 31B). This opening clause is typical of *sharī'a* court rulings (*hukm-i shar'*) issued as "deeds" on single sheets of paper in nineteenth-century Qajar Iran. These "deed"-style *ḥukm*s should be distinguished from legal rulings issued in the question-and-answer style examined above.[35]

The scribe has left a gap after the introductory clause (Figure 31C). In the lines of the ruling that follow, Ḥājj Mullā Muḥammad Kāẓim establishes the legal transfer of the properties of a certain Ḥājjī Muḥammad Riḍā Tājir Khurāsanī to his wife and later via his wife to his grandson, Āqā Shaykh Muḥammad Ḥasan. The possession of Ḥājjī Muḥammad Riḍā Tājir Khurāsanī's properties after his

34 Document no. 14126A14, WWQI, no. 3613, Āstān-i Quds Collection, Mashhad.
35 For an example of a legal ruling by Sangalajī issued in the "deed" style, see Riḍā'ī 2008, 190.

death by all his other heirs based on the claim of inheritance was therefore illegal and void. These heirs in accordance with Ḥājj Mullā Muḥammad Kāẓim's ruling had to vacate possession of the said properties and deliver them to Āqā Shaykh Muḥammad Ḥasan. The ruling is dated end of Shaʿbān 1296/August 1879.

On the bottom right-hand margin next to the date of the ruling, Ḥājj Mullā Muḥammad Kāẓim has written a short note in Arabic in *naskh* script: *naʿm, qad ḥakamtu bi-dhālika ka-dhālika wa-l-ḥukmu li-llāh al-ʿaliyyu l-aʿlā* (yes, I judged it as it is (mentioned), but judgement belongs to God, the Exalted) (Figure 31D). This clause, which uses the Arabic first-person past-tense construction *ḥakamtu* (I judged), explicitly establishes the fact that Ḥājj Mullā Muḥammad Kāẓim had acted as a judge when he issued the ruling. The text therefore could not be confused with his non-binding legal opinion on the facts of the case. The document contained his binding judicial decision in a lawsuit. Sangalajī, in turn, always added the Arabic clause *al-amr kamā suṭira wa-zubira* at the top of the sheet in his own handwriting to indicate that a document contained the text of his binding judicial decision in a lawsuit (see Figure 26).[36] This made it impossible to mistake the text of such rulings he issued as non-binding legal opinions. Like Ḥājj Mullā Muḥammad Kāẓim, Sangalajī also frequently made use of Arabic first person past-tense constructions such as *ḥakamtu* (I judged) and *qaḍaytu* (I adjudicated), as we shall see below. Not all *sharīʿa* practitioners active in Iran in this period used such first-person Arabic past-tense clauses when issuing legal rulings as binding judicial decisions. As we shall see in Chapter 6, this in turn made it possible to circumvent the enforcement of their rulings by claiming that they were non-binding legal opinions.

Ḥājj Mullā Muḥammad Kāẓim affixed his rectangular seal with the inscription *al-mutawakkil ʿalā l-llāh ʿabduhu muḥammad kaẓim* in *nastaʿlīq* twice on the document. The first seal appears next to his marginal note establishing that he had acted as a judge in the case (Figure 31D). The second seal is next to a second marginal note, written on the bottom right-hand corner of the document (Figure 31E). According to this note, Āqā Shaykh Muḥammad Ḥasan appeared before Ḥājj Mullā Muḥammad Kāẓim on 19 Shawwal 1296/6 October 1879, that is, over a month after the initial ruling was issued. He swore an oath establishing his right to the properties of his deceased grandfather. It is likely, therefore, that the ruling of Ḥājj Mullā

36 The Safavid *shurūṭ* of Mīr Qawām al-Dīn Shīrāzī provides the following list of third-person Arabic clauses which, he terms *sijills*, which judges could add to documents containing their judgements: *jarā dhālika ka-dhālika wa-ashhadtu bi-dhālika; jaryānuhu hākadha bi-maḥdarī; jarat al-qiṣṣa al-maṣfūra wifq al-masṭūr ladayya al-faqīr and al-amr hādha hākadha jarā bi-maḥdarī namaqahu*, see Riḍāʾī 2021, 132. Sangalajī's usage of the clause *al-amr kamā suṭira wa zubira* to indicate his binding judicial decision therefore clearly derives from earlier Safavid practice.

Muḥammad Kāẓim had still not been enforced by this date. In the new note, Ḥājj Mullā Muḥammad Kāẓim reiterates the content of his initial ruling, confirming that the heirs of the deceased Ḥājjī Muḥammad Riḍā Tājir Khurāsanī were to deliver possession of his properties, including the income they derived from the years they held possession illegally, to Āqā Shaykh Muḥammad Ḥasan.

At the top right-hand corner of the sheet are two ratifications of the ruling of Ḥājj Mullā Muḥammad Kāẓim. Such ratifications of the binding force of legal rulings were known as *imḍā-yi ḥukm*. The ratification issued by Sangalajī in November 1879 (Figure 29F) reads as follows:

> In the name of God, the Exalted. The *ḥukm* issued by Ḥājj Mullā Muḥammad Kāẓim, may God bless him, is to be obeyed and complied with and is binding (*muṭāʿ wa muttabaʿ wa mumḍā ast*). Written by the miserable wretch at the beginning of Dhū l-Ḥijja 1296/November 1879. [Seal]: *muḥammad ṣādiq b. muḥammad mahdī al-ḥusaynī al-ṭabāṭabāʾī.*

The second ratification is by a cleric with an oval seal with the following inscription in *naskh*: *al-ʿabd muḥammad raḥīm* (see Figure 31G). Muḥammad Raḥīm reiterates Mujtahid-i Sangalajī's ratification and adds an additional clause in Arabic on the necessity of obeying the ruling: *yajib ittbāʿuhu wa-lā yajūz radduhu* (it must be obeyed, and it is not permitted to contradict it). As we shall see in Chapter 5, in nineteenth-century Iran, such ratifications of rulings were often written by Imāmī scholars whose ability to carry out *ijtihād* was widely recognised in order to reinforce the binding force of the ruling.

The final element of the document can be found on the verso of the sheet. As we have noted earlier, precisely where Sangalajī wrote a *sijill* on the recto of the document, his registrar would write a registration note on the verso confirming that the document had been copied into Sangalajī's *sharīʿa* court register. This practice applied not only to legal rulings issued by Sangalaji himself but also his ratifications of the legal rulings of other scholars. In this case, exactly where Sangalajī's ratification appears on the recto, the verso of the document has the registration note "it has been registered" (*thabt shud*). This registration note was written by one of Sangalajī's registrars, who uses an oval seal with the inscription *muḥammad ḥusayn 1286* in *nastaʿlīq* (see Figure 32H). As we shall see in the section below, the registration of such rulings ratified by Sangalajī in his register was a selective process. Though the text of the ruling ratified by Sangalajī was copied verbatim into his register, other marginal additions to the document, such as in this case the ratification by the cleric Muḥammad Raḥīm, were not always transcribed into the register. The text of Sangalajī's own ratification is of course always faithfully reproduced in his register.

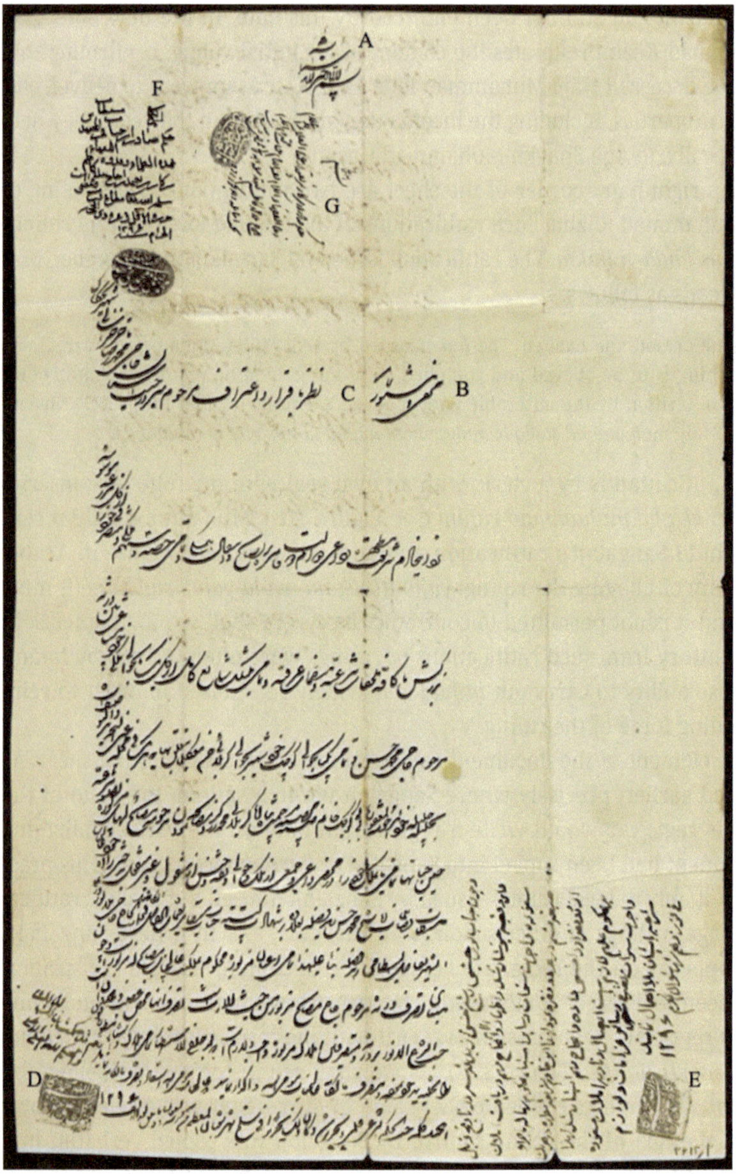

Figure 31: Recto of a "deed"-style legal ruling of Ḥājj Mullā Muḥammad Kāẓim dated Shaʿbān 1296/ August 1879, ratified by Sangalajī in Dhū l-Ḥijja 1296/November 1879. 34 x 22 cm. © Document no. 14126A14, WWQI, no. 3613 Āstān-i Quds Collection, Mashhad.

Figure 32: Verso of a "deed"-style legal ruling of Ḥājj Mullā Muḥammad Kāẓim dated Shaʿbān 1296/ August 1879, ratified by Sangalajī in Dhū l-Ḥijja 1296/November 1879. 34 x 22 cm. © Document no. 14126A14, WWQI, Āstān-i Quds Collection, Mashhad.

2.6 The Recording Practice of Sangalajī's *Sharīʿa* Court Registers

In the previous section, we saw how a legal ruling by Sangalajī and his ratification of the ruling of another scholar were issued on two sheets of paper. The latter ruling had a registration note on the verso where Sangalajī's ratification appeared on the recto, suggesting that the ruling and ratification were registered in Sangalajī's *sharīʿa* court. In this section, we will examine what "registration" or recording of different types of legal documents in Sangalajī's *sharīʿa* court registers involved in practice. Our analysis will focus on the two surviving *sharīʿa* court registers from Sangalajī's *sharīʿa* court. Nobuaki Kondo has provided an important quantitative analysis of the content of the two registers along with translations of several examples of legal rulings and contracts.[37] Riḍāʾī, meanwhile, has described some of the recording practices used by the scribes of the registers in his introduction to his partial facsimile edition of the first register.[38] This earlier research is, however, far from exhaustive. We are in fact only beginning to decipher the rich content of the two thick registers which combined have approximately 864 bifolia (1,730 pages). This page count is based on the sequence numbering (seq.) of the digital images of the pages of the two registers. All references below to the pages of the register follow the sequence number of the digital images held by Harvard University.[39]

The first register (S1) measures 65 cm × 23 cm × 17 cm and contains approximately 328 bifolia (656 pages). The first entry in S1 appears on S1: page 5 (S1: 5). It consists of witness testimony by Sangalajī in an inheritance case. The testimony is dated 5 Shaʿbān 1284/2 December 1867. The last entry in S1, a summary of a settlement contract, appears on S1: 656. The settlement contract is dated 6 Shawwāl 1280/15 March 1864. It was validated by Sangalajī at the beginning of Ṣafar 1286/May 1869. Between 1284–1286/1867–1868, at least three different scribes at Sangalajī's *sharīʿa* court recorded, in succession, entries in S1. This is visible from the shifts in the layout and script of the entries. I refer to each scribal hand with a different letter: A, B, C etc. S1 had at least three different scribal hands: A (S1: 5–284), B (S1: 284–480) and C (S1: 481–656). However, it is important to note here that each entry is composed of two segments in two different scripts, a segment in Arabic *naskh* script and one in Persian *shikasta-nastaʿlīq* script. It is not clear if both the *naskh* and *shikasta-nastaʿlīq* segment were written by the same scribe, by two different scribes, or by Sangalajī and a scribe.

37 Kondo 2017, 44–45.
38 Riḍāʾī 1387 sh./2008, 6–17.
39 WWQI, document nos. 902A2 (Sangalajī I) and 902A3 (Sangalajī II).

The second register (S2) measures 60 cm × 23 cm × 17 cm. It has approximately 536 bifolia (1074 pages). The first entry appears on S2: 5. It records a settlement contract dated 26 Jamādī II 1291/10 August 1874 validated by Sangalajī on 25 Dhū l-Ḥijja 1292/22 January 1876. The last legible entry on S2: 1076 is dated Dhū l-Qaʿda 1293/ November-December 1876. A preceding entry, however, is dated 15 Jamādī I 1294/ 28 May 1877 (S2: 1072). There are at least four clearly distinguishable scribal hands: D (S2: 5–514); E (S2: 515–800), F (S2: 831–936) and G (937–1076). As in the case of S1, it is not clear whether the *naskh* and *shikasta-nastaʿlīq* segments of a given entry were the work of one or two scribes. The scribal hands between S2: 801–830 are not easy to distinguish. S2: 801–809, for example, appears to be in an entirely different hand: H. The entries between S2: 810–830, on the other hand, appear to have been written by scribal hands that have already recorded earlier entries in the register, in particular F. In brief, several different people working at Sangalajī's *sharīʿa* court recorded entries in his registers. This is confirmed by the evidence of the registration notes and seals appearing on original documents which suggest Sangalajī employed several different registrars simultaneously. It is not unlikely that the registrars who added their registration note and seal onto original documents were also the scribes who recorded the original documents in the registers.

Before we examine this recording practice, however, a few codicological remarks are in order. Regrettably, I have been unable to consult the two registers *in situ* at the National Archives of Iran in Tehran (NLAI). I therefore rely exclusively on digital images of the two registers in my analysis. Riḍāʾī has suggested that the leather binding of the two registers is Russian though this is difficult to confirm. An embossed paper mark A. Lepeshkin no. 5 is visible at the top right-hand corner of S2: 814. This does suggest that the paper used for S2 and probably also for S1 is of Russian provenance.

2.6.1 Structure, Layout and Language of the Entries

2.6.1.1 The *Dafʿa* Horizontal Line

Despite minor differences, depending on the scribe in question, each of the entries on the pages of the two registers follows a specific format. The entries are arranged in two vertical columns at the centre of the page. They are separated from each other by horizontal lines which run across the width of each column. The origins of these horizontal lines known as *dafʿa* are from the shorthand Persian accounting script known as *siyāq*. In *siyāq*, the letters of the word *dafʿa* are extended in a specific manner.[40] First the *dāl* is extended as a short single stroke.

40 See for example Kāshānī 1395 sh./2016, 170–171.

The letters *fāʾ* and the final *hāʾ* retain their usual position, but the *ʿayn* is extended as a longer stroke (see Figure 33). When the two extended components are joined together, they form a single horizontal line cipher which begins with a slight curve upwards and ends with a small circumflex (Figure 34).

Figure 33: *dafʿa* written in *siyāq*.[41]

Such horizontal *dafʿa* lines are also found embedded in the middle of the text of individual entries to arrange a list of items, for example, of properties, or witness testimonies. Each listed property or witness testimony thus appears with a separate horizontal line above it.

Figure 34: *dafʿa* extended as a horizontal line in Sangalajī's *sharīʿa* court register, S1: 65. © MS no. 67032/692, NLAI, Tehran.

2.6.1.2 Two Languages and Scripts

In addition to the use of such horizontal lines to arrange the text of entries, the other main structural feature of the entries is the division of each entry into two segments. The first segment uses Arabic *naskh* and the second Persian *shikasta nastaʿlīq*. The reason for using two different scripts was to separate the "important" Arabic text Sangalajī wrote in original documents in his own hand from the text of the rest of the document written in Persian by a scribe. It is difficult, however, to confirm whether any of the *naskh* segments that appear in the register, though they bear some resemblance to Sangalajī's handwriting in original documents, were written by Sangalajī himself. Directly below the *naskh* segment is the summary, in the case of contracts, or verbatim record, in the case of legal rulings, of the main text (*matn*) of the original document. This segment of the entry was recorded in *shikasta-nastaʿlīq* script and was written, as in the case of the original document, by the scribe. It is difficult to prove that Sangalajī wrote any of the *shikasta-nastaʿlīq* segments of the entries in the registers himself.

41 Kāshānī 1395 sh./2016, 170.

2.6.2 A Comparison of Two Pages, S1: 65 and S2: 682

We shall now examine how the two constituent parts of each entry – the *naskh* segment and the *shikasta-nastaʿlīq* segment – come together in more detail by comparing the entries in two pages: S1: 65 and S2: 682. S1: 65 has four entries and S2: 682 contains five entries. S1: 65 and S2: 682 are unusual because they each contain an entry with a segment which has not yet been filled in by the scribe. The entries in S1: 65 are copied by scribe A while those in S2: 682 are copied by scribe F.

2.6.2.1 S1: 65

The date the entries were copied into the register is recorded at the top of the sheet S1: 65 by scribe A (Figure 35). The date is written after the Arabic word *yawm*, meaning "day", as follows: *yawm 13 dhū l-ḥijja al-ḥarām 1284*/6 April 1868. As we shall see, the way the registration date is recorded at the top of the page is one way of identifying the different scribal hands. Another way is by analysing the horizontal strokes used to separate entries. Scribe A starts the line with a short stroke upwards, then straightens it and finally ends with a small circumflex.

In S1: 65, the first entry (Figure 35, 1), which begins on the top right-hand corner of the sheet, records the summary of a settlement contract (*muṣālaḥa-nāma*) dated 27 Shawwāl 1284/21 February 1868. The *naskh* segment which would normally record Sangalajī's Arabic *sijill* on the settlement contract, however, has been left blank. The boundaries of the property involved in the transaction are also left blank. They are not listed under the four horizontal strokes between lines four and five of the entry. This might be because the scribe who wrote the entry had insufficient information regarding these details, or alternatively did not see the need to fill these in given the fact that the contract was not judicially certified by Sangalajī. We have also seen earlier that there could be a delay between when a contract was drafted and when it was judicially certified by Sangalajī. This occurred especially if the contract was produced in a different *sharīʿa* court in Tehran and later taken to Sangalajī for the addition of his *sijill*. In general, if a contract was drafted in Sangalajī's own *sharīʿa* court, there is a relatively short gap between the date it was drafted, the addition of a judicial attestation by Sangalajī, and its recording in the register. In this case, the settlement contract is dated 27 Shawwal 1284/21 February 1868. Based on the date at the beginning of the page, it was thus registered over a month later, on 13 Dhū l-Ḥijja 1284/6 April 1868. This suggests that it was probably produced in a different *sharīʿa* court and later shown to Sangalajī who for reasons that are not clear refrained from adding his *sijill* to it. The contract was nevertheless copied into his register.

The second entry (Figure 35, 2) records the summary of a conditional sale deed (*bayʿ-i sharṭ*) dated 10 Dhū l-Ḥijja 1284/3 April 1868. This deed was judicially certified three days later by Sangalajī on [1]3 Dhū l-Ḥijja 1284/6 April 1868 and recorded in the register on 13 Dhū l-Ḥijja 1284/6 April 1868. This suggests that the document was produced in Sangalajī's *sharīʿa* court.

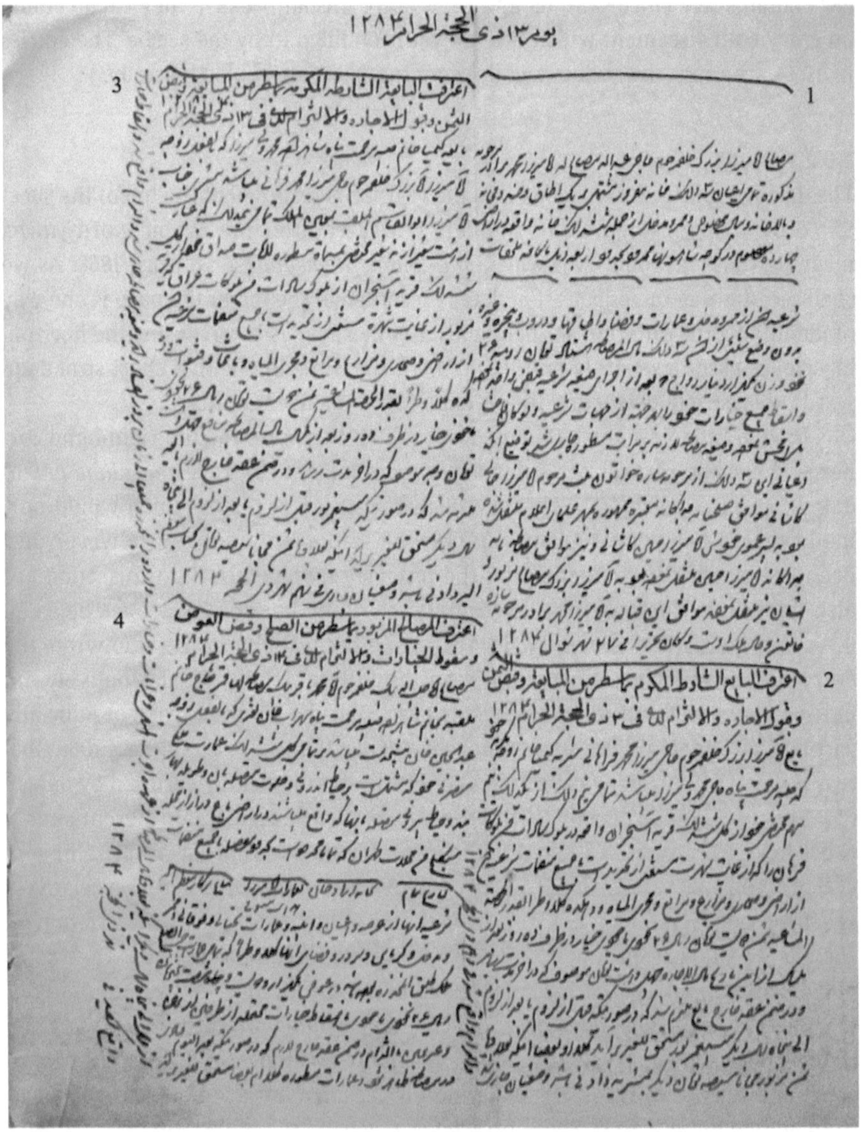

Figure 35: S1: 65, Scribe A. © MS no. 67032/692, NLAI, Tehran.

The third entry (Figure 35, 3) on the top left-hand column contains the summary of another conditional sale deed dated 9 Dhū l-Ḥijja 1284/2 April 1868, which Sangalajī judicially certified on 13 Dhū l-Ḥijja 1284/6 April 1868. This deed was registered on the same day it was judicially certified, on 13 Dhū l-Ḥijja 1284/6 April 1868, suggesting that the original deed was also produced in Sangalajī's *sharīʿa* court.

The fourth entry (Figure 35, 4) records the summary of a deed of settlement dated Dhū l-Ḥijja 1284/March-April 1868. For some reason, the scribe has left a gap for the day of the month of Dhū l-Ḥijja 1284 that the deed was written on, but this has not been filled in. This settlement deed was judicially certified by Sangalajī on 14 Dhū l-Ḥijja 1284/7 April 1868, that is a day after the date 13 Dhū l-Ḥijja 1284/6 April 1868 recorded at the top of the page. As with the other two previous entries, the short gap between the date of Sangalajī's *sijill* and its registration suggests that the original deed was produced in Sangalajī's *sharīʿa* court. The three entries which record Sangalajī's *sijill* as it appeared in the original deeds do not reproduce, however, the *sijill*s of other scholars that no doubt also appeared in these documents, nor the testimonies of witnesses. The main text of the deeds is also not transcribed verbatim in the entries but summarized. Finally, scribe A makes up for the lack of space on the sheet by writing lines vertically between the two columns of text or on the margins. The way the margins were used to write additional text that could not be fitted into the column entries is another way of distinguishing the different scribal hands.

2.6.2.2 S2: 682

Having examined the recording practice of scribe A, we are now ready to examine S2: 682 by scribe F (Figure 36). Scribe F, in contrast to scribe A, uses the Arabic preposition *fī* (on) followed by the date, instead of the noun *yawm* (day) to record the registration date at the top of the page. In S2: 682, however, there is no date visible at the top of the page. We can work out, however, by comparing the entries and registration date on the previous and following page, that the entries in S2: 682 were recorded on 13 Ramaḍān 1294/21 September 1877. Unlike scribe A, the horizontal strokes used by scribe f to separate the entries are almost completely straight. Scribe F, like scribe A, follows the same recording structure of the entries. There is a *naskh* segment for Sangalajī's own Arabic text in the original document and a Persian *shikasta-nastaʿlīq* segment for the remaining text of the document written by a scribe.

In S2: 682 as in S1: 65 we have an example of an entry that has not yet been filled in completely. In this case, though Sangalajī's *sijill* has been filled in the *naskh* segment of the fourth entry (Figure 36, 4), the *shikasta-nastaʿlīq* segment is missing. The text of the *sijill* dated 22 Rajab 1294/2 August 1877 is: *al-amr kamā suṭira wa-zubira wa-ḥakamtu bi-ʿazl al-sābiqayn wa-naṣb al-lāḥiqayn ḥurrira fī 22 rajab al-murajab 1294* (the matter is as it is recorded, and I issued a judgement on the dismissal of the previous two and the appointment of the two that are mentioned in this document. Written on 22 Rajab 1294/2 August 1877). The first part of the *sijill, al-amr kamā suṭira wa-zubira,* was used by Sangalajī on all his legal rulings issued as binding judicial decisions. We saw earlier how this appears on the recto of a *sharī'a* court ruling by Sangalajī dated Dhū al-Ḥijja 1281/April 1865. The recorded entry of the *sijill* reproduced in the register, however, omits the pious formula *bisimihi ta'āla* that Sangalajī uses in his *sijill* on the original document. The reference in the second part of the *sijill* suggests a case where Sangalajī, based on his own judicial authority as a *mujtahid,* dismissed two legal guardians, or possibly administrators of an endowment, and appointed others in their place.

As the scribe has not filled in the text of the ruling in the *shikasta-nasta'līq* segment, however, the precise circumstances of the case are not known. It is not clear why the registration of this ruling remained incomplete. There is a delay of over a month between the date of the *sijill* of Sangalajī on the ruling, 22 Rajab 1294/2 August 1877, and its registration in the register on 13 Ramaḍān 1294/21 September 1877. This type of delay between Sangalajī's intervention on the original document and its subsequent registration is common. There was often in fact a registration "backlog" of such original documents in the *sharī'a* court. The result was that documents were often registered later.

In the case of S2: 682, entry one records a ruling issued by Sangalajī in the question-and-answer style (Figure 36, 1). The question is dated 11 Sha'bān 1294/21 August 1877. Sangalajī added a reply to it on 23 Sha'bān 1294/2 September 1877. It was finally registered on 13 Ramaḍān 1294/21 September 1877. Entry two also contains a question-and-answer style ruling (Figure 36, 2). The question is undated, but Sangalajī's reply is dated 23 Sha'bān 1294/2 September 1877. Entry three is the summary of a conditional sale deed. The text of the deed is dated to the beginning of Ramaḍān 1294/September 1877 (Figure 36, 3) Sangalajī added his *sijill* to it on 7 Ramaḍān 1294/15 September 1877. It was registered on 13 Ramaḍān 1294/21 September 1877. Entry five is an undated question-and-answer ruling by Sangalajī dated 13 Ramaḍān 1294/21 September 1877 (Figure 36, 5). This document was registered on the same date that it was produced. Finally, unlike scribe A, scribe F does not squeeze overflow text from an entry in straight vertical lines in between the columns or on the margins, but as a spiral. This is clearly visible in the case of the third entry.

2.6.3 Identifying and Reading the Entries I: Legal Rulings

The specific set of formulas Sangalajī used in all his interventions on legal documents allows the reader of the register to quickly identify the type of record in each entry. An entry containing a *naskh* segment beginning with the affirmative Persian adverb *balī*, meaning yes, invariably marks the beginning of a legal ruling

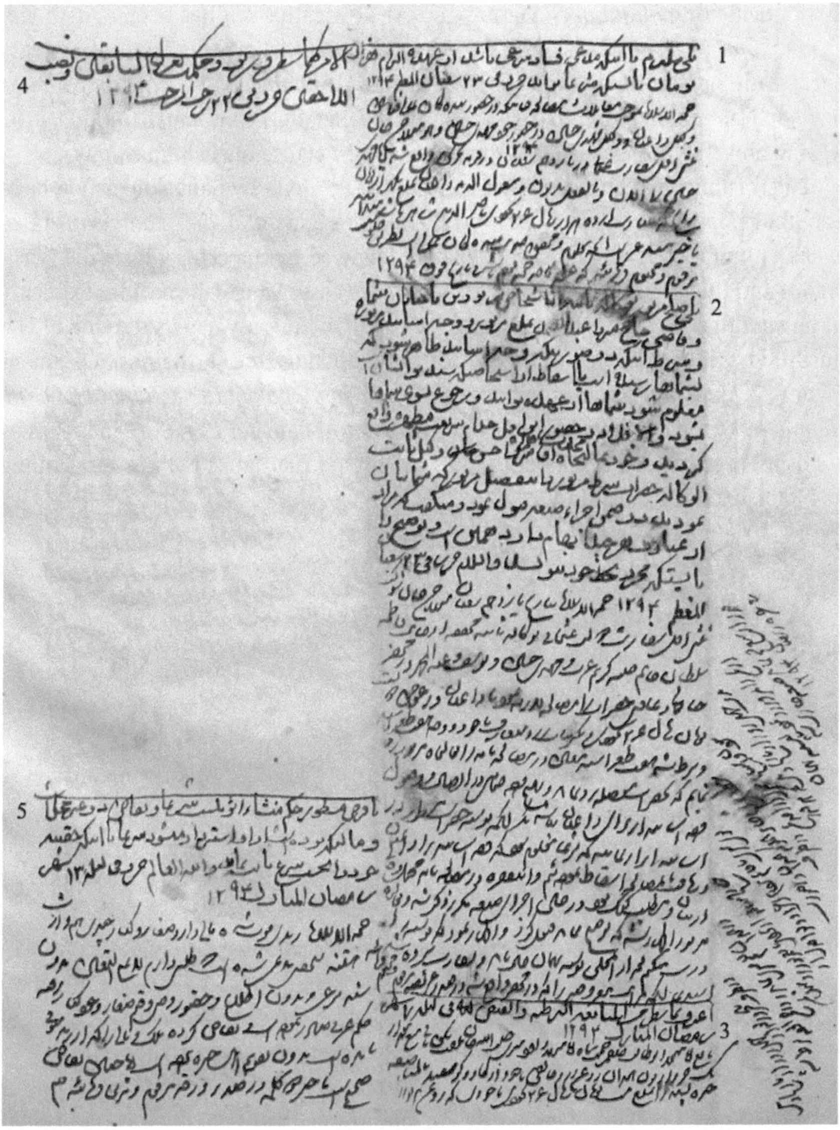

Figure 36: S2: 682, Scribe F © MS no. 67032/692, NLAI, Tehran.

issued by Sangalajī in the form of an answer to a question. The *balī* is clearly visible at the start of the *naskh* segment of entries one and two in S2: 682. Not all replies to questions, however, begin with *balī*. Entry five in S2: 682, for example, does not begin with *balī*. Nevertheless, the *shikasta-nastaʿlīq* segment opens with the honorific title *ḥujjat al-islām*, to which the evocative *alif* has been added: *hujjat al-islamā* (O Proof of Islam!). As we have seen earlier, this form of address marked the beginning of a question. In addition to *ḥujjat al-islamā*, other honorifics such as *qiblat al-anamā* (O Guide of the People!) and *sharīʿat-madārā* (O Legal Scholar!) were also used in the introductory clause of such questions.

Legal rulings which were issued in the "deed" style by Sangalajī, as we have seen above, have the following *sijill* in the *naskh* segment: *al-amr kamā suṭira wa-zubira.* In most cases, this was immediately followed by the clause *ḥurrira fī* (written on) and then the date. However, in some rare cases Sangalajī specifies explicitly in the *sijill* that he issued the judgement verbally before it was written down. The fourth entry in S2: 722, for example, has the following *sijill* in the *naskh* segment (Figure 37, 1): *al-amr kamā suṭira wa-zubira wa-laqad ḥakamtu shafāhan bi-mā yaṣiḥḥu al-ḥukm bihi sharʿan ḥurrira fī 4 shahr rabīʿ al-mawlūd 1294* (The matter is as it is as it is recorded, and I adjudicated verbally in accordance with its legal ruling on 4 Rabīʿ II 1294/18 April 1877).

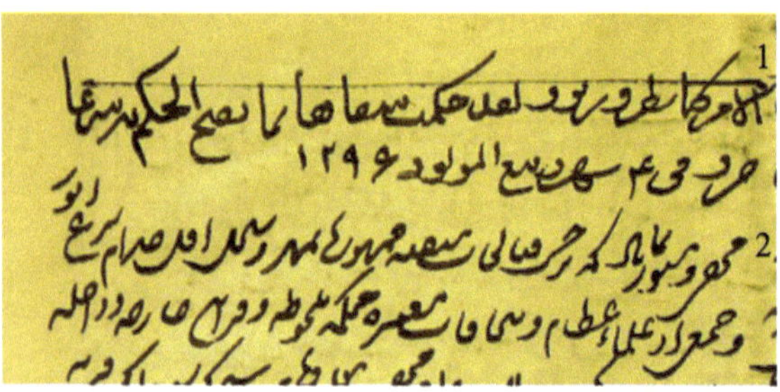

Figure 37: S2: 773, entry no. 4. © MS no. 67032/692, NLAI, Tehran.

Moreover, the text of such "deed-style" legal rulings usually open with the Persian clause *makhfī wa masṭūr namānad ki* (let it not remain hidden or concealed that) (Figure 37, 2). As we have seen in Section 2.5.2, this opening clause was typical of legal rulings issued by Sangalajī and other clerics in the "deed" style.

If the *naskh* segment begins with the Persian clause *ānchih-rā ki* (whatever) or *ḥukm-i ṣādir az* (the ruling issued by), or the Arabic clause *hādha l-ḥukm al-ṣādir min* (this ruling issued by) followed by the name of an individual, it marks the start of a ratification by Sangalajī of another cleric's ruling. Yet another Arabic clause of ratification used by Sangalajī begins: *ḥukm al-ḥākim al-muṭāʿ muṭāʿun nāfidhun* (the ruling of the judge who is to be obeyed is binding). For example, in S1: 539, Sangalajī's ratification in the first entry is: *ḥukm al-ḥākim al-muṭāʿ māḍin nāfidhun hasbamā ḥakama ḥurrira fī 14 rabīʿ I 1285* (the ruling of the judge to be obeyed is binding and effective as he has judged it, written on 14 Rabīʿ I 1285/5 July 1868). Below such ratifications, the text of the ruling that Sangalajī ratified is recorded, usually under headings such as *ṣūrat-i ḥukm* (copy of the ruling) or *ṣūrat-i khaṭṭ wa muhr* (copy of the handwriting and seal of) followed by the name of the cleric. If the ruling involved witness testimonies, these too were transcribed from the original document under the rubric *ṣūrat-i shahādat* (copy of the witness testimonies). As a rule, the ratifications of other clerics of a given ruling are not transcribed in the register. There are, however, rare exceptions which appear under the heading *ṣūrat-i imḍā* (copy of the ratification). This happened, in particular, if Sangalajī was asked to issue a certified a copy of a ruling which contained ratifications (S2: 868–869).

In the third entry in S2: 783, Sangalajī's ratification copied in the *naskh* segment reads as follows: *ānchih-rā ki jināb mustaṭāb sharīʿatmadār sayyid al-mujtahidīn āqā-yi ḥājjī mīrzā maḥmūd marqūm namūda-and muṭāʿ wa muttabaʿ wa mumḍā ast ḥar-rahu al-aqall fī 13 shahr rabīʿ al-thānī 1296* (whatever the leader of jurists Ḥājjī Mīrzā Maḥmūd has written is to be obeyed and is binding. Written by the miserable

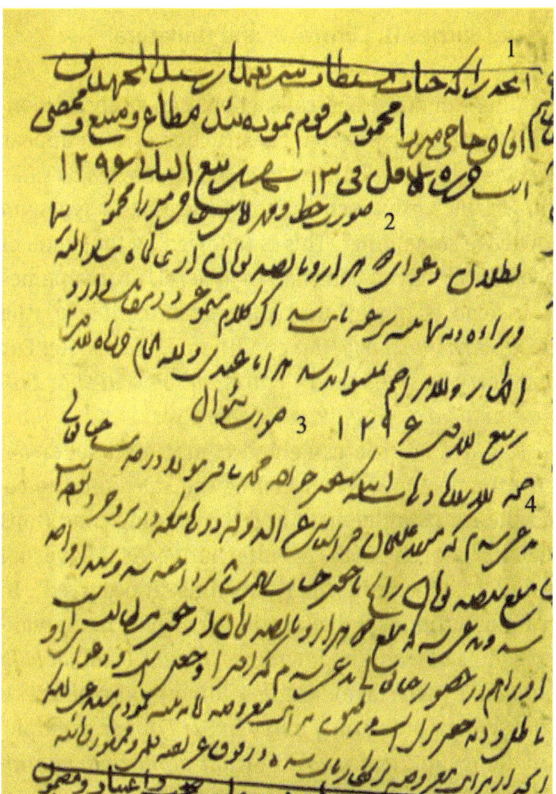

Figure 38: S2: 783, entry no. 3. © MS no. 67032/692, NLAI, Tehran.

wretch on 13 Rabīʿ II 1294/27 April 1877) (Figure 38, 1). The scribe does not indicate if the ruling of Ḥājjī Mīrzā Maḥmūd had been ratified by any other cleric prior to or after Sangalajī's ratification of the ruling. Below Sangalajī's ratification is the heading *ṣūrat-i khaṭṭ wa muhr-i āqā-yi ḥājjī mīrzā maḥmūd* (copy of the writing and seal of Ḥājjī Mīrzā Maḥmūd). Though the presence of the seal in the original document is mentioned in such headings, the entries never reproduce the inscription (*sajʿ-i muhr*) of the seal. Instead, the *shikasta-nastaʿlīq* segment only transcribes the text of Ḥājjī Mīrzā Maḥmūd's ruling, which in this case was issued as the answer to a question (Figure 38, 2). The question is recorded after the reply under the heading *ṣūrat-i suʾāl* (copy of the question) (Figure 38, 3). The text of the question starts with the usual address *ḥujjat al-islamā* (O Proof of Islam!) (Figure 38, 4). The entry as a whole thus consists of three parts in the following order: the text of Sangalajī's ratification of Ḥājjī Mīrzā Maḥmūd's ruling, the answer by Ḥājjī Mīrzā Maḥmūd, and the question to Ḥājjī Mīrzā Maḥmūd.

2.6.4 Identifying and Reading the Entries II: Contracts and Unilateral Declarations

Like legal rulings, entries containing summaries of transactions can easily be identified in the register by their Arabic past-tense verbal constructions which appear in the *naskh* segment recording Sangalajī's *sijill* on the document. Sangalajī's *sijill*s for contracts usually begin with Arabic verbs such as *iʿtarafa*, used as a synonym for *aqarra*, meaning "to acknowledge something". This is followed by the name of the individual or parties involved in the given contract. In general, proper names are not specified in the *sijill*. Instead, Sangalajī uses titles such as *al-bāyiʿ* (the seller), al-*muṣāliḥ* (the settler), *al-bāyiʿ al-shāriṭ* (the conditional seller), etc. For example, the *sijill* in the second entry in S1: 65 reads: *iʿtarafa al-bāyiʿ al-shāriṭ al-mukarram bi-mā suṭira min al-mubāyaʿa wa-qabḍ al-thaman wa-qabūl al-ijāra wa-l-iltizām ladayya fī 3 dhū l-ḥijja 1284* (the esteemed conditional seller acknowledged what is written (in the document) concerning the sale, and the receipt of the purchase sum and the rental agreement and the binding conditions before me on 3 Dhū l-Ḥijja 1284/27 March 1868). An alternative Arabic verbal construction introducing the *sijill* uses the verb *waqaʿ*, meaning "it occurred". In such cases, the type of contract or unilateral declaration that was being validated is specified with terms such as *al-waqf* (endowment), *al-bayʿ* (sale) *al-ṣulḥ* (settlement), *al-dayn* (debt), *al-nikāḥ* (marriage), *al-ṭalāq* (divorce) or *al-tawkīl* (power of attorney). The *naskh* segment of the only entry in S2: 778, for example, contains the following *sijill* by Sangalajī: *qad waqʿa al-waqf al-mazbūr min al-wāqif al-muwaffaq ʿalā nahj al-mazbūr wa-l-sharāʾiṭ al-masṭūra wa-l-tawliya wa-l-niẓāra wa-l-niyāba kamā suṭira wa-fuṣila fī l-waraqa bi-maḥdarī fī 25 rabīʿ al-

mawlūd 1296 (the mentioned endowment was constituted by the successful endower in my presence on 25 Rabīʿ 1296/19 March 1879 as mentioned and according to the stipulations recorded and its administration, supervision and deputyship is as it is described and explained in the document) (Figure 39).

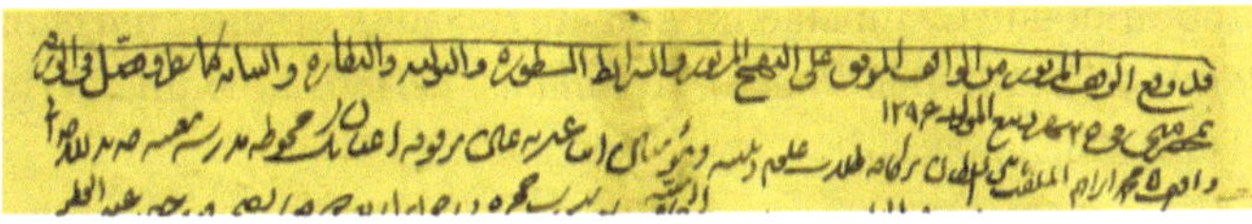

Figure 39: S2: 778, entry no. 1. © MS no. 67032/692, NLAI, Tehran.

The simplest transactions that are recorded are acknowledgments of debt. They provide us with a good example of how the contents of deeds were summarized in their register entries. In S2: 915, the seventh entry begins with the date of Sangalajī's *sijill*, abbreviated as follows: 22. J. I. 96 (22 Jamādī I 1296) (Figure 40). This practice, however, is particular to the scribe that registered this acknoweldgement and is not followed by the other scribes of the registers. Below the abbreviated date is the text of Sangalajī's *sijill* in *naskh*: *iʿtarafa bi l-dayn al-mazbūr ladayya fī 22 jamādī al-ūlā 1296* (he acknowledged the stated debt before me on 22 Jamādī I 1296/14 May 1879). Under Sangalajī's *sijill* is the *shikasta-nastaʿlīq* segment. This segment records the details of the acknowledgement using four sub-headings: *madyūn* (debtor); *dāʾina* (female creditor); *dayn* (amount owed) and *muddat* (time). Finally, the date is recorded but without specifying the day of the month. The one-month period of repayment of the debt probably began from the date of Sangalajī's *sijill* on the original deed, that is 22 Jamādī I 1296/14 May 1879.

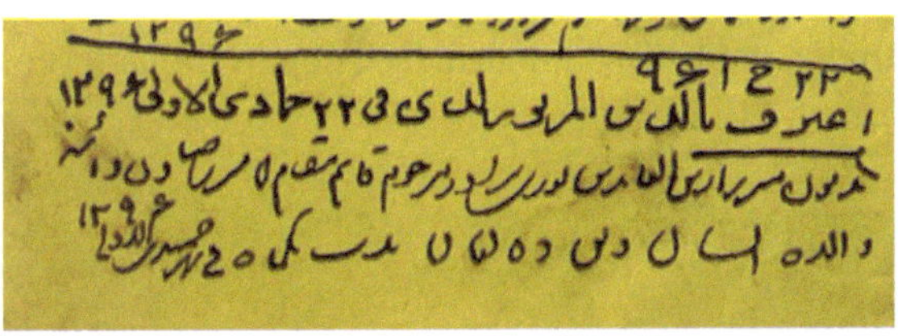

Figure 40: S2: 915, entry no. 7. © MS no. 67032/692, NLAI, Tehran.

Text

١. ٢٢ ج ١۶٩
٢. اعترف بالدين المزبور لدى فى ٢٢ جمادى الاولى ١٢٩۶
٣. مديون: ميرزا زين العابدين نورى، برادر مرحوم قائم مقام آقا ميرزا صادق؛ دائنه:
٤. والده ايشان؛ دين: ده تومان؛ مدت: يک ماه؛ فى شهر جميدى الاولى ١٢٩۶

Translation
1. 22. J. I. 96.
2. [Sangalajī's *sijill* in *naskh*]: The debtor acknowledged the mentioned debt before me on 22 Jamādī I 1296/14 May 1879.
3. [Summary of the deed in *shikasta-nastaʿlīq*]: Debtor (*madyūn*): Mīrzā Zayn al-ʿĀbidīn Nūrī, brother of late Qāʾim Maqām Āqā Mīrzā Ṣādiq. Creditor (*dāʾina*):
4. His mother (*wālida-yi īshān*). Debt (*dayn*): 10 *tūmān*s. Period: 1 month. (Written) in Jamādī I 1296/April-May 1878.

In the *shikasta-nastaʿlīq* segments of other entries containing contracts we also find a similar process of summarizing the content of an actual deed using nouns such as *bāyiʿ* (seller), *mushtarī* (buyer) or for settlement contracts constructions such as *muṣāliḥ* and *muṣāliḥ lahu* before the names of the parties involved. What follows is a brief summary of the contract and its date. Neither the witness testimonies nor the *sijill*s of other scholars besides Sangalajī that appeared in the original deed are reproduced in the register entry.

2.6.5 Annulement

As we have noted earlier, legal acts were annulled in Iran by removing their seals from the original deed. How was this reflected in the registers? If a particular contract was annulled or became void, the scribe indicated this in the register by crossing it out. Like the horizontal *dafʿa* lines that appear above each entry, the type of stroke the scribes of Sangalajī's registers used to cancel entries also has its origins in the Persian accounting *siyāq* shorthand script. The Arabic numeral 9 was used to cross out entries. The number 9 was extended as a vertical line across the entry.[42] In the third entry in S2: 599, the heads of two Arabic 9 numerals are clearly visible above the horizontal line on an annulled deed of power of attorney

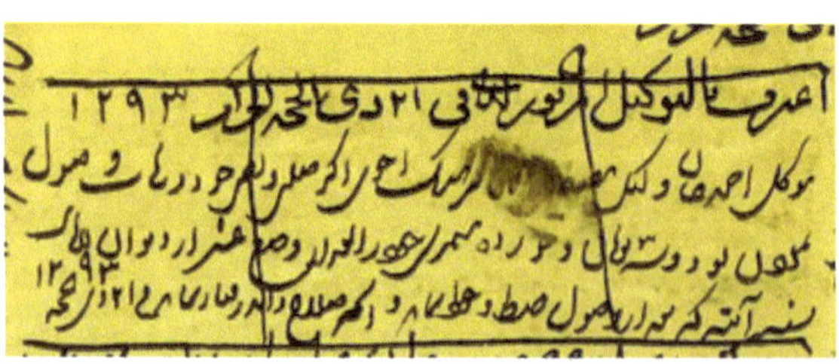

Figure 41: S2: 599, entry no. 3. © MS no. 67032/692, NLAI, Tehran.

42 See Kāshānī 1395 sh./2016, 85.

dated 21 Dhū l-Ḥijja 1293/7 January 1877, which was validated by Sangalajī and registered on the same day (Figure 41). When exactly the deed was annulled or became void and was crossed out by the scribe is not specified in this particular case. There are relatively few such crossed-out entries in the registers. This might be because Sangalajī's *sharīʿa* court was not informed of a subsequent cancellation of an original deed that had been registered earlier, a problem which is mentioned in the leagl ruling we examined earlier (see section 2.5.1).

In some cases, the scribes wrote an additional note confirming when Sangalajī's seal had been removed from the original deed. For example, the first entry in S1: 61 contains the summary of a document recording a series of transactions made by a certain Jahāngīr Khān on 28 Dhū l-Qaʿda 1284/22 March 1868. According to its *sijill*, the document was validated by Sangalajī on the same day, 28 Dhū l-Qaʿda 1284/22 March 1868. The entire entry, however, is crossed out with three vertical-number nine *siyāq* strokes. At the bottom of the entry, the scribe has written the following note: This document became void on 5 Dhū l-Ḥijja 1284/25 March 1868 and the seal of his excellency (i.e. Sangalajī) was removed from it (*īn niwishta bi-tārikh-i yawm-i panjum-i shahr-i dhū l-ḥijja 1285 bāṭil shud wa muhr-i jināb āqā kishīda shud*). Based on the date at the top of the page and the other entries, the entry was probably registered on 3–4 Dhū l-Ḥijja 1284/27–28 March 1868, that is, a day or two before it was crossed out and the scribe added the remark on the removal of the seal.

Another way of cancelling a deed was to write a *sijill* of cancellation. A rare example of this occurs in the fourth entry in S1: 289 registered on 9–10 Rajab 1284/6–7 November 1867 (Figure 42). On 10 Rajab 1284/7 November 1867, Sangalajī confirms the cancellation of a conditional sale written as a settlement contract dated 10 Dhū l-Ḥijja 1283/15 April 1867. The *naskh* segment containing Sangalajī's *sijill* reads as follows: *qad saḥḥa wa-waḍaḥa faskh al-muṣālaḥa al-masṭura ladayya fī 10 rajab al-murajab 1284* (The cancellation of the said settlement contract was established before me on 10 Rajab 1284/7 November 1867).

According to *Wajīzat al-taḥrīr*, a *shurūṭ* manual from the Qajar period completed in 1254/1829–1830, the use of the Arabic verb *waqaʿ* in the *sijill* implied that the legal matter occurred before the judge or scribe, whereas if the verbs *waḍaḥa*, *saḥḥa* and *ittaṣaḥa* were used in the *sijill*, it meant that the proceedings had not taken place before the judge or scribe but became established later for them.[43] In

43 Iṣfahānī 1393 sh./2014, 25: "*bi-dān ki dar sijillāt farq miyān-i waqaʿ wa waḍaḥa an ast ki waqaʿ ʿalāmat-i ān ast ki ān amr dar ḥuḍur-i ān ḥākim-i sharʿ ya muḥarrir guzāshta, wa waḍaḥa wa ṣaḥḥa wa ittaṣaḥa ʿalāmat-i ān ast ki an amr dar ḥudūr-i ān ḥakim yā ān mūḥarrir naguzāshta, nihāyat bar ān wāḍiḥ shuda.*" For other examples where Sangalajī uses a *sijill* with *waḍaḥa* see the third entry in S1: 75. Sangalajī confirms the power of attorney (*al-tawkīl*) granted elsewhere to an individual to collect a debt. Similarly, the fifth entry in S1: 29 confirms the outcome of

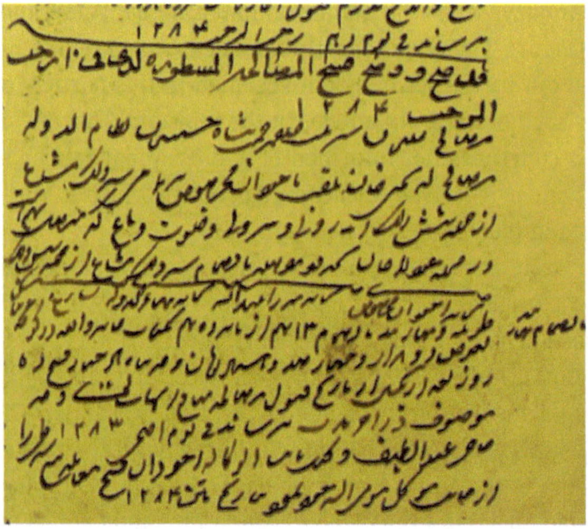

Figure 42: S1: 289, entry no. 4. © MS no. 67032/692, NLAI, Tehran.

this case, it is not clear where the original settlement contract dated 10 Dhū l-Ḥijja 1283/15 April 1867 was drafted and where it was annulled.

If Sangalajī followed the practice outlined in *Wajīzat al-taḥrīr*, then his use of the verbs *waḍaḥa* and *saḥḥa* in his *sijill* indicate that both the authentication of the original contract and its annulment had occurred elsewhere. When the contract was shown to him on 10 Rajab 1284/7 November 1867, he simply confirmed its cancellation. The register also contains other *sijill*s, beginning for example with *saḥḥa*, such as *qad saḥḥa al-iʿtirāf,* which might indicate that the deed in question was not originally drafted and certified in Sangalajī's *sharīʿa* court.[44] This does not necessarily mean, however, that all entries which begin with *iʿtarafa* or *qad waqaʿ sijill*s are from deeds that were produced in Sangalajī's *sharīʿa* court. Only a more thorough comparison than is possible here of original deeds and copies with their transcribed register entries will allow us to determine whether the site of production can be distinguished based on the formula Sangalajī used for his *sijill* and which was later recorded in the register.

---

proceedings in an inheritance dispute and the first three entries in S1: 290 which confirm sales that had occurred in other *sharīʿa* courts.

44 For examples of *sijill*s which begin with *qad saḥḥa al-iʿtirāf,* see the first entry in S1: 300; the first two entries in S1: 313, for *qad saḥḥa* the fifth entry in S1: 305.

2.6.6 Certifying the Authenticity of Originals

In addition to annulment, the entries in the register demonstrate that Sangalajī and his *sharī'a* court spent a considerable amount of time authenticating legal documents, both originals and their copies. Sangalajī was often asked to verify whether the handwriting (*khaṭṭ*) of the *sijill* and seal (*muhr*) in an original document belonged to a given scholar. The *sijill* of each scholar in this period, as we have seen, was highly distinctive in terms of its formal aspects and formulae. Nevertheless, it is not clear precisely how Sangalajī identified the handwriting and seals of his contemporaries and scholars who had died in his lifetime. It is likely that he was only able to do this for the narrow circle of scholars that he collaborated closely with in Tehran and whose documents often appeared at his *sharī'a* court for his validation. In the first entry in S2: 789, for example, Sangalajī confirms the authenticity of the *sijill* and seal of the deceased Āqā Sayyid Ismā'īl, most likely Sayyid Ismā'īl Bihbahānī (d.1295/1878), on an original settlement contract after the latter's death (Figure 43). From other entries in the registers, we know that Sangalajī often ratified the rulings of Sayyid Ismā'īl Bihbahānī, when the latter was still alive, and would therefore be expected to be familiar with the handwriting of his *sijill* and his seal. The entry is divided into three parts. The *naskh* segment begins with Sangalajī's note of authentication (Figure 43, 1):

> The above *sijill* is written in the handwriting of the deceased Āqā Sayyid Ismā'īl, may God exalt his rank. The seal is also the seal of the deceased and is genuine and authentic. Written by the miserable wretch (Sangalajī) on the night of 4th Jamādī I 1296/26 April 1879.

Below this is the text of Sayyid Ismā'īl Bihbahānī's own *sijill*, dated 9 Jamādī II 1283/19 October 1866, under the heading *ṣūrat-i khaṭṭ wa muhr-i marḥūm āqā sayyid ismā'īl* (copy of the handwriting and seal of the deceased Āqā Sayyid Ismā'īl) (Figure 43, 2). Finally, under the heading *ṣūrat-i muṣālaḥa-nāma* is a copy of the settlement contract dated 4 Rabī' I 1283/17 July 1866, which Sayyid Ismā'īl Bihbahānī had judicially certified on 9 Jamādī II 1283/19 October 1866 (Figure 43, 3). Though the page has no registration date on the top, judging from the date of the other entries on the page and those in the previous and subsequent pages, the document's registration must have occurred between 21–26 Jamādī II 1296/13–18 May 1879.

In some cases, Sangalajī was asked to confirm the authenticity of his own *sijill* and seal on legal documents he had judicially certified earlier. For example, in the second entry in S2: 127, Sangalajī confirms the authenticity of his own *sijill* and seal on a conditional sale deed dated 8 Ramaḍān 1271/25 May 1855 (Figure 44). The *naskh* segment contains the following note by Sangalajī:

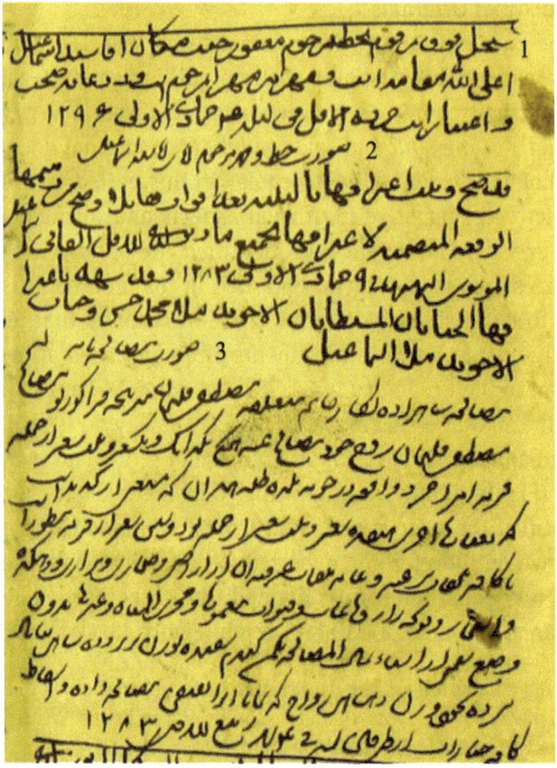

Figure 43: S2: 789, entry no. 1. © MS no. 67032/692, NLAI, Tehran.

> The handwriting (*khaṭṭ*) of the *sijill* is of the lowest of the servants of the pure *sharīʿa* (Sangalajī) and the seal is the previous seal of the lowest of the servants of the illuminated *sharīʿa* (Sangalajī). Written on 17 Shawwal 1293/5 November 1876.[45]

This note is significant because it confirms that Sangalajī wrote his *sijill*s on all original documents himself. Below this is the copy of Sangalajī's *sijill* on the conditional sale deed under the heading: "copy of the handwriting and old seal of the Proof of Islam (i.e. Sangalajī)" (*ṣūrat-i khaṭṭ wa muhr-i qadīm-i jināb ḥujjat al-islām*). Once again, however, no inscription of the seal is provided in such entries. The next segment records the text of Sangalajī's *sijill* dated 18 Ramaḍān 1271/4 June 1855: *iʿtarafa al-bāyiʿ al-shāriṭ bi-jamīʿ mā suṭira ladayya fī 18 shahr ramaḍān al-mubārak 1271* ("the conditional seller acknowledged all that is written

45 S2: 127: "*khaṭṭ-i sijill khaṭṭ-i īn aqall-i khuddām-i sharīʿat-i muṭaḥḥara ast wa muhr muhr-i sābiq-īn aqall-i khuddām-i sharīʿat-i anwar ast ḥurrira fī 17 shawwāl 1292.*"

before me on 18 Ramaḍān 1271/4 June 1855"). The final segment of the entry records the summary of the conditional sale deed. From the date of the entries in the following page, the registration of this entry probably occurred on that same date that Sangalajī issued his note, that is, 17 Shawwāl 1293/5 November 1876.

If Sangalajī had doubts about the authenticity of an original document such as a legal ruling, he refrained from ratifying it. The fourth entry in S1: 68 contains in the *shikasta-nastaʿlīq* segment the text of a legal ruling issued in the "deed" style by a certain Ākhūnd Mullā ʿAlī Qāpūzābādī, dated 25 Dhū l-Qaʿda 1284/19 March 1868 (Figure 45). Sangalajī's ratification, however, is missing in the *naskh* segment. The scribe has written the following remark instead in the margins: "This is the ruling of Ākhūnd Mullā ʿAlī Qāpūzābādī but since it was not in the latter's handwriting, his excellency (i.e. Sangalajī) did not ratify it." (*īn ḥukm-i jināb āqā ākhūnd mullā ʿalī qāpūzābādi ast wa chūn khaṭṭ-i ākhūnd nabūd jināb āqā imḍā nafarmūdand*). In this case, we see that although the ruling was not ratified by Sangalajī, once it had arrived in his *sharīʿa* court it was nevertheless registered by his scribes.

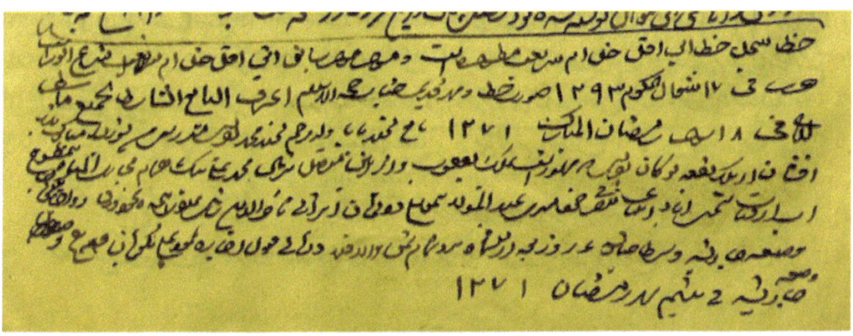

Figure 44: S2: 127, entry no. 2. © MS no. 67032/692, NLAI, Tehran.

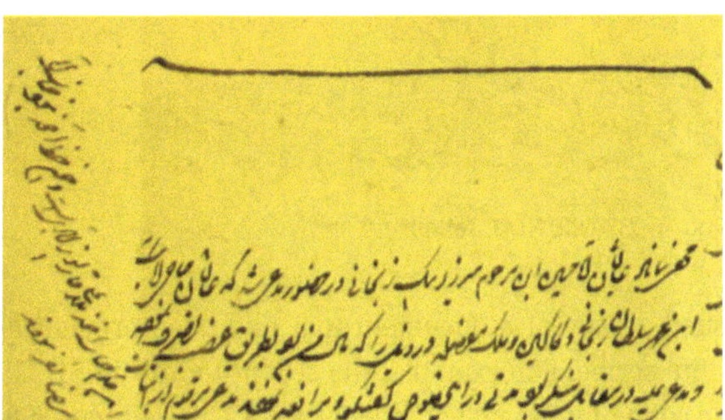

Figure 45: S1: 68, entry no. 4. © MS no. 67032/692, NLAI, Tehran.

2.6.7 Certifying the Authenticity of Copies

Besides authenticating original documents (*aṣl*), Sangalajī's *sharīʿa* court also routinely authenticated copies or transcripts (*sawād/rū-niwisht*). When Sangalajī confirms the authenticity of a copy of an original deed, he explicitly notes the number of *sijill*s and seals the original deed contained. For example, in the fifth entry in S1: 47, Sangalajī authenticates a copy of a document containing the summary of a sale deed on its recto and a settlement contract on the verso. Sangalajī's *sijill* in the *naskh* segment reads: "the copy is similar to its original, containing twenty-seven seals and twenty-eight *sijill*s. The verso contains four seals and a *sijill*. Written on the night of 20 Dhū l-Qaʿda 1284/14 March 1868" (*al-sawād muṭābiq li-aṣlihi al-mushtamal ʿalā sabʿa wa-ʿishrīn khāṭaman wa-thāmaniya wa-ʿishrīn sijillan wa-l-ẓahr mushtamal ʿalā ʿarbaʿ amhārin wa-sijillun wāḥidun ḥurrira fī layla 20 dhī l-qaʿda al-ḥarām 1284*) (Figure 46). Due to the decentralisation of judicial authority among Imāmī scholars in Iran in this period, it was common for legal documents, as in this case, to contain multiple *sijill*s and seals belonging to different scholars. The *shikasta-nastaʿlīq* segment records the summary of the sale deed dated Rajab 1249/14 November–13 December 1833 on the recto and a summary of the settlement contract dated 5 Shawwal 1271/21 June 1855 on the verso of the document. Based on the registration date at the top of the page and the subsequent page, the entry was registered on 20 Dhū l-Qaʿda 1284/14 March 1868. The entry does not, however, specify whether the copy of the sale deed and settlement contract which Sangalajī judicially certified was brought to his *sharīʿa* court from outside or whether the copy was produced by the scribes of his *sharīʿa* court.

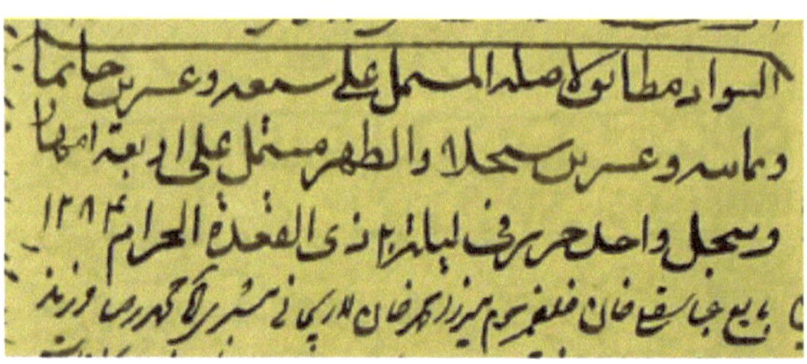

Figure 46: S1: 47, entry no. 5. © MS no. 67032/692, NLAI, Tehran.

If Sangalajī's *sharīʿa* court issued a copy of a document that had been previously registered, this was noted by the scribe. For example, the seventh entry in S1: 115 records a question-and-answer ruling by Sangalajī dated 3 Rabīʿ I 1285/24 June 1868. Directly below the text of the question-and-answer ruling, under an additional horizontal line, the scribe has recorded Sangalajī's *sijill*, confirming the authenticity of a copy of the document: *al-sawād muṭābiq li-aṣlihi ḥarrarahu al-aqall fī 4 n-h-w-m-y shahr rabīʿ al-awwal 1285* ("the copy is identical to the original written by the miserable wretch on 4 Rabīʿ I 1285/25 June 1868"). Coded letters, such as *n-h-w-m-y* in this case, were sometimes added by Sangalajī in his *sijills*, as we have seen earlier. Below Sangalajī's *sijill* in the *naskh* segment of the entry is the following note in the *shikasta-nastaʿlīq* segment by the scribe: *sawād hamīn niwishta ast ki thabt shuda ast* ("the copy is the same as what was registered") (Figure 47).

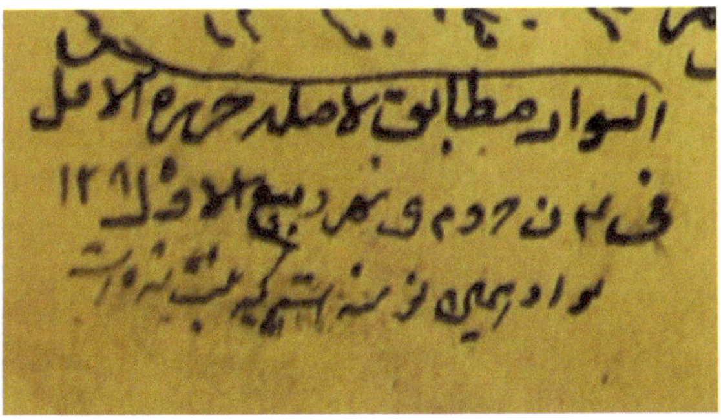

Figure 47: S1: 115, entry no. 7. © MS no. 67032/692, NLAI, Tehran.

In some cases where a copy was issued based on a previously registered original, the date of the original registration was also noted by the scribe. For example, in the four entry in S2: 641, Sangalajī authenticates a copy of a marriage contract that had been registered earlier. The *naskh* segment of the entry reads as follows: "the copy is identical to the original containing seventeen seals and fourteen *sijills*, written by the miserable wretch on 9 Rabīʿ II 1294/23 April 1877".[46] Below this in the *shikasta-nastaʿlīq* segment the scribe has written: "copy of the marriage contract of Mīrzā Sayyid ʿAlī Akbar and Hājar Khānum, daughter of the deceased Mīrzā Abū l-Qāsim Mustawfī al-Mamālik. Its original was registered in Ramaḍān 1285/December 1868–January 1869 in the *thabt-i kull*"[47] (Figure 48). The precise meaning of *thabt-i kull* here is unclear. It might simply be a reference to Sangalajī's *sharīʿa* court registers, which contained a more complete entry of the document under the entries for Ramaḍān 1285/December 1868–January 1869. Since the original marriage contract had already been registered earlier, its text was not reproduced when the copy was issued.

---

46 S2: 641, entry no. 4: "*al-sawād muṭābiq li-aṣlihi al-mushtamal ʿalā sabʿa ʿashara muhran wa ʿarabata ʿashara sijillan ḥarrahu al-aqall fī 9 rabīʿ al-thānī 1294.*"

47 S2: 641, entry no. 4: "*sawād-i qabāla-yi nikāḥ-i mīrzā sayyid ʿalī akbar . . . hājar khānum bint marḥūm . . . abū l-qāsim ki aṣl-i-an dar ramaḍān 1285 dar thabt-i kull ḍabt ast.*"

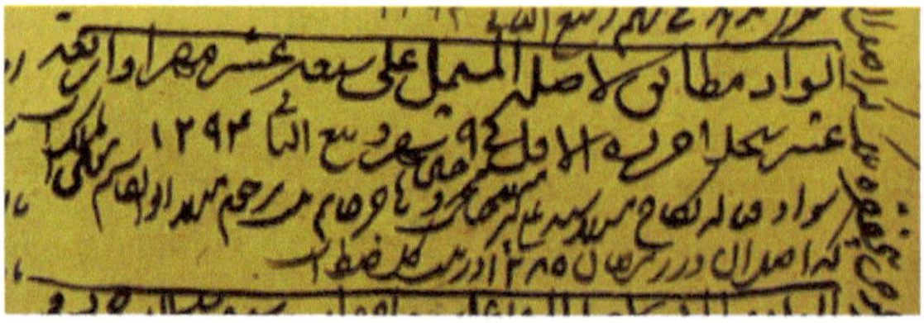

Figure 48: S2: 641, entry no. 4. © MS no. 67032/692, NLAI, Tehran.

It was also possible for the *sharīʿa* court to issue copies of documents that had been judicially certified by Sangalajī, but which, for one reason or another, had not been recorded in the registers. The first entry in S1: 133 records the summary of a settlement contract (*muṣālaḥa-nāma*) dated 16 Safar 1271/8 November 1854, which Sangalajī had judicially certified on 18 Shawwal 1271/4 July 1855. The scribe first records in *naskh* the *sijill* of Sangalajī on the copy of the document: "the copy is identical to the original which contains on its recto and verso thirteen seals and on its recto twelve *sijills*, written by the miserable wretch on the night of 25 Rabīʿ I 1285/15 August 1868".[48] Notable here is the usage of *matn* to refer to the recto of the sheet, where the main text or *matn* of the document appears, and *ẓahr* to refer to the back of the sheet, or verso. This is followed by the following remark in *shikasta-nastaʿlīq* by the scribe: "The original document was sealed by his excellency's blessed seal on 18 Shawwal 1271/4 July 1855 but was not registered, therefore it is being registered now".[49] Below this is the *naskh* segment reproducing Sangalajī's *sijill* on the original settlement contract and a *shikasta-nastaʿlīq* segment recording a summary of the deed. In this case, the original settlement contract had been judicially certified by Sangalajī but was ultimately not registered, probably because it dates to the period before Sangalajī had begun to maintain registers. Similarly, the second entry in S1:133 issues a copy of and transcribes a *waqf* deed that Sangalajī had also judicially certified on 18 Shawwāl 127/4 July 1855, but which had not been registered.

2.6.8 Reissues, Duplicates, and Revisions

In cases where a previously registered document was issued as a copy based on its registered entry and not the original document, Sangalajī would write a remark to this effect on the issued copy, and this remark would be transcribed in

48 S1: 133, entry no. 1: "*al-sawād muṭābiq li-aṣlihi al-mushtamal matnan wa ẓahran ʿala thālatha ʿashara khāṭaman wa matnan ʿala ithnay ʿashara sijillan ḥarrahu al-aqall fi layla 25 shahr rabīʿ al-awwal 1285.*"

49 S1: 133, entry no. 1: "*aṣl-i īn niwishta dar 18 shawwāl 1271 bi-muhr-i mubārak-i jināb āqā risīda wa thabt nashuda li-hādha dar īn tārikh ki sāwad shuda thabt mī-shawad.*"

the margins next to its registered entry. For example, in S1: 203, the fourth entry records a settlement contract dated 16 Shaʿbān 1285/2 December 1868, which Sangalajī validated on the same day. On the left-hand margin of the entry is the following remark by Sangalajī: "It is correct based on its valid registration. Written on 11 Rabīʿ I 1292/17 April 1875" (Figure 49).[50]

In another example, the first entry in S2: 706 records a question-and-answer ruling dated 16 Jamādī II 1294/28 June 1877. Next to the entry on the right-hand

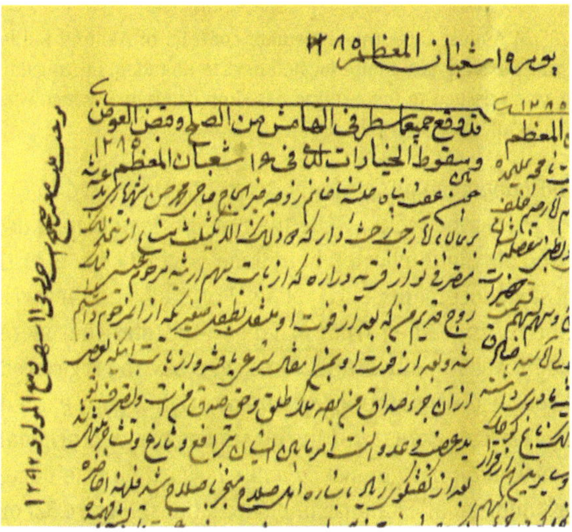

Figure 49: S1: 203, entry no. 4. © MS no. 67032/692, NLAI, Tehran.

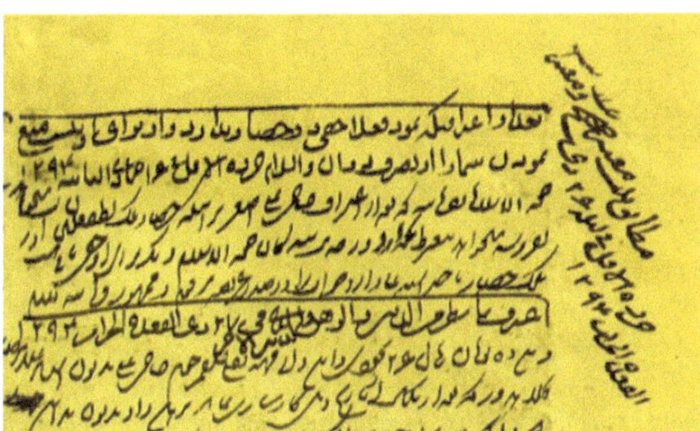

Figure 50: S2: 706, entry no. 1. © MS no. 67032/692, NLAI, Tehran.

50 S1: 203, entry no. 4: "*bar ḥasb-i thabt-i muʿtabar ṣaḥīḥ ast ḥurrira fī 11 shahr-i rabīʿ al-mawlud 1292.*"

margin is the following remark by Sangalajī, reproduced by the scribe from the issued copy: "It is accurate based on its valid registration. Written by the miserable wretch on the night of 26 Dhū l-Qaʿda 1294/2 December 1877".[51] (Figure 50).

There were also cases where individuals had registered documents at Sangalajī's *sharīʿa* court but then subsequently lost the originals. They would refer to Sangalajī for new originals to be issued based on their registered entries. Each time this happened, the scribe recorded this in the register. For example, the fourth entry in S1: 167 has the following note by the scribe in *shikasta-nastaʿlīq*:

> On the night of 5 Jamādī I 1285/24 August 1868, the settlement contract of Ākhūnd Mullā Yaʿqūb and Mīrzā Beg concerning six *dāng* of a house located next to Khandaq, in Sangalaj, one of the quarters of Tehran, was reissued to the Ākhūnd based on its original which was registered on 27 Dhū l-Ḥijja 1281/23 May 1865.[52]

The Arabic feminine noun *al-muthannā*, meaning "double", was the term used to describe such reissued duplicates. The scribe would write the remark *al-muthannā ast tak nuskha-yi awwal mafqūd ast* (it is the duplicate; the unique original copy is lost) next to the registered entries of such documents. Such reissued copies based on register entries, should, however, be distinguished from original duplicates that were made when the original document was initially drafted. In such cases, the registered entry of the original document specified whether more than one original copy existed using formulas such as: *dhālika l-kitāb nuskhatān* (this document has two original copies) (Figure 51) or *al-kitāb nuskhatān matnan-wa sijillan wa-shurūṭan* (the document has two originals with text, judicial attestations, and stipulations) (Figure 52) or simply *nukshatān* (two original copies) (Figure 53).[53] Some scribes added this remark at the bottom of the entry while others added it next to the *naskh* segment at the top.

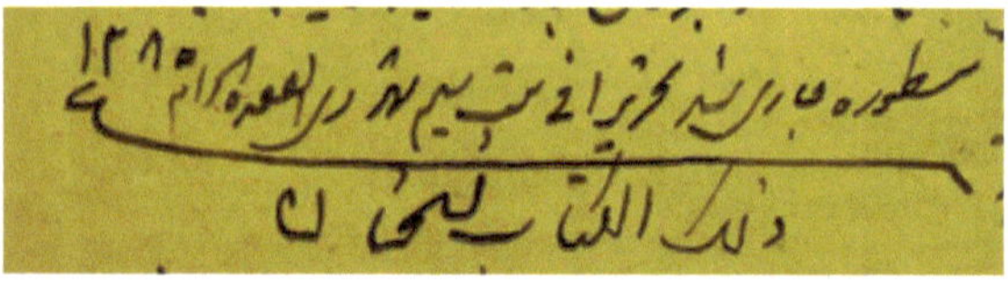

Figure 51: S1: 284, entry no. 3. © MS no. 67032/692, NLAI, Tehran.

51 S2: 706, entry no. 1: "*muṭābiq-i thabt-i muʿtabar ṣaḥīh ast wa muʿtabar ast ḥarrarahu al-aqall fī layla 26 dhī l-qaʿda al-ḥarām 1294.*"

52 S1: 167, entry no. 4: "*aṣl-i qabāla dar tārīkh-i 27 dhī l-ḥijja 1281 thabt shuda būd mujaddadan az rūy-i thabt niwishta shuda wa bi-ākhūnd dāda shud tā wāḍiḥ bāshad.*"

53 In S1: 537, Fig. 24, instead of *nuskhatān* the scribe has written *nuskhata(y)n*. See also Riḍāʾī 1387 sh./2008, 12.

Figure 52: S1: 537, entry no. 1. © MS no. 67032/692, NLAI, Tehran.

In S2: 915, the first entry contains the summary of a settlement contract dated 18 Jamādī I 1296/10 May 1879. The word *nuskhatān* is written diagonally by the scribe across the *naskh* segment containing Sangalajī's *sijill*, also dated 18 Jamādī I 1296/10 May 1979 (Figure 53). The fact that the *sijill* and the contract have the same date suggests the settlement contract was drafted in Sangalajī's own *sharīʿa* court and had not come from outside. This is confirmed, moreover, by the remark that two originals were produced.

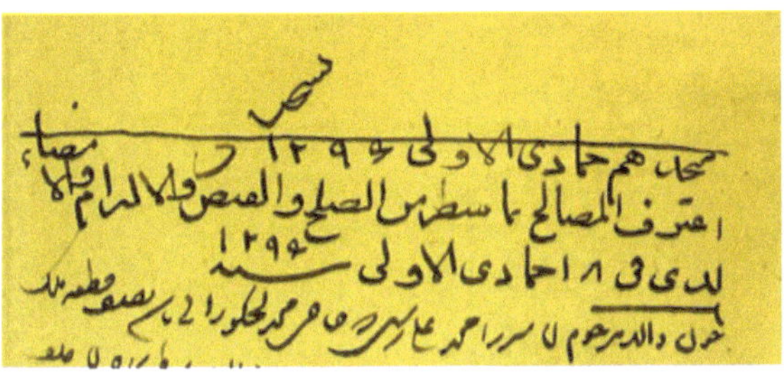

Figure 53: S2: 915, entry no. 1. © MS no. 67032/692, NLAI, Tehran.

If an original deed underwent modification and was re-registered, Sangalajī's scribes took care to note this. The fifth entry in S1: 53 contains a question-and-answer ruling issued by Sangalajī. The reply is dated 24 Dhū l-Qaʿda 1284/18 March 1868. The scribe has crossed out the entry using the vertical number nine *siyāq* strokes and has written the following remark in the margin: "this document has been modified in terms of its *sijill*s and text and has been written and registered twice"[54] (Figure 54).

Such meticulous registration practice was important because it was not uncommon that within the context of a dispute, parties would refer to Sangalajī's registers. For example, in the sixth entry in S1: 73, Sangalajī confirms the necessity of acting upon the stipulations of a particular settlement contract based uniquely on its registered entry:

54 S1: 53, entry no. 5: "*Īn niwishta sijillan wa matnan taghyīr dāda shud wa dū martaba niwishta wa thabt shud.*"

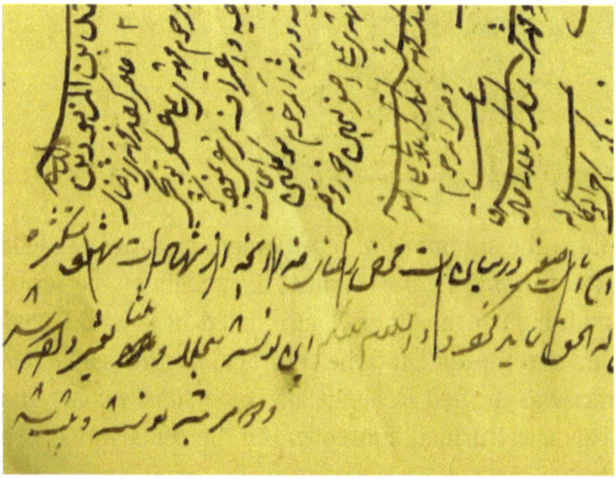

Figure 54: S1: 53, entry no. 5. MS no. 67032/692, NLAI, Tehran.

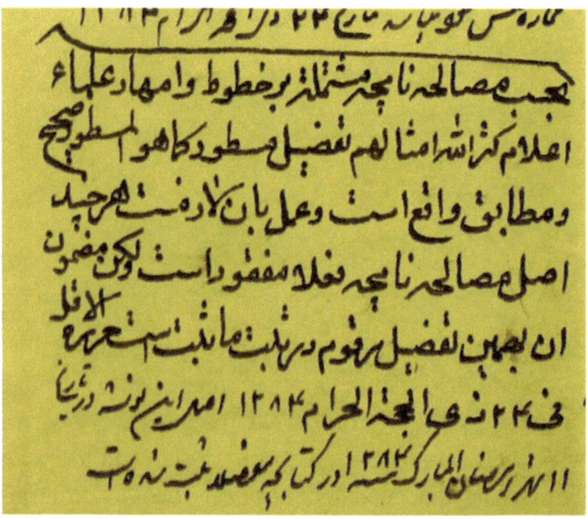

Figure 55: S1: 73, entry no. 6. MS no. 67032/692, NLAI, Tehran.

Based on the settlement contract containing the handwriting and seals of the exalted learned scholars, may God increase their number, the said details are accurate and must be acted upon. Even though the original settlement contract is now lost, its content with the same details is recorded in our register-archive. Written by the miserable wretch on 24 Dhū l-Ḥijja 1284/17 April 1868".[55]

55 S1: 73, entry no. 6: *"aṣl-i muṣlāḥa-nāmcha fiʿlan mafqūd ast wa lākin maḍmūn-i ān bi-hamīn tafṣīl marqūm dar thabt-i mā thabt ast."*

In the *shikasta-nasta'līq* segment, the scribe specifies the date the original lost settlement contract was recorded in the registers: "the original document was recorded in detail in the register (*kitābcha*) on 11 Ramaḍān 1284/6 January 1868"[56] (Figure 55).

2.6.9 Indicating Additional Notes and Blank Spaces

As we have seen earlier, the Arabic numeral nine was used to create strokes to annul entries, based on *siyāq* accounting practice. The Arabic numeral three, on the other hand, was used to add additional notes relating to a given entry in the margins. For example, in the *naskh* segment of the fifth entry of S1: 497, the scribe records Sangalajī's confirmation of the authenticity of the *sijill* and seal of the deceased Ḥājj Mullā Mīrzā Muḥammad on a settlement deed. The *sijill* and the settlement deed are dated the beginning of Rabī' I 1278/6 September 1861. Sangalajī's confirmation is dated Shawwāl 1284/January–February 1868. The scribe has added the Arabic numeral three above the entry and on the right-hand margin next to it (Figure 56). The Arabic numeral three signals an additional note by Sangalajī on the original deed on 6 Dhū l-Qa'da 1285/18 February 1869, that is, almost a year after his first note confirming the authenticity of Ḥājj Mullā Mīrzā Muḥammad's *sijill* and seal. The additional note reaffirms the validity of the settlement contract based on the authentic *sijill* and seal of the deceased Ḥājj Mullā Mīrzā Muḥammad.

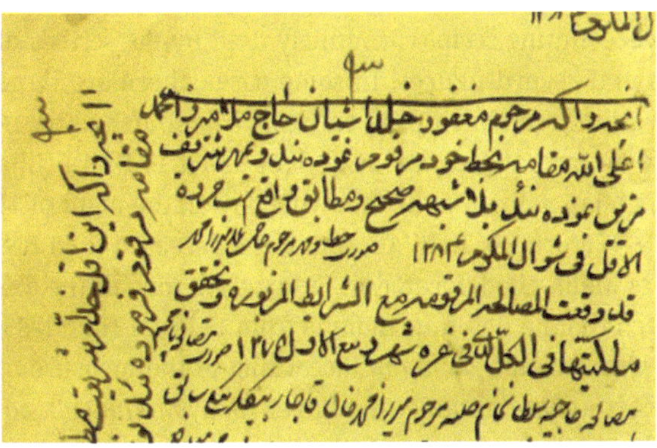

Figure 56: S1: 497, entry no. 5. © MS no. 67032/692, NLAI, Tehran.

56 S1: 73, entry no. 6: "*aṣl-i īn niwishta dar tārīkh-i 11 ramaḍān al-mubārak sana 1284 dar kitābchih mufaṣṣalan thabt shuda ast.*"

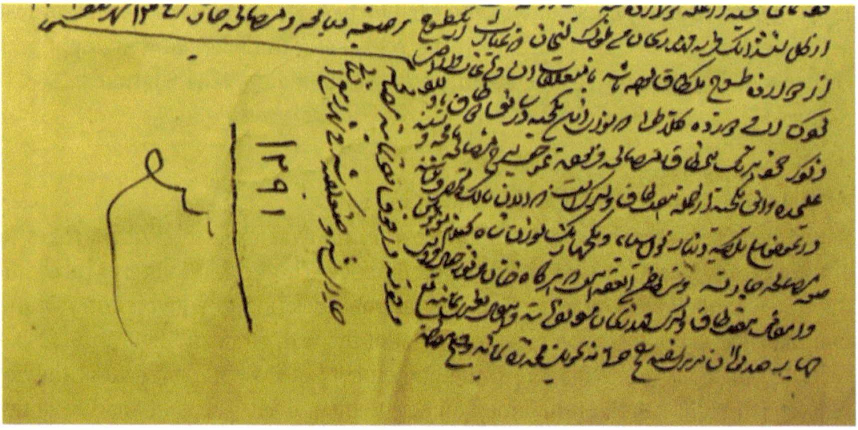

Figure 57: S2: 509, entry no. 3. © MS no. 67032/692, NLAI, Tehran.

Another remark in the form of a cipher that is found in the registers is *bayāḍ shud* or *bayḍa shud*, shortened to *bayḍa*. This clause, meaning left blank, is often encountered in Persian documents to signal the end of the text of the document and to prevent any further additions in blank spaces (Figure 57).

2.6.10 The Use of *Siyāq* in the Entries

The Persian shorthand *siyāq* accounting script is routinely used by the scribes of the registers to write words and record figures. In some cases, there are large blocks of *siyāq* text embedded in the middle of the entries.[57] The fourth entry in S1: 470, for example, records an acknowledgement of debt dated 13 Dhū l-Ḥijja 1285/27 March 1869, which Sangalajī validated the following day on the night of 14 Dhū l-Ḥijja 1285/28 March 1869 (Figure 58). Luṭf ʿAlī, son of the deceased Riḍā Bēg Zand, resident of the village of Malik-ābād, located in Fashawiyya (one of the districts of Tehran), acknowledged that he had four months from 13 Dhū l-Ḥijja 1285/27 March 1869 to deliver 25 *kharwār* and 45 *mann* (according to the measure of Tabriz) of wheat without defect and acceptable to a baker (*bī-ayb-i khabbāz pasand*) and 10 *kharwār* of barley to the associates of Khān Bībī Khānum, daughter of Ẓahīr al-Dawla, in Tehran. Sangalajī's *sijill* appears in *naskh* at the top of the entry. The amount of the debt is recorded both in words in the text of the entry in

57 See for example S1: 460–461 which records the *waqf* deed of Mīrzā Yūsuf Mustawfī al-Mamālik dated Ramaḍān 1284/December 1867–Jaunary 1868 judicially certified by Sangalajī on 18 Dhū l-Qaʿda 1284/12 March 1868.

shikasta-nastaʿlīq and under the two *dafʿa* headings in *siyāq* between the second and third line of the main text of the entry. We have therefore a combination of three scripts: *naskh*, *shikasta-nastaʿlīq* and *siyāq*.

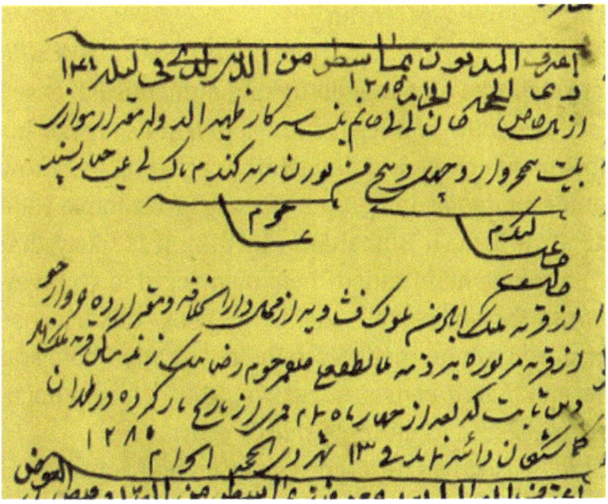

Figure 58: S1: 470, entry no. 4. © MS no. 67032/692, NLAI, Tehran.

Conclusion

The *sharīʿa* courts of Qajar Iran followed different registration and archival procedures. The Tammāmī *shaykh al-islām* court registered legal deeds on small pieces of paper known as *fard*, thus creating a "*fard*-archive". Sangalajī's use of registers resulted in a "register-archive" made up of bound codex registers. The use of *fard* can be traced to the fiscal administration Safavid of Iran and probably even earlier. What unites the Tammāmī Shiraz *fard* papers and Sangalajī's registers from Tehran is their recourse to the Persian shorthand accounting script known as *siyāq*, used to write both numerals and words. In Sangalajī's case, we have seen for example the use of *dafʿa* horizontal lines and the number nine for cancelling entries, features which are well known from *siyāq* manuals. There was in this technical sense an overlap between the administrative world of the *mustawfiyān*, the accountants responsible for producing and archiving documents relating to the income and expenditure of the state, and the scribal world of the *muḥarrirān*, the scribes responsible for producing and archiving *sharīʿa* court documents.

The use of *siyāq* notwithstanding, in the decentralised post-Safavid period, each *sharīʿa* court had its own set of scribal (script, layout, ciphers), linguistic (formulae), material (paper or cloth), sealing and archival practice (registers, *fard*, originals, copies). It is possible, therefore, to identify different *sharīʿa* courts. There were not only regional differences or urban rural distinctions, but also differences within a given locality, such as the difference between the practices of Sangalaji and other judicially active jurists in Tehran.

As we have seen from our analysis above, a document with Sangalajī's *sijill* was unmistakable. In turn, Sangalajī was able to identify and authenticate, based on their unique formal aspects, the *sijill*s and legal rulings (*ḥukm-i sharʿ*) of his contemporaries. From the documents copied in Sangalajī's registers, we know that he worked closely with other *mujtahid*s in Tehran, such as for example Ḥājjī Mullā ʿAlī Kanī (d. 1888) and Sayyid Ismāʿīl Bihbahānī (d. 1878). It is likely that each of these Tehran-based *mujtahid*s maintained their own register-archives, just like Sangalajī, which have so far not come to light. We know this because original legal deeds from Tehran contain on their verso the registration note and seals of the registrars of different *sharīʿa* courts, suggesting that a single document was often simultaneously registered in multiple *sharīʿa* courts.

In Bihbahānī's case, he initially used two different seals. The first was used to seal his *sijill* on the recto of legal documents, and the second was affixed on the verso precisely where his *sijill* appeared on the recto. It is not clear if he had already begun to maintain a register at this stage. Later, however, we notice an additional seal on the verso of documents where his *sijill* and seal appeared on the recto. This is the seal of his registrar, a certain Muḥammad Ḥasan Tihrānī. Unlike the registrars employed by Sangalajī, Muḥammad Ḥasan did not write a separate remark like *thabt shud* (it was registered). Instead, the inscription on his seal indicated that the document had been registered: *muḥammad ḥasan thabt namūda* (Muḥammad Ḥasan registered it).[58] Though details such as the use of different types of seals by a single cleric or the way in which a registration note was written by his registrar may appear minor, they were crucial for identifying the authenticity of documents.

In addition, we know from other surviving *sharīʿa* court registers in Tehran that the registration practice of *sharīʿa* courts was by no means identical. In Tehran, we are faced with an informal corpus of registers maintained by private *mujtahid*s. Each of these exhibit their own recording idiosyncrasies and are thus different from the more standardized *qāḍī* court registers (*sijillāt al-maḥākim al-sharʿiyya*) of Ottoman towns. The logic of the entries in the only other *sharīʿa* court register that has been examined so far from Tehran, the register of Shaykh

58 See Riḍāʾī 1386 sh./2007, 44–55.

Faḍlullāh Nūrī, shows differences from Sangalajī's registers.[59] When Nūrī, for example, records the copy of a deed he authenticated, he does not specify how many *sijill*s and seals the original deed contained as Sangalajī does. Moreover, Nūrī does not reproduce the text of his own *sijill* on original deeds or copies he validated. He simply notes that the document contained his *sijill* and seal. For example, at the end of an entry recording the summary of a conditional sale dated 27 Dhū l-Qaʿda 1304/17 August 1887, Nūrī notes "*muhr wa sijill dārad bi īn ʿalāmat: ḥ-y-b-l-b k-f-kh-g-ḍ-ʿ-dh*" (it contains a seal and a *sijill* with these signs: *ḥ-y-b-l-b k-f-kh-g-ḍ-ʿ-dh*).[60] Based on our comparison with actual documents, it is clear that what Nūrī actually means here is that the deed contained *his* seal and *sijill*. The registered entry, however, did not copy the text of his *sijill* on the document, but only recorded the coded letters of his *sijill* in each case.

As more original documents, copies, and their registered entries are compared from Tehran during the nineteenth and early twentieth centuries, we will begin to understand how such decentralised *sharīʿa* courts relied on each other to authenticate, ratify, annul, register, and issue copies of different types of legal documents. In other words, we can conceive of a system of interdependent local register-archives which could be consulted in cases of dispute. Since there was no uniform record-keeping practice, however, it is likely that some of these register-archives had a far more ad hoc approach to archival practice compared to the scrupulous attention to detail of Sangalajī's *sharīʿa* court. In addition, it should be noted that Sangalajī's registers are among the few known examples of such registers that recorded not only transactions but also legal rulings. As we have seen, Sangalajī registered not only all rulings he issued himself, but also those issued by others which he ratified or authenticated. In contrast, Nūrī does not record rulings. This could be because Sangalajī's registers date from a period when Sangalajī was a recognised *mujtahid*, capable of issuing rulings himself and ratifying the legal rulings of other scholars.[61] Sangalajī's registers shed light on how transactions and legal rulings were recorded together in a *sharīʿa* court register in Iran in the pre-modern period. In this sense, Sangalajī's registers are as unique as the "*fard* archive" of the Tammāmī *shaykh al-islām sharīʿa* court of Shiraz, which is the only known example so far of *sharīʿa* court transactions summarized on *fard* papers for archival purposes.

---

59 On the register of Shaykh Faḍlullāh Nūrī, which covers the period Rabīʿ II 1303–Dhū l-Qaʿda 1306/January 1886–July 1889, see Kondo 2017, 43–45. An edition of this register was published in 2006, see Ittiḥādiyya and Rūḥī 1385 sh./2006.

60 Ittiḥādiyya and Rūḥī 1385 sh./2006, 245.

61 Kondo 2017, 91.

Chapter 4
The Validity of the *Waqf* of Luṭf ʿAlī Khān Turshīzī

Introduction

The previous three chapters have focused on reconstructing who the *sharīʿa* practitioners of Iran were between the sixteenth to twentieth centuries and the scribal and archival practices of their *sharīʿa* courts. This chapter and the following two chapters reconstruct, based on surviving sources, endowment (*waqf*) disputes that took place in nineteenth and early twentieth century Iran. The objective is to understand how *sharīʿa* practitioners, in this case *mujtahid*s, intervened in actual disputes by issuing legal rulings (*ḥukm-i sharʿ*). In this chapter, I will investigate how multiple *mujtahid*s issued legal rulings in a long-drawn-out dispute relating to the endowment of a certain Luṭf ʿAlī Khān Turshīzī. I will begin by introducing the sources and the principal actors – the litigants and the *mujtahid*s they referred to. This will be followed by a reconstruction of litigation focusing on how legal rulings were obtained and used in practice by litigants. I will conclude this case study with a discussion on what the dispute reveals about the role of the Imāmī *mujtahid* as a *qāḍī* and *muftī* in Qajar Iran.

1 The Sources

The legal controversy over the validity of the endowment of Luṭf ʿAlī Khān Turshīzī (d.1215/1800–1) was a cause célèbre in early Qajar Iran. It brought into conflict two of the leading Imāmī *mujtahid*s active in Iran at the time: Mullā Aḥmad Narāqī (d.1245/1829) and Sayyid Muḥammad Bāqir Shaftī (d.1260/1844) (see Figure 57).[1]

Narāqī was convinced the endowment had not been properly constituted as a *waqf* and had been lawfully sold by Luṭf ʿAlī Khān's children to the royal physician of Fatḥ ʿAlī Shāh (r. 1797–1834). Shaftī, after initial doubt, became certain the endowment was valid and the sale had been illegal. The documentary sources which survive from the dispute are limited. A transcript of Luṭf ʿAlī Khān's *waqf*

1 For Shaftī's biography, see Tunikābūnī 1396 sh./1976, 135–151, Āshtiyānī 1325 sh./1946, 24–35 and Schneider 2002, 240–273. For Narāqī, see Tunikābūnī 1396 sh./1976, 139–142 and Khwānsārī 1987, 233–241.

https://doi.org/10.1515/9783111239736-005

Figure 59: A Qajar-era portrait of Sayyid Muḥammad Bāqir Shaftī (d.1260/1844).[2]

deed has survived.[3] The transcript also contains a legal ruling Shaftī issued in the dispute, judicially certifying the validity of the *waqf*.[4] Several other documents have only survived as copies reproduced in theoretical legal texts.[5] These texts were produced after a legal debate on the validity of the *waqf* that occurred between Shaftī and Narāqī. From Narāqī's side, the case has been preserved in his collection of question and answers on the *sharīʿa* (Per. *suʾāl wa jawāb*) compiled while he was still alive by one of his students, Muḥammad b. Muḥammad Yusūf

2 I have been unable to trace where the original portrait is preserved.

3 See Mihrābādī, III, 1336 sh./1957, 638–640.

4 See Mihrābādī, III, 1336 sh./1957, 638–641.

5 In the 1940s, Muḥīṭ Ṭabāṭabāʾī found several documents relating to litigation of the dispute in the library of the *imām-jumʿa* of Zavārih, see Ṭabāṭabāʾī 1354 sh./1975.

al-Mīma'ī al-Jūshqānī.[6] Jūshqānī has preserved details of the endowment dispute in the form of a long question (*su'āl*) that was written to Narāqī, along with Narāqī's answer (*jawāb*). The question includes not only a copy of Shaftī's legal ruling on the case, but also two early rulings issued by Mīrzā-yi Qummī (d.1231/1816) and Shaykh Muḥammad Ḥusayn Ḥā'irī Iṣfahānī (d. 1254/1838–39).[7] Mīrzā-yi Qummī, Shaftī, and Narāqī were the most significant *mujtahids* active in Iran during this period. Shaykh Muḥammad Ḥusayn Ḥā'irī Iṣfahānī was destined to become one of the most prominent *mujtahid*s based in the shrine cities of Iraq, Najaf and Karbala, after the completion of his work on the principles of jurisprudence, *al-Fuṣūl al-gharwiyya fī l-uṣūl al-fiqhiyya*, which he completed in Najaf in 1232/1817. He is often referred to by the name Ṣāḥib Fuṣūl.

From Shaftī's side the case has been preserved in the detailed theoretical treatise he wrote to defend his ruling.[8] The treatise contains a copy of the request for an opinion (*istiftā'*) that was written to Shaftī asking him for his ruling, the ruling he issued at the time, and the rebuttal (*raddiyya*) that Narāqī wrote in response. The main component of the treatise, however, consists of Shaftī's refutation of Narāqī's *raddiyya*.

Besides the rulings and the theoretical writings produced by Shaftī and Narāqī, there is also a brief account of the dispute by one of the main litigants involved: the poet, Mīrzā Muḥammad 'Alī Ṭabāṭabā'ī (d.1248/1832), known as Vafā. Vafā's account appears in an autobiographical entry in the *Tadhkira-yi Ma'āthir al-Bāqiriyya*, a biographical dictionary of poets that he composed between 1242–1247/1826–1831.[9] In addition to Vafā's narrative, some of Vafā's invective poetry (*hajw*) against his opponents in the dispute has also survived.[10]

6 The *nisba* al-Mīma'ī al-Jūshqānī suggests he came from the village of Jūshqān-Mīma near Kāshān, generally referred to as Jūshqān-Qālī after its finely woven carpets, see the entry 'Jūshqān' in Dihkhudā (URL: https://www.parsi.wiki/fa/wiki/207425/جوشقان, Accessed 1 May 2023). These types of *su'āl wa-jawāb* collections are comparable to *fatwā* compilations in the Sunnī world. Narāqī's collection of *su'āl wa-jawāb* survives in two volumes, see Ṭabāṭabā'ī 1354 sh./1975, 15–22. An edition based on five manuscripts was recently published, see Ustādī 1380 sh./2001, 357–371.

7 For Mīrzā-yi Qummī's biography, see Tunikābūnī 1372 sh./1994, 51–54; Khwānsārī 1987, 125–127.

8 The treatise entitled *Risāla fī 'adam luzūm al-qabḍ idhā ja'ala al-wāqif al-tawliya li-nafsihi* has been published based on a manuscript in a private collection, see Shaftī 1379 sh./2001.

9 Zavārihī 1385 sh./2007, for the autobiographical entry see: 296–314. For a discussion of the dates of composition of the text, see Humā'ī 1327 sh./1948, 138.

10 Much of Vafā's invective poetry against his opponents has survived in the collection of poems (*dīwān*) of Yaghmā Jandaqī, his close friend and fellow poet, see Ṭabāṭabā'ī, 1344 sh./ 1965, 182–184.

In what follows, I will use the surviving sources to reconstruct litigation in the dispute, focusing on how rulings were obtained and used by the parties involved.

2 Historical Reconstruction

In approximately the year 1215/1800–1, Luṭf ʿAlī Khān, a native of Turshīz in Khurāsān, inherited a large amount of land in the region of Zavārih, a small town in Isfahan province.[11] Luṭf ʿAlī Khān decided to build a school (*madrasa*) for the poor Ṭabāṭabāʾī *sayyids* (descendants of the Prophet) living in Zavārih to whom he was related maternally.[12] Once the construction work had begun, Luṭf ʿAlī Khān had an endowment (*waqf*) deed drawn up constituting all the lands he had inherited as an endowment for the *madrasa.*[13] Luṭf ʿAlī Khān appointed himself the first administrator (*mutawallī*) of the endowment, and designated, a leading member of the local *ʿulamāʾ* of Zavārih: Mullā ʿAbd al-ʿAẓīm Bīdgulī Kāshānī, to take over as administrator after his death. In the same year, 1215/1800–1, Luṭf ʿAlī Khān died. Soon after his death, Luṭf ʿAlī Khān's children sold all the lands their father had constituted as *waqf* to the shah's physician (*ḥakīm-bāshī*), Mīr Sayyid Ḥusayn Ṭabīb, who had ancestral ties to Zavārih and its region. In theory, the sale of Luṭf ʿAlī Khān's lands to the royal physician was illegal, because *waqf* land was inalienable and could not be sold. The earliest surviving ruling issued in the case suggests that the loophole invoked by the parties to justify the sale was that Luṭf ʿAlī Khān's endowment had failed to meet one of the conditions required to constitute a valid *waqf* according to Imāmī law: the transfer of possession of endowed property (*al-qabḍ wa-l-iqbāḍ*).

---

11 Turshīz, modern–day Kāshmar, is situated around two hundred kilometres southwest of Mashhad. Luṭf ʿAlī Khān belonged to the Arab ʿĀmirī tribe. According to the Mihrābādī, Luṭf ʿAlī Khān was returning to Turshīz after a pilgrimage to Karbala and had stopped en route in Zavārih, where a section of the ʿĀmirī tribe was settled. During Luṭf ʿAlī Khān's stay in Zavārih, his brother–in–law Muḥammad Ḥusayn Khān ʿĀmirī was assassinated. Luṭf ʿAlī Khān inherited a large area of land belonging to Muḥammad Ḥusayn Khān in the region. It is these lands that included the fields (*mazraʿa*) of Ḥasanābād, Mazdābād (Hurmuzābād) and Shahrāb, which Luṭf ʿAlī Khān constituted as *waqf* for his madrasa, see Mihrābādī, III, 1336 sh./1957, 638–639.

12 Zavārihī 1385 sh./2007, 305: *"bi-sabab-i nisbat–i ummī ki bā sādāt–i balada–yi mazbūra dāsht"*.

13 For the text of the *waqf* deed, see Mihrābādī, III, 1336 sh./1957, 638–640. Muḥammad Naṣīr al-Ḥusaynī, the *shaykh al – islām* of Turshīz wrote the authentication clause (*sijill*) on the validity of the *waqf* onto the deed. This suggests the deed was probably drawn up in Turshīz, not Zavārih. The *waqf* deed is dated simply with the year 1215/1800–1801.

2.1 A Legal Loophole? The Transfer of Possession of Endowed Property

Muslim jurists agree that there are four requirements to constitute a valid (*ṣaḥīḥ*) *waqf*: (1) a founder (*al-wāqif*); (2) the property to be made *waqf* (*al-mawqūf*); (3) the beneficiaries (*al-mawqūf ʿalayh*) and (4) the declaration or act of founding (*ʿaqd*). Imāmī jurists and some Sunnī jurists add a fifth requirement: (5) the *waqf* can only become binding and irrevocable (*lāzim*) after the property to be made *waqf* is transferred (*iqbāḍ*) by the founder to the possession (*qabḍ*) of the administrator (*mutawallī*) or to the beneficiaries.[14]

Luṭf ʿAlī Khān's children maintained that although Luṭf ʿAlī Khān's *waqf* had met the first four requirements, it had failed to meet the fifth one. This was because when Luṭf ʿAlī Khān had declared his intention to constitute the *waqf* and appoint himself as the *mutawallī*, the lands to be made *waqf* were not in his possession (*qabḍ*) but had been leased out to someone else on a rental contract.[15] Since Luṭf ʿAlī Khān had died before the rental contract ended, a transfer of possession of *waqf* property to the *mutawallī*, in this case to the founder, had, strictly speaking, not taken place. The *waqf* was therefore invalid, and the lands belonged to his children as their inheritance.

2.2 Conflicting Legal Rulings

2.2.1 The Ruling of Mīrzā-yi Qummī

The earliest known legal ruling in support of the claims being made by Luṭf ʿAlī Khān's children and the royal physician was issued by Mīrzā-yi Qummī (d.1231/1816). The text of Mīrzā-yi Qummī's ruling has been preserved by Narāqī's student, Jūshqānī.[16] Jūshqānī's recording of Mīrzā-yi Qummī's ruling is interesting. Jūshqānī is careful to mark the beginning and end of the verbatim quote of the text of the ruling. He also demonstrates that he is aware that the *mujtahid* here was acting as a *muftī*, issuing a ruling on a hypothetical situation that had been presented to him, and that he was not judicially certifying a a claim like a *qaḍī*. As we shall see, Jūshqānī nevertheless experienced some anxiety regarding the binding force of such

14 R. Peters et al."Wakf", *EI*², IX, 59. The Persian term *qabḍ wa-iqbāḍ* (Arabic: *al-qabḍ wa-l-iqbāḍ*) translates literally as 'possession and transfer'; *iqbāḍ wa-qabḍ*, 'transfer and possession' is also used interchangeably. In early Imāmī Shīʿī legal texts the term *qabḍ* is used alone with *iqbāḍ* being implied. For the views of Imāmī jurists on the requirement of *qabḍ*, see Kondo 2003, 115–116; Tawīsrkānī 1379 sh./2000), 25–33 and Tawīsrkānī 1376 sh./1998, 25–33.

15 Document no. 2.

16 Document no. 1b.

rulings issued as opinions in a case. In fact, Jūshqānī uses the dispute over Luṭf ʿAlī Khān's endowment to put his own question to his teacher Narāqī on the binding force of such rulings.

Mīrzā-yi Qummī's ruling gives us no clues regarding the context in which it was issued. Based on the use of expressions such as *har-gāh* (whenever), *dar mā naḥnu fīhi* (in the hypothetical situation we are in) and *mafrūḍ* (it is supposed), there can be little doubt that the ruling was issued in the question-and-answer format and that the question had presented the facts of the case hypothetically without specifiying names and places.[17] From the evidence of the reply, the question must have been about the validity of a *waqf* constituted from leased land. Mīrzā-yi Qummī confirmed that the *waqf* of leased land was invalid unless it could be established that the administrator or the beneficiaries had taken possession (*qabḍ*) of the land to be endowed from the lessee.[18] Since the administrator had died before this could happen in the hypothetical situation described to him, the endowment was invalid.

2.2.2 The Ruling of Ṣāḥib Fuṣūl

The first real challenge to the sale that had taken place between Luṭf ʿAlī Khān's children and the royal physician came in the form of a ruling issued by the prominent jurist Shaykh Muḥammad Ḥusayn Ḥāʾirī Iṣfahānī better known as Ṣāḥib Fuṣūl (d. 1254/1838–39). It is not clear if the ruling was issued by Ṣāḥib Fuṣūl during the period when he was in Isfahan or while he was living in the shrine cities of Iraq. Like the ruling issued by Mīrzā-yi Qummī, Ṣāḥib Fuṣūl's ruling uses expressions such as *dar ṣūrat-i mafrūḍa* (in this hypothetical situation), which suggests that the question that was submitted to him also presented the facts of the case hypothetically.[19] According to Ṣāhib Fuṣūl, a rental lease was no obstacle to land being endowed as *waqf.* However, the lands could not be removed from the possession of the lessee during the rental period.[20] Ṣāḥib Fuṣūl argued that when leased land

17 Document no. 1b.

18 Document no. 1b: "*magar bi-īn nahw ki mawqūf ʿalayh yā mutawallī qabḍ bi-idhn-i mustaʾjir qabḍ kunad . . . wa binā bar ʿadam-i fawriyyat-i qabḍ hargāh baʿd az inqiḍāʾ-i muddat-i ijāra bi-qabḍ-i mawqūf ʿalayh yā mutawallī qabḍ bi-dahad khūb ast*". This could happen according to Mīrzā-yi Qummī if the administrator or the beneficiaries took possession of the lands with permission of the lessee during the rental period, but it was better if they took possession after the expiry of the rental contact since *qabḍ* did not have to occur immediately (*fawriyat*) upon the constitution of the *waqf.*

19 Document no. 1c.

20 Document no. 1c: "*amlāk-i mawqūfa-rā az yad-i mustaʾjir qabl az inqiḍāʾ-i muddat-i ijāra intizāʿ namī-tavān kard*".

was made into *waqf*, transfer of possession (*qabḍ*) to the administrator or the beneficiaries could be inferred from other signs. Ṣāḥib Fuṣūl then proceeded to give four instances in the case which he felt suggested that some form of *qabḍ* had occurred.

The four instances cited in Ṣāḥib Fuṣūl's reply are as follows: (1) the permission (*idhn*) of the founder to the lessee to spend rental income from the lands on the madrasa; (2) the ability of the second administrator (*mutawallī*) to renew the lease of the lands after the death of the founder; (3) the use of rental income from the lands to pay the expenses of the *waqf*, and (4) the endorsement of the *waqf* status of the lands by the descendants of the founder.[21] As we shall see, Ṣāḥib Fuṣūl's argument that some form of *qabḍ* had occurred was considered weak. For most jurists, the fact that the founder as the first administrator had not taken possession of the land as *waqf* before he died was compelling evidence that no *qabḍ* had occurred in the case. The permission of the founder to the lessee to disburse rental income from the lands on the expenses of the madrasa was not considered a form of *qabḍ*. The lease had been made out on lands that were private property. The rental income therefore could not be considered *waqf* revenues or a sign that the the stipulations of the *waqf* deed were being acted upon.

2.2.3 The Poet Vafā Becomes a Claimant

Though we do not know who asked Ṣāḥib Fuṣūl for his ruling on the endowment, it is quite likely that he was consulted by Vafā, a young poet of Zavārih. Vafā was studying medicine in Isfahan when he heard about the attempt by Luṭf ʿAlī Khān's children to sell their father's lands and thus deprive their maternal cousins, the Ṭabāṭabāʾī sayyids, of a school in Zavārih. If Vafā was behind the ruling issued by Ṣāḥib Fuṣūl, then his efforts came to nothing. Mīr Sayyid Ḥusayn Ṭabīb, the royal physician, was an influential man with connections in Zavārih. He could count on the support of the new administrator's own son, Ḥājjī Mullā Muḥammad ʿAlī, but also Mīrzā ʿAbd al-Bāqī Shīrāzī, the local governor and tax collector of Ardistān (*nāʾib al-ḥukūma wa mustawfī-yi ardistān*). In the face of such powerful enemies, the poet could only hurl invective at them.[22]

21 Document no. 1c: "*imḍā-yi waratha–yi wāqif waqfiyyat–rā*". The last reason might possibly be a reference to the signatures on the *waqf* deed. There is at least one non–*ʿulamāʾ* attestation which could have belonged to a descendant of Luṭf ʿAlī Khān, see the attestation of Muṣṭafā Qulī Khān: Mihrābādī, III, 1336 sh./1957, 640–641.

22 Muḥīṭ Ṭabāṭabāʾī 1344 sh./ 1965, 182–4; Mīrzā ʿAbd al-Bāqī, for instance, was ridiculed as follows: "*tā zadī ṭabl-i ʿarr u nīz ʿamal / shud bi-khar khalq-i mardumiyyat badal / bugusastī zi mardumān u shudī / mutaffiq bā ṭabīb-i duzd-i daghal / ān ṭabībī ki az qawāʾid-i ṭibb farq nakarda sanda az ṣandal / ān ḥusaynī ki juz ghūr-i yazīdash / natawānam zadan bi hīch mathal*" (When you began to imitate a donkey, you turned into one, / you left the human race when you became an

Ṣāḥib Fuṣūl's ruling made no difference to the *status quo* in Zavārih. Luṭf ʿAlī Khān's lands remained firmly in the hands of the royal physician. Work on the construction of Luṭf ʿAlī Khān's madrasa had ground permenantly to a halt. It seemed that Vafā's opponents had won – they had outfoxed him. Then suddenly – almost miraculously – one of the most powerful jurists in Isfahan, possibly in Iran, Sayyid Muḥammad Bāqir Shaftī (d.1260/1844), decided to support Vafā's cause.

2.2.4 The Question to Sayyid Muḥammad Bāqir Shaftī

Shaftī's involvement in the case first came when he was solicited – probably by Vafā – for a ruling on the validity of the endowment. Initially, Shaftī ruled against the validity of the *waqf*. Not long afterwards, we do not know precisely when, Shaftī changed his mind and issued a new ruling – this time in support of the validity of the endowment. Defending his decision to issue a new ruling in the case, Shaftī explained that he had not given the matter enough thought the first time:

> . . . when a group of believers asked me for my view after considerable reflection on the problem, I issued an opinion (*aftaytuhu bi-dhālika*) to that effect [that the endowment was valid]. This was after I had initially replied without proper study that it [the endowment] was invalid due to *qabḍ wa-iqbāḍ* not having occurred . . . .[23]

Though the original question submitted to Shaftī and his initial answer or ruling have not survived – the document was perhaps destroyed by a disappointed Vafā – the question used to obtain the new ruling has been preserved.[24] The question is a good example of how the specific details of a case were omitted using expressions such as 'a certain person' (*shakhṣī*) and 'certain lands' (*baʿḍī amlāk*) when the ruling sought was a legal opinion on the case. Like in the question to Ṣāḥib Fuṣūl, the question to Shaftī also provides some evidence that *qabḍ* has occurred. The lessee had been authorized by the founder to use rental income from the lands for the expenses of the *madrasa* and its construction, and the lessee had

accomplice of that thief, the doctor, / a physician for whom herbs and excrement are the same, / a Ḥusaynī *sayyid* who is like Yazīd!).

23 Shaftī 1379 sh./2001, 64–65: "*wa lidhā lammā istaftā minnī baʿḍu ahli l-īmānī aftaytuhu bi-dhālika, baʿda t-taʾmmuli fī l-masʾalati wa-aṭrāfihā, baʿda mā ajabtuhu fī awwali l-amrī min ghayri tadqīqi n-naẓarī fīhā bi l-fasādi li-ʿadami taḥaqquqi l-qabḍi wa-l-iqbāḍi, thumma lammā taʾammaltu l-masʾalata wa-mustanada l-qabḍi wa-l-iqbāḍi tabayyana lī anna l-ḥaqqa khilāfu dhālika [fa]-katabtu fī maqāmi l-jawābi bi ṣ-ṣiḥḥati wa-l-luzūm*".

24 Document no. 2.

spent the money as he was instructed.[25] The facts as presented in the question, however, hinge on the fact that when the endowment was constituted, (1) the founder had intended it to be used for a specific purpose (*ṣīgha-yi waqf-i ān amlāk rā bi-īn jihat-i makhṣūṣa jārī namūd*) and (2) that he had appointed himself the administrator during his lifetime (*tawliyat-i waqf ra mā-dāma ḥayātuhu bi-jihat-i nafs-i khud qarār dād*).[26] It is precisely these two conditions that were going to form the basis of Shaftī's new ruling (see below).

The presentation of the facts of the case in the question ends by asking whether the lands were *waqf* and following the stipulations of the *waqf* deed binding or private property belonging to the heirs of the founder as their inheritance, given that *qabḍ* had not taken place (*naẓar bi ʿadam-i taḥaqquq-i iqbāḍ wa qabḍ*).[27] This last conditional clause is important because it anticipates Shaftī's reply. Shaftī was going to argue that absence of *qabḍ* occurring in this case did not affect the validity of the *waqf*.

2.2.5 Shaftī's New Ruling

Shaftī's new ruling declared the endowment to be valid.[28] Shaftī did not argue, however, as Ṣāḥib Fuṣūl had done, that the *waqf* was valid because some form of *qabḍ* had taken place. Instead, Shaftī turned the case in a completely new direction. According to Shaftī, *qabḍ* was not required in the case. The endowment was valid despite the fact that there had been no transfer of possession of the land to be endowed to the administrator or beneficiaries.

The reason for this, according to Shaftī, was that the endowment had been founded for a specific purpose, and the founder had appointed himself administrator during his lifetime. This was, as we have seen, already mentioned in the presentation of the facts of the case in the question. According to Shafī, the validity of a *waqf* that was constituted in this way was not contingent upon *qabḍ* taking place. In support of his new ruling, Shaftī cited the following evidence from the Qurʾān and the reports attributed to the infallible Twelver Shīʿī Imāms:

1. Qurʾān 5:1[29]
2. The authentic report of Muḥammad b. al-Ḥasan al-Ṣaffār[30]
3. The authentic report of Muḥammad b. Muslim[31]

---

25 Document no. 2.
26 Document no. 2.
27 Document no. 2.
28 Document no. 1d.
29 Document no. 1d.
30 Document no. 1d.
31 Document no. 1d.

The way the evidence is presented in the ruling suggests that Shaftī was aware that the text he was producing was going to be read by other *mujtahids*. He therefore took steps to give his ruling enough authority from the sources to make it look credible. It is doubtful whether the average reader would have understood the code-like references to the Qurʾānic verses and traditions Shaftī cited in support of his ruling. For instance, Shaftī simply quotes the Qurʾānic verse 5:1 by its opening words: *awfū bi l-ʿuqūd.* The reports are quoted in abbreviated form, mentioning the narrator, the collection where they were recorded, and the relevant section, for instance: the 'the authentic report (*ṣaḥiḥā*) of Muḥammad b. Muslim from Abū Jaʿfar (the fifth Imām al-Bāqir, d. 732), peace be upon him, narrated (*al-marwiyya*) in *al-Kāfī* and *al-Tahdhīb*.[32] If there was any doubt that these references were not intended for the uninitiated, the text suddenly switches to Arabic and then back into Persian. The way such legal rulings issued as an answer to a question can be contrasted with legal rulings issued as judicial certifications of a claim. The language used in a legal ruling judicially certifying a claim was always as clear and explicit as possible because it was meant to be read and understood by the political authorities responsible for its enforcement.

2.2.6 The Question to Mullā Aḥmad Narāqī

Shaftī's intuition that his new ruling would not go unanswered was correct. Soon after it was issued, his ruling found its way to Kāshān. Shaftī explains what happened as follows:

> This is the *jawāb* (answer) I wrote to this *istiftā*ʾ (request for a legal opinion) a short while ago. I have been informed that this *jawāb* was taken to some scholars (*ʿulamā*ʾ) in Kāshān, but it did not please them and provoked a rebuttal (*radd*)[33]

The "scholars in Kāshān" Shaftī was referring to was in fact one man: Mullā Aḥmad Narāqī. It is likely that it was Vafā's opponents who had taken Shaftī's ruling to Narāqī. They must have sensed that Shaftī's new ruling on the case was dangerous. Though Shaftī's ruling was only issued as a legal opinion on the facts of the case, Vafā could easily rewrite the same question, but this time specify Luṭf ʿAlī Khān's name and the name and location of the lands involved. The ruling Shaftī would now potentially issue to the same question would constitute a judicial certification of the *waqf* claim, which Vafā could use to try and repossess the

32 On Imāmī Shīʿī *ḥadīth* literature see for example Kohlberg 2014 and Rajani 2021.
33 Shaftī 1379 sh./2001, 67: *"īn jawābī ast ki muddatī qabl dar jawāb-i istiftāʾ qalamī shuda dar īn waqt madhkūr shud ki īn jawāb dar dār al-muʾminīn-i kāshān bi baʿḍī az ʿulamāʾ risida marḍī-i īshān nashuda,ʿinān-i qalām dar maydān-i radd-i īn jilva dād".*

lands. Mīrzā-yi Qummī's opinion on the case was less significant now that Shaftī had demonstrated that the *waqf* in this case was valid even without *qabḍ* having occurred.

This was probably what prompted Vafā's opponents to go to Kāshān to ask Narāqī for his opinion on Shaftī's new ruling. Narāqī was perhaps the only *mujtahid* left in Iran who could silence Shaftī. It was a dangerous gamble. Narāqī could, after all, end up endorsing Shaftī's view. It was a risk, however, that Vafā's enemies appeared willing to take and, at least in the short term, it seems to have paid off. We do not know precisely how Narāqī was consulted by Vafā's opponents. It is possible that a question was drafted and Narāqī was provided with copies of the rulings that had been issued by Mīrzā-yi Qummī, Ṣāḥib Fuṣūl, and Shaftī. Narāqī's student, Jūshqānī, copied the earlier rulings into a long question (*su'āl*) that was addressed to Narāqī along with Narāqī's reply (*jawāb*).[34] The question (*su'āl*) to Narāqī contains the following:

a. The facts of the case and the request for Narāqī's view
b. The ruling of Mīrzā-yi Qummī
c. The ruling of Ṣāḥib Fuṣūl
d. The new ruling of Shaftī
e. Jūshqānī's additional question to Narāqī on the case

The answer (*jawāb*) is made up of:

f. Narāqī's rebuttal (*raddiyya*) of Shaftī's new ruling
g. Narāqī's answer to Jūshqānī's additional question

As Shaftī quotes Narāqī's rebuttal in full in the detailed theoretical defense he wrote in 1233/1818 against it, it would seem that Narāqī's rebuttal had already been written before this date. What is not clear, however, is if the remaining elements of the question to Narāqī and his answer were also written at the same time or rather compiled later from disparate documents by Jūshqānī. According to the question (*su'āl*) as it is recorded by Jūshqānī, it was not Vafā's opponents, but the local scholars responsible for validating and annulling contracts of the region (*arbāb-i ʿaqd wa ḥall-i wilāyat*) that approached Narāqī for his view.[35] This could be perfectly true. Vafā's opponents may have used intermediaries. The *su'āl* also presents Narāqī in the role of an arbiter asked to decide between the legal opinions of 'the jurists of the age' (*mujtahidān-i zamān*): Mīrzā-yi Qummī, Ṣāḥib

34 Document no. 1a-g.

35 Document no. 1a: *"chigūnagī-rā bi ʿard-i sāmī risānīda ṣūrat-i baʿḍī fatāwī-rā ki ṣādir shuda nīz bi – naẓar-i sāmī bi-risānand wa ān-chi ra'y-i sharīf dar ān bāb bar ān gardīd bi-ān ʿamal namūda raf-i nizāʿ namāyand".*

Fuṣūl, and Shaftī. This might be how the case had been presented to Narāqī, but it could also be a later interpolation by Jūshqānī. Similarly, the *su'āl* does not present the case hypothetically to Narāqī, like in the question to Shaftī. It specifies the name of the founder, Luṭf ʿAlī Khān, the location of the lands, and the new administrator, Mullā ʿAbd al-ʿAzīm Bīdgulī. It is possible that Vafā's opponents or their intermediaries risked specifying such details in their question because they knew in advance what to expect from Narāqī, or alternatively, that these details were added by Jushqānī later to a new version of the question.

Jūshqānī's own additional question in the case uses the rulings of Mīrzā-yi Qummī, Ṣāḥib Fuṣūl, and Shaftī quoted verbatim to ask Narāqī about the problems *mujtahid*s caused for their non-*mujtahid* followers (*muqallidīn*) when they issued conflicting rulings. Jūshqānī's question is already anticipated in the beginning of the *su'āl*, when Jūshqānī notes that the scholars of the region came to Narāqī because the contradictory rulings issued by the *mujtahid*s of the age were causing increasing strife and conflict (*mansha'-i izdiyād-i tanāzuʿ wa tashājur*). From the preceding discussion it seems likely that Jūshqānī created a new question-and-answer text at a later stage based on the original rulings and rebuttals in the case. In so doing, he was able to preserve both Narāqī's view on the case as well as on a problem that the case itself had brought up – the conflicting rulings of *mujtahid*s.

2.2.7 Narāqī's Rebuttal of Shaftī's New Ruling

According to Narāqī, the arguments presented by Shaftī in his new ruling lacked any basis in the law (*bī-wajh*) and were in fact irregular (*gharīb*).[36] According to Narāqī, Shaftī's suggestion that there was no evidence to suggest that *qabḍ* was a universal requirement for constituting a valid *waqf* was not true. As evidence that *qabḍ* was a universal requirement, Narāqī cited:

1. The transmitted consensus of opinion of Imāmī jurists on the requirement of *qabḍ*[37]
2. A rescript (*tawqīʿ*) of the Twelfth Imām[38]
3. An argument from logic[39]

---

36 Shaftī 1379 sh./2001, 69:"*ān-chi muftī [Shaftī] dar bayān-i ʿadam-i ishṭirāṭ [-i qabḍ] bayān namūda bī-wajh ast, balkah bisyār gharīb ast*" "What the *muftī* [Shaftī] has expressed on the non-requirement [of *qabḍ*] is without basis but also very strange indeed."
37 Ustādī 1380 sh./2001, 225–230.
38 Ustādī 1380 sh./2001, 225–230.
39 Ustādī 1380 sh./2001, 225–230.

Narāqī also rejected Shaftī's use of Qur'ān 5:1 and the reports of al-Ṣaffār and Muslim to argue that *qabḍ* was not required in the specific circumstances of the case at hand. As far as Narāqī was concerned, the report of al-Ṣaffār had nothing to do with the issue of *qabḍ*, while the report of Muslim quoted by Shaftī was compelling proof that *qabḍ* was in fact a requirement in the case. The text of Narāqī's rebuttal also included several additional arguments from what Narāqī calls the *ghayr-i manqūlāt*, that is, evidence not based directly on the transmitted texts (the Qur'ān and the sayings of the Imāms) or on the transmitted consensus of Imāmī jurists.

2.2.8 Shaftī's Theoretical Defense of his New Ruling

Not long after Narāqī's *raddiyya* was written, it reached Shaftī in Isfahan. Narāqī's attack prompted Shaftī to write a detailed theoretical defense of his ruling. According to Shaftī, Narāqī's arguments were even more baseless than his own (*bisyār bī-wajh*) and disgraceful (*bī-waqʿ*).[40] The treatise which Shaftī wrote to defend his new ruling and respond to Narāqī's *raddiyya* was completed in Ramaḍān 1233/July 1818. Shaftī seems to have been aware right from the beginning that he was not going to stand much chance trying to prove that *qabḍ* had somehow occurred in the case. Not surprisingly he makes no attempt, as Ṣāḥib Fuṣūl had done, to prove it had. Instead, the focus of the first part of Shaftī's rebuttal was to prove that neither the transmitted texts (*al-nuṣūṣ*) nor the transmitted consensus of Imāmī jurists (*al-ijmāʿ al-manqūla*) on the requirement of *qabḍ* covered the circumstances of the case at hand. It was necessary, therefore, to do as he had done and exercise deductive effort (*ijtihād*), to come up with a new ruling from the sources of the law.

Shaftī felt that when the consensus of Imāmī jurists had been formed, it had never considered a situation where the founder had appointed himself administrator during his lifetime and the lands were not in his possession, or what Shaftī called *fī mā naḥnu fīhi* ('the hypothetical situation we are in'). The same was true as far as the transmitted texts were concerned. The traditions were related almost without exception to *waqf*s being constituted for the benefit of family members, and never for a specific public purpose like building a madrasa. Based on this, Shaftī argued that unless it could be proven that the requirement of *qabḍ* mentioned in the texts and the consensus did in fact cover the circumstances of the

---

40 Shaftī 1379 sh./2001, 69: "*bar har kas ki fī l-jumla rabṭ dar mabāḥith-i fiqh wa mabānī-yi ān dāshta bāshad, ẓāhir ast ki jamīʿ-i ānchi madhkūr shuda bisyār bī-wajh wa bī-waqʿ ast*" "To anyone with a grounding in jurisprudence and its rules, it will become evident that everything that has been mentioned [in Narāqī's rebuttal] is completely without basis and highly contemptible."

case, or what Shaftī called *wa-law fī mā naḥnu fīhi* ('even in the hypothetical situation we are in'), it was necessary to infer a new ruling from the sources. This did not mean, Shaftī argued, that he did not accept that *qabḍ* was a universal requirement to constitute a valid and irrevocable *waqf*. Shaftī felt Narāqī had misunderstood him. According to Shaftī, the very opening lines of his ruling were loud and clear (*yunādī bi andā ṣawtin*) that he was specifying a situation where *qabḍ* was not required, but that he was not disputing the requirement itself.[41] Instead, what he was trying to argue was that Narāqī's insistence on clinging (*tamassuk*) to the requirement of *qabḍ* mentioned in the texts and the consensus was useless in this particular case. This section is followed by Shaftī's rebuttal of Narāqī's rebuttal of his use of Qur'ān 5:1 and the sayings of al-Ṣaffār and Muslim. Shaftī also refutes Narāqī's use of a rescript (*tawqīʿ*) attributed to the Twelfth Imam and Narāqī's argument from logic. The final section of the rebuttal deals with Narāqī's arguments from the *ghayr-i manqūlāt*. It did not take long for Narāqī to respond to Shaftī's rebuttal. Narāqī asked his brother, Abū al-Qāsim b. Muḥammad Mahdī Narāqī (d.1265/1849), to write a rebuttal on his behalf refuting Shaftī's treatise. It was given the title *Mulakhkhaṣ al-maqāl fī dafʿ al-qīl wa-l-qāl* (A brief discourse in refutation of tittle-tattle).[42]

2.2.9 Jūshqānī's Additional Question and Narāqī's Answer

Before returning to the story of the dispute, we will examine Jūshqānī's additional question on the case and Narāqī's answer to it.[43] Jūshqānī's question is written in the form of a request for a clarification of a doubt (*shubha-ī*) he had about the case of Luṭf ʿAlī Khān's endowment. It sheds light on how legal opinions issued by *mujtahids* were perceived in early Qajar Iran.

Jūshqānī begins his question by mentioning the Imāmī Uṣūlī doctrine of emulation (*taqlīd*), according to which it was obligatory for all believers who were not *mujtahids* themselves (also known as *muqallids*) to follow the rulings of a *mujtahid*

---

41 This is not strictly speaking true. Shaftī does mention in his ruling that there was no evidence to suggest that *qabḍ* was a universal requirement. It is precisely this section which Narāqī meant to refute by citing the consensus of Imāmī jurists, the rescript from the Twelfth Imām, and the same traditions of al-Ṣaffār and Muslim that had been used by Shaftī, see document no. 1d.

42 MS. no. 3136, Kitāb-khāna-yi ʿĀyatullāh Marʿashī Najafī, Qum. I have not examined the contents of this manuscript. There appears to be another rebuttal by a different author, Sayyid Abū Ṭālib b. Abū Turāb Ḥusaynī Qāʾinī (d.1293/1876–7), entitled *Ṣafwat al-Maqāl*. The contents appear to be identical to *Mulakhkhaṣ al-Maqāl*. The text was completed on 3 Jamādī II 1282/24 October 1865 and the manuscript in Kitāb-khāna-yi ʿĀyatullāh Marʿashī was copied on 14 Muḥarram 1287/16 April 1870. See MS no.3132, Kitāb-khāna-yi ʿĀyatullāh Marʿashī Najafī, Qum.

43 See document no. 1e and document no. 1g.

on points of law.[44] The ruling of the *mujtahid* would be equivalent for them to the ruling of God. Jūsqhānī then notes that in the case at hand, the descendants of Luṭf ʿAlī Khān were the *muqallids* of Mīrzā-yi Qummī.[45] The administrator and those who wanted to revive the *madrasa* were the *muqallids* of Shaftī. Mīrzā-yi Qummī issued a ruling saying the endowment was invalid. Shaftī's ruling said it was valid. Based on the Uṣūlī doctrine of *taqlīd*, it was binding for both sides to do as their *mujtahids* had ruled; however, since the rulings of the two *mujtahids* were contradictory in the case, disputes had arisen.[46] Since the ruling of the *mujtahid* for his *muqallid* was equivalent to the ruling of God (*ḥukmullāh*), Jūshqānī now asked anxiously: How it was possible that in this case the rulings of God could cause so much strife and sedition?[47]

In his answer, Narāqī begins by explaining that rulings (*ḥukms*) were of two types: actual (*wāqiʿī*) rulings and apparent (*ẓāhirī*) rulings. The rulings which God had decreed were actual rulings, but their meanings were only known by the Prophet and the infallible Imāms. During the period of occultation (*dar zamān-i sadd-i bāb al-ʿilm*), access to God's actual rulings was no longer possible. Actual rulings could not be accessed merely through use of the intellect; they required the presence of the Prophet or the infallible Imāms. Access to God's apparent rulings was still possible, however, through the intellectual efforts of the *mujtahid*. Narāqī now proceeds to recapitulate the Imāmī Uṣūlī doctrine of *taqlīd*, of which he was a leading exponent in Qajar Iran.

Narāqī then explained that in problems or questions (*masāʾil*) which related exclusively to the non-*mujtahid* believer (*muqallid*) and where there was no dispute involved (*ki mutaʿlliq bi khud-i ū ast wa bas wa munāzaʿī az barāy-i ū nīst*), the *muqallid* was bound (*mukallaf*) to follow the opinion (*fatwā*) of whichever *mujtahid* he was emulating.[48] The opinion (*fatwā*) of the *mujtahid* would be equivalent to God's apparent ruling for the *muqallid*. In problems which came up between two or more people and involved an argument (*takhāṣum*) or a dispute (*tanāzuʿ*), however, the mere emulation (*taqlīd*) of the opinion (*fatwā*) of a *mujtahid* did not suffice.[49] Instead, to determine what God's apparent ruling was required judicial proceedings before a *mujtahid* (*muḥtāj bi-tarāfuʿ dar khidmat-i mujtahid*).[50] The ruling the *mujtahid* issued after such judicial proceedings would

44 Document no. 1e.
45 Document no. 1e.
46 Document no. 1e.
47 Document no. 1e.
48 Document no. 1g.
49 Document no. 1g.
50 Document no. 1g.

now be considered God's apparent ruling in the case and would be binding (*lāzim al-ittibāʿ*) upon the claimant and defendant to follow.[51]

After citing an example to illustrate what he meant, Narāqī concludes his reply by adding that only those rulings which a *mujtahid* issued that related to the specific details of a case (*ḥukm dar khuṣūṣ-i wāqiʿa*) were binding. This was not the case for rulings issued as an answer to a request for a legal opinion on the case (*na īn ki bi mujarrad-i istiftāʾ bāshad*).[52] None of the rulings that had been issued thus far in Luṭf ʿAlī Khān's case, that is, the ruling of Mīrzā-yi Qummī, the ruling of Ṣāḥib Fuṣūl, or the ruling of Shaftī, were thus binding. These rulings were merely issued as answers to a request for a legal opinion. They were not the outcome of judicial proceedings before a *mujtahid* on the specific details of the case.

Narāqī's clarification was necessary due to the Uṣūlī doctrine of *taqlīd*. For the masses, who were non-*mujtahid* followers (*muqallids*), all the rulings their *mujtahid* issued were perceived as binding. Jūshqānī expresses the view of the masses when he says the supporters (*muʿāwinīn*) of the descendants of Luṭf ʿAlī Khān, presumably also *muqallids* of Mīrzā-yi Qummī, felt that their actions were motivated by a sense of religious duty and piety (*bar birr wa taqwā*). By frustrating Vafā's attempts to revive the *waqf*, they felt they were upholding Mīrzā-yi Qummī's ruling. The fact that Mīrzā-yi Qummī had not issued the ruling as the outcome of judicial proceedings or even the fact that the text was merely hypothetical and had no specific details mentioning the name of the endowment, the lands, the claimant, or the founder, made no difference. Everyone knew Mīrzā-yi Qummī was referring to Luṭf ʿAlī Khān's endowment, and that was all that mattered. The ruling he issued was in their eyes equivalent to the verdict of God, and, as the *muqallids* of Mīrzā-yi Qummī, they were bound to follow it.

In the Sunnī context, the term *fatwā* was used to distinguish the *muftī*'s non-binding legal opinion in litigation from the *qāḍī*'s binding judicial decision (*ḥukm*) in a case. In Qajar Iran, the term *fatwā* was rarely used. Instead, irrespective of whether the jurist acted as a *muftī* or a *qāḍī*, his ruling was referred to as a *ḥukm-i sharʿ*. This significant Qajar shift in nomenclature explains why Narāqī had to draw distinctions in the binding force of rulings *mujtahids* issued as legal opinions on a case versus their judicial certification of a claim. In practice, unless there was some sort of challenge, however, such distinctions were rarely drawn. In some cases, they were even strategically obscured, as we shall see in the case study examined in the following chapter.

51 Document no. 1g.
52 Document no. 1g.

It is quite likely that ordinary litigants like Luṭf ʿAlī Khān's children were able to use Mīrzā-yi Qummī's ruling to validate the sale of Luṭf ʿAlī Khān's vast lands in Zavārih. There were limits, however, to the probative force of a legal opinion. A legal opinion might work as a legal permit if you were already in possession of the disputed object. If, however you were not in possession of it, the probative force of a legal opinion was significantly reduced. To confiscate a disputed object in practice still required a ruling which judicially certified a claim. The more specific the text of the ruling judicially certifying the claim, the better; otherwise, it could be construed as being a legal opinion, and its binding force could be challenged. Litigants seem to have understood this, because several years after Shaftī's legal opinion on the validity of Luṭf ʿAlī Khān's endowment, Shaftī issued an explicit ruling judicially certifying the claim of *waqf*.

2.2.10 Shaftī's Ruling Judicially Certifying the *Waqf* Claim and its Enforcement

Seven years after Shaftī wrote his theoretical defense against Narāqī's rebuttal, he issued a new legal ruling in the case.[53] The ruling was issued on 19 Rajab 1240/ 9 March 1825. This ruling was not a legal opinion which discussed the facts of the case hypothetically. The ruling explicitly declared that all the lands which belonged to the deceased Luṭf ʿAlī Khān were *waqf* and that Luṭf ʿAlī Khān's heirs had no right to these lands. The sale they had concluded with the royal physician was therefore illegal. Those in possession of the lands had to surrender them with immediate effect and hand control of them over to the administrator of the endowment. The judicial ruling also made it obligatory for those in possession of the lands to pay the administrator the arrears of more than twenty years' worth of rental income from the lands.

It is not clear why it took seven years after the defense of his legal opinion for Shaftī to issue a ruling judicially certifying the *waqf* claim. It is possible that Shaftī had issued similar rulings between 1233–1240/1818–1825 that have not survived. Alternatively, it could be that Narāqī's rebuttal had been powerful enough to stop him from issuing a ruling which judicially certified the *waqf* claim.

If so, we are forced to admit that the strategy of Vafā's opponents in taking the case to Kāshān before Narāqī had been at least partly successful. Moreover, it means that what Narāqī had issued was not a mere theoretical rebuttal intended for jurists and their students, but it had some impact on actual litigation. Jūshqānī clearly felt that what Narāqī had been asked to write would decide between the rulings issued by Mīrzā-yi Qummī, Ṣāḥib Fuṣūl, and Shaftī. Jūshqānī does not term the text Narāqī had been asked to write a rebuttal. Instead, he uses the

53 Document no. 3.

terms ruling (*ḥukm-i sharʿī*) and exalted opinion (*raʾy-i sharīf*).[54] According to Jūshqānī, whatever Narāqī wrote would be enforced (*ʿamal namūda*) in order to settle the dispute (*raf-i nizāʿ*).[55] This suggests that not only were legal opinions perceived to have some probative force, but that they could also take the form of a relatively long rebuttal.

The probative force of Narāqī's rebuttal must also have derived from the fact that it made it clear which claim Narāqī would judicially certify if asked to do so. In this way, his theoretical rebuttal functioned as a warning to Vafā. Any attempt by Vafa to seek a judicial ruling on the case from Shaftī would result in a similar action from his opponents before Narāqī. Vafā's opponents had thus managed to re-validate their claim to the lands after the death of Mīrzā-yi Qummī by referring to Narāqī. Tunikābūnī has an interesting anecdote where he notes that an impasse – he may even be referring to this very case – had once occurred between Narāqī and Shaftī in a particularly troublesome litigation. In the end, Narāqī and Shaftī wrote their theoretical views on the case, which were presented before a third jurist in Iraq who endorsed Narāqī's view.[56] It is likely that something similar was going on between 1818–1825 in the dispute over Luṭf ʿAlī Khān's endowment and that an Imāmī juristic consensus had emerged in favour of Narāqī's view.

In such a situation, Shaftī might have preferred to wait until he was certain that any further ruling he issued in the case had the political support necessary to remove the disputed lands from the possession of royal physician and circumvent the legal obstacle created by Narāqī's rebuttal. The appointment in 1240/1825 of Fatḥ ʿAlī Shāh's fifteen-year-old son Sayf al-Dawla (1224–1299/1809–1882) to the post of governor of Isfahan seems to have created just such an opportunity. The

54 Document no. 1e; Jūshqānī asks Narāqī to clarify his doubt after first issuing the 'requested *ḥukm-i sharʿī*' (*ḥukm-i sharʿī-yi maqṣūd*) on the case. The use of '*ḥukm-i sharʿī*' here is an early nineteenth century example of the use of this term.

55 Document no. 1a.

56 Tunikābūnī 1396 sh./1976, 54: "*dar baʿḍī az awqāt mīyān-i īshān [Narāqī] wa marḥūm ḥujjat al-islām [Shaftī] munāzaʿa shud dar murāfaʿa-ī pas dāwarī bi-ānjā kishīd ki ṭarafayn tafṣīl-i madrak-i khiyāl-i khud-rā niwisht dar khidmat-i marḥūm āqā sayyid muḥammad khalaf-i marḥūm āqā sayyid ʿalī firistādand ān marḥūm sukhan-i mullā aḥmad [Narāqī] rā tarjīḥ dāda*" (At some point there was a dispute between him [Narāqī] and the Ḥujjat al-Islām [Shaftī] in a litigation, the judging of the case was so troublesome that the two sides wrote details of what they thought appropriate and sent it to Sayyid Muḥammad son of Sayyid ʿAlī. Sayyid Muḥammad preferred Narāqī's view). Sayyid Muḥammad Ṭabāṭabāʾī (d.1242/1827) also known as Mujāhid was the son of Sayyid ʿAlī Ṭabāṭabāʾī (d.1231/1816). Sayyid ʿAlī was a leading student of the leading Uṣūlī jurist Muḥammad Bāqir Bihbahānī.

young Sayf al-Dalwa quickly came under Shaftī's tutelage.[57] Shaftī's rulings from this period onwards were exceedingly powerful. It is likely that Shaftī now felt assured that a ruling he issued on the case of Luṭf ʿAlī Khān's endowment could no longer be stopped. The theoretical defense Shaftī had written of his own ruling must have also helped to diminish the probative force of Narāqī's *raddiyya* and add weight to his own ruling. In the very same year of Sayf al-Dawla's appointment, 1240/1825, Shaftī issued a ruling which judicially certified the *waqf* claim. This ruling was not issued on a separate document but transcribed directly onto the *waqf* deed of Luṭf ʿAlī Khān Turshīzī.

Initially, Shaftī appears to have ordered the new administrator of the endowment, Mullā ʿAbd al-ʿAẓīm Bīdgulī, to recover the lands from the royal physician.[58] According to Vafā, Bīdgulī felt it was beneath his dignity to get involved in the restitution process.[59] This probably also had to do with the fact that Bīdgulī's son was implicated in the sale. Once it had become established that Bīdgulī, his former teacher, had no intention of pursuing the matter, Vafā says he had no choice but to act himself.

When Vafā initially emerged as a claimant, he had managed to convince Shaftī and a few other *mujtahid*s to appoint him to the post of supervisor (*nāẓir*) of Luṭf ʿAlī Khān's endowment.[60] How Vafā did this is not clear. It is likely that he exploited the fact that he was related maternally to Luṭf ʿAlī Khān, as indeed all the Ṭabaṭabāʾī *sayyid*s of Zavārih were. Vafā must have also demonstrated that the new administrator, Bīdgulī, had not done enough to stop the sale of the lands. Vafā's appointment to the post of supervisor was significant because his right to act on behalf of the endowment could not be challenged.

2.2.11 Intrigues of the Opposition

Almost as soon as Shaftī's ruling judicially certifying the claim of *waqf* was issued, Vafā's troubles began. Vafā describes this period of litigation in vivid detail in his autobiographical account. Vafā's enemies realized that without Shaftī's support, Vafā did not stand a chance. The only way to defeat Vafā was to estrange him from Shaftī. Vafā's enemies informed Shaftī that Vafā had recited obscene verses about him in Zavārih.[61] Almost exactly at the same time, another plot was hatched.

57 For Shaftī's relations with Sayf al-Dawlā, see Masjidī, 1381sh/2003, 67–90.
58 Zavārihī 1385 sh./2007, 306.
59 Zavārihī 1385 sh./2007, 306.
60 Zavārihī 1385 sh./2007, 306.
61 Zavārihī 1385 sh./2007, 307.

Aware of Shaftī's hatred for *ṣūfīs*, letters stating that Vafā was a *ṣūfī* began to circulate.[62] Shaftī recived one of these letters and was furious.[63] It was decided that an example would be made out of Vafā. Vafā would be brought in chains to the courthouse (*dār al-qaḍāʾ*), and the *ḥudūd* - the penalties prescribed by the *sharīʿa* - would be imposed on him as a warning to other *ṣūfīs*.[64] In fright, Vafā escaped to his hometown, Zavārih.[65]

Vafā's opponents, though, had not finished with him. They arranged for an official to go to Zavārih to find witnesses who had heard the scandalous verses.[66] The witnesses would be brought to Isfahan and the obscene poetry would be read to Shaftī so he could judge for himself.[67] Luckily for Vafā, the plot failed. When asked to recite the offending verses, the main witnesses, Bīdgulī's son and his associates, could only come up with:

> Behind Simnān is Dāmghān!
> The river of Gurgān lies in between!
> On the far side is Turkmenistan!
> Sugar is from Māzandarān![68]

The verses were fabricated nonsense. They could hardly be construed as invective against Shaftī.[69] Vafā, referring to the verses, quotes the great medieval skeptic and freethinker, Ibn al-Rawandī (d.c.339/950), condemned as a heretic:

> This is what troubled minds
> and turned a skilled artist into an atheist.[70]

---

62 Zavārihī 1385 sh./2007, 308.
63 Zavārihī 1385 sh./2007, 308.
64 Zavārihī 1385 sh./2007, 308. Vafā's reference to the *dār al-qaḍāʾ* here is quite possibly a reference to Shaftī's own private *sharīʿa* court where he lived in the Bīdābād quarter of Isfahan. Shaftī, quite unsually for jurists of the time, maintained a band of young toughs (*lūṭīs*) who implemented the *ḥudūd*.
65 Zavārihī 1385 sh./2007, 308.
66 Zavārihī 1385 sh./2007, 309.
67 Zavārihī 1385 sh./2007, 309. Vafā mentions the following Arabic verse in his description of that difficult time: *matā yanjalī l-laylī dh-dhunūnī l-kawādhibu / wa-yabdū ṣ-ṣabāḥa ṣ-ṣidqī min kulli jānibu* (When will the night of deception and lies end and the morning of truth begin?).
68 Zavārihī 1385 sh./2007, 309: *"pusht-i simnān dāmghān ast ay khudā / rūd-i gurgān dar mīyān ast ay khudā/ ān ṭaraf tar turkamān ast āy khudā / shikar az māzandarān ast ay khudā".*
69 According to Masjidī, the verses might possibly be interpreted as a critique of Shaftī's family. Muḥīṭ, however, thinks that the verses were simply written by Vafā in his account to represent the type of absurdities his opponents had come up with. They were not the actual verses that were read to Shaftī. See Zavārihī 1385 sh./2007, 27; Ṭabāṭabāʾī 1344 sh./ 1965), 182–183.
70 Zavārihī 1385 sh./2007, 309: *"hādha l-lladhī tarka l-awhāmu hāʾiratan wa-ṣayyara l-ʿālima n-naḥrīri zindīqan".*

Vafā's innocence was established. It took him longer to clear the charge of Ṣūfism, however. Vafā did this in part by composing poems in praise of Shaftī and the impressive Sayyid Mosque, which Shaftī was building at great personal expense in the Bīdābād quarter of Isfahan.[71] Vafā also began to collect poems other poets had sung in praise of Shaftī or the Sayyid Mosque.[72] These poems were later assembled in a biographical dictionary which Vafā dedicated to Shaftī, entitled *Tadhkira-yi Ma'āthir al-Bāqiriyya.*[73] As Vafā's ties with Shaftī improved, Vafā came into contact with the young governor of Isfahan: Sayf al-Dawla. Sayf al-Dawla, an aspiring poet, was not averse to learning a thing or two from a sharp wit like Vafā. Vafā includes a long poem in praise of Sayf al-Dawla at the end of the *Tadhkira-yi Ma'āthir al – Bāqiriyya.*[74] With help from Sayf al-Dawla's officials, Vafā was able to get Shaftī's *waqf* ruling enforced. More than twenty years after Luṭf ʿAlī Khān Turshīzī's death, his *waqf* lands were returned to the control of the administrator, and his madrasa was revived in Zavārih.[75]

Conclusion

The dispute over the validity of Luṭf ʿAlī Khān Turshīzī's endowment involved some of the most prominent *mujtahid*s of Iran and the shrine cities of Iraq. Mīrzā-yi Qummī, Ṣāḥib Fuṣūl, Shaftī, and Narāqī were not just locally recognised *mujtahid*s involved in petty litigation in a town quarter. They were eminent Imāmī Uṣūlī professors who spent most of their time training students to become *mujtahid*s. Given their perceived legal knowledge, their ruling was generally sought almost as soon as a case involved a complicated theoretical problem. This was done by writing a question and requesting an answer. The facts of the case at hand were presented hypothetically in the question without reference to specific names and places. We do not know who wrote the question that was submitted to these jurists. It is likely it was written by the leading students of Mīrzā-yi Qummī, Ṣāḥib Fuṣūl, Shaftī, and Narāqī. The student writer of the question clearly had a

71 Zavārihī 1385 sh./2007, 310.

72 Zavārihī 1385 sh./2007, 59.

73 The autobiographical entry which appears at the end of the *Tadhkira* was written in 1242/1826. It is quite likely Vafā had already begun to gather material for the *Tadhkira* before this date, see Humā'ī, 1327sh/1948, 138.

74 Zavārihī 1385 sh./2007, 312–314.

75 Several disputes broke out after Vafā's death over the *waqf* between Vafā's children and the sons of the administrator Mullā ʿAbd al-ʿAzim Bīdgulī, for a summary see: Ṭabāṭabā'ī 1354 sh./1975, 15–17.

good grasp of the rulings of his Uṣūlī professor respondent.[76] In this way he was well placed to give legal advice to the litigant that had come to seek the ruling. The way the question was drafted seems to have anticipated its answer. In this sense it functioned as a legal vest for a conclusion that had already been reached through some form of informal legal discussion, probably between the student writer of the question and the litigant. In this case we have two surviving recensions of the question. One recension that has come down to us is recorded by Jūshqānī, Narāqī's student, and the other is preserved in Shaftī's theoretical defense of his ruling. We do not, however, possess the original documents containing the question-and-answer rulings issued in the case.

According to Jūshqānī, the litigants referred to Mīrzā-yi Qummī, Ṣāḥib Fuṣūl, Shaftī or Narāqī because they were followers (*muqallids*) of these *mujtahids*. This seems unlikely, given the fact that in each case, the litigants happened to be *muqallids* of precisely those *mujtahids* whose rulings suited their interests. There seems, instead, to have been prior reconnaissance by the litigants to determine precisely which *mujtahid* was likely to support their case. This reconnaissance did not always work. Shaftī's initial legal ruling on the case, which has not survived, seems to have been of no use to the party that requested it and was revoked by Shaftī. Given the charismatic authority of the *mujtahids* involved in the dispute over Luṭf ʿAlī Khān's endowment, the rulings they had issued, even though mere legal opinions, were perceived to have probative or binding force. The respective rulings of Mīrzā-yi Qummī and Narāqī in the case helped the royal physician hold on to Luṭf ʿAlī Khān's lands for over twenty years. There were limits, however, to this perceived binding force. A legal opinion, even from a *mujtahid* like Shaftī, was insufficient to confiscate the disputed lands and revive the *waqf*. This explains why Shaftī ultimately issued a legal ruling which judicially certified the *waqf* claim. This ruling was not written in the question-and-answer style, but in the "deed" style. It is not known if the ruling was issued as a separate document. The only surviving recension has come down to us as it was recorded directly onto Luṭf ʿAlī Khān's *waqf* deed.

Remarkably, for almost twenty years before the issuance of this judicial ruling, which specified the places involved and the names of the individuals related to the case, the dispute over Luṭf ʿAlī Khān's endowment seems to have been fought using rulings that were theoretical legal opinions. Both parties, as we have seen, consulted eminent Imāmī Uṣūlī *mujtahids* for their opinion on the theoretical problem

---

76 See Kondo 2009, 72. The student of the Uṣūlī professor was supposed to be fully conversant with his teacher's rulings and method such that he was able to come up with the same ruling as his professor in a case.

of *qabḍ* which was crucial to their respective claims. Neither side seemed willing to submit to judicial proceedings such as arbitration by a *mujtahid* or to negotiate an amicable settlement. Instead, each side tried to validate or invalidate the legal opinion the other side had obtained. This in turn forced the *mujtahids* involved to defend their view. In some cases, as we have seen, their legal rulings turned into lengthy academic rebuttals issued in the form of a separate treatise.

In the absence of a clear state-enforced separation in this period of the jurisdiction of *qāḍī* and *muftī*, a *mujtahid* like Shaftī could issue a legal opinion on the case and at the same time issue a judicial certification of a claim. This increased the probative force of the legal opinion considerably, because Shaftī's legal opinion directly anticipated his judicial certification of the claim of one side in the case. Confusingly, both texts, legal opinions and judicial certifications of claims are simply termed *ḥukm-i sharʿ* in Qajar sources, though they were not equal in terms of their probative force. The term *fatwā* is encountered far less frequently in reference to legal opinions, unlike in the Hanafi Ottoman or Central Asian context. The term *istiftāʾ* was sometimes used to refer to the question when the facts were presented hypothetically.

The text of Shaftī's ruling judicially certifying the claim of *waqf* does not describe prior litigation in the dispute or record the claim of the claimant and the reply of the defendant. There is also no mention in the text of the ruling that the evidence of the defendant was reviewed. This is important because, as we shall see in the next chapter, a ruling issued as a judicial certification of a claim that was not the outcome of proceedings (1) before a scholar both sides recognised as a *mujtahid*, and (2) where the evidence of both sides was reviewed, could not bring closure to a dispute.

In this case, however, Shaftī's own influence in Isfahan and the support of the officers of Sayf al-Dawla meant his judicial certification of the claim of *waqf* was sufficient to remove the lands from the possession of the royal physician and to revive the *waqf*. Narāqī's opinion and the theoretical rebuttal he wrote may have helped to act as a legal obstacle for some time. In practice, however, only a valid counter judicial certification of the claim issued by a recognised jurist could prevent the restitution of lands and force, as we shall see in the next chapter, an unwilling side to submit to arbitration or a negotiated settlement.

Chapter 5
Resolving a Land Dispute in Astarābād

Introduction

The previous chapter examined the nature and function of the Imāmī *mujtahid*'s legal ruling (*ḥukm-i sharʿ*) issued as an opinion in an endowment dispute in Qajar Iran. We saw, for example, how a ruling from a powerful *mujtahid* could be used as a legal permit to sell valuable *waqf* land. At the same time, we noted that there were limits to the binding force of rulings issued as an opinion. Even if such a ruling was issued by a leading *mujtahid*, in practice, to remove disputed land from the possession of the defendant required a ruling that judicially certified a legal claim to ownership. Under the influence of the dominant Imāmī Uṣūlī doctrine of *taqlīd*, the emulation of the *mujtahid* by the non-*mujtahid* believer, ordinary people tended to view any ruling issued by a *mujtahid* as binding. The *mujtahids* and their students, on the other hand, were quite aware of the difference between a ruling issued as a non-binding opinion and a ruling issued as a binding judicial certification of a claim in a dispute.

In this chapter we will examine the procedural problems surrounding legal rulings issued by scholars in Qajar Iran as a judicial certification of a claim in an endowment dispute involving two villages in the countryside of Astarābād (present day Gurgān) called Chūplānī and Mīr-Maḥalla.[1] The lands belonging to Chūplānī and Mīr-Maḥalla were used to cultivate husked rice (*shaltūk*). The rice was cultivated in paddy fields irrigated by the Tarang River, which passed between the two villages. The villages enjoyed ancient rights to the waters of the Tarang River and neighboring streams which was supplied to the lands through a system of canals (*qanāts*). As water was essential for paddy cultivation, the villages were very valuable, but also the object of repeated conflict. During the reign of Fatḥ ʿAlī Shāh (r.1797–1834), a local group of Ḥusaynī *sayyids* (descendants of the Prophet through his grandson al-Ḥusayn) in Astarābād, known as the Dirāzgīsū ('long-haired'), claimed they were entitled to a share of the annual rice yield of Chūplānī and Mīr-Maḥalla. According to the sayyids, the two villages had originally been *waqf* land endowed by their ancestor Mīr Rūḥullāh al-Ḥusaynī in the Safavid period. Later, however, they had been usurped by the ruling Qajar khans of Astarābād. The Qajar khans, who ruled Astarābād and its region as provincial governors

1 Chūplānī and Mīr-Maḥalla are located thirty-seven kilometres northeast of Gurgān, capital of Golestān province, in north-central Iran.

https://doi.org/10.1515/9783111239736-006

(*bēglerbēgī*), rejected the *waqf* claim of the sayyids.[2] As far as they were concerned, the villages were not *waqf*, but rather private property which they had legally acquired. Initially, the sayyids tried to have their status as administrators and beneficiaries of the two endowed villages, Chūplānī and Mīr-Maḥalla, recognised. When this failed, they decided to contest the possession of the two villages by the Qajar khans.

Litigation by the sayyids came to focus on the legal rulings issued by two scholars: Āqā Muḥammad Mahdī Kalbāsī (d. 1278/1861–2) and Ḥājjī Mullā Riḍā Astarābādī (d.*c*.1251/1835). Both rulings judicially certified the *waqf* claim of the Dirāzgīsū sayyids.

Āqā Muḥammad Mahdī's ruling made it compulsory for the Qajar khans to recognise the rights of the Dirāzgīsū as beneficiaries or administrators of the *waqf* lands or to vacate possession. Ḥājjī Mullā Riḍā Astarābādī's ruling required the Qajar khans to return possession of the two villages and their lands (*radd-i amlāk*) to the Dirāzgīsū sayyids. The Qajar khans, who were responsible for enforcement as provincial governors of Astarābād and its region, refused to enforce these legal rulings. They claimed they did not recognise either Āqā Muḥammad Mahdī or Ḥājjī Mullā Riḍā Astarābādī as *mujtahid*s. The legal rulings they had issued in the case were therefore not valid. The use of this strategy demonstrates how significant the Imāmī Uṣūlī requirement of *ijtihād* had become in Qajar Iran in dispute resolution involving the evaluation of evidence by scholars according to *sharīʿa* norms.

In the face of this and other strategies by the Qajar khans to circumvent enforcement, the sayyids were forced to repeatedly ratify the binding force of the two legal rulings and certify the ability to carry out *ijtihād* of the scholars that issued them. It did not help that the Qajar khans had also been able to judicially certify their own claim to the ownership of the two villages. The Qajar khans possessed several legal rulings from some of the most powerful *mujtahid*s of Astarābād and the Caspian region, which confirmed their right to ownership of the lands as private property (*milk*). Nevertheless, the repeated attempts made by the Dirāzgīsū sayyids – over the course of thirty years – to ratify the binding force of the legal rulings of Āqā Muḥammad Mahdī and Ḥājjī Mullā Riḍā Astarābādī finally paid off. They were able to force the Qajar khans to agree to submit to arbitration over the lands twice and finally to accept a negotiated settlement over the village of Chūplānī. The Dirāzgīsū had less success with the more fertile village of Mīr-Maḥalla. The village remained in private hands well into the late Qajar period. In what follows, I first present the principal actors involved in the dispute.

2 For the use of the title *bēglerbēgī* in Iran, see P. Jackson, "Beglerbegī" *EIr*., IV, fasc.1, 84.

This is followed by a description of the surviving sources and a reconstruction of litigation based on these sources. I conclude the chapter with a discussion on the intervention of *mujtahid*s in judicially certifying legal claims in Qajar Iran.

1 Principal Actors: Dramatis Personae

1.1 The Claimants: Sayyid Faḍlullāh Astarābādī and the Dirāzgīsū Sayyids

The claimants listed in the earliest documents relating to the dispute are the two Dirāzgīsū sayyids, Mīr Mūsā and his brother Mīr Taqī. The driving force behind the claim of the Dirāzgīsū sayyids, however, was Mīr Mūsā's son, Sayyid Faḍlullāh Astarābādī. Sayyid Faḍlullāh was the prayer leader (*pīsh-namāz*) of the Friday Mosque of Astarābād.[3] He had spent time in Isfahan studying under the leading *mujtahid*, Sayyid Muḥammad Bāqir Shaftī (d.1260/1844), whom we encountered in the previous chapter.[4]

1.2 The Defendants: ʿAbbās Khān Qājār Bēglerbēgī and his Descendants

Sayyid Faḍlullāh's formidable opponent, the defendant in the dispute, was ʿAbbās Khān Qājār Bēglerbēgī, who reigned as governor of Astarābād from 1251–1255/1835–1839.[5] After ʿAbbās Khān's death, it was his descendants who would

3 Sutūda and Dhabīḥī 1354 sh./1975, VI: 142–143: "*āqā sayyid faḍlullāh astarābādī pīsh-namāz-i masjid-i jāmiʿ-i astarābād*".
4 Shaftī gave Sayyid Faḍlullāh a licence (*ijāza*) either to transmit Imāmī Shīʿī *ḥadith* or to practice *ijtihād*. I have not been able to trace the text of this *ijāza*. There are several manuscripts containing Shaftī's *ijāzāt*, see for instance MS no. 11548, *Majmūʿa-yi ijāzāt-i ḥujjat al-islām sayyid muḥmmad bāqir bi-ʿidda-ī az ʿulamāʾ*, Kitāb-khāna-yi Shūrā-yi Majlis, Tehran, for the list of *ʿulamāʾ* Shaftī awarded an *ijāza* to, including Sayyid Faḍlullāh al-Astarābādī, see the first folio. In a legal agreement (document no. 53) dated 1263/1847, Sayyid Faḍlullāh is referred to as a *mujtahid*.
5 The period for which the various governors of Astarābād were in power is based mainly on the Qajar chronicle of Muḥammad Ḥasan Khān Iʿtimād al-Saltana (1843–1896), *Tārīkh-i Muntaẓam–i Nāṣirī*, 1363–1367 sh./1984–1988, I-III, and on the administrative decrees published in Sutūda and Dhabīḥī, 1354 sh./1970, VI. When precisely ʿAbbās Khān Qājār assumed the governorship of Astarābād is not mentioned by Iʿtimād al-Saltana. A *farmān* from Muḥammad Shāh addressed to him and dated Rabīʿ II 1251/ August 1835 suggests he was already in control of local government by this date (see document 16). In the year 1252/1836, he is referred to as *bēglerbegī* of Astarābād and is ordering troops, see Iʿtimād al-Saltana 1363–1367 sh./1984–1988, III, 1636: "*bi mawjib-i amr-i aqdas-i ʿabbās khān qājār bēglerbēgī-yi astarābād*"; another *farmān* of Muḥammad Shāh addressed to him dated Rabīʿ II 1255/June 1839 (document no. 18) suggests he was still in power in Astarābād.

oppose the Dirāzgīsū. ʿAbbās Khān and his family belonged to the Qūyūnlū clan ('the flock keepers') of the Qājār tribe. ʿAbbās Khān was thus directly related to the royal family in Tehran. In Astarābād, another faction of the Qajar tribe, the Develū clan ('the camel-herders'), had long challenged the right of the Qūyūnlū to rule. The post of *bēglerbēgī* of Astarābād during this period often rotated between members of these two clans.[6] As we shall see, the Dirāzgīsū enjoyed brief possession of the two villages during the reign of ʿAbbās Khān's successor, Muḥammad Nāṣir Khān Develū (r.1256–1263/1840–1847).[7] Some leading Qūyūnlū Qājār khans also appear to have supported Sayyid Faḍlullāh's cause, but little is known about their involvement in the dispute.[8]

1.3 The Scholars (*ʿUlamāʾ*) of Isfahan

The first stage of litigation by the Dirāzgīsū depended almost entirely on Sayyid Faḍlullāh's close ties with the *ʿulamāʾ* of Isfahan. Sayyid Faḍlullāh initially involved Āqā Muḥammad Mahdī Kalbāsī (Karbāsī).[9] Āqā Muḥammad Mahdī, like Sayyid Faḍlullāh, was a student of Shaftī and had ended up marrying Shaftī's daughter.[10] When the Qajar khans refused to recognise Āqā Muḥammad Mahdī as a *mujtahid*, it was to Āqā Muḥammad Mahdī's father-in-law – Shaftī – that Sayyid Faḍlullāh turned. After Shaftī's death, Sayyid Faḍlullah and the Dirāzgīsū approached Āqā Muḥammad Mahdī's father, Ḥājjī Muḥammad Ibrāhīm Kalbāsī (d. 1261/1844–5), for a certification of his son's ability to carry out *ijtihād*. Like Shaftī, Kalbāsī was a leading *mujtahid* based in Isfahan.[11] In fact, his prestige was rivalled only by Shaftī. Shaftī, Kalbāsī, and Āqā Muḥammad Mahdī's brother, Shaykh Jaʿfar, were all destined to play a key role in the first stage of litigation.

6 See for instance Neyestani, "Gorgān, vii. From the Safavids to the End of the Pahlavi Era," *EIr.*, XI, fasc. 2, 154–162 and Hambly 1991, VI, 104–43.
7 Document no. 19; document no. 20.
8 An example is Mūsā Khān b. Mahdī Qulī Khān Qūyūnlū Qājār who is mentioned in document no. 14a and document no. 42.
9 Khwānsārī 1987, 89; for his involvement in a *waqf* dispute case in Tehran, see Kondo 2003, 119.
10 Khwānsārī 1987, 89.
11 Khwānsārī 1987, 83–89.

1.4 The *ʿUlamāʾ* of Astarābād

In addition to prominent *ʿulamāʾ* of Isfahan, Sayyid Faḍlullāh could count on the support of several *ʿulamāʾ* in Astarābād.[12] The following, for instance, were repeatedly called upon to judicially certify the claim of the Dirāzgīsū or authenticate their documents: Mullā ʿAbbās ʿAlī,[13] Mullā ʿIsā Kandābī, Mullā Ḥājjī Āqā Bābā,[14] Mullā Riḍā ʿAlī Chiyākandī, Mullā Isḥāq, and Mullā Aḥmad. Equally important for the Dirāzgīsū was an Astarābādī *mujtahid* living in Tehran: Sayyid Naṣrullāh al-Ḥusaynī.[15] The support of these Astarābādī *ʿulamāʾ* for the Dirāzgīsū never wavered. They were critical to any success that the sayyids eventually had. The most important supporter of the Dirāzgīsū claim, however, was also one of the oldest *mujtahid*s of Astarābād: Ḥājjī Mullā Riḍā Astarābādī.[16] Ḥājjī Mullā Riḍā Astarābādī had been a leading student of the chief Uṣūlī *mujtahid* in Iraq, Muḥammad Bāqir Bihbahānī.[17] He belonged to the first group of Bihbahānī's students who returned to Iran.

When Ḥājjī Mullā Riḍā returned to Astarābād from Iraq, he was recognised as a *mujtahid* and took an active part in the administration of justice according to the *sharīʿa* in the town.[18] In the 1790s, however, he appears to have fallen out with the Qajar khans of Astarābād after he issued a ruling making it compulsory for them to return Chūplānī and Mīr-Maḥalla to the Dirāzgīsū. This ruling was never enforced. Despite the strong support the Dirāzgīsū enjoyed in Astarābād, Tehran and Isfahan, there were several leading Astarābādī *ʿulamāʾ* who certified the counterclaim of the Qajar khans to the two villages. We know the names of three jurists who supported the Qajar khans, though there may have been more. The first was Sharīʿatmadār Ākhūnd Mullā Muḥammad ʿAlī Ashrafī (d.c.1264/

---

12 The single most important source for the biographies of the *ʿulamāʾ* of Qajar Astarābād to have come to light so far is the text *Sharḥ-i ḥāl-i ʿulamāʾ wa udabāʾ-i Astarābād*, completed in Rajab 1294/July 1877 by Muḥammad Ṣāliḥ b. Muḥammad Taqī b. Muḥammad Ismāʿīl Astarābādī. The text was edited and published by Masīḥ Dhabīḥī. See Dhabīḥī 1348 sh./1969, 91–103. Muḥammad Ṣāliḥ was the son of Mullā Muḥammad Taqī, one of the main jurists involved in the dispute. For Muḥammad Ṣāliḥ's autobiography, see Dhabīḥī 1348 sh./1969, 197–213.

13 Dhabīḥī 1348 sh./1969, 153–154.

14 Dhabīḥī 1348 sh./1969, 153.

15 Dhabīḥī 1348 sh./1969, 187.

16 Dhabīḥī 1348 sh./1969, 149–154. When Muḥammad Ṣāliḥ was writing his biographies of the *ʿulamāʾ* of Astarābād in 1877, a madrasa which Ḥājjī Mullā Riḍā Astarābādī had founded in Astarābād in the quarter of Naʿlbandān was not yet finished. Ḥājjī Mullā Riḍā Astarābādī endowed his library to this madrasa. The madrasa has been revived in Gurgān today and is known as the Madrasa-yi ʿIlmiyya–yi Raḍawiyya. Ḥājjī Mullā Riḍā Astarābādī's full name is given as Mullā Muḥammad Riḍā b. Muḥammad Ṣādiq Astarābādī.

17 Dhabīḥī 1348 sh./1969, 150.

18 Dhabīḥī 1348 sh./1969, 163.

1848). Sharīʿatmadār, as he is referred to in the sources, was the *imām-jumʿa* (prayer leader of the Friday Mosque) of Astarābād during the reign of Muḥammad Shāh (r.1834–1848).[19] When the Dirāzgīsū were finally able to force the Qajar khans to an arbitration, it was Sharīʿatmadār who was chosen to arbitrate the dispute. The second jurist who supported the Qajar khans was Mullā Muḥammad Taqī Astarābādī (d.1272/1855).[20] Mullā Muḥammad Taqī had spent most of his life outside Astarābād in Isfahan, Najaf, and Karbala, studying with leading Uṣūlī *mujtahids* from whom he received *ijāzas*.[21] He spent the last fourteen years of his life in Astarābād and appears to have held the post of *imām-jumʿa* for some time.[22] It is quite likely he was Sharīʿatmadār's successor to this post.

After Sharīʿatmādār, Mullā Muḥammad Taqī was asked to arbitrate in the land dispute between the Dirāzgīsū sayyids and the Qajar khans. The third jurist who supported the Qajar khans was Raʾīs al-ʿUlamāʾ (d.1284/1867).[23] It seems that Raʾīs had also been asked to act as arbiter but died before he could.[24] He made the fatal decision to accompany an expeditionary force that left Astarābād to fight a group of Yomut Turkmen.[25] At a fierce battle that took place at Āq Qalʿa,

19 Sutūda and Dhabīḥī 1354 sh./1975, VII, 248–249. The inscription (*sajʿ-i muhr*) of his oval seal was: *al-mutawakkil ʿalā allāh muḥammad ʿalī 1246/1830–1.*

20 Dhabīḥī 1348 sh./1969, 179–182. Muḥammad Ṣāliḥ mentions four clerics with the name Mullā Muḥammad Taqī in Astarābād: (1) his own father, Mullā Muḥammad Taqī b. Muḥammad Ismāʿīl, (2) Mullā Muḥammad Taqī al-Nawkandī (p.154), (3) Mullā Muḥammad Taqī, the brother of Ākhūnd Mullā Muḥammad Kāzim al-Astarābādī (p.165), and (4) Mullā Muḥammad Taqī who settled in Langrūd (p.194–195). The latter three appear to have been minor *ʿulamāʾ* in comparison with the author's father, Mullā Muḥammad Taqī b. Muḥammad Ismāʿīl. Since the case of the Dirāzgīsū and Qajar khans was adjudicated in each generation by individuals who have the longest biographical entries, it is likely the Mullā Muḥammad Taqī involved in this dispute was Muḥammad Ṣāliḥ's father. Like the other major jurists of Astarābād who were involved in the dispute, Mullā Muḥammad Taqī b. Muḥammad Ismāʿīl is also said to have presided over the administration of *sharīʿa* justice in Astarābād (*chahārdah sāl bar riyāsat-i sharʿiyya-yi astarābād awqāt gudharānīd*). He held the post of *imām-jumʿa* (*dar masjid-i jāmiʿ-i astarābād imāmat farmūd*), possibly after the death of Sharīʿatmadār Ashrafī. Regrettably, the inscription (*sajʿ-i muhr*) of the main ratification in the case issued by Mullā Muḥammad Taqī is illegible (document 4b). The inscription of the square seal on a later ratification which might have been issued by him is: *muḥammad al-taqī imāmī* [. . .] (document 5).

21 Dhabīḥī 1348 sh./1969, 180.

22 Dhabīḥī 1348 sh./1969, 181.

23 Dhabīḥī 1348 sh./1969, 182–185. Raʾīs's full name was Mullā Muḥammad Riḍā Astarābādī. He is not, as often happened, to be confused with the Mullā Muḥammad Riḍā b. Muḥammad Ṣādiq Astarābādī, founder of the Madrasa–yi Raḍawiyya, whose ruling formed the basis of the claim of the Dirāzgīsū. The documents refer to the former as Raʾīs and the latter as Ḥājjī Mullā Riḍā Astarābādī. Raʾīs was born in the village of Fūjard and is often given the *nisba* Fūjardī.

24 Sutūda and Dhabīḥī 1354 sh./1975, VI, 228–230.

25 For an eyewitness account of this battle, see Kashmīrī (undated), 75–97.

he was killed with a cannonball fired by Īshān - chief of the Yomut Turkmen.[26] Raʾīs was proclaimed a martyr (*shahīd*) in Astarābād, and his memory and influence persisted long after his death. The last major Astarābādī *mujtahid* involved in the dispute was Muḥammad Ṣādiq al-ʿAqīlī.[27] By the time he intervened in the case in the 1870s, the dispute between the Dirāzgīsū and the Qājār khans had been going on for almost a century. Despite strong opposition, al-ʿAqīlī decided the best way to end the dispute once and for all was not arbitration, which had proved ineffective, but a negotiated settlement. In concluding this section, it is worth noting that besides the Iṣfahānī *ʿulamāʾ* that Sayyid Faḍlullāh involved in the case, the adjudication of the dispute was brought each time before individuals who from the biographical sources appear to have been the leading local *mujtahids* of Astarābād of their time (see Figure 60).

Ḥājjī Mullā Riḍā Astarābādī c.1790s

Sharīʿatmadār Mullā Muḥammad ʿAlī Ashrafī, *imām-jumʿa* of Astarābād, c. 1846-47

Mullā Muḥammad Taqī, *imam-jumʿa* of Astarābād, c.1848-50

Raʾīs al-ʿUlamāʾ c.1867-68

Muḥammad Ṣādiq al-ʿAqīlī c.1871-2

Figure 60: The *ʿulamāʾ* of Astarābād involved in the land dispute from the late eighteenth century onwards.

2 The Sources: The Archive of the Dirāzgīsū Sayyids

In the 1970s, Manūchihr Sutūda and Masīḥ Dhabīḥī transcribed and published a corpus of over one hundred documents belonging to the Dirāzgīsū sayyids of Astarābād.[28] Fifty-six documents are concerned with the dispute between the Dirāzgīsū

26 Kashmīrī (undated), no.4 year 5, 61: *"Īshān-i malʿūn bā tīp-i buzurg wa baydaq risida marḥūm raʾīs al-ʿulamāʾ rā dar sar-i tīp shahīd karda."*
27 Dhabīḥī 1348 sh./1969, 191–192.
28 The Dirāzgīsū documents were in two separate collections belonging to Ḥujjat al-Islām Āqā Riḍā Maybudī and Āqā Sayyid Ḥusayn Burūmand, see the introduction in Sutūda and Dhabīḥī 1354 sh./1975, VII, 27. The Dirāzgīsū archive is one of several archives of sayyid groups in Astarābād published in *Az Āstarā tā Astarābād*. The other main sayyid groups are the descendants of

and the Qajar khans over Chūplānī and Mīr-Maḥalla.[29] All references to the documents of the Dirāzgīsū henceforth refer to these fifty-six documents (see the appendix). Document numbers in the tables marked with an asterisk are originals (*aṣl*); all unmarked documents are transcripts (*sawād*). I have divided important documents into their constituent parts, which are marked with letters of the alphabet. If a document is not examined in detail in the historical reconstruction, I have included a summary of its content in the tables. I will now briefly describe the documents and their significance.

Ten documents are related to the legal rulings of Āqā Muḥammad Mahdī and Ḥājjī Mullā Riḍā Astarābādī (Table I, document nos. 1–10). Besides documents relating to the two rulings, there are legal documents which shed light on the Dirāzgīsū

Mīr Findiriskī and the Shīrangī sayyids, who were often at odds with the Dirāzgīsū over boundaries and water rights. The Dirāzgīsū documents are almost without exception about the *waqf* of their ancestor Mīr Rūḥullāh. My reconstruction is based on the documents relating to the villages of Chūplānī and Mīr-Maḥalla in the countryside of Astarābād. There was also, however, litigation in the Qajar period over *waqf* properties belonging to Mīr Rūḥullāh in the quarter of Pāy–i Sarw, today in the centre of the modern town of Gurgān, see for instance Sutūda and Dhabīḥī 1354 sh./1975, VII, 239–248.

29 The pre-Qajar documents in the Dirāzgīsū archive mainly relate to the village of Chūplānī. The earliest Safavid document is a witness statement (*istishhād-nāma*) dated Ṣafar 1005/October 1596 (Sutūda and Dhabīḥī 1354 sh./1975, VII, 222–224), requesting testimony about theft of water belonging to Chūplānī. The document suggests Chūplānī was already *waqf* land by this period because it refers to the stipulations of the founder (*bi-maḍmūn-i wāqif*). This is confirmed by another witness statement dated Dhū al-Qaʿda 1005/June 1597 (Sutūda and Dhabīḥī 1354 sh./1975, VII, 225–227). According to this document, Chūplānī and another village, ʿAlawī-kālata, belonged to Mīr Ibrāhīm Chūplānī, who constituted them as a *waqf* for his descendants (*waqf karda bar awlād-i khud*). The witness statement requests testimony that the sale of the two villages after Mīr Ibrāhīm's death to a certain ʿUlyār Beg was illegal. Another witness statement dated Rajab 1095/June 1684 (Sutūda and Dhabīḥī 1354 sh./1975, VII, 227–230) suggests that Mīr Rūḥullāh's father, Amīr Kamāl al-Dīn Maḥmūd, acquired possession of Chūplānī through his mother, who had inherited the village from her brother Mīr Ghiyāth al-Dīn Muḥammad. The witness statement asks for confirmation that Mīr Ghiyāth al-Dīn Muḥammad had constituted Chūplānī as a *waqf* for the benefit of his descendants (*bi-awlād waqf namūda*). The genealogical link between Mīr Ibrāhīm Chūplānī and Mīr Rūḥullāh is unclear from these Safavid era witness statements. The Dirāzgīsū claim was based on the constitution of the village as *waqf* by Mīr Rūhullāh, see his *waqf-nāma*: document 12. There are very few pre-Qajar documents in the archive of the Dirāzgīsū relating to the village of Mīr-Maḥalla. The most significant is an original deed of gift dated 10 Rabīʿ II 942/18 October 1535, where a certain Muḥammad Ṣāliḥ transfers the field (*mazraʿa*) of Mīr-Maḥālla to Mīr Rūḥullāh's father, Kamāl al-Dīn Maḥmūd (see Sutūda and Dhabīḥī 1354 sh./1975, VII, 63–64). In some Qajar documents Chūplānī is referred to as a *mazraʿa* (field), not a *qarya* (village) (see document 3), but the earliest Safavid documents use *qarya*. Mīr-Maḥalla is usually referred to as a *qarya* in the Qajar documents, but the earliest Safavid document in the archive uses *mazraʿa*.

claim to the two villages. These include transcripts of the Safavid-era *waqf* deed of Mīr Rūḥullāh (Table I, document nos. 11–12) and a transcript of a witness statement (*istishhād-nāma*) containing testimonies about the illegal sale of the two villages to the Qajar khans and another witness statement concerning punishment inflicted by ʿAbbās Khān Qājār to supporters of the Dirāzgīsū (Table I, document nos. 13–14).

The documents of the Dirāzgīsū also include a number of royal decrees issued by the shah (Table II, document nos. 15–24) and provincial decrees issued by the governors of Astarābād (Table II, document nos. 25–32). As these documents were made in official chanceries, they tend to be formulaic. Nevertheless, they can sometimes reveal what was being demanded by the Dirāzgīsū at various stages in the dispute and whether these demands were being met or not. In some cases, the petitions requesting these decrees have survived (Table III, document nos. 33–35). One of these petitions was written not by the Dirāzgīsū but by their opponent: ʿAbbās Khān (document no. 34). It is not clear how this document entered the archive of the Dirāzgīsū. Like the letters described below, it is likely that many of these documents once formed part of Sayyid Faḍlullāh's private archive. The corpus was probably assembled by Sayyid Faḍlullāh himself or his authorized agent (*wakīl*) in the case - Mullā Muḥammad ʿAlī.

By far the most revealing source in the archive is a rather chaotic collection of letters (Table III, document nos. 36–51). Most of these letters are not dated. The author and recipient must be worked out from the content. Some of these letters were written by the Dirāzgīsū, while others appear to have been written by their supporters. They are addressed to various political authorities, including the shah and ʿAbbās Khān. They are often polemical in tone and cite evidence from the Qurʾān and traditions to prove that it was a divine duty to respect the rights of the Dirāzgīsū, who were descendants of the Prophet. There are several letters in the archive which were clearly exchanged between two or more Astarābādī *ʿulamā*ʾ. I have drawn extensively on these *ʿulamā*ʾ letters.

These letters document a passionate legal debate between two rival camps in Astarābād in the 1860s over the legal rulings that had been issued so far in the case and the best way to resolve the dispute. Besides the letters of the Astarābādī *ʿulamā*ʾ, there are also a few letters by Sayyid Faḍlullāh's *wakīl*, Mullā Muḥammad ʿAlī. These letters explain the practical difficulties of litigation against a powerful defendant like ʿAbbās Khān. A few letters appear to have been exchanged between Qajar officials in Astarābād and officials in the royal court in Tehran. This correspondence might have been carried out on behalf of Sayyid Faḍlullāh, who wanted to keep the royal court informed about ʿAbbās Khān's attempts to evade arbitration.

Finally, the Dirāzgīsū documents also contain several contracts and legal agreements (Table IV, document nos. 52–56). The most important of these is a transcript of a binding agreement signed at the royal court where both sides agree to arbitration before the *imām-jum'a* of Astarābād, Sharī'atmadār Muḥammad 'Alī Ashrafī. In concluding this section, most of the dated documents appear to have been produced during the reign of Muḥammad Shāh (r.1834–1848). This was a period of intense litigation by Sayyid Faḍlullāh. He tried everything he possibly could to get the rights of the Dirāzgīsū to their ancient *waqf* lands recognised. Initially, Sayyid Faḍlullāh and the Dirāzgīsū seem to have been willing to let 'Abbās Khān retain possession of the lands if he recognised their rights to a share of its revenues. When 'Abbās Khān refused to do this, Sayyid Faḍlullāh demanded the lands be returned to the Dirazgīsū.

3 Historical Reconstruction

3.1 Stage 1: The Rulings of the *'Ulamā'* of Isfahan in Astarābād

The earliest Qajar-era document in the Dirāzgīsū archive is a *farmān* of Fatḥ 'Alī Shāh dated Dhū al-Qa'da 1240/June 1825.[30] The document suggests that by this date 'Abbās Khān was in possession of Chūplānī and Mīr-Maḥalla. The document also reveals something about the nature of the dispute between the Dirāzgīsū and 'Abbās Khān. The Dirāzgīsū claimed that the two villages were private *waqf* land

30 Document 15. Precisely how or when the Qajar khans came to acquire possession over Chūplānī and Mīr-Maḥalla is not clear from the sources. According to Fatḥ 'Alī Shāh's *farmān*, the lands had been granted to 'Abbās Khān and Riḍā Khān in a tax revenue assignment (*tuyūl*): *"panj dāng az qaraya-yi mīr-maḥalla . . . wa shīsh dāng az qarya-yi chūplānī-yi astarābād-i rustāq ki bi-tuyūl . . . 'abbās khān wa riḍā khān muqarrar ast"*. The revenue assignment suggests that the two villages had become part of crown land *(khāliṣajāt-i dīwānī)*. This is confirmed by the fact that the revenues were to be paid to the Dirāzgīsū sayyids, Mīr Mūsā and Mīr Taqī, out of the total tax collection *(muwāfiq-i jam' -i dīwānī)* of the villages. There are instances of revenue assignments superimposed on crown land. What is unusual, however, is for a revenue assignment to be made out on private *waqf* lands whose beneficiaries and administrators were restricted, as in the case of Chūplānī and Mīr-Maḥalla. We know that after the collapse of the Safavid dynasty, a large amount of land was abandoned, usurped, or turned into crown land. It seems that in the case of Chūplānī and Mīr-Maḥalla, two things occurred. Not only did the private *waqf* lands become crown land, but they were also illegally bought by the Qajar khans (Sutūda and Dhabīḥī 1354 sh./1975, VI, 262–268), according to the Dirāzgīsū. In other words: a *tuyūl* granted on crown land, which was formerly a private family *waqf*, was turned into private property *(milk)*. 'Abbās Khān is thus said to have 'inherited' the two villages from Riḍā Khān as private property (document 50). The Dirāzgīsū seem to have been more successful in getting their rights to another former *waqf* village which belonged to them recognised: 'Alawī-kālata. This village also appears to have become part of crown land, but unlike Chūplānī and Mīr-Maḥalla, it had not been granted in a *tuyūl* to the Qajar khans, see document no. 16: *"qarya-yi 'alawī-kālata ki bi-khāliṣa-yi dīwān ma'mūl ast dar qadīmu l-ayyām az amlāk-i waqfī-yi ajdād-i āqā sayyid faḍlullāh būda"*.

which belonged to them (*amlāk-i arbābī-yi mawqūfī*).[31] Since the real 'owner' of all *waqf* property was God, the 'ownership' of the Dirāzgīsū was as administrators and beneficiaries of the *waqf* land. In recognition of their 'ownership' of the *waqf* land, 'Abbās Khān had to pay them one-tenth of the annual revenues of the two villages.[32] This one-tenth is referred to in the *farmān* as the right of the land (*ḥaqq al-arḍ*) of the sayyids.[33]

The one-tenth share of revenues is significant because according to Mīr Rūḥullāh's *waqf* deed, the administrator of the endowment was entitled to one-tenth of the yield of the endowed lands.[34] This suggests that the two Dirāzgīsū sayyids, Mīr Mūsā and Mīr Taqī, mentioned in the royal decree, claimed this amount from 'Abbās Khān as administrators of the two endowed villages. We do not know if 'Abbās Khān paid any heed to Fatḥ 'Alī Shāh's *farmān*.[35] A decade later, Abbās Khān was in power as governor of Astarābād, and the dispute between him and the Dirāzgīsū sayyids does not appear to have shown any signs of improving.[36] Mīr Mūsā's son, Sayyid Faḍlullāh, seems to have decided that the Dirāzgīsū needed to make it clear to 'Abbās Khān that if he continued to refuse to pay them what was rightfully theirs, then his possession of the two villages was illegal (*ghaṣb*) and an act of oppression (*'udwān*). To do this, Sayyid Faḍlullāh obtained a legal ruling from a scholar living in Isfahan.

3.1.1 Why Isfahan?

Isfahan was in many ways a natural choice. During this period, some of the most prominent *mujtahids* in Iran lived and taught there, notably Sayyid Muḥammad Bāqir Shaftī and Ḥājjī Muḥammad Ibrāhīm Kalbāsī. It was just the place where a strongly worded ruling against the oppressive *bēglerbēgī* of Astarābād could be safely issued. Moreover, Sayyid Faḍlullāh was well-known in Isfahan. He had

---

31 Document no. 15: *"muqarrar ast muwāfiq-i waqf-nāmajāt-i mu'tabar wa aḥkām-i 'ulamā' amlāk-i arbābī-yi mawqūfī-yi 'ālī jinābān . . . āqā sayyid mūsā wa āqā mīr taqī astarābādī mībāshad . . . az hādhi al-sana takhā-qūy īl wa mā ba'da-hā har sāla bar sabīl-i istimrār ḥaqq al-arḍ-i sādāt-i 'ālī darajāt rā az qarār-i dah wa yak muwāfiq-i jam'-i dīwānī kārsāzī-i ānhā namūda . . .".*

32 Document no. 15. The revenues were to be paid in kind from the *jam'-i dīwānī*, the total tax collection of the two villages.

33 Document no. 15.

34 Document no. 12: *"ba'd az jam'-i manāfi' yak 'ushr rā bi-'unwān-i ḥaqq al-tawliya ṣarf-i ma'īshat"*; Mīr Mūsā's son, Sayyid Faḍlullāh, also demands his right to revenues of the village to be paid as the 'stipend of the administrator' (*ḥaqq al-tawliya*).

35 Document no. 15. Fatḥ 'Alī Shāh's *farmān* is not addressed to 'Abbās Khān but to his son, the governor of Astarābād, Muḥammad Qulī Mīrzā Mulk-Ārā (r. 1229–1249/1813–1833). It was Mulk – Ārā's duty to ensure 'Abbās Khān paid the yearly amount.

36 Document nos. 16, 17, and 18.

spent several years there as a student training to become a *mujtahid* under Shaftī. Sayyid Faḍlullāh, however, did not ask Shaftī to issue the ruling. Rather, he asked Shaftī's son-in-law and former student Āqā Muḥammad Mahdī Kalbāsī (d.1278/1861–2) to issue it. This could be because Shaftī was too busy, or perhaps Sayyid Faḍlullāh merely wanted to use the ruling as a warning. ʿAbbās Khān would have known that Faḍlullāh's next move would inevitably involve Āqā Muḥammad Mahdī's father-in-law – arguably the most powerful jurist alive in Iran. Perhaps Sayyid Faḍlullāh did not approach Shaftī in the first instance because he still hoped that ʿAbbās Khān would recognise the rights of the Dirāzgīsū to the lands. The text of the ruling of Āqā Muḥammad Mahdī does seem to confirm this.[37]

Sayyid Faḍlullāh is not mentioned as the claimant in the text. His father, Mīr Mūsā, and his uncle, Mīr Taqī, who must have been the oldest surviving descendants of Mīr Rūḥullāh at the time, are listed as beneficiaries of the two *waqf* villages. There can be little doubt, though, that it was Sayyid Faḍlullāh, with his ties to Isfahan, who was behind the issuance of the ruling. Just as the ruling does not mention Sayyid Faḍlullāh, it does not refer directly to ʿAbbās Khān – the defendant who was in possession of the land at the time. The ruling offers 'the possessor' of the villages two alternatives. He could either choose to possess the lands legally or vacate possession. The first option meant recognising that as beneficiaries and administrators of the *waqf* land, the Dirāzgīsū had to be paid their share of revenues from the two villages promptly ever year. The second option would involve returning the lands back to the Dirāzgīsū so that they could lease the two villages to other landowners. ʿAbbās Khān had no intention of following either option. Before I examine how Āqā Muḥammad Mahdī's ruling was challenged by ʿAbbās Khān, we must consider briefly how it was issued.

3.1.2 The Issuance of Āqā Muḥammad Mahdī's Ruling

Āqā Muḥammad Mahdī's ruling was issued on 25 Muḥarram 1251/23 May 1835. It is tempting to think that Sayyid Faḍlullāh simply sent his agent, Mullā Muḥammad Ismāʿīl, to Isfahan to get it. It might on the other hand have been brought by someone from Isfahan after a brief correspondence between Sayyid Faḍlullāh and Āqā Muḥammad Mahdī. According to the text, the ruling was issued based on the testimony of reliable witnesses (*bi-shahādat-i shuhūd-i muʿtabara*) and the writings of several *ʿulamāʾ* (*niwishtijāt-i chandī az ʿulamāʾ*).[38] The *waqf*-deed of Mīr Rūḥullāh which the Dirāzgīsū had in their archive is not mentioned, though it was probably sent as well. The ruling is not preceded by a protocol of claims by both sides, nor

37 Document no. 1.
38 Document no. 1.

does it contain the text of witness depositions or a précis of prior litigation. It is therefore not clear who the reliable witnesses referred to in the ruling were. It could be that witnesses from Astarābād travelled to Isfahan to give oral testimony before Āqā Muḥammad Mahdī. This is unlikely, because according to strict rules of evidence in Islamic law, to prove that lands were *waqf* would have required many witnesses to make the trip from Astarābād to Isfahan.[39] It is far more likely that Āqā Muḥammad Mahdī was sent a written witness statement (*istishhād-nama*) containing a copy of oral testimonies which had been certified by Astarābadī *ʿulamāʾ*. We know that Dirāzgīsū had such a document in their archive, and it is possible that this was what was shown to Āqā Muḥammad Mahdī.[40] We shall return to the significance of this document when discussing the ruling of Ḥājjī Mullā Riḍā Astarābādī.

3.1.3 Āqā Muḥammad Mahdī's Ruling in Astarābād

For two years, attempts by Sayyid Faḍlullāh to use Āqā Muḥammad Mahdī's ruling in Astarābād do not seem to have worked. The reason for this is not clear. We know that ʿAbbās Khān had shown documents proving his ownership of the lands to the *imām-jumʿa* of Astarābād, Sharīʿatmadār Mullā Muḥammad ʿAlī Ashrafī. Sharīʿatmadār is said to have certified that the villages were private property belonging to ʿAbbās Khān.[41] There were thus two opposing judicial certifications. The claimant, Sayyid Faḍlullāh, had a ruling certifiying the lands were *waqf* and belonged to the Dirāzgīsū. The defendant, ʿAbbās Khān, had a ruling certifying that the lands were private property (*milk*). Usually, if two opposing legal claims – *waqf* and private property – had been judicially certified, this should have forced arbitration between the two sides. In this case it did not. From later documents, we know that ʿAbbās Khān challenged the validity of the ruling Sayyid Faḍlullāh had brought from Isfahan. ʿAbbās Khān claimed it had been issued by a non-*mujtahid*; therefore, it was not legally valid. This, along with Sharīʿatmadār's certification that the lands were private property, seems to be the main reason why Āqā Muḥammad Mahdī's ruling had no discernible effect in Astarābad.[42] It also helps to explain why Sayyid Faḍlullāh sought a ratification of the ruling from Sayyid Muḥammad Bāqir Shaftī.

---

39 See the case study in chapter 6.

40 Document no. 13. On the *istihhād-nāma* see chapter 6.

41 Document no. 48: *"wa marḥūm sharīʿatmadār . . . ṣarīḥ niwisht ki chuplānī milk-i ʿabbās khān ast"*. From later documents, we know that there were other jurists besides Sharīʿatmadār who had also certified that the lands were private property in this stage of litigation, see for instance document 34.

42 Document no. 18.

3.1.4 Sayyid Muḥammad Bāqir Shaftī's Ratification

On 3 Jamādī II 1253/4 September 1837, Sayyid Muḥammad Bāqir Shaftī wrote the following line above the ruling of Āqā Muḥammad Mahdī: "It is obligatory for everyone to follow the stipulations of this writing" (*bar qāṭiba lāzim ast ʿamal bi-muqtaḍā-yi īn niwishta namūda bāshand).*[43] Shaftī had ratified the binding force of Āqā Muḥammad Mahdī's ruling. What Shaftī's ratification (*imḍā-yi ḥukm*) did not make clear, however, was whether Āqā Muḥammad Mahdī was a *mujtahid* or not. Shaftī had merely confirmed that the ruling of Āqā Muḥammad Mahdī was valid and enforceable. The question of the ability of Sayyid Muḥammad Bāqir Shaftī's son-in-law to exercise *ijtihād* remained unresolved.

3.1.5 Shaftī's Ratification in Astarābād

Meanwhile, however, the ratification of Āqā Muḥammad Mahdī's ruling by Shaftī had confirmed the ruling was legally valid and binding. Sayyid Faḍlullāh could now use it in litigation. Sayyid Faḍlullāh petitioned the royal court in Tehran at least once.[44] On 25 Rajab 1256/September 1840, a *farmān* was issued by Muḥammad Shāh and addressed to the new governor of Astarābād, Muḥammad Nāṣir Khān Develū Qājār, who had taken over from ʿAbbās Khān.[45] The *farmān* ordered Muḥammad Nāṣir Khān to check if the two villages were crown land, and if it turned out that they were not (*dar ṣūratī ki khāliṣa nabāshad*), to deliver 'possession' of the lands to Sayyid Faḍlullāh. The *farmān* was based among other documents on the ratification issued by Shaftī.[46] Muḥammad Nāṣir Khān in turn issued a series of provincial decrees ordering a certain Qurbān ʿAlī Āqā-yi Qājār to deliver possession of Chūplānī and Mīr-Maḥalla to Sayyid Faḍlullāh's agents.[47] Sayyid Faḍlullāh and his brothers were formally recognised, for the first time, as administrators (*mutawallī*) of the two *waqf* villages. The share of revenues they intended to claim was the stipend due to the administrator of a *waqf* (*ḥaqq al-tawliya*).[48]

A note on one of the provincial decrees which was written and sealed by Muḥammad Nāṣir Khān suggests the transfer of possession of the lands was carried out by Qurbān ʿAlī Āqā-yi Qājār.[49] According to a provincial decree dated Shawwāl 1256/December 1840, however, it seems that possession of the village of Mīr-

43 Document no. 1.
44 Document no. 33.
45 Document no. 19.
46 Document no. 19.
47 Document nos. 25 and 26.
48 Document no. 26.
49 Document no. 26.

Maḥalla had not yet been transferred to Sayyid Faḍlullāh or his agents. The decree orders a payment to be made of revenues from Mīr-Maḥalla to Sayyid Faḍlullāh as a government stipend (*mustammarī-yi dīwānī*).[50] This suggests that the village of Mīr-Maḥalla, at least, was still either in the possession of ʿAbbās Khān or the local government. Another document, a legal agreement dated Rabīʿ I 1257/ May 1841, does suggest that Sayyid Faḍlullāh held some form of possession. The agreement was signed between Sayyid Faḍlullāh and a landowner named Malik Kāẓim and his son. In this document, Sayyid Faḍlullāh authorises them to collect revenues from peasants farming on the lands of Chūplānī and Mīr-Maḥalla or making use of its waters.[51] This may, however, simply be an attempt by Sayyid Faḍlullāh to take the revenue collection into his own hands, even though the lands were in ʿAbbās Khān's possession.

The documents are never completely clear about what is meant by the Dirāzgīsū being in 'possession'. Did Qurbān ʿAlī Āqā-yi Qājār really deliver possession of the two villages to Sayyid Faḍlullāh's agents, or did he merely deliver revenues he collected from ʿAbbās Khān? As we shall see, as the intensity of the conflict between ʿAbbās Khān and Sayyid Faḍlullāh increased, several revenue collectors (*muḥaṣṣil*) had to be dispatched from the royal court to Astarābād to collect and deliver (*īṣāl wa wuṣūl*) the payments. At least legally speaking, however, Sayyid Faḍlullāh had been awarded 'possession' of the lands. The *farmān* of Muḥammad Shāh and the provincial decrees of Muḥammad Nāṣir Khān from this period made it clear that if ʿAbbās Khān believed the lands belonged to him as private property (*milk*), he would have to submit to arbitration.[52] ʿAbbās Khān, of course, had no intention of doing anything of the sort. One reason for this appears to be that the imām-*jumʿa* of Astarābād, Sharīʿatmadār, had confirmed that the only basis of Sayyid Faḍlullāh's legal claim to 'possession' of the lands was Shaftī's ratification of Āqā Muḥammad Mahdī's ruling.[53]

3.1.6 Ḥājjī Muḥammad Ibrāhīm Kalbāsī's Ratification

In 1260/1844, Sayyid Muḥammad Bāqir Shaftī died in Isfahan. In Astarābād, 'possession' of the two villages which the Dirāzgīsū sayyids had enjoyed for around three years from 1256–1260/1840–1843 also came to an end.[54] Now that Shaftī was

50 Dhabīḥī 1348 sh./1969, 164.
51 Document no. 52.
52 Document no. 19; Document no. 26b.
53 Document no. 48: *"wa marḥūm sharīʿatmadār niwishtijāt-i mutʿaddida niwisht ki āqā sayyid faḍlullāh mustanad-i taṣarruf-i ū ḥukm-i ḥujjat al-islām [Shaftī] būda wa bas."*
54 Document no. 2: *"mawqufun ʿalayhim [sādāt-i dirāzgīsū] si chahār sāl qabl taṣarruf-i mālikāna namūd[and] wa bi-ṭarīq-i waqfiyyat ʿamal namūdand ḥāl baʿd az fawt wa marḥūm shudan-i sarkār*

dead, ʿAbbās Khān felt that the ruling of Āqā Muḥammad Mahdī was no longer binding. Sayyid Faḍlullāh and the Dirāzgīsū realized they needed to ratify it again as quickly as possible. We know from documents in the Dirāzgīsū archive that they sent a question to Āqā Muḥammad Mahdī's father, Ḥājjī Muḥammad Ibrāhīm Kalbāsī, asking him for a new ratification of the ruling.[55] This time, the Dirāzgīsū were careful to ask not only for a ratificiation (*imḍā-yi ḥukm*) of Āqā Muḥammad Mahdī's ruling but also a certification (*taṣdīq*) that Āqā Muḥammad Mahdī was a *mujtahid*.[56] What this meant according to the question was that whenever (*har-gāh*) a ruling of Āqā Muḥammad Mahdī's was shown in Astarābād, it should be considered legally valid and binding (*nāfidh*).[57] The Dirāzgīsū wanted to make it absolutely clear that Āqā Muḥammad Mahdī's rulings were those of a recognised *mujtahid*. Their binding force was not dependent on the ratification of another recognised living jurist. The Dirāzgīsū did not want to see a repeat of what had happened after Shaftī's death.

3.1.7 The Issuance of Ḥājjī Muḥammad Ibrāhīm Kalbāsī's Ratification

On Friday 16 Rajab 1260/1 August 1844, Ḥājjī Muḥammad Ibrāhīm Kalbāsī ratified his son's ruling. The ratification also included an explicit certification of his *ijtihād*. Kalbāsī confirmed that Āqā Muḥammad Mahdī was indeed a *mujtahid*. All legal rulings issued by Āqā Muḥammad Mahdī were valid and binding, and it was compulsory to enforce them. According to Kalbāsī, Āqā Muḥammad Mahdī was not only a qualified *mujtahid*, but in his view, he was the most learned jurist of his time (*az sāʾirīn aʿlam mī-dānam*) after Shaftī's death. Kalbāsī also referred to the accepted (*maqbūla*) report narrated by ʿUmar b. Hanzala, from the sixth Imām, Jaʿfar al-Ṣādiq. In accordance with the report, Kalbāsī noted, to disobey the ruling of a qualified jurist like Āqā Muḥammad Mahdī was equivalent to an act of polytheism (*wa-huwa fī ḥadd al-shirk bi-llāh*).[58] An indication that Kalbāsī was serious about what he was saying is that he sealed the text of this ratification three times. There was, however, a problem. Kalbāsī had not written the ratification himself. A scribe wrote it. When Kalbāsī's ratification reached Astarābād, no one believed he had issued it. The ratification was assumed to be forged. For most of the rest of that year, 1260/1844, Sayyid Faḍlullāh and the Dirāzgīsū tried to certify

. . . ḥujjat al-islām [shaftī] mīkhwāhand bidūna tarāfuʿ taṣarruf dar ān amlāk kunand ʿabbās khān."

55 Document no. 2.

56 Document no. 2.

57 Document no. 2.

58 For a translation of this important report attributed to the sixth Imāmī Shīʿī *imām* Jaʿfar al-Ṣādiq (d. 765) and used to justify the judicial authority of the Imāmī Shīʿī jurist, see Calder 1979, 104.

that the text of the ratification issued by Ḥājjī Muḥammad Ibrāhīm Kalbāsī was authentic.

3.1.8 Certifying the Issuance of Ḥājjī Muḥammad Ibrāhīm Kalbāsī's Ratification

The main problem with Kalbāsī's ratification seems to have been that it was not written directly above the original (*aṣl*) ruling of Āqā Muḥammad Mahdī. This was how Shaftī's ratification had been issued.[59] Kalbāsī's ratification, however, had been issued separately as a reply to the question written to him by the Dirāzgīsū. This would explain why the Dirāzgīsū had to go to such lengths to prepare a new document where they tried to introduce all three texts together: the text of the ruling of Āqā Muḥammad Mahdī, the text of the question they had sent to Ḥājjī Muḥammad Ibrāhīm Kalbāsī, and the text of the ratification Kalbāsī had issued.[60] Once this document was prepared, the Dirāzgīsū asked Āqā Muḥammad Mahdī's brother, Shaykh Jaʿfar, to certify the authenticity of all three texts. Shaykh Jaʿfar must have had access to the original ruling issued by his brother, the original question of the Dirāzgīsū, and the original ratification his father had issued above the petition. These originals were probably kept in the Kalbāsī family archive in Isfahan.

Shaykh Jaʿfar confirmed that the ratification had indeed been issued by his father, Ḥājjī Muḥammad Ibrāhīm Kalbāsī, on Friday 16 Rajab 1260/1 August 1844. Shaykh Jaʿfar noted that though the text of the ratification had been written by a scribe, his father, Ḥājjī Muḥammad Ibrāhīm Kalbāsī, had taken great care to write a small sentence in Arabic in his own handwriting above it: *ṣadara ʿannī wallāhu al-ʿālim* (it was issued by me, God is the Knower)[61] so that its authenticity could not be disputed. Kalbāsī's seal and the line *ṣadara ʿannī wallāhu al-ʿālim* was sufficient proof that Kalbāsī had issued the text of the ratification.[62]

Probably because he felt Shaykh Jaʿfar's certification was not going to be enough for the sceptics in Astarābād who supported ʿAbbās Khān, Sayyid Faḍlullāh also asked an Astarābādī jurist to countersign Shaykh Jaʿfar's certification. This was done by Naṣrullāh al-Ḥusaynī, a well-respected Astarābādī jurist who lived in Tehran. Naṣrullāh al-Ḥusaynī notes in his ratification that he had been asked several

59 Document no. 1b; we know from the certified transcript of Āqā Muḥammad Mahdī's ruling that Shaftī's ratification had been written directly above the ruling in the original document.
60 Document no. 2.
61 This is a common clause in Qajar *sharīʿa* documents. In full, it reads as follows: *wa-l-lāhu al-ʿālim bi-ḥaqāʾiq al-umūr wa-l-aḥkām* ('God alone is the Knower of the True Nature of Affairs and Rulings').
62 Document no. 2.

times to verify the authenticity of Kalbāsī's ratification (*chunān ki mukarraran dīda shūda*).[63] Āqā Maḥmūd b. Muḥammad ʿAlī Bihbahānī Kirmānshāhī (d.1269/1852–3), a grandson of the famous Uṣūlī jurist in Iraq, Muḥammad Bāqir Bihbahānī, was also asked to ratify Shaykh Jaʿfar's certification.[64] Āqā Maḥmūd notes that he issued his ratification of Shaykh Jaʿfar's certification based on the testimony of witnesses. This was not the usual procedure to confirm the authenticity of rulings and their ratifications. In general, verifying the authenticity of a ruling or ratification simply involved comparing the original text with its transcript. The authenticity of the transcript of Āqā Muḥammad Mahdī's ruling and Shaftī's ratification had been certified in this manner.[65] In this case, the recourse to witness testimony was to ensure doubts could not be raised about Shaykh Jaʿfar's certification.

What is surprising is that Kalbāsī was not asked to certify the authenticity of his own ratification himself. Kalbāsī was clearly still alive, because Shaykh Jaʿfar uses the expression 'may God extend his shadow' (*adāmā allāhu taʿālā ẓilālahu*) after mentioning his name.[66] It could be that Kalbāsī was too old and weak, and that Shaykh Jaʿfar was therefore asked to write the certification. Based on the issuance of Kalbāsī's ratification of Āqā Muḥammad Mahdī's ruling, Kalbāsī generally seems to have preferred, as some jurists did, to use scribes. This might explain why he did not follow the explicit instructions of the Dirāzgīsū to issue the ratification in his own handwriting.[67] Kalbāsī's use of a scribe may not have raised eyebrows in Isfahan. In Astarābād, however, it made it easier to raise doubts – real or invented – about the authenticity of the ratification he had issued.

3.1.9 Ḥājjī Muḥammad Ibrāhīm Kalbāsī's Ratification in Astarābād

Sayyid Faḍlullāh's attempts to certify the authenticity of the issuance of Ḥājjī Muḥammad Ibrāhīm Kalbāsī's ratification do not seem to have worked. ʿAbbās Khān was able to successfully retain legal possession of the disputed lands.[68] On what legal basis ʿAbbās Khān remained in possession of the lands is not clear from the sources. As we mentioned earlier, Sharīʿatmadār had certified that the lands were private property belonging to ʿAbbas Khan. We also know from a later petition ʿAbbās Khān wrote to the royal court that he had been able to get several other

63 Document no. 2.
64 Document no. 2.
65 Document no. 1.
66 Document no. 2.
67 Document no. 2: "*dū kalama bi-khaṭṭ-i mubārak wa muhr-i sharīf imḍā bi-farmāʾīd wa l-salām.*"
68 Document no. 34.

jurists in the region to certify his claim to the lands as private property.[69] The shah also appears to have issued a decree in ʿAbbās Khān's favour which stated that Sayyid Faḍlullāh had no legal claim in the case.[70]

Sayyid Faḍlullāh appears to have been acutely aware of the problems he had created by seeking rulings in the case from jurists in Isfahan. Besides the problem of constantly having to certify the authenticity of the issuance of these texts for an Astarābādī audience, there was also the difficulty of getting ʿAbbās Khān to recognise the *itjihād* of a relatively unknown *mujtahid* like Āqā Muḥammad Mahdī residing in Isfahan. Sayyid Faḍlullāh realised that if the Dirāzgīsū were to have any chance of success, they needed to base their claim on a legal ruling issued by a local *mujtahid* of Astarābād. Fortunately for Sayyid Faḍlullāh, there had been an Astarābādī jurist who had issued a ruling in favour of the Dirāzgīsū whose *ijtihād* ʿAbbās Khān could not possibly challenge.

3.2 Stage 2: The Revival of Ḥājjī Mullā Riḍā Astarābādī's Ruling

We do not know exactly when Sayyid Faḍlullāh and the Dirāzgīsū decided to turn their attention to a legal ruling that had been issued in the 1790s by Ḥājjī Mullā Riḍā Astarābādī (d.*c.*1251/1835). The ruling had made it compulsory for two of ʿAbbās Khān's predecessors, Riḍā Khān (r.1200–1207/1785–1792) and Imām Qulī Khān (r.1207–1214/1792–1799), to return the disputed lands to the Dirāzgīsū. It is not clear why Sayyid Faḍlullāh obtained a new ruling from Isfahan in 1251/1835 instead of simply using Ḥājjī Mullā Riḍā Astarābādī's ruling in the first place. One reason may be that Ḥājjī Mullā Riḍā Astarābādī was still alive in Astarābād. Since the ruling was never enforced by ʿAbbās Khān's predecessors, Sayyid Faḍlullāh probably did not think it was likely ʿAbbās Khān would agree to enforce the ruling while he was in power. Sayyid Faḍlullāh might have therefore felt it was best to avoid the risk of further embarrassment for the revered old *mujtahid* and obtain a new ruling in the case from outside Astarābād. Sayyid Faḍlullāh probably still believed at the time that it was possible to convince ʿAbbās Khān to recognise the right of the Dirāzgīsū to a share of revenues from Chūplānī and Mīr-Maḥalla. A flexible ruling like the one issued by Āqā Muḥammad Mahdī, which gave ʿAbbās Khān the option to recognise the Dirāzgīsū claim, was thus deemed more suitable than Ḥājjī Mullā Riḍā Astarābādī's old ruling. Sayyid Faḍlullāh could of course have asked someone in Astarābād to issue the new ruling. There were

69 Document no. 34.
70 Document no. 34.

probably few Astarābādī jurists, however, who would have been willing to give Sayyid Faḍlullāh and the Dirāzgīsū such a ruling against the governor. Moreover, since the local jurists in Astarābād and its region must have been aware of the issuance of Ḥājjī Mullā Riḍā's ruling, they would not have agreed to issue a new ruling on the case. Obtaining a ratification of a ruling issued by a jurist of Ḥājjī Mullā Riḍā's stature was also probably not easy to obtain.

3.2.1 From a Share in Revenues to a Return of the Lands (*Radd-i Amlāk*)

In the 1840s, however, the situation in Astarābād was quite different from the 1830s. Ḥājjī Mullā Riḍā Astarābādī was dead and ʿAbbās Khān was no longer in power as governor. After the debacle with Āqā Muḥammad Mahdī's ruling and the ratifications issued by Shaftī and Kalbāsī, Sayyid Faḍlullāh must have realized that no revenue payments were ever going to be paid to the Dirāzgīsū by ʿAbbās Khān. ʿAbbās Khān's continued refusal to recognise their rights had meant that the only way forward was to demand a definitive restitution of the lands (*radd-i amlāk*). For this purpose, Ḥājjī Mullā Riḍā Astarābādī's ruling was perfect. ʿAbbās Khān could not claim he did not recognise Ḥājjī Mullā Riḍā Astarābādī to be a *mujtahid*. ʿAbbās Khān was known to have enforced other rulings of Ḥājjī Mullā Riḍā Astarābādī when he was governor and when Astarābādī was still alive. The only problem was that it was fifty years since Ḥājjī Mullā Riḍā Astarābādī had issued his ruling in favour of the Dirāzgīsū against Abbās Khān's predecessors. The first step, therefore, was to make the issuance of the ruling by Ḥājjī Mullā Riḍā Astarābādī publicly known again.

3.2.2 Certifying the Issuance of Ḥājjī Mullā Riḍā Astarābādī's Ruling

An original undated document in the archive of the Dirāzgīsū sheds some light on how the issuance of Ḥājjī Mullā Riḍā Astarābādī's ruling was made publicly known.[71] The document begins with the clause *makhfī namānad ki* (let it be known that). The verbatim text of the ruling of Ḥājjī Mullā Riḍā Astarābādī is then transcribed. The next segment requests anyone to write in the margins and seal the document if: (1) they had either seen, heard, or were aware of the ruling, or had been witnesses to its issuance[72], or (2) recognised Ḥājjī Mullā Riḍā Astarā-

71 Document no. 3.

72 Document no. 3: "*har-ki az ḥājjī-yi mujtahid-i mazbūr ḥukm-rā dīda wa muṭalliʿ ast wa shāhid bar ḥukm-i īshān būda yā az īshān istimāʿ namūda bāshad*".

bādī to be a *mujtahid*,[73] or (3) could testify that ʿAbbās Khān enforced Ḥājjī Mullā Riḍā Astarābādī's rulings in Astarābād and/or recognised him as a *mujtahid*.[74]

Fourteen Astarābādī *ʿulamāʾ* certified the authenticity of the text of Ḥājjī Mullā Riḍā Astarābādī's ruling and the fact that he had issued it. Several *ʿulamāʾ* also confirmed that ʿAbbās Khān had previously recognised Astarābādī as a *mujtahid*. Most of the *ʿulamāʾ* involved in preparing the document are the usual suspects who supported the Dirāzgīsū, such as for instance Naṣrullāh al-Ḥusaynī and Mullā ʿAbbās ʿAlī.[75] The text of Astarābādī's ruling, however, is also certified by Sharīʿatmadār Mullā Muḥammad ʿAlī Ashrafī, the *imām-jumʿa* of Astarābād.[76] Sharīʿatmadār does not confirm that ʿAbbās Khān recognised Astarābādī as a *mujtahid*, but he certifies that Astarābādī was a *mujtahid*. Since none of the statements on the document are dated, we do not know whether they were written at the same time, perhaps at a meeting convoked by Sayyid Faḍlullāh, or at different times. What is significant, however, is that this is the first tangible sign we have of the appearance of the *imām-jumʿa* of Astarābād among the documents of the Dirāzgīsū. As we noted earlier, Sharīʿatmadār is known to have certified documents of ʿAbbās Khān. From the 1840s onwards, however, Sharīʿatmadār appears to have endorsed the Dirāzgīsū cause. ʿAbbās Khān does not seem to have been aware that Sayyid Faḍlullāh had been certifying documents of the Dirāzgīsū before his most powerful clerical supporter.

3.2.3 The Issuance of Ḥājjī Mullā Riḍā Astarābādī's Ruling on a Witness Statement

Most of the Astarābādī *ʿulamāʾ* who certified the text of Ḥājjī Mullā Riḍā Astarābādī's ruling do not make it clear where the original (*aṣl*) ruling had been issued. From the testimony of Mullā ʿAlī Akbar,[77] Mullā Riḍā Chiyākandī and Mullā Muḥammad Taqī, however, it seems the original ruling had been written directly on to an original (*aṣl*) witness statement (*istishhād-nāma*).[78] An undated transcript (*sawād*) of a witness

73 Document no. 3: *"ya khud-i īshān ḥājjī-rā mujtahid-i nāfidh al-ḥukm [mī-dānand]"*.

74 Document no. 3: *"wa khud-i ʿālī jāh ʿabbās khān aḥkām-i ān-rā dar astarābād nāfidh mī-dānand"*.

75 Document no. 3.

76 Document no. 3.

77 Dhabīḥī 1348 sh./1969, 176–177.

78 Document no. 3: *"ḥukm dar matn muwāfiq bā ṣurat-i ḥukm-i īshān ast ki bi-khaṭṭ wa muhr-i sharīf-i īshān dar istishhād masṭūr wa mamhūr ast"*; see also the testimony of Mullā Riḍā Chiyākandī: *"wa dar aṣl-i istishhād az ḥājjī-yi marhum shinīdam muhr kardam"*. Mullā Muḥammad Taqī's ratification also provides further evidence that the ruling of Ḥājjī Mullā Riḍā Astarābādī was issued on an original (*aṣl*) witness statement.

statement has survived among the documents of the Dirāzgīsū.[79] Though this transcript contains several certifications by various Astarābādī *ʿulamāʾ*, it does not contain a copy of the ruling of Ḥājjī Mullā Riḍā Astarābādī.

It is quite likely that Sayyid Faḍlullāh and the Dirāzgīsū had in their archive the original witness statement with the original ruling of Ḥājjī Mullā Riḍā Astarābādī inscribed in it. They also possessed, however, a certified transcript of the witness statement which omitted the ruling. It is this certified transcript that Sayyid Faḍlullāh used to obtain the ruling of Āqā Muḥammad Mahdī. Sayyid Faḍlullāh did not want the Iṣfahānī *ʿulamāʾ* to know that a ruling had already been issued on the case in Astarābād by Ḥājjī Mullā Riḍā Astarābādī. If the *ʿulamāʾ* of Isfahan were aware that a ruling had already been issued in the dispute the 1790s in Astarābād, they would only have ratified it and would not have issued a new ruling. Qajar *ʿulamāʾ* were aware that new rulings issued in a case that had already been decided had the potential to create chaos. Consequently, if they became aware that a ruling had already been issued by a jurist in a case, then all subsequent *ʿulamāʾ* would generally either ratify (*imḍā*) or invalidate (*naqḍ*) the initial ruling. This would explain why even as late as the 1860s, the local Astarābādī *ʿulamāʾ* never issued a new ruling in the dispute between the Dirāzgīsū sayyids and the Qajar khans. Litigation had come to focus, instead, on either ratifying or invalidating Ḥājjī Mullā Riḍā Astarābādī's ruling.

Moreover, as we have seen, during the first stage of litigation, Sayyid Faḍlullāh was not after a restitution of the lands (*radd-i amlāk*). He did not seek therefore a ratification of Ḥājjī Mullā Riḍā Astarābādī's ruling from Isfahan. What he was after was a new ruling. The only way to supress the fact that a prior ruling was issued was to send a transcript (*sawād*) of the witness statement without it to Isfahan. This transcript –with Ḥājjī Mullā Riḍā Astarābādī's ruling suppressed – seems to be the witness statement which has survived today in the Dirāzgīsū archive. The original witness statement containing Ḥājjī Mullā Riḍā Astarābādī's ruling and seal which was shown by Sayyid Faḍlullāh to Astarābādī *ʿulamāʾ* to certify the issuance of the ruling is no longer extant. Before we proceed further, we must briefly consider the content of the transcript of the witness statement which has survived because it sheds light on how the Dirāzgīsū had initially based their claim to the two villages before the period of ʿAbbās Khān.

79 Document no. 13.

3.2.4 Mīr Mūsā and Mīr Taqī's Witness Statement

The witness statement contains four elements: the request for testimonies, testimonies by witnesses, certifications by Astarābād *'ulamā'*,[80] and certifications of the authenticity of the transcript. The request for testimony solicits witness testimonies from:

1. Witnesses who were aware that the village of Mīr-Maḥalla and the village of Chūplānī were lands belonging to the deceased Sayyid Riḍā and the deceased Mīr 'Imād, both sons of Mīr Rūḥullāh al-Ḥusaynī, and that these lands were constituted as a *waqf* for Mīr Ruḥūllāh's male descendants (*awlād-i dhukūr*);[81]
2. Witnesses who had heard Mīr 'Imād's daughter, Bīja Sharaf, make an acknowledgement (*iqrār*) while she was alive that the lands in question were constituted as a *waqf* for Mīr Ruḥūllāh's male descendants;[82]
3. Witnesses who knew that the present beneficiaries of the *waqf* lands were Mīr Mūsā and his brother Mīr Taqī, and that the possession of the *waqf* lands by anyone else was illegal, and that the sale of Mīrzā Muḥammad 'Alī Hirawī and others to the deceased Muḥammad Riḍā Khān was illegal.[83]

From the request it is clear that Mīr Mūsā and Mīr Taqī were alive when the witness statement was prepared, since they are referred to as the present *(al-ḥāl)* beneficiaries of the *waqf* lands. Muḥammad Riḍa Khān mentioned in the document is the governor of Astarābād, Riḍā Khān (r.1200–1207/1785–1792).[84] We can assume therefore that this witness statement was produced in the 1790s before the death of Mīr Mūsā around 1255/1838.[85]

3.2.5 Bīja Sharaf's Legal Acknowledgement (*Iqrār*)

The main reason for creating the witness statement was to prove that Mīr Rūḥullāh's *waqf* had been constituted in favour of his male descendants only *(waqf-i*

---

80 An example of one of the *'ulamā'* certifications is document no. 13: "Based on the testimonies of a group of reliable people, the contents of a valid *waqf-nāma*, and the seals of the sayyids and the *'ulamā'* on this document, it has become evident and clear to this lowest slave of God that 5 *dāng* of the village of Mīr-Maḥalla and Chūplanī in its entirety are an endowment for the benefit of the said male descendants, and the beneficiaries are now Mīr Mūsā and Mīr Taqī. God is the Knower [Place of the seal of Mullā 'Isā]".

81 Document no. 13a.

82 Document no. 13.

83 Document no. 13.

84 He is also called Riḍā Khān Qūyūnlū, see document no. 13.

85 Sutūda and Dhabīḥī 1354 sh./1975, VII, 74–75.

awlād-i dhukūr). Though this is already mentioned in Mīr Rūḥullāh's *waqf* deed, it appears that the written document was not enough. Oral testimony was required to confirm that Mīr Rūḥullāh's *waqf* had been constituted exclusively for his male descendants. According to the witness testimonies, after the death of Mīr Rūḥullāh, control of the two villages was inherited by two of his sons: Sayyid Riḍā and Mīr ʿImād. After their death, Mīr ʿImād's daughter, Bīja Sharaf, inherited possession of the lands. Bīja Sharaf's husband, a certain Mīrzā Muḥammad ʿAlī Hirawī, sold the villages to the governor of Astarābād, Riḍā Khān (see Figure 59).

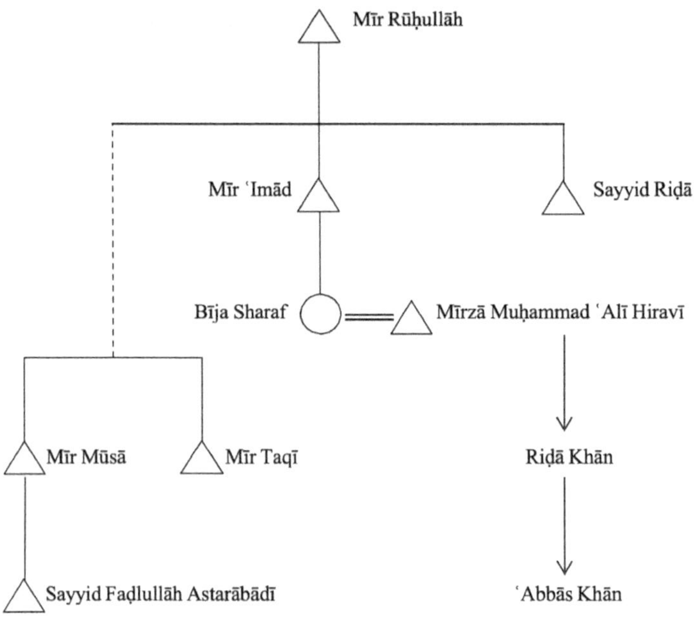

Figure 61: A partial reconstruction of possession of the *waqf* of Mīr Rūḥullāh founded in Muḥarram 1052/ April 1642.[86]

86 Mīr Rūḥullāh had at least two other sons besides Mīr ʿImād and Sayyid Riḍā named Mīr Ghiyāth al-Dīn and Mīr Kamāl al-Dīn (Sutūda and Dhabīḥī 1354 sh./1975, VI, 432–433). It is not clear from the sources which of Mīr Rūḥullāh's sons Sayyid Faḍlullāh Astarābādī's father Mīr Mūsā traced his descent from. We know Sayyid Faḍlullāh was Mīr Mūsā's son from Sutūda and Dhabīḥī 1354 sh./1975, VII, 74–75: *"jināb āqā sayyid faḍlullāh astarābādī . . . marḥūm maghfūr jannat riḍwān ārām-gāh āqā mīr mūsā wālid-i ān jināb"*. ʿAbbās Khān inherited the disputed lands from Riḍā Khān and his son Imām Qulī Khān b. Riḍā Khān, see document no. 50: "*hamān yad-i riḍā khān wa irth az ū mustamirr bāshad*".

If Bīja Sharaf had acquired control of the villages from her father Mīr ʿImād as an inheritance, then the lands were private property (*milk*) and the sale to Riḍā Khān was legal. Similarly, if Bīja Sharaf had acquired possession of the two villages as an administrator of the *waqf*, the sale might still be construed as legal. It could be assumed, as it was in the 1860s, for instance, that there had been some legal pretext which had permitted the sale of the *waqf* lands by the administrator. Bīja Sharaf's acknowledgement (*iqrār*), therefore, that the lands had been constituted as a *waqf* in favour of Mīr Rūḥullāh's male descendants was significant. It was proof that she had not inherited control of the lands as private property from her father Mīr ʿImād. At the same time, it was evidence that her control, as a female descendant of Mīr Rūḥullāh had been provisional until such a time when Mīr Rūḥullāh's male descendants were old enough to become administrators.

Since Bīja Sharaf neither owned the land as private property nor was a *de jure* administrator of the *waqf*, the sale that had occurred to Riḍā Khān was illegal. In fact, anyone whose possession of the lands derived from Bīja Sharaf possessed the lands illegally. It is probably shortly after these witness testimonies were collected that Ḥājjī Mullā Riḍā Astarābādī wrote his ruling on the necessity of the return of the lands to Mīr Mūsā and Mīr Taqī. This ruling, as we have already mentioned, was written directly on to their original witness statement, but it was never enforced. Perhaps after the ruling failed to work, the Dirāzgīsū felt it was easier to simply demand a share of revenues from the land rather than attempt a full-scale restitution of the two villages. The *farmān* of Fatḥ ʿAlī Shāh issued in Dhū al-Qaʿda 1240/June 1825, which recognises the right of Mīr Mūsā and Mīr Taqī to one-tenth of the revenues of Chūplānī and Mīr-Maḥalla, was probably based on a transcript of Mīr Mūsā and Mīr Taqī's witness statement without Astarābādī's ruling.

Similarly, Āqā Muḥammad Mahdī, as we have discussed above, must also have based his ruling on a similar transcript of Mīr Mūsā and Mīr Taqī's witness statement. In the 1840s, however, Sayyid Faḍlullāh began to make use of the original witness statement of Mīr Mūsā and Mīr Taqī. This witness statement preserved Astarābādī's ruling in Astarābādī's own handwriting and with Astarābādī's seal. Sayyid Faḍlullāh was determined to make another attempt to regain control of Chūplānī and Mīr-Maḥalla from the Qajar khans.

3.3 Stage 3: Attempts to Enforce Arbitration

3.3.1 The Attempt at Arbitration before Sharīʿatmadār Ashrafī

An undated petition ʿAbbās Khān wrote to the royal court is significant because it is the only record we have of ʿAbbās Khān's view of the land dispute. According to the document, Sayyid Faḍlullāh had initiated an invalid lawsuit (*daʿwa-yi bāṭila karda*) over the village of Mīr-Maḥalla in the past.[87] The failed process referred to by ʿAbbās Khān here is probably a reference to Sayyid Faḍlullāh's use of Āqā Muḥammad Mahdī's ruling. ʿAbbās Khān notes that in response to Sayyid Faḍlullāh's attempt, he had sent rulings of the jurists of Astarābād, Sārī, Bārfurūsh and the entire Caspian region to the shah.[88] The shah, having examined these rulings, issued a decree that Sayyid Faḍlullāh had no legal claim in the case. Sayyid Faḍlullāh, following the issuance of the *farmān*, dropped the matter. Now, however, according to ʿAbbās Khān, he had begun to disturb the peasants of Mīr Maḥalla again. ʿAbbās Khān informs the shah that his agent, Ḥājjī Mīrzā Khānjān, was sending someone to the royal court to collect a firm decree which could be used to prevent Sayyid Faḍlullāh from creating further trouble. The petition ends by noting that if, despite the rulings of the jurists which ʿAbbās Khān had sent to the royal court, Sayyid Faḍlullāh still felt he had a claim to make, then he should prepare himself for arbitration. If not, he should relinquish his claim over Mīr-Maḥalla.[89]

The document is the first indication we have that ʿAbbās Khān was willing to submit to arbitration over the lands. The reasons for this are not entirely clear. It seems that after the failure of Āqā Muḥammad Mahdī's ruling, Sayyid Faḍlullāh began an intense campaign from 1844–1847 to force ʿAbbās Khān to accept arbitration. The polemical letters that survive in the Dirāzgīsū archive probably date from this period. A letter by a jurist named Sayyid Muḥammad Bāqir addressed to ʿAbbās Khān stresses that the dispute between him and Sayyid Faḍlullāh must be resolved via arbitration.[90] We also know that Sayyid Faḍlullāh signed a legal agreement on 21 Jamādī I 1263/7 May 1847 with a certain Qulī Khān Yūzbāshī.[91] The document authorises Qulī Khān Yūzbāshī to collect revenues from Mīr-Maḥalla and Chūplānī on behalf of Sayyid Faḍlullāh. It also refers to several more documents that Sayyid Faḍlullāh had been able to obtain in the intervening period in support of his claim. These documents include a *taʿlīqa* decree from the Prime Minister (*ṣadr-i aʿẓam*), Ḥājjī Mīrzā Āqāsī (d.1264/1848), and a *raqam* decree ratifying the *taʿlīqa* from the new governor of Astarābād, Sulaymān Khān Qūyūnlū Qājār (r.1257–1267/1840–1850).[92]

It was probably Qulī Khān Yūzbāshī's attempts to tax the peasants of Mīr-Maḥalla that had provoked ʿAbbās Khān's initial petition. We know that ʿAbbās

87 Document no. 34.
88 Document no. 34.
89 Document no. 34.
90 Document no. 51.
91 Document no. 53.
92 Document no. 30.

Khān sent at least two further petitions to the royal court during this period.[93] In a petition sent to the royal court in Rajab 1263/July 1847, ʿAbbās Khān is said to have formally agreed to arbitration with Sayyid Faḍlullāh before the *imām-jumʿa* of Astarābād, Sharīʿatamdār Ashrafī.[94] ʿAbbās Khān's reason for choosing Sharīʿatmadār was probably because Sharīʿatmadār had endorsed his claim to the lands during the period when Sayyid Faḍlullāh had brought Āqā Muḥammad Mahdī's ruling from Isfahan. What ʿAbbās Khān does not seem to have known was that Sayyid Faḍlullāh and the Dirāzgīsū had also been paying visits to Sharīʿatmadār. When ʿAbbās Khān proposed Sharīʿatmadār as arbiter, the Dirāzgīsū agreed.

3.3.2 The First Binding Agreement at the Royal Court

On 12 Shaʿbān 1263/26 July 1847, Sayyid Faḍlullāh's agent, Mullā Muḥammad Ismāʿīl, and Ḥājjī Mīrzā Khānjān, representing ʿAbbās Khān, signed a binding agreement (*iltizām-nāmcha*) at the royal court in Tehran.[95] Both sides agreed to present themselves either in person or via their proxies for arbitration before Sharīʿatmadār in Astarābād. Whatever ruling Sharīʿatmadār issued would be recognised as the verdict of God (*ḥukmullāh*). If either side failed to show up for the arbitration, they would face punishment. A revenue collector (*muḥassil*) named Naqd ʿAlī Bēg was appointed by the royal court to ensure that both sides appeared before Sharīʿatmadār for the arbitration. Naqd ʿAlī Bēg was also supposed to send a report to the royal court with the outcome.[96] The transcript of the binding agreement that has survived does not specify an exact date when the arbitration was to occur. We know from a letter which Sayyid Faḍlullāh's agent, Mullā Muḥammad Ismāʿīl, wrote to Sayyid Faḍlullāh that it proved impossible to compel ʿAbbās Khān to come for the arbitration: "First of all, where is the Bēglerbēgī? . . . When he was encamped at Siyāh – Bālā, the shah's *muḥassil* and Āqā Mīr Abū l-Qāsim went up to see him and said: 'Come let us go before Sharīʿatmadār' – they heard insults in reply."[97] The Dirāzgīsū did appear before Sharīʿatmadār, and Sharīʿatmadār

93 Document no. 35.
94 Document no. 35.
95 Document no. 54.
96 Document no. 54.
97 Document no. 42: *"awwalan ānki kū bēglerbēgī . . . dar zamānī ki dar ūrdū-yi siyāh-bālā būdand muḥassil-i shāhī bā āqā mīr abū al-qāsim raftand wa bā īshān guftand ki biyā khidmat-i sharīʿatmadār jawāb bi durushtī shinidand"*. This important letter is undated, and I have worked out who the recepient and the author are from the content. There is little doubt, however, that the *malja' al-anām* referred to in the document is Sayyid Faḍlullāh, and that the *wakīl* is his agent Mullā Muḥammad Ismāʿīl, whose writing style is instantly recognisable among the documents of the Dirāzgīsū archive.

endorsed their claim. ʿAbbās Khān was furious with Sharīʿatmadār. He summoned Sharīʿatmadār's brother, Ḥasan Khān, in Ashraf, a small town in the Caspian region. Ḥasan Khān was subjected to the bastinado and then tied up and asked to pay a fine of two hundred *tūmāns.*[98] News soon spread about what had happened, and an angry mob of Sharīʿatmadār's supporters gathered to attack ʿAbbās Khān's men and free the brother of the *imam-jumʿa* of Astarābād. ʿAbbās Khān's men had to content themselves with the few *tūmāns* they found in Ḥasan Khān's pocket, and quickly set him free.[99] The Dirāzgīsū tried to document these acts of violence perpetrated by ʿAbbās Khān. They petitioned witnesses to give testimony about what had happened so that it could be used as proof later.[100]

3.3.3 ʿAbbās Khān's New Petition to the Royal Court

In Rabīʿ I 1264/February 1848, ʿAbbās Khān sent a new petition to the royal court.[101] ʿAbbās Khān claimed that eight months had passed since the binding agreement was signed and that neither Sayyid Faḍlullāh nor his representative had appeared before Sharīʿatmadār.[102] Based on a note that had been scribbled in the margin of the binding agreement both sides had signed and sealed, ʿAbbās Khān requested the lands remain in his possession until Sayyid Faḍlullāh or his representative were ready for arbitration.[103] Sayyid Faḍlullāh and the Dirāzgīsū were shocked by ʿAbbās Khān's lies. Sayyid Faḍlullāh left Astarābād for Tehran to

98 Document no. 42: *"khabar bi ʿālījāh beglerbegī risīd ki jināb sharīʿatmadār niwishta dāda-and, dar ashraf barādār-i jināb sharīʿatmadār iḥḍār farmūdand wa muʾākhadha-yi ziyādī kardand ki barādar-i tū dah hizār tūmān bi-man ḍarar zada ast mablagh-i diwist tūmān ū rā jarīma namūdand dar ḥuḍūr-i khud ū rā bastand chūn ahālī-yi ashraf muṭalliʿ shudand khwāstand ki bi – hujūm-i ʿāmm birawand wa barādar-i jināb sharīʿatmadār rā biyāwarand si chahār tūmān ki dar jīb dāsht giriftand wa ū rā rahā kardand".*

99 Document no. 42; a representative of Sharīʿatmadār living in Sārī was also fined by ʿAbbās Khān. In the letter, in light of the recent events, Mullā Muḥammad Ismāʿīl asks Sayyid Faḍlullāh if he could be relieved of his duties as *wakīl* of the Dirāzgīsū: "As I have said regarding what happened to Sharīʿatmadār's brother and his representative: I too have relatives in Māzandarān, and my family and I often make trips there, so I fear the same thing will happen to us" *(chūn mulāḥiẓa-yi īn awḍāʿ namūdam jurʾat na-namūdam ki iẓhār-i wikālat az janib shumā namāyam awwalan ān ki ʿarḍ shud ki bar sar-i barādar wa mansūb-i sharʿīatmadār chi āwardand banda ham dar māzandarān wābasta-hā dāram ʿalāwa ān ki banda wa bandazāda-hā gāh gāhī bi-māzandarān āmad wa shud dārim bar mā hamān mī-rawad bar sar – i barādar-i sharīʿatmadār wa mansūb-i īshān rafta).*

100 Document no. 14; *ʿabduhu al-rājī muḥammad* appears to have been the only person brave enough to respond to the Dirāzgīsū request for witness testimony.

101 Document no. 35.

102 Document no. 37.

103 Document no. 37.

explain to the shah personally what had really happened.[104] At the royal court, Sayyid Faḍlullāh presented a witness statement signed by several *ʿulamāʾ* and notables confirming that attempts had been made to summon ʿAbbās Khān for arbitration, but that he had refused.[105] In Rabī II 1264/March 1848, a letter was written from the royal court to another *muḥaṣṣil*, Ibrāhīm Bēg Tufangdār, in Astarābad, giving him details about what had happened so far.[106]

Ibrāhīm Bēg was ordered upon receipt of the letter to obtain a decree from the governor of Astarābād, Sulaymān Khān Qūyūnlū Qājār, and to use it to summon representatives of the two sides for arbitration before Sharīʿatmadār.[107] This time, if either side failed to appear, Ibrāhīm Bēg was to ask Sharīʿatmadār to write a note confirming who had appeared and who had not.[108] This document was to be sent along with Ibrāhīm Bēg's report to the royal court.[109] We know from an undated letter in the archive of the Dirāzgīsū that Ibrāhīm Bēg's efforts to bring ʿAbbās Khān's agent, Ḥājjī Mīrzā Khānjān, before Sharīʿatmadār did not succeed.[110] Sayyid Faḍlullāh's agent, Mullā Muḥammad Ismāʿīl, did appear and managed to get Sharīʿatmadār to write a note confirming that he had come for the arbitration.[111] Following two failed attempts to bring the two sides before Sharīʿatmadār, in Jamādī I 1264/April 1848, ʿAbbās Khān sent yet another petition to the royal court.[112] ʿAbbās Khān suggested that if Sayyid Faḍlullāh was willing, the arbitration of the case should be carried out by another jurist in Astarābād. The jurist ʿAbbās Khān had in mind was Mullā Muḥammad Taqī.

3.3.4 The Attempt at Arbitration before Mullā Muḥammad Taqī

As noted in the introduction to this chapter, Mullā Muḥammad Taqī had spent a considerable amount of time outside Astarābād studying with leading Uṣūlī jurists. When he returned to Astarābād, in around 1258/1842–3, his erudition was

---

104 Document no. 37. Sayyid Faḍlullāh also appears to have got a *taʿlīqa* decree from the Prime Minister, Ḥājjī Mīrzā Āqāsī, confirming that ʿAbbās Khān had not come for the arbitration, which he had somehow managed to attach to the original binding agreement that had been sealed by ʿAbbās Khān's agent. Apparently, only one original of the agreement was kept at the royal court. This might explain why the Dirāzgīsū archive only has a transcript of this important document.
105 Document no. 37: *"wa istishhād rā ham ibrāz namūda"*.
106 Document no. 37.
107 Document no. 37.
108 Document no. 37.
109 Document no. 37.
110 Document no. 38.
111 Document no. 38.
112 Document no. 38.

widely acknowledged. He is said to have held the post of *imām-jumʿa* of Astarābād, though precisely when is not clear. Like Sharīʿatmadār, Mullā Muḥammad Taqī also seems to have initially supported ʿAbbās Khān. He is said to have written the following about the ruling of Ḥājjī Mullā Rīḍā Astarābādī and the status of the two villages: "I have made thorough investigations, but its [the ruling's] validity has not become evident and [the disputed lands] are private property (*man faḥṣ-i bisyār kardam wa iʿtibārash maʿlūm nashud wa milk ast*)".[113]

As in the case of Sharīʿatmadār, the problem seems to be that Mullā Muḥammad Taqī issued this certification before examining the documents of the Dirāzgīsū. When Mullā Muḥammad Taqī did eventually see Mīr Mūsā and Mīr Taqī's original witness statement with Ḥājjī Mullā Riḍā Astarābādī's ruling, he realised that there could be no doubt whatsoever that Astarābādī had indeed issued a ruling in favour of the Dirāzgīsū some fifty years ago. Moreover, the ruling had been issued based on evidence, witness testimonies confirming an illegal sale of the land to the Qajar khans. The importance of Mīr Mūsā and Mīr Taqī's original witness statement for Mullā Muḥammad Taqī is confirmed by the fact that he issued his ratification of Astarābādī's ruling next to Astarābādī's ruling on this document.[114]

What is unclear from the sources is when Sayyid Faḍlullāh first showed the documents of the Dirāzgīsū to Mullā Muḥammad Taqī. It seems that Sayyid Faḍlullāh's agent, Mullā Muḥammad Ismāʿīl, had asked Sharīʿatmadār whether it was permissible for further legal proceedings to take place after the ruling Sharīʿatmadār had issued ratifying Ḥājjī Mullā Riḍā Astarābādī's ruling.[115] Sharīʿatmadār said it was not permissible.[116] The ratification he had issued was final.[117] Perhaps because they knew the ratification would have no binding force unless it was the outcome

113 Document no. 48.

114 Document no. 35b: "*bismillāh ʿazza shaʾnuh; muḥaqqaq wa huwaydā gardīd ki marḥūm . . . ḥājjī mullā riḍā aʿlā allāh maqamahu ḥukm bi-radd-i amlāk-i marqūma bi-ḥaḍarāt-i marqūmīn karda-and wa dar īn si saṭr-i janb niwishta-and wa ḥukm-i īshān lāzim al-ittibāʿ ast [jāy-i muhr-i mullā muḥammad taqī]*". Mullā Muḥammd Taqī's ratification was copied in later transcripts of the witness statement. The actual text of Ḥājjī Mullā Riḍā Astarābādī's ruling, however, written in three lines next to it (*dar īn si saṭr-i janb*), was not.

115 Document no. 37; it appears it was Sharīʿatmadār's reply to this question that led to the bastinado and fine imposed on his brother by ʿAbbās Khān.

116 Document no. 37: "*chunān ki istiftāʾ shuda iʿāda-yi īn murāfaʿa fawq-i ḥukm wa imḍāʾ-yi ʿulamāʾ ḥarām wa ghayr-i jāʾiz*".

117 Document no. 37; Sayyid Faḍlullāh's agent was convinced that the ratification that had been issued to the Dirāzgīsū by Sharīʿatmadār had the binding force to end the dispute, even though it had not been the outcome of arbitration.

of a real arbitration, the Dirāzgīsū agreed, as ʿAbbās Khān had suggested, to take the case before Mullā Muḥammad Taqī.

3.3.5 The Second Binding Agreement at the Royal Court

The process of bringing the two sides to arbitration before Mullā Muḥammad Taqī was as chaotic as in the case of Sharīʿatmadār. Once again, the two sides signed a binding agreement at the royal court in Tehran.[118] A new decisive clause was added to the agreement. If one of the sides failed to appear for arbitration, victory would automatically be granted to the side that appeared.[119] The *muḥaṣṣil* entrusted with the task of enforcing the binding agreement was Ḥājjī Āqā Bēg Yūzbāshī, Superintendent of the Royal Store of Carpets (*yūzbāshī-yi farrāsh-khāna -yi mubāraka*).[120] Ḥājjī Āqā Bēg Yūzbāshī was already in Astarābād trying to collect Sayyid Faḍlullāh's pension and enforce the ratification Sharīʿatmadār had issued to the Dirāzgīsū.[121] Following ʿAbbās Khān's petition to the royal court, Ḥājjī Āqā Bēg Yūzbāshī's duties were now to bring the two sides for arbitration before Mullā Muḥammad Taqī.[122] As before, however, neither ʿAbbas Khān nor his agent, Ḥājjī Mīrzā Khānjān, could be compelled to appear before Mullā Muḥammad Taqī.[123] According to the terms of the new binding agreement, Sayyid Faḍlullāh and the Dirāzgīsū had won, or so it seemed. In the same month, Jamādī II 1264/ May 1848, however, queries began to be raised about Ḥājjī Mullā Riḍā Astarābādī's *ijtihād*.

We know this from a petition which the Dirāzgīsū wrote to Mullā Muḥammad Taqī, asking for a ratification of Astarābādī's status as a *mujtahid* and the binding force of the ruling he had issued.[124] It was a rather desperate attempt by ʿAbbās Khān to circumvent the enforcement of the ruling. Ḥājjī Mullā Riḍā Astarābādī's juristic credentials were solid. He was a student of the great Uṣūlī jurist Muḥammad Bāqir Bihbahānī himself and among the first group of scholars returning from Iraq to Iran in the Qajar period trained and recognised as *mujtahids*. Naturally, his death had made it easier to cast doubts about his *ijtihād*. The Dirāzgīsū had been preparing for this. Sayyid Faḍlullāh, as we have seen, had already approached several Astarābādī *ʿulamāʾ* to certify that Ḥājjī Mullā Riḍā Astarābādī

118 Document no. 35.
119 Document no. 35.
120 Document no. 35.
121 Document no. 35.
122 Document no. 35.
123 Document no. 35.
124 Document no. 4; this document was probably prepared when the Dirāzgīsū appeared for arbitration before Mullā Muḥammad Taqī.

was a *mujtahid*, that ʿAbbās Khān had recognised him as such and that he used to enforce his rulings.[125] These certifications were clearly not enough. On 20 Jamādī II 1264/24 May 1848, Mullā Muḥammad Taqī issued a new certification to the effect that the deceased Ḥājjī Mullā Riḍā Astarābādī was indeed a *mujtahid*. Mullā Muḥammad Taqī also ratified the ruling issued by Ḥājjī Mullā Riḍā Astarābādī.[126] Despite this, in 1267/1850–1, Mullā Muḥammad Taqī was again asked to certify Astarābādī's *ijtihād* and ratify his ruling.[127] From this period onwards, the question of Astarābādī's *ijtihād* did not resurface. ʿAbbās Khān and Sayyid Faḍllulāh were both dead. The dispute was now carried on between ʿAbbās Khān's children and the Dirāzgīsū. As we shall see, ʿAbbās Khān's children turned the focus of litigation away from the validity of Astarābādī's ruling based on his qualifications as a *mujtahid* to the circumstances surrounding the issuance of the ruling. This was a strategic decision. None of the Astarābādī *ʿulamāʾ* had been willing to concede that Ḥājjī Mullā Riḍā Astarābādī was not a *mujtahid*. There were, however, some powerful jurists who were not convinced that the ruling had been issued as a binding judgement in the case.

3.4 Stage 4: The Debate over the Legal Rulings in the Case and the Settlement

3.4.1 The Ruling of Raʾīs al-ʿUlamāʾ

Shortly after the death of Mullā Muḥammad Taqī in 1272/1855, Raʾīs al-ʿUlamāʾ (d.1284/1867) is said to have written the following sentence about Ḥājjī Mullā Riḍā Astarābādī's ruling: *ān ḥukm muʿtabar nīst* (that ruling is not valid).[128] This meant trouble for the Dirāzgīsū. Until this point they appear to have enjoyed some measure of possession over the village of Chūplānī.[129] Mīr-Maḥalla, however, remained in ʿAbbās Khān's hands and been inherited by his children.[130] Using Raʾīs's ruling, ʿAbbās Khān's children now managed to reconfiscate Chūplānī from

125 Document no. 3.
126 Document no. 4.
127 Document no. 5.
128 Document no. 48.
129 After the arbitration with Mullā Muḥammad Taqī, the Dirāzgīsū appear to have been in possession of Chūplānī, though they had transferred parts of it which were unproductive to a local government official. See document no. 46.
130 Document no. 55; according to a settlement contract between the Dirāzgīsū and a minister in the local government of Astarābād dated Shaʿbān 1276/October 1860, Mīr-Maḥalla seems to have remained in ʿAbbās Khān's hands despite the arbitration proceedings before Sharīʿatmadār Ashrafī and Mullā Muḥammad Taqī.

the Dirāzgīsū.[131] Therefore, around twenty-five years after Sayyid Faḍlullāh obtained his ruling from Isfahan against ʿAbbās Khān, the dispute between the sayyids and the khans, *daʿwā-yi sādāt wa khawānīn* as it was called, was back to where it had started. The Dirāzgīsū were not in possession of either Chūplānī or Mīr-Maḥalla. Once again, they were claimants in the dispute. In the aftermath of Raʾīs al-ʿUlamā's invalidation (*naqḍ*) of Ḥājjī Mullā Riḍā Astarābādī's ruling, an intense legal debate broke out among the *ʿulamāʾ* in Astarābād.[132] The *ʿulamāʾ* of Astarābād became divided into two rival camps. There were *ʿulamāʾ* who strongly opposed a negotiated settlement. They argued that the claim of the Dirāzgīsū to the lands based on the ruling of Ḥājjī Mullā Riḍā Astarābādī was still valid despite Raʾīs al-ʿUlamāʾ's so-called invalidation. They claimed that the possession of Chūplānī by ʿAbbās Khān's children based on the ruling of Raʾīs was invalid. ʿAbbās Khān's children had no right to initiate a new round of legal proceedings in the case (*tajdīd-i murāfaʿa*) based on a new ruling.[133] This was not legally permissible (*murāfaʿa kardan jāʾiz nīst*).[134]

The other group, led by Raʾīs al-ʿUlamāʾ himself, claimed that the ruling issued by Ḥājjī Mullā Riḍāʾ Astarābādī was not the type of ruling that could end a dispute between two sides (*qāṭiʿ-i nizāʿ-i ṭarafayn*).[135] It was not the kind of ruling that brought about closure such that no further litigation was permissible. Raʾīs and others had examined documents of both sides and thought, based on what they had seen, that ʿAbbās Khān's children had a stronger claim to the lands as their inheritance than the Dirāzgīsū. It was, they argued, in the best interests of the

131 Document no. 46.

132 Much of what we know about this legal debate comes from four anonymous letters (document nos. 47, 48, 49 and 50) in the archive of the Dirāzgīsū written by A, B, C and D. This correspondence appears to have occurred shortly after A, B, C, and D had inspected the documents of the Dirāzgīsū and the documents of ʿAbbās Khān's children. A, B, C and D all seem to have been jurists who supported the Dirāzgīsū. They differed, however, on how the dispute with ʿAbbās Khān's children should be resolved. Letter A was written by a jurist who opined, based on the documents of the two sides, that the claim of the Dirāzgīsū was stronger. He presents several arguments in favour of the validity of Ḥājjī Mullā Ridā Astarābādī's ruling and opposes a settlement. B was shocked to find that ʿAbbās Khān's children had rulings from the very same jurists who had given rulings to the Dirāzgīsū. B considerd that based on the documents, the claim of the Dirāzgīsū to the lands was not defensible. B therefore proposed a settlement as the best way forward. Like B, C's opinion was that settlement was the best option for the Dirāzgīsū. Like A, D opposed a settlement. As far as D was concerned, any jurist who supported a settlement was a supporter of ʿAbbās Khān's children and an enemy of the Dirāzgīsū. D ends his letter categorically: the sayyids will not accept a settlement (*sādāt bi-ṣulḥ rāḍī namī shawand*).

133 Document nos. 7–10.

134 Document nos. 7–10.

135 Document no. 9.

Dirāzgīsū to negotiate an amicable settlement with the descendants of ʿAbbās Khān. If not, they warned, the Dirāzgīsū risked losing everything.

3.4.2 The Binding Force of the Text

In what follows I will summarize the legal debate that took place among the Astarābādī *ʿulamaʾ*. This debate is of considerable interest as it sheds light on how rulings issued by scholars in such land disputes were perceived and discussed. The first question that had to be resolved was the nature of Ḥājjī Mullā Riḍā Astarābādī's ruling.[136] Was Astarābādī's text the type that had the binding force to permanently deprive ʿAbbās Khān's children of their claimed inheritance of the two villages (*qāṭiʿ-i ʿudhr-i marḥūm bēglerbēgī*)?[137] Initially the debate centered on the text of the ruling itself, but it later moved to the circumstances of the issuance of the text. The text of Ḥājjī Mullā Riḍā Astarābādī's ruling was as follows:

> A group of reliable people have given witness testimony regarding the said circumstances. The ruling of the *sharīʿa* to be obeyed and followed is the compulsory return of the said lands to the said people.[138]

According to the *ʿulamāʾ* who supported a settlement, the text was not a judgement issued in a lawsuit, because it lacked any expression of self-intent. This was seen as a crucial requirement for helping to distinguish whether Astarābādī had meant to issue a judicial decision or was merely asserting what the ruling of the *sharīʿa* was on the case, in other words his legal opinion.[139] When they wanted to

---

136 Document no. 8.

137 Document no. 7; Naṣrullāh al-Ḥusaynī considered that even if there was any doubt, which there should not be, whether Ḥājjī Mullā Riḍā Astarābādī's ruling had the binding force to do this, the ruling issued by Āqā Muḥammad Mahdī and the ratifications issued by Sharīʿatmadār Ashrafī were more than sufficient to deprive the children of ʿAbbās Khān of the two villages.

138 Document no. 3.

139 This was discussed based on the theoretical distinction between an assertion (*khabar*) and an origination (*inshāʾ*). See especially document no. 9. The jurists who supported a settlement construed the text of Astarābādī's ruling as a *khabar*, while jurists who opposed a settlement construed the text as an *inshāʾ*. All *fatwā*s were deemed to be *khabar* – an assertion or a report. They could either be believed (*taṣdīq*) or disbelieved (*takhdhīb*) by the litigant who requested them. A ruling that was written, however, as an *inshāʾ* was not subject to being believed or disbelieved. Its binding force was inherent, and like a judgement at the end of a lawsuit, the litigant had no choice before it. He chould not choose to accept it or reject it. There is so far no study of the view of Imāmī jurists on this distinction, as it relates to judicial practice. One of the main differences between a text written as a *khabar* and one written as an *inshāʾ* was the presence or absence of self-intent. For the significance of self-intent in Islamic legal acts and the *khabar/inshāʾ* distinction, see Jackson 1996, 170–177 and Messick 2001, 151–178.

make it explicit that they were acting as judges, Qajar jurists tended to include speech act declarations in Arabic in their rulings such as 'I judged' (*ḥakamtu*) or 'I made it binding' (*alzamaytu*). Alternatively, this could be expressed in the form of a clause at the end of the ruling as follows: *hākadha qaḍaytu wa-alzamaytu wa-llāhu khayru l-ḥākimīn* (thus I have judged and made binding and God is the best of judges).[140] A far more common way, however, to express self-intent was to use a passive construction explaining what had become established and confirmed for the jurist acting as a judge based on the evidence. This is the way for instance Āqā Muḥammad Mahdī's ruling is constructed: "For this servant of religious scholars it has become established and confirmed that . . ." (*barāy-i īn khādim-i ʿulamāʾ-i dīniyya muḥaqqaq wa thābit shud ki*).[141]

Astarābādī, however, had made no reference to himself in his ruling. His ruling did not have an explicit speech act declaration, nor did it use a passive construction which would have helped to indicate he was acting as a judge. References to the self were important because, unlike in the Ottoman world or Central Asia, the Qajar jurist combined the role of *qāḍī* and *muftī*. If the text of his ruling did not make it absolutely clear that he was issuing a judicial decision, it could always be construed as an opinion. Since there was no state regulation controlling how legal documents had to be issued, Qajar jurists tended to compose the text of their rulings as they saw best. While some took great care to ensure they were clear and precise about the type of ruling they issued, others were notoriously vague and ambivalent. This caused problems when the binding force of the text was challenged.

The *ʿulamāʾ* who opposed a settlement were irritated by the idea that the lack of an expression of self-intent in the text meant it was not issued as a judicial decision. They argued that the very same jurists who supported a settlement routinely ratified rulings which contained neither expressions of self-intent nor even the word *ḥukm* as binding judicial decisions.[142] Moreover, it could be inferred

---

140 See Ṭabāṭabāʾī, 1361 sh./1982, 380, 413 for examples of rulings with these clauses at the end.

141 Other examples include: 'For this servant of the victorious Qajar state, certain knowledge has been obtained that' (*bar dāʿī-yi dawām-i dawlat-i qāhira ʿilm-i qaṭʿī ḥāṣil gardīd ki*) (Sutūda and Dhabīḥī 1354 sh./1975, VI, 255) or 'for this servant of the chosen, pure, infallible Imāms, may God's blessing be upon them, it has become apparent and evident that' (*bar īn khādim-i akhyār aʾimma-yi aṭhhār ʿalayhim ṣalawātu llāhi l-māliki l-ghaffār ẓāhir wa āshkār gardīda ki*) (Bīgdilī 1367 sh./1988, 247).

142 Document no. 50, D: *"dar bisyār jāhā dīdam ki shumā bar ḥukm-i baʿḍ ki lafẓ-i qaḍaytu wa alzamaytu nadāsht wa lafẓ-i ḥukm muḥaqqaq irjāʿ nashuda imḍā niwishtīd īn nīz mithl-i ān waqāʿī ast"* ("I have seen in many places that you have ratified [as binding judicial decisions] rulings of others which did not have the words "I judged" (*qaḍaytu*) or "I have made binding" (*alzamaytu*). In fact even the word *ḥukm* was not specified. This too [the case of Astarābādī's ruling] is like those instances"). Naṣrullāh al-Ḥusaynī, a staunch supporter of the Dirāzgīsū, notes that jurists

from circumstantial evidence that the text had been issued as a judicial decision in a lawsuit. There was no doubt that there had been some form of request for reliable witness testimony (*muṭālaba-yi shuhūd*).[143] The text also seemed to imply the presence of a claimant and a defendant (*ḥuḍūr-i khaṣmayn*) since it required a return of the lands from one party to another.[144] Finally, the way the text was formally written (*kitābat*), its use for instance of the word *luzūm* making an action compulsory, was proof that it had been issued as a judicial decision in the case.[145] The *ʿulamāʾ* who supported a settlement were not convinced. Even if one accepted the premise that it had been issued as a judicial decision, it was not clear if Astarābādī had reviewed the evidence of both parties when he wrote the ruling. Here the debate turned to the circumstances of issuance (*kayfiyyat-i ṣudūr*) of the text.

3.4.3 The Circumstances of Issuance

This problem seems to have been caused by the fact that Ḥājjī Mullā Riḍāʾ Astarābādī's original ruling was written onto Mīr Mūsā and Mīr Taqī's witness statement. His ruling could therefore be interpreted as a judicial decision certifying the claim of the claimant based on their evidence alone, in the absence of the defendant. Astarābādī's ruling did not make it clear if he had also taken the evidence of the defendant into account when he wrote it. Such a ruling could not be said to be a binding judgement which had definitively settled the dispute in favour of one side issued in the absence of the other side. Rather, it was merely a judicial certification of the claim of one side. Since there was no way to decisively resolve this problem, the debate now turned to other documents in the archives of the two sides.

3.4.4 The Documents of Possession of the Qajar Khans

First the documents proving possession (*al-athār al-taṣarruf*) of the villages by the Qajar khans were discussed. These included sale deeds proving that the Qajar khans had bought the two villages. They also included rental contracts which proved that as owners of the two villages, the Qajar khans had leased the lands to other individuals. The *ʿulamāʾ* who supported a settlement opined that even if the

---

who had doubts over the binding force of the text would not accept it if they themselves had issued such a ruling, and others raised similar doubts, see document 7.

143 Document no. 9: *"maḥmūl ast bar maʿnī-yi ḥukm khuṣūṣan bā inḍimām-i qarāʾin min ḥuḍūr-i khaṣmayn wa muṭālaba-yi shuhūd-i muʿtabara"*.

144 Document no. 9.

145 Document no. 8.

lands had formerly been *waqf*, given the sheer number of documents proving continuous possession by the Qajar khans of Chūplānī and Mīr-Maḥālla since the beginning of the Qajar period, the assumption had to be that some sort of legal sale of the *waqf* lands had occurred.[146] Many of the documents proving the possession of the two villages by the Qajar khans had sealed attestations in the handwriting of the preeminent scholars (*aʿyān wa akābir*) of Astarābād.[147] The only way to explain this was that an authoritative jurist had at the time issued a ruling permitting the sale of the *waqf* land (*mujawwiz-i bayʿ-i waqf*) to the Qajar khans.[148] This would also explain why Ḥājjī Mullā Riḍā Astarābādī's ruling on the necessity of a return of the lands to the Dirāzgīsū (*radd-i amlāk*) had never been enforced.[149] The lands had by then legally become private property (*milk*) and were no longer *waqf*. The *ʿulamāʾ* who opposed a settlement rejected this argument. They said they too had inspected the so-called *al-athār al-taṣarruf* of the Qajar khans but had found them to be fundamentally problematic. The *aʿyān wa akābir* of Astarābād merely verified that the transcripts of these documents corresponded to their originals.[150] There was not a single well-known scholar who certified the legal validity of these contracts.[151] In addition, if one examined what was written in the contracts themselves, the purchase sum given of under two hundred and fifty *tūmān*s for both the two villages was far too low.[152] These were valuable lands. Mīr-Maḥalla had ancient water rights to the Tarang river and its rent alone was a thousand *kharwār* of grain; its sale for such a paltry sum must have been illegal.[153] It was also improbable that the ruling of an authoritative jurist who permitted the sale of the *waqf* land had somehow acted as a legal obstacle preventing Astarābādī's ruling from being enforced.[154] A far more likely reason for the non-enforcement of Astarābadī's ruling was that

146 Document no. 48, B.
147 Document no. 48, B: *"bar khuṭūṭ wa khawātim-i aʿyān wa akābir-i astarābād"*.
148 Document no. 48, B.
149 Document no. 48, B.
150 Document no. 50, D: *"ammā niwishtijāt-i qājār wa khawānīn az qabāla wa bunchāq ki muhr maʿrūfī dar ānhā nīst muntahā īnki sawād muṭābiq-i aṣl ast muhr-i bisyār dārad az muʿtabarīn wa ghayrihim wāfī dalāl namīshawad"*.
151 Document no. 50, D.
152 Document no. 50, D: *"ijāra-yi mīr-maḥalla hizār kharwār astarābādī wa āb-i ān qarya rūd-khāna-yi ʿaẓīma-yi tarang ast wa ḥāl marḥūm [Riḍā Khān] ān qarya rā az fulān wa fulān kharīda bi mablagh-i kami ki har du qarya [Chūplānī wa Mīr-Maḥalla] bi yik ṣad wa panjāh tumān namī risad"*.
153 Document no. 47, A.
154 Document no. 47, A: *"gharaḍ-i dāʿī īn ast ki shumā bar sabīl-i iṭlāq ihtimāl-i taḥqīq-i bayʿ-i waqf bi-wāsiṭa-yi wujūd-i mujawwiz bā ṣudūr-i ḥukm az ḥākim-i awthaq bar khilāf-i ḥukm-i bi waqf az zamān-i marḥimat panāh ḥājjī mullā riḍā astarābādī ṭābā tharāhu tā zamān-i mā nadahīd"*.

the powerful Qajar khans had no interest in enforcing a ruling that had gone against them, and the weak Dirāzgīsū were unable to do anything about it.[155]

3.4.5 Territorial Jurisdiction

The discussion now turned to the other rulings and ratifications that had been issued. Most of the *ʿulamāʾ* supporting a settlement rejected the ruling of Āqā Muḥammad Mahdī and the ratification of Shaftī.[156] The general sentiment in Astarābād in the 1860s was resentment at Sayyid Faḍlullāh's decision to get a ruling from Isfahan. The Astarābādī *ʿulamāʾ* thought that a long-standing dispute involving two villages in the countryside of Astarābād should never have been taken to Isfahan. This was expressed in a saying that was widely circulated at the time: 'the dead of Astarābad should be washed in Astarābad' (*bā murda-yi astarābād dar astarābād mī-shūyand*).[157] Moreover, as some pointed out, Āqā Muḥammad Mahdī had been in no position to evaluate whatever oral or written evidence had been presented to him.[158] Although there does seem to have been an awareness of problems raised by a ruling issued in a different territorial jurisdiction, the validity of Āqā Muḥammad Mahdī's ruling or Shaftī's ratification of it were never explicitly challenged, because they had been issued in Isfahan.

For most *ʿulamāʾ* involved in the case, Āqā Muḥammad Mahdī's ruling or Shaftī's ratification were perfectly valid as judicial decisions. It made no difference that they were issued in Isfahan and concerned two villages eight hundred kilometres away in Astarābād. The real problem, as in the case of Astarābādī's ruling, was that neither Āqā Muḥammadī Mahdī's ruling nor Shaftī's ratification was preceded by a summary of litigation. It was difficult to work out, therefore,

155 Document no. 47, A: *sādāt kasānī hastand bi-qadr-i pūst-i pīyāz az īshān kārī sākhta namī-shawad*"; Document no. 50, D.

156 Document no. 48, B: "*dar īn wāqiʿa aḥqar al-anām ḥukm-i ṣādir az marḥūm āqā muḥmmad mahdī rā muʿtabar namīdānam aṣl-i kayfīyyat rā mīdānam wa niwishta-yi marḥūm āqā-yi ḥujjat al-islām [Shaftī] rā man giriftam dar īn ki ān ḥukm-i muʿtabar wā qāṭiʿ-i nizāʿ nīst*"; "*az faqara-yi ḥukm-i āqā muḥammad mahdī bugdhārīd ān qaṭʿan ghayr-i muʿtabar ast bi-ān jamīʿ-i wujūh muḥtamal ast jāʾiz nabāshad*".

157 The "washing" here is a reference to Islamic rites of purification before the burial of a dead body.

158 Document no. 50, D: "*guftam ki muʿāmalāt-i astarābād rā ʿulamāʾ-yi ān balad bihtar wuqūf dārand chūn khuṭūṭ wa amhār wa aḥwālāt-i ʿulamāʾ wa akhbār wa umūr-i wāqiʿa wa shawāhid-i mutaḍammina wa qarāʾin-i wāfiyya rā chūn ahl al-bayt-and adrī-and*" ("I said that the *ʿulamāʾ* of Astarābād are better informed about transactions which take place in the town, because they are better acquainted with the handwriting, seals and circumstances of the *ʿulamāʾ* and the particulars of a case and with what is authentic and reliable evidence, being inhabitants of the town").

whether ʿAbbās Khān's claim had been reviewed, and whether these rulings could be construed as having brought about a closure of the lawsuit.

3.4.6 The Ruling in the Defendant's Absence

This case study has so far demonstrated two ways in which *ʿulamāʾ* were approached by litigants. The Dirāzgīsū approached Āqā Muḥammad Mahdī and Shaftī in ʿAbbās Ḵhān's absence. The attempts at arbitration before Sharīʿatmadār Ashrafī and Mullā Muḥmmad Taqī, however, were instances where both parties mutually agreed to present themselves before these clerics. In the latter case, there was no problem regarding the judicial competence of these mutually chosen arbiters (*maḥḍar-i sharʿ-i marḍī al-ṭarafayn*). Both sides had agreed to recognise the *ḥukm* they would issue as binding. In the former case, however, there was no such mutual agreement regarding the judicial competence of the judges chosen by the claimant.

Qajar jurists were divided regarding the probative force of a ruling issued in the defendant's absence if the defendant claimed he did not recognise the judicial competence of the claimant's judge. According to Mīrzā-yi Qummī (d.1231/1816), a *ḥukm* issued by a judge to a claimant in the absence of the defendant remained valid and probative even if the defendant claimed he did not recognise the judge's judicial competence.[159] The *ḥukm* only became invalid if the defendant could prove that the claimant's judge was judicially incompetent. Mīrzā-yi Qummī's model for *sharīʿa* litigation before arbitration was thus pro-claimant. It meant that the claimant could, immediately upon the issuance of a *ḥukm* which judicially certified his claim, appeal to the Qajar authorities to confiscate the disputed object from the defendant. This in turn would compel the defendant to accept arbitration over the disputed object. Mullā Aḥmad Narāqī (d.1245/1829), however, proposed a different solution. Narāqī's proposed framework for *sharīʿa*

159 Ustādī 1380 sh./2001, 363: "*ẓāhir shud az ān-chi bayān kardīm ki bi-mujarrad-i ḥukm-i ḥākim bar muddaʿā ʿalayh-i ghāʾib ḥukm mī shawad bi – istiḥqāq-i muddaʿī akhdh-i māl-i muddaʿā bihi rā wa ibqāʾ-i māl dar yad-i ū wa jāʾiz nīst istirdād az ū mā-dāmī ki muddaʿā ʿalayh ithbāt-i ʿadam-i qābiliyyat-i ānhā nakarda ast na īn ki mujarrad ʿadam-i qābiliyyat dar nazd-i muddaʿā ʿalayh kāfī bāshad dar ʿadam-i jawāz-i intizāʿ-i māl az ū wa ibqāʾ-i māl dar yad-i ū*" ("It will have become evident from all that we have explained that upon the mere issuance of a ruling by a judge [to a claimant] against a defendant who is absent, it is permissible [for the claimant] to confiscate the disputed object and retain possession of it. It is not permissible to restitute it [the disputed object] from the claimant so long as the defendant has not proved the incompetence [of the judge]. The simple claim by the defendant that he does not recognise the competence of the judge who issued a ruling to the claimant is not sufficient for him to retain possession of the disputed object and to prevent its confiscation from him"). I am indebted to Hossein Modarressi Ṭabāṭabāʾī for drawing my attention to this important Uṣūlī theoretical discussion on judicial procedure.

litigation before arbitration is pro-defendant. Narāqī argued that no *ḥukm* issued in the absence of the defendant could be binding unless the defendant recognised the judicial competence of the claimant's judge.[160]

Narāqī notes that in his time it was quite common for a claimant to go to a remote town and judicially certify his claim before an incompetent judge and then try and use the *ḥukm* that was issued to confiscate the disputed object from an innocent defendant in his hometown.[161] The defendant would now be forced – according to Mīrzā-yi Qummī's model - to first locate the claimant's judge and then find witnesses to testify that the judge was judicially incompetent. Narāqī argued that this involved undue difficulty (*ḥaraj*) for the defendant. The defendant, instead, had to be free to recognise or reject the judicial competence of the claimant's judge. If the defendant rejected the judicial competence of the claimant's judge, it was the claimant who had to establish that his chosen judge was judicially competent. The claimant would have to do this before a second judge whose judicial competence both sides recognised. It was only after the second

160 Ustādī 1380 sh./2001, 365: "*ẓāhir ān ast ki ithbāt-i qābiliyyat wa fiqāhat wa ʿadālat-i ḥākim bar zayd ast na ʿamr wa qabl az murāfaʿa dar naz-i ḥākimī dīgar ki musallam-i ṭarafayn bāshad wa ṣudūr-i ḥukm az ū bar qābiliyyat-i ḥākim zayd rā ʿalā ẓāhir al-sharʿ tasalluṭ-i akhdh-i muddaʿā bihi az ʿamr nabāshad*" ("What is evident is that proving competence and the knowledge of jurisprudence and the good morals of the judge is upon Zayd [the claimant], not upon ʿAmr [the defendant]. Before an arbitration has occurred before a [second] judge that is accepted by both sides and a ruling is issued by him regarding the competence of the [first] judge, Zayd, based on what is evident according to the *sharīʿa*, has no power to confiscate the disputed object from ʿAmr").

161 Ustādī 1380 sh./2001, 357–371: "*dar akthar-i bilād wa qurā jamʿī ghayr-i mutadayyinīn hastand ki bidūna istiḥqāq wa qābiliyyat bar masnad-i ḥukūmat nishasta wa ḥukm mīkunand wa nihāyat-i amr īn ast ki dar hamān balad ya qarya-yi khud-i īshān ʿadam-i qābiliyyat-i īshān maʿlūm ast, wa dar wilāyāt-i dīgar majhūl wa ghayr-i maʿrūf-and, pas har ki ḥukmī khwāhad az yakī az īshān bi-gīrad wa jamʿī rā shāhid bar ān ḥukm girifta, wa dar wilāyāt-i dūrdast ki khabar az ḥāl-i īn ḥākim nadārand* [*mī-tawānand*] *amwāl-i muslīmīn rā az yad-i īshān intizāʿ* [*kunand*] *wa mutaṣarrif-i bī-chāra bāyad bi aṭrāf bidūwad tā ān ḥākim rā paydā kunad wa baʿd az ān ʿadam-i qābiliyyat-i ū thābit kunad, wa jamʿī az ʿudūl hamrāh-i khud bibarad tā īn marḥalah rā dar nazd-i ḥākim-i sharʿ-i wāqiʿī thābit kundad wa shakkī nīst ki ḥarajī ast ʿaẓīm*" ("In most towns and villages, a group of impious people who are neither eligible nor competent to judge have seated themselves on the seat of judgeship and are judging cases. The result is this: though their incompetence is widely known in the town or village in which they live, in other provinces they are unheard of or less well known. Now whoever likes receives a *ḥukm* from one of these individuals, finds some people to witness the issuance of that *ḥukm* and then goes to a far-off province whose inhabitants know nothing about the judge that issued the *ḥukm*, and they try to use his ḥukm to confiscate the property of believing Muslims. The poor possessors [of the property] must run here and there to try to find that judge and then prove that he is not fit to judge, and [they have to] take witnesses [from the town where the judge resides] with them to a real judge (*ḥākim-i sharʿ-i wāqiʿī*) to do this. There can be no doubt that all this involves great difficulty (*ḥaraj*)").

judge had issued a certification of the judicial competence of the claimant's judge that the *ḥukm* that had been issued to the claimant acquired probative force in litigation. Before this happened, the claimant could not use the *ḥukm* to compel the defendant to accept arbitration over the disputed object.

The repeated attempts made by the Dirāzgīsū to certify the *ijtihad* of Āqā Muḥammad Mahdī and then Hājjī Mullā Riḍā Astarābādī suggests that by the mid-nineteenth century, it was Narāqī's and not Qummī's procedural framework which was followed. The claimants had to establish the judicial competence of their chosen judges. This hypothesis will, however, remain inconclusive since we do not possess the defendant's archive in this case and know relatively little about ʿAbbās Khān's *sharīʿa* litigation against the Dirāzgīsū.

3.4.7 The Circumstances of the Issuance of the Rulings and the Ratifications

It had become impossible to determine on the basis of the text alone whether the various rulings and ratifications in the archive of the Dirāzgīsū had been issued to the Dirāzgīsū before or after arbitration with the Qajar khans. The text of the ratifications of Ḥājjī Mullā Riḍā's ruling merely said that Ḥājjī Mullā Riḍā's ruling was binding. That, however, did not help to establish whether the ratification had been issued after the evidence of the Dirāzgīsū and the Qajar khans had been weighed side by side or not. Although during the lifetime of Sharīʿatmadār and Mullā Muḥammad Taqī it was easy to confirm the circumstances in which their ratifications were issued, after their death, in the archive of the Dirāzgīsū, they looked like ordinary ratifications of a ruling issued to a claimant in the absence of the defendant. As we saw, moreover, ʿAbbās Khān had never really appeared for arbitration. In reality, therefore, none of the rulings or ratifications in the archive of the Dirāzgīsū had been the outcome of arbitration. Ḥājjī Mullā Riḍā Astarābādī's ruling was probably the only one which might possibly have been the outcome of arbitration.

As we saw, however, this too could not be determined decisively. Litigation in the third stage revealed a major weakness in the way rulings and ratifications were issued. If there was no summary of court proceedings, the circumstances of issuance would always remain ambiguous. In turn, this made it easier to challenge the binding force of the ruling or ratification. It could always be claimed in the next generation that the ruling was not a product of arbitration. This seems to have been the dilemma in the late 1860s. It had become impossible to distinguish the binding force of the rulings and their ratifications after the death of the jurists that had issued them, based simply on their texts. This problem was further complicated by the fact that the same jurists had issued rulings or ratifications to both sides at different times based on evidence presented to them seperately by either side (see Table 1).

Table 1: A partial reconstruction of the conflicting legal rulings and ratifications in the archives of the claimant (Dirāzgīsū) and the defendant (the descendants of ʿAbbās Khān Qājār Bēglerbēgī) in Astarābād, ca. 1868.

Jurists who issued rulings or ratifications to the Dirāzgīsū which endorsed their claim to the two villages as *waqf*:	Jurists who issued rulings or ratifications to ʿAbbās Khān's descendants which endorsed their claim to the two villages as private property (*milk*):
1. Sayyid Muḥammad Bāqir Shaftī	1. Sayyid Muḥammad Bāqir Shaftī
2. Sharīʿatmadār Ashrafī	2. Sharīʿatmadār Ashrafī
3. Mullā Muḥammad Taqī	3. Mullā Muḥammad Taqī
4. Raʾīs al-ʿUlamāʾ	4. Raʾīs al-ʿUlamāʾ

It turned out that ʿAbbās Khān's children also had a ruling from Shaftī in their archive in support of their claim to the lands.[162] An inspection of the Dirāzgīsū archive, meanwhile, revealed that Raʾīs al-ʿUlamāʾ had in fact also ratified Ḥājjī Mullā Riḍā Astarābādī's ruling earlier in the dispute.[163] In brief, the descendants of ʿAbbās Khān might also claim, as the Dirāzgīsū were trying to do now, that one of the ratifications in their archive had settled the dispute decisively in their favour such that no further litigation was permissible by the Dirāzgīsū. It was this problem, more than anything else, which seems to have convinced some Astarābādī *ʿulamāʾ* who might have been initially opposed to a settlement that it was in fact the only way forward. Astarābādī *ʿulamāʾ* who had inspected the archive of ʿAbbās Khān's descendants made it clear that as long as the *bēglerbēgī*'s descendants had ratifications issued by Shaftī, Sharīʿatmadār, Mullā Muḥammad Taqī, and Raʾīs in their possession, they would be able to undermine the legal basis of the claim of the Dirāzgīsū. In such circumstances, another round of arbitration would not help the Dirāzgīsū. In fact, if such a course of action were taken, chances were the Dirāzgīsū might lose everything.[164] A settlement, on the other hand, would at least guarantee that the Dirāzgīsū would regain some control over parts of their ancestral lands.

162 Document no. 48, B: "*baʿd az īnki niwshtahā-yi marḥūm āqā-yi raʾīs wa āqā-yi sharīʿatmadār wa āqā-yi ḥujjat al-islām [Shaftī] dīdam ki dar yad-i waratha-yi marḥūm ʿabbās khān beglerbegī būd . . .*".

163 Document no. 50, D: "*wa ʿulamāʾ-i baʿd az marḥūm ḥājjī mullā riḍā baʿd az istiḥḍār hama imḍā-yi ḥukm-i īshān [ḥājjī mullā riḍā] niwshtand ḥattā marḥūm ākhūnd raʾīs-i shahīd wa marḥūm ḥājjī mullā muḥammad taqī illā ān ki ākhar bi-jihat īn ki īn ḥukm bar mawḍūʿ-i fatwāʾī ast na ḥāṣil-i khuṣūmat bi-ḥasb-i āthār-i taṣarruf chīzī niwsihtand*".

164 Document no. 49, C. C stressed that if the children of ʿAbbās Khān petitioned officials in the government, based on the documents in their archive, it was likely that the Dirāzgīsū would be deprived of the lands.

3.4.8 The Division of the Village of Chūplānī

On 11 Jamādī I 1288/29 July 1871, a jurist named Muḥammad Ṣādiq al-ʿAqīlī volunteered to broker the settlement.[165] Slightly more than half of Chūpalānī was given to the Dirāzgīsū sayyids while the rest was kept by the children of ʿAbbās Khān.[166] No side would be allowed henceforth to make a legal claim about Chūpalnī against the other side.[167] The justification for the settlement that was recorded in the deed was that it was in the best interests of the *waqf* and the preservation of social harmony and because it had become impossible, based on the conflicting rulings in the case, to determine whether the village of Chūplānī was *waqf* land belonging to the Dirāzgīsū or private property belonging to ʿAbbās Khān's descendants:

> Because the binding *sharīʿa* rulings of the two sides in the dispute were conflicting and contradictory (*aṭrāf-i nizāʿ aḥkām-i muṭāʿa-yi sharʿiyya-yi mutaḍādda wa mutanāqiḍa dar dast dāshtand*), and the *ʿulamāʾ* had caused huge controversy (*ikhtilāf-i ʿaẓīm namūda būdand*) deciding between the earlier and the later rulings (*wārid wa mawrūd*) and the abrogating and abrogated rulings (*nāsikh wa mansūkh*) and those which were valid and those which were not (*iʿtibār wa ʿadam-i ānhā*), therefore, taking the best interests of the *waqf* into account, and with the permission of the beneficiaries and the *mutawallī* and those that have legal authority, and for the benefit of future generations, after they [Niẓām al – ʿUlamāʾ and Ḥājjī Āqā ʿAlī] were granted powers of attorney [by the children of ʿAbbās Khān], a settlement (*ṣulḥ*) was negotiated.[168]

For some unspecified reason, the rich and fertile village of Mīr-Maḥalla does not seem to have been part of the negotiations. Its fate is unclear. Several documents appear to suggest that it continued to remain in private hands, and that the Dirāzgīsū as late as the 1920s had been unable to get their claim over it recognised.[169]

---

165 Document no. 10; Document no. 56.

166 Document no. 56. The deed further specified that the sayyids were to be paid for damages and losses for the preceding years. Niẓām al-ʿUlamāʾ ʿAbdullāh Mīrzā and Ḥājjī Āqā ʿAlī-yi Astarābādī would be responsible for collecting these payments from the children of ʿAbbās Khān and giving them to the sayyids.

167 Document no. 56.

168 Document no. 56.

169 Two documents suggest that the sayyids were never able to regain possession of Mīr-Maḥalla. The first document (Sutūda and Dhabīḥī 1354 sh./1975, VI, 553–556) is an assignment of revenue (*tuyūl*) dated 1282/1865–1866 in which Mīr-Maḥalla is granted by Nāṣir al-Dīn Shāh (r. 1264–1313/1848–1896) to a certain Malik ʿAbbās Yūzbāshī in exchange for maintaining and mustering troops. The second document (Sutūda and Dhabīḥī 1354 sh./1975, VII, 205–207) dated Rabīʿ II 1340/December 1929 is a settlement contract between the Dirāzgīsū sayyids and Āqā Mīrzā Jaʿfar, son of Āqā Ramzān ʿAlī, authorised proxy of the merchants (*wakīl al-tujjār*) of Astarābād. According to the agreement, the Dīrāzgīsū sayyids rented out the village of Mīr-Maḥalla (not in their possession) on a lease of one hundred and ten lunar years to Āqā Mīrzā Jaʿfar, provided that he or his representative spent between one to a maximum of ten thousand *tūmāns* over the

In sum, even though Muḥammad Ṣādiq al-ʿAqīlī ratified the binding force of both Astarābādī's ruling and Āqā Muḥammad Mahdī's ruling, he was compelled to accept that a negotiated settlement, not further arbitration, was the only way to resolve a land dispute between a group of local Ḥusaynī sayyids and the ruling Qajar elite.

Conclusion

In both the first and the second stage of litigation, we have seen that the judicial competence of scholars who issued legal rulings to the claimant was rejected by the defendant. Contesting judicial competence in the context of this case meant rejecting the scholar's *ijtihād*. This forced the claimants in the dispute to certify the scholar's *ijtihād* before other *mujtahid*s whose *ijtihād* was recognised. In the case of Āqā Muḥammad Mahdī, it was his father, Ḥājjī Muḥammad Ibrāhīm Kalbāsī, who certified his *ijtihād*. For Ḥājjī Mullā Riḍā Astarābādī, the Dirāzgīsū persuaded a very large number of Astarābādī *ʿulamāʾ*, including Sharīʿatmadār and Mullā Muḥammad Taqī, to certify his *ijtihād*. These certifications of *ijtihād* shed light on the function of the *mujtahid* and his ruling in *sharīʿa* litigation. By certifying that Āqā Muḥammad Mahdī and Ḥājjī Mullā Riḍā Astarābādī were *mujtahid*s, or in the language of the documents, *mujtahid-i nāfidh al-ḥukm*, the Dirāzgīsū confirmed that they could issue a valid and binding legal ruling in *sharīʿa* litigation.

This was important to establish because according to the dominant Imāmī Uṣūlī doctrine, only qualified *mujtahid*s could act as judges in *sharīʿa* litigation. Rulings of a non-*mujtahid* were theoretically invalid unless they were ratified by a *mujtahid*. In Ḥājjī Mullā Riḍā Astarābādī's case, there was a consensus among the Astarābādī *ʿulamāʾ* that he was indeed a *mujtahid*. This in turn meant that any ruling he had issued judicially certifying the *waqf* claim was binding and could be used by claimants – the Dirāzgīsū – to repossess Chūplānī and Mīr-Maḥalla. In contrast, we have no surviving certifications of the *ijtihād* of Āqā Muḥammad

---

first twelve lunar years in judicial proceedings to regain control of Mīr-Maḥalla from all usurpers whose possession derived from ʿAbbās Khān (*wa īn maṣārif-i intizāʿ dar waraqa makhṣūṣ ast bi-rishta-yi ʿabbās khānī mina al-ṣadr ilā al-sāqa*). If after twelve years Āqā Mīrzā Jaʿfar or his representative had not succeeded, the sayyids would have the option to cancel the agreement or to extend it for another twelve years, and this would continue until possession of Mīr-Maḥalla had been secured. Once possession of Mīr-Maḥalla was secured, 2 ½ *dāng* would remain leased out to Āqā Mīrzā Jaʿfar in exchange for a nominal rent of 5 *tūmāns* at the local rate, while 2 ½ *dāng* would be entrusted to the *mutawallī* of the *waqf* and its beneficiaries – the Dirāzgīsū sayyids. According to this document, the village of Mīr-Maḥalla was owned in the 1920s by Ḥājjī Ḥusayn Āqā Amīn al-Ḍarb Tihrānī.

Mahdī from any of the Astarābādī *'ulamā'*. The Dirāzgīsū were forced to go to Isfahan to certify his *ijtihād*. Was this because the Astarābādī *'ulamā'* did not consider Āqā Muḥammad Mahdī to be a *mujtahid*? The Astarābādī *'ulamā'* were probably not able to establish the *ijtihād* of a scholar from Isfahan.

Attempts by the Dirāzgīsū to resolve the question of Āqā Muḥammad Mahdī's *ijtihād* through his father's certification only made matters worse. If doubt remained over Āqā Muḥammad Mahdī's ability to carry out *ijtihād*, many considered that it was not legally permissible for Sayyid Faḍlullāh to use his ruling to certify the Dirāzgīsū claim. It is probably for this reason that Sharī'atmadār is reported to have said that the only basis for Sayyid Faḍlullāh's claim was Shaftī's ratification. Shaftī, unlike Āqā Muḥammad Mahdī, was not a local scholar but a leading Imāmī *mujtahid* in Iran whose *ijtihād* was beyond doubt. His *ijtihād* was acknowledged well beyond the province of Isfahan. It was even recognised outside Iran. This meant that Shaftī's ratification was recognised as legally binding in *sharī'a* litigation in Astarābād.

It was unlikely, however, for the ruling of Āqā Muḥammad Mahdī, a relatively unknown scholar, to be considered binding in *sharī'a* litigation in Astarābad. Similarly, the binding force of Ḥajjī Mullā Riḍā Astarābādī's ruling might also be challenged in Isfahan. There was thus a distinction in the binding force of legal rulings issued in litigation by locally recognised *mujtahid*s compared to the leading Imāmī *mujtahid*s of their time. This is clearly visible in the certifications that were issued concerning Ḥajjī Mullā Riḍā Astarābādī's *ijtihād*. Some of these certifications emphasize that, though he was a *mujtahid*, his rulings were only considered legally valid and binding (*nāfidh*) in the province of Astarābād (*dar īn wilāyat nāfidh al-ḥukm būdand*).[170] Others, more generous, insisted that the binding force of his rulings extended well beyond the confines of Astarābād (*dar īn wilāyat wa sā'ir-i buldān bi-lā rayb wa shakk*).[171] In theory, the ruling of a qualified *mujtahid* was considered legally valid in *sharī'a* litigation. In practice, there were territorial limits to its binding force. These territorial limits depended on how widely recognised the *ijtihād* of the scholar who issued the ruling was. Since this was subjective, the binding force of legal rulings issued in litigation by a less well-known *mujtahid* outside his hometown or community was limited.

Litigation in the first and second stage also exposed a weakness in the Uṣūlī theory of judicial procedure (*qaḍā'*). If the validity of the legal ruling in litigation was dependent on the *ijtihād* of the judge, then a ruling issued by a scholar whose *ijtihād* was not recognised by one of the parties in a dispute could be considered

170 Document no. 3.
171 Document 3.

invalid. In the first and second stage, ʿAbbās Khān claimed he did not consider the scholars who had issued rulings to the Dirāzgīsū to be *mujtahid*s. Imāmī Uṣūlī *mujtahid*s were aware of the procedural problem of one side refusing to recognise the *itjihād* of a given scholar in litigation and tried to come up with a procedural framework to resolve this. In theory, according to Narāqī, if the defendant contested the judicial competence (*qābiliyyat*) of the judge who had issued a ruling to the claimant, then there had to be an arbitration over the competence of the judge. This arbitration was to be carried out by a second judge whose competence was accepted by claimant and defendant.[172] Only after the arbitration had occurred would the ruling the first judge had issued to the claimant have any binding force in litigation. In contrast, Mīrzā-yi Qummī argued that the ruling issued to the claimant, had immediate binding force irrespective of the defendant's refusal to acknowledge competence. It could be used to immediately confiscate the disputed object from the defendant. Restitution of the disputed object back to the defendant only occurred if the defendant was able to prove the incompetence of the judge who issued the ruling to the claimant.[173] In practice, the Dirāzgīsū seem to have tried to get around the problem of the competence of Ḥājjī Mullā Riḍā Astarābādī by insisting that ʿAbbās Khān had enforced rulings of Ḥājjī Mullā Riḍā Astarābādī while he was governor of Astarābād. This enforcement was in their view an important sign that he recognised Ḥājjī Mullā Riḍā Astarābādī's *ijtihād*.

Besides the problem of *ijtihād*, the case also revealed the problem of the absence of centralised recording and registration procedures relating to legal rulings in Qajar Iran. In chapter two we saw how some individual *mujtahid*s maintained private registers which recorded legal rulings. There is little evidence so far to suggest that this was a widespread practice. In this case, we have seen that the Dirāzgīsū had to prepare a new legal document where they asked local Astarābādī *ʿulamāʾ* to certify the issuance of Ḥājjī Mullā Riḍā Astarābādī's legal ruling in the previous generation. This suggests there was no formalized, centrally regulated registration of legal rulings in Astarābād during the period of Ḥājjī Mullā Riḍā Astarābādī which could be consulted. In the case of the *ʿulamāʾ* of Isfahan, they were probably not aware of the issuance of Astarābādī's ruling in the previous generation. It was therefore possible for Āqā Muḥammad Mahdī to issue an entirely new ruling in the case based on the evidence presented to him. Conversely, neither Sharīʿatmadār nor Mullā Muḥammad Taqī, nor indeed any of the Astarābādī *ʿulamāʾ* involved in the case who were aware of the issuance of Ḥājjī Mullā Riḍā Astarābādī's ruling issued a new legal ruling in

172 Ustādī 1380 sh./2001, 365.
173 Ustādī 1380 sh./2001, 363.

the case. They were only willing to ratify or invalidate the original ruling of Ḥājjī Mullā Riḍā Astarābādī.

In addition to the problem of the registration of legal rulings, there was no formal regulation regarding how legal rulings were written and issued. It was impossible to determine from the text of Ḥājjī Mullā Riḍā Astarābādī's ruling if it had been issued as the outcome of arbitration after he reviewed the evidence of both sides, or was based on the evidence presented by one side only, or was his legal opinion in the case. This was significant as in the absence of state-enforced jurisdictional boundaries, the *mujtahid* could act either as a *muftī* or a *qāḍī* when he issued a legal ruling. As we have seen in chapter three, some *mujtahid*s were explicit in the way they wrote their rulings and clearly specified when they acted as a judge. This was done for example using Arabic speech act declarations such as *qaḍaytu* (I judged) or providing a description of proceedings which described prior review of evidence of both parties or stated that the evidence of only one side had been reviewed.[174] Other *mujtahid*s, however, were less meticulous, leaving the binding force of their rulings open to interpretation after their death, as demonstrated by the case we have examined here.

174 For examples of Qajar era legal rulings issued as judicial decisions with a protocol of claims by the claimant and defendant and the review of evidence of both sides by the judge, see for example a ruling of the *shaykh al-islām* of Neyrīz dated Rabīʿ II 1303/January 1886 in Bhalloo and Rezai 2017, and two rulings of Mīrzā Luṭf ʿAlī (d. 1262/1845), *imām-jumʿa* of Tabriz dated 12 Rabīʿ I 1255/26 May 1839 and and 6 Rabīʿ II 1259/6 May 1843 in Werner 2000, 372–375 and Riḍāʾī 1383 sh./2005, 29–39. For an example of a ruling issued as a judicial decision which explicitly states it was issued in the absence of the other side, see S1: 611, a register copy of a *ḥukm-i sharʿ* issued by Sangalajī on 26 Shawwāl 1285/9 February 1869 with the remark *al-ghāʾib ʿalā ḥujjatihi idhā aḥḍara*.

Chapter 6
Reviving the *Waqf* of Mīrzā Aḥmad Kafrānī

Introduction

The previous chapter focused on the how legal rulings issued by jurists who judicially certified a claim were used and interpreted in a long-drawn-out land dispute between the Dirazgisu sayyids of Astarābād and the ruling Qajar khans. The claim of the sayyids to the disputed lands was based on the premise that these lands were constituted as a family *waqf* by their ancestor Mīr Ruḥullāh during the Safavid period. The turbulent socio-political transition between the fall of the Safavid dynasty from 1722 onwards and the rise of the Qajars in the late eighteenth century resulted in the conversion of many formerly *waqf* lands into crown land (*khālisa*) or private property (*milk*). In the case of the lands Mīr Ruḥullāh had constituted as *waqf*, both appear to have occurred. Though the sayyids had a copy of Mīr Rūḥullāh's *waqf* deed (*waqf-nāma*) in their archive, we saw that the evidence of the *waqf* status of their lands remained contingent on oral witness testimony. In this case, the testimony was based on a legal acknowledgement (*iqrār*) made by one of Mīr Rūḥullāh's descendants, a woman named Bīja Sharaf. Witnesses testified to having heard Bīja Sharaf declare that the lands were constituted as a *waqf* for Mīr Rūḥullāh's male descendants. Any sale therefore that had occurred of the *waqf* was illegal. This reported *iqrār* by Bīja Sharaf was documented through multiple oral witness testimonies recorded in a document that was drawn up for two Dirāzgīsū sayyids, Mīr Mūsā and Mīr Taqī.

The name given to this type of document was *istishhād-nāma*, which I translate here as "witness statement".[1] It was in fact the main legal instrument used to record multiple oral witness testimonies in Iran from at least the Safavid period onwards. Its use was particularly widespread in claims of *waqf*. This chapter will focus on the function of *istishhād-nāma*s in *waqf* disputes in Iran. We will begin by providing some theoretical background on the significance of oral witness testimony in relation to *waqf* claims. This will be followed by an analysis of how such oral testimony came to be recorded in early modern Iran in written artefacts known as *istishhād-nāma*. The third part of the chapter will focus on the role played by *istishhād-nāma*s in an endowment dispute involving another *waqf*

1 This translation is not entirely satisfactory. The *istishad-nāma* certificate usually contains several sealed witness testimonies. The term *shahādat-nāma* was used to refer to document containing a single sealed witness deposition.

https://doi.org/10.1515/9783111239736-007

founded in the Safavid period which became the object of dispute in the Qajar era. This *waqf* was revived in early twentieth-century Isfahan through a legal ruling of a *mujtahid* which was based on multiple oral witness testimonies recorded in several *istishhād-nāmas*.

1 Witnessing and *Waqf* according to Imāmī Shīʿī Law

According to Imāmī Shīʿī law, a widespread or common report known technically as *al-samāʿ*, *al-shiyāʿ* or *al-istifāḍa* could be used as evidence to establish different types of legal claims. For example, al-Muḥaqqiq al-Ḥillī, known as al-Muḥaqqiq al-Awwal (c. 1205–1277), says in *Sharāʾiʿ al-islām*:

> The authority of the judge is established through a widespread report, and likewise paternity (*al-nasab*), ownership of property without qualification (*al-milk al-muṭlaq*), death, marriage and *waqf*.[2]

Al-Muḥaqqiq adds a precision concerning the case of *waqf*, noting that since *waqf* was meant to be eternal, if widespread report was not admissible as evidence, then *waqf*s would become invalid with the passage of time and the death of (the original) witnesses (of their founding).[3] Contemporary Imāmī Shīʿī *mujtahids* such as Khumaynī (d. 1989) have used the Persian term *lisān-i mardum* or "on the tongue of the people" to describe this sort of widespread report attesting to a claim. A widespread report, however, can only be used as proof (*ḥujja*) if it is widespread enough to yield certain or satisfactory knowledge (*al-mufīd li l-ʿilm aw al-iṭmināN*) and not just suspicion (*ẓann*) about the claim. Besides the widely transmitted report, three other means of proving *waqf* are mentioned: (1) the acknowledgement (*iqrār*) of the possessor (or after his death by his heirs) that the land is *waqf* (*iqrār dhī l-yad*); or (2) transactions upon the stipulations of the *waqf* without opppostion and (3) *al-bayyina al-sharʿiyya*, which refers to the evidence of two just male witnesses (*ʿadlayn*) or its equivalent.[4]

In practice, this theory materialised in Iran in the form of a specific legal document in Persian: the *istishhād-nāma*, which was used to establish various types of legal claims, including those relating to *waqf*. The *istishhād-nāma* collected in writing the oral testimonies of witnesses who had heard (*shuhūd-i samāʿī*) that

2 Al-Ḥillī 1409/1989, 862: "*tuthbitu wilāyat al-qāḍī bi l-istifāḍa wa-kadhā yuthbitu bi l-istifāḍa al-nasab, al-milk al-muṭlaq wa-l-mawt wa-l-nikāḥ wa-l-waqf.*"

3 Al-Ḥillī 1409/1989, 919: "*inna l-waqf li l-taʾbīd, fa-law lam tusmaʿ fīhi l-istifāḍa la-buṭilat al-wuqūf maʿa imtidād al-waqf wa-fanāʾ al-shuhūd.*"

4 Khūmaynī 1390/1970, II, 85.

such and such land, for example, was *waqf*. Alternatively, to strengthen the claim further, as we saw in the previous chapter, such witnesses could also report, for example, an *iqrār* made by the possessor that the land in question was *waqf* or that they had knowledge of transactions in accordance with the stipulations of the founder of the *waqf*, as stated for example in his deed of endowment (*waqf-nāma*). Before examining how this occurred in an actual dispute we will first look at the formal structure of the *istishhād-nāma*.

2 Formal Aspects of the *Istishhād-nāma* in Early Modern Iran

2.1 A Zand *Istihhād-nāma* from Isfahan, c. 1175/1762

The earliest *istishhād-nāma* exemplars to have survived date from the Safavid period, though it is possible that this documentary practice is much older. An eighteenth-century *istishhād-nāma* produced in Isfahan under Zand rule (1751–1794) gives us a sense of how the *istishhād-nāma* was recorded by *sharīʿa* courts before the Qajar period. The *istishhād-nāma* is in the form of a vertical roll (*ṭūmār*) made by gluing together multiple sheets of paper (Figure 62–64).[5] There are horizontal fold lines visible on the recto and a vertical fold line on the right-hand side of the sheet (Figure 63). The *istishhād-nāma* itself appears to have been pasted at some point onto another document to preserve it and prevent further damage. A *basmala* from the second document is visible from a lacuna in the *istishhād-nāma* (Figure 63G). The *istishhād-nāma* contains several lacunae (Figure 63E) and tearing is also visible along the horizontal and vertical fold lines. The *istishhād-nāma* consists of three different parts: the request for testimonies (Figure 63D), marginal witness testimonies which are sealed (for example Figure 62C) and a sealed legal ruling (Figure 62A). The six-line request for testimonies is written by the scribe in *naskh* script. It begins with the following introductory clause: "witness testimony is requested from the sayyids and notables of Isfahan and the peasants and farmers and inhabitants of . . . may it be protected, whoever knows and is aware that" (*istishhād wa istikhbār wa istifhhām mī-rawad az jamīʿ-i ḥaḍarāt-i sādāt wa fuḍalā-yi ʿālī-maqām-i iṣfahān wa ruʿāyā wa mazārʿiān wa ahālī [. . .] bi l-amn wa l-amān ki har ki ʿalīm wa wāqif būda bāshad ki*). There is a lacuna in the second line of this opening clause where the name of the place of the lands is mentioned.

5 File no. 612/3 G-9, Sāzmān-i Awqāf wa Umūr-i Khayriyya, Isfahan. I am indebted to Sayyid Ṣādiq Ḥusaynī Ishkawarī for images of this document from the digital archive of Majmaʿ-i Dhakhāʾir-i Islāmī, file no. 111. For an edition of the *istishhād–nāma* see Ishkawarī 1388 sh./2009, VII, 232–245. Regrettably, the roll dimensions were not noted during the digitsation.

The next segment of the request for testimony records the claim itself, namely, that 6 *dāng* of the village of Jayān and 5 *dāng* and 9 *ḥabba* of the village of Andavān Qahāb in the region of Isfahan were constituted as *waqf* to the shrines of ʿAlī in Najaf and al-Ḥusayn in Karbala, that the administration of the endowment has continued in lineal succession from father to son without interruption until the present time, and that the present administrator (*mutawallī*) of this *waqf* was Shaykh Aḥmad b. Shaykh ʿAbdallāh.[6] Shaykh Aḥmad was clearly behind the production of the roll, but his name appears to have been deliberately torn out of the document by a later owner of the roll at various places, including above the last line of the request for testimony (Figure 63E) and from the legal ruling (Figure 62A). The last segment of the request for testimony asks witnesses to write and seal their testimony on the bottom and in the margins (*dar dhayl wa ḥawāshī*) of the document so that it could serve as proof when required (*ki ʿinda al-ḥājat ḥujjat būda bāshad*). The request for testimony ends with the Quranic verse: "for indeed God never lets the reward of those who do good go to waste" (Q: 11: 115).

Seventy-five witnesses have recorded their testimonies around the margins and above and below the six-line request for testimony, each confirming the claim using slightly different expressions. Most of these testimonies were written onto the document by the witnesses in their own hand and are sealed. These sealed autograph witness testimonies can be contrasted with the testimonies of peasants and farmers from the two villages, which were recorded by a scribe directly below the request for witness testimony (Figure 63F). All the testimonies carry a tiny remark, *ṣaḥḥa* (it is correct), written on the top right-hand side of the text of the testimony (see for example Figure 63F). The testimonies are all undated. The final element of the *istishhād-nāma* roll is a legal ruling which judicially certified the *waqf* claim based on the recorded witness testimonies and Shaykh Aḥmad's role as its administrator. This legal ruling is dated Dhū l-Qaʿda 1175/May–June 1762 (Figure 62A). It is recorded on the top left-hand corner of the roll above the six-line request for testimony and is sealed. Regrettably, the seal is illegible. It is not clear if the scholar who wrote this ruling is the same person who wrote the *ṣaḥḥa* remarks on the testimonies. It is also difficult to determine if the entire process of production of the roll took place when the ruling was written, or if it occurred over time as new autograph testimonies were gradually added onto the roll.

6 The *waqf* itself was constituted by a woman, Gawharshāh Bīgam b. Mīrzā Ismāʿīl, on 22 Rajab 1071/23 March 1661 in the Safavid period. For an edition of her *waqf* deed, see Ishkawarī 1388 sh./2009, VII, 220–231.

Figure 62: Start of the Zand *istishhād-nāma* roll (*ṭūmār*) from Isfahan, dated Dhū l-Qaʿda 1175/ May–June 1762. © File no. 612/3 G-9, Sāzmān-i Awqāf wa Umūr-i Khayriyya, Isfahan.

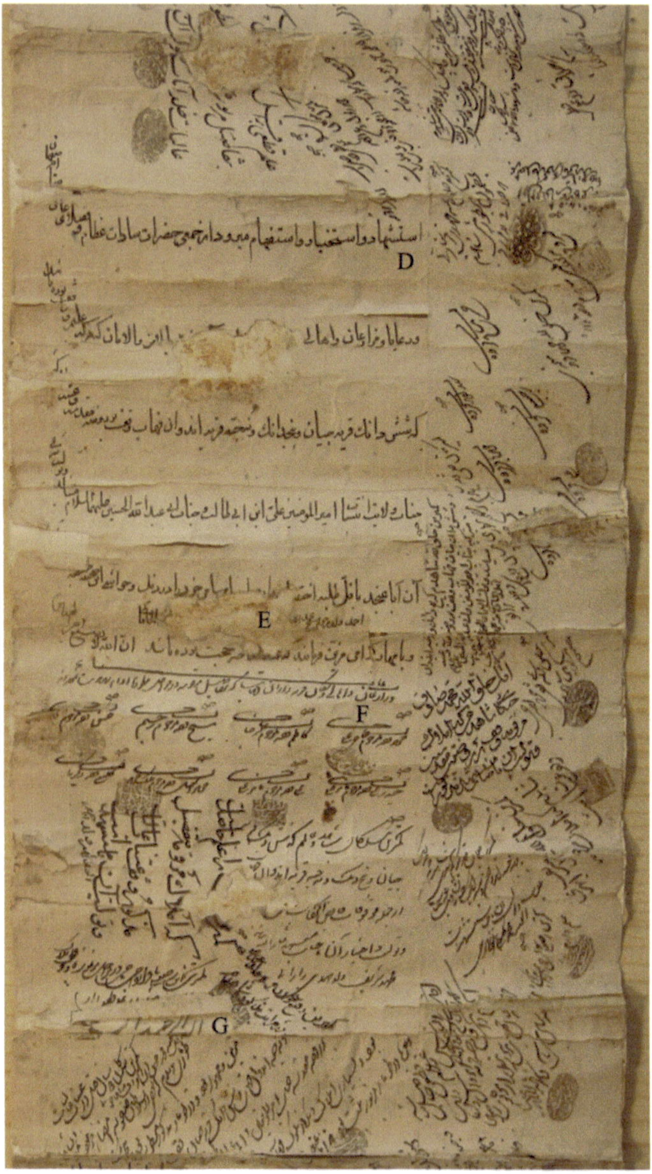

Figure 63: Six-line request for testimonies section of the Zand *istishhād-nāma* roll.

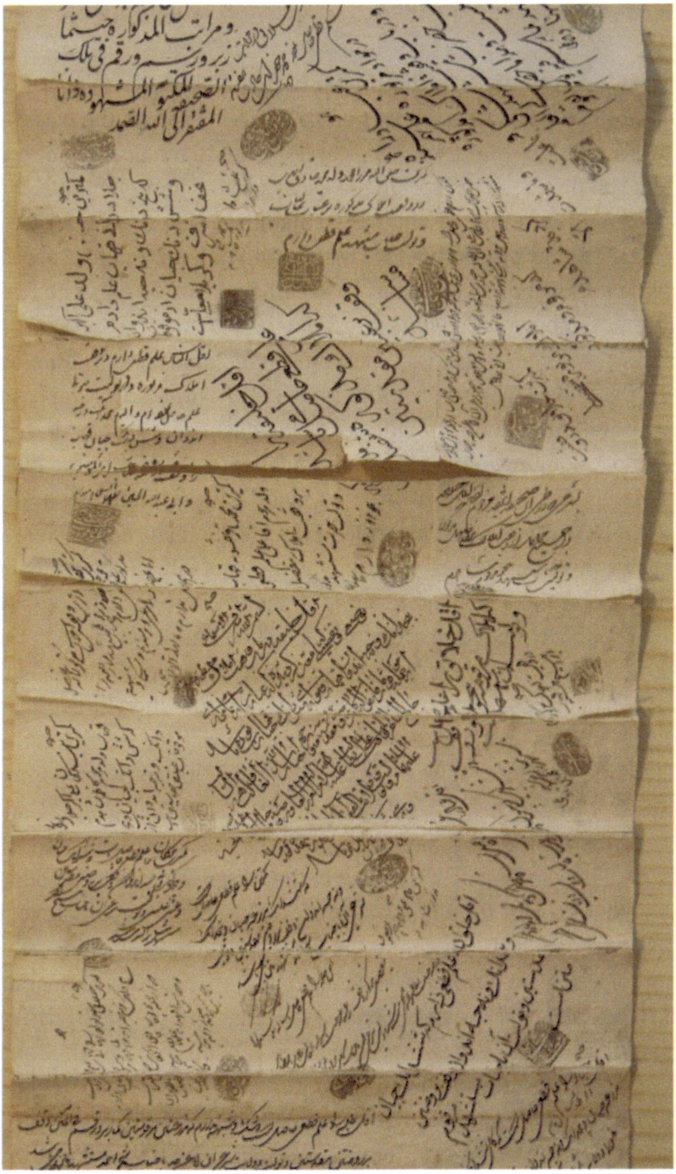

Figure 64: Witness testimonies recorded below the request for testimonies in the Zand *istishhād-nāma* roll.

2.2 A Qajar *Istishhād-nāma* dated 1280/1864

In the Astarābād case we examined in the previous chapter, we noted that the legal ruling of Ḥājjī Mullā Riḍā Astarābādī was originally recorded on the witness statement of Mīr Mūsā and Mīr Taqī itself. This corresponds to the practice of the Zand *istishhād-nāma* roll discussed earlier. In the Qajar period, however, both the request for tesimony and the marginal witness testimonies tended to be written by a scribe, while legal rulings based on such *istishhād-nāmas* were not recorded onto the *istishhād-nāma* itself but were issued on seperate sheets. We also no longer find the *saḥḥa* remark above each witness testimony.

As an example, we will consider a Qajar-era *istishhād-nāma* written on blue paper in Isfahan in 1280/1864.[7] The sixteen-line request for witness testimony in *naskh* script asks the inhabitants of the villages of Rūydashtīn to testify that 12 out of 70 *ḥabba* of land belonging to the village of Jundān, around a hundred kilometres southeast of Isfahan, was constituted as *waqf* for the *imām-zāda* ʿAlī b. Muḥammad b. Zayd b. Mūsā al-Kādhim shrine in the village (Figure 65).

According to the request for witness testimony, the ownership of the lands in question was unknown, and the lands had reverted to the crown (*majhūl al-ḥāl wa khāliṣa ast*). Making it publicly known that the lands, which had been ruined and uncultivated (*makhrūba būdan wa lam yazraʿ shudan*) since the time of the Afghan conquest (*az awān-i ghalaba-yi afghān tā kunūn*), were *waqf* would therefore ensure they were revived, and thereby help to raise the funds nessecary for repairs to the shrine and to pay its staff and Qurʾān reciters, as well as to light its lamps (*bi-maṣārif -i khayr az taʿmīr-i ʿimārāt wa makhārij-i khuddām wa qariyān-i qurʾān wa afrūkhtan-i maṣābīḥ*). The request for witness testimony is dated Shaʿbān 1280/February 1864.

There are over sixty-four testimonies recorded in the *istishhād-nāma* around the margins of the sixteen-line request for witness testimony. The spatial organisation of the marginal witness testimonies in relation to the request for witness testimony is quite different from the Zand-era *istishhād-nāma* examined earlier. The reason for this is that each of the elements of the document was written and organised by the same scribe. The marginal testimonies are recorded into columns on the left – and right-hand margin of the request for witness testimony. Most of the testimonies end with the date of the Islamic *hijrī* lunar year 1280/1864 in which they were recorded. It is not certain if they were all recorded on the *istishhād-nāma* by the scribe at the same time or if they were first collected individually on a separate document over time and later transferred onto the *istishhād-nāma*. The testimonies are short and

7 I am indebted to Sayyid Ṣādiq Ḥusaynī Ishkawarī for images of this document from the digital archive of Majmaʿ-i Dhakhāʾir-i Islāmī, file no. 490. For an edition of this document, see the appendix.

Figure 65: A Qajar era *istishhād-nāma* dated Shaʿbān 1280/February 1864, relating to the *waqf* lands belonging to the *imām-zāda* ʿAlī b. Muḥammad b. Zayd b. Mūsā al-Kāẓim shrine in the village of Jundān near Isfahan © File no. 490, digital archive, Majmaʿ-yi Dhakhāʾir-i Islāmī, Qum.

appear to have been solicited mainly from individuals who lived in neighboring villages. The witnesses are grouped according to the villages they are from. The village name is indicated in a note above the testimony of the first individual from a given village, for example: witnesses from Qūrṭān (var. Qūrtān) village (*shuhūd-i qarya-yi qūrṭān*). Each testimony is recorded under a preposition *īn* (this), or adjective such as *aqall* (the lowest), or honorific *ʿālī ḥaḍrat*, with letters extended, or simply below the *dafʿa* horizontal stroke written as a cipher.[8] Most of the testimonies are recorded by the scribe in *shikasta-nastʿalīq* script, though some are recorded in *naskh* script. It is possible that the use of different scripts served to distinguish either two different occasions on which these testimonies were added onto the sheet or groups of individuals. Two of the marginal witness testimonies recorded in *naskh* script, for example, read as follows (Figure 66):

(A) This lowest of cultivators (*aqall al-zāriʿīn*) of the village of Suhrān, Rajab ʿAli has heard (*ismāʿ karda-am*) from the fathers (*ābāʾ*) and white beards (*rīsh-sifīdān*) and has acquired certain knowledge (*ʿilm-i qaṭʿī*) of what is in the text that 12 *ḥabba* of land belonging to the village of Jundān is a *waqf* of the *imāmzāda* shrine and is in ruins [from the time of the Afghans until now]. 1280/1864. Oval seal: *payrū-yi dīn-i nabī ismāʿīl.*

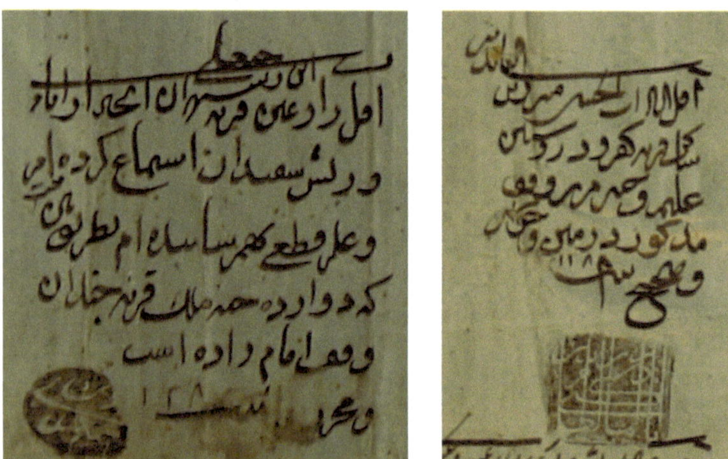

Figure 66: Detail of two testimonies (A, left and B, right) from the *istishhād-nāma* of *imām-zāda* ʿAlī b. Muḥammad b. Zayd b. Mūsā al-Kāẓim shrine in Jundān © File no. 490, digital archive, Majmaʿ-yi Dhakhāʾir-i Islāmī, Qum.

8 In a few instances, the extended first word in *siyāq* is the honorific *ʿālī-jināb*.

(B) The lowest of Ḥusaynī sayyids (*aqall al-sādāt*), Mīr Zayn al-ʿĀbidīn, resident of the village of Kafrūd, Rudashtīn. [I have] knowledge and know from report (*ʿilm wa khabar*) that the said *waqf* in the text [of the document] and in the magins, is true." 1280/1864. Square seal: *yā imām zayn al-ʿābidīn adriknī.*

Each testimony is sealed individually by the witness. The seals of each witness appear to have been affixed after their testimony was recorded onto the document by the scribe. This contrasts with the practice of the Zand *istihhād-nāma* roll above where, in general, each witness first affixed his seal onto the the *istishhād-nāma* and then wrote his testimony in his own hand.

The main purpose of the multiple oral witness testimonies recorded in such *istishhad-nāmas* was to function as proof that the lands in question were *waqf.* Even if the original *waqf* deed was available, as we shall see in the case of Mīrzā Aḥamd Kafrānī's *waqf* (see below), it was, nevertheless, the multiple oral testimonies of living witnesses that was cruicial to the *waqf* claim. This suggests that in establishing *waqf* claims, common report or hearsay was more significant than the written evidence of an authentic *waqf* deed.

In concluding this section, the production of an *istishhād-nāma* was above all a social act. Like a modern petition, it brought together large numbers of signatories, thus spreading awareness of a *waqf* claim within communities and applying social pressure on individuals who had acted unlawfully, for example, either by transforming a *waqf* into private property or by diverting *waqf* revenues for uses other than those stipulated by the founder of the *waqf.* In some cases, as in the example of the *istishhād-nāma* of the *imām-zāda* ʿAlī b. Muḥammad b. Zayd b. Mūsā al-Kāẓim, reviving former *waqf* land which had become crown land over time was seen as a pious act which helped to sustain a religious shrine. In what follows, we will examine how the *istishhād-nāma* was used as a legal instrument in the Qajar period to revive a Safavid family *waqf.*

3 The *Waqf* of Mīrzā Aḥmad Kafrānī, 1240–1332/1825–1913

3.1 Sources

Before we proceed to a historical reconstruction of the dispute over the *waqf* of Mīrzā Aḥmad Kafrānī in Isfahan, a few remarks concerning the sources are in order. The original (*aṣl*) documents relating to the *waqf* of Mīrzā Aḥmad Kafrānī do not appear to have survived, or are still in the possession of his descendants. What we have today are transcripts (*sawād*) of 48 original documents, probably made after 1330/1912, when the case was referred to Mullā Muḥammad Ḥusayn

Fishārakī (1266–1353/1850–1935), a leading *mujtahid* and member of the *ʿulamāʾ* of Isfahan (see Figure 67).

Figure 67: Muḥammad Ḥusayn Fishārakī (1266–1353/1850–1935), the main *mujtahid* involved in reviving Mīrzā Aḥmad Kafrānī's *waqf.*

The original documents were transcribed by one hand onto pieces of paper which are attached to a copy of the *waqf-nāma* in the form of an annex (*ḍamīma*). To record seals that appeared in the original documents, the copyist uses the words "place of the seal of (*maḥall-i muhr-i*)", followed by the name of the owner of the seal. Similarly, any handwriting which appeared in the owner's own hand in the original documents is indicated by the words "handwriting of (*dast-khaṭṭ -i*)" followed by the name. These transcribed documents were deposited at some point in the provincial *waqf* archive of Isfahan (Sazmān-i Awqāf wa Umūr-i Khayriyya).[9] They were edited and published by Ṣādiq Ḥusaynī Ishkawarī in 2009.[10] In what follows, we will use the edited documents to reconstruct litigation in the dispute over Mīrzā Aḥmad Kafrānī's endowment.

9 File no. 7 A 663, Sāzmān-i Awqāf wa Umūr–i Khayriyya, Isfahan.
10 Ishkawarī 1388 sh./2009, III, 238–457. For a list of the documents, see the appendix.

3.2 Historical Reconstruction

3.2.1 Mīrzā Aḥmad Kafrānī (d. after 988/1580) and his *Waqf*

Mīrzā Aḥmad Kafrānī lived during the reign of the second Safavid shah, Ṭahmāsp I (r. 930–84/1524–1576). So far, the only reference to him I have found is in the *Tadhkira* of Taqī al-Dīn Awhadī Balyanī (973–1050/1565–1640), *ʿArafāt al-ʿĀshiqīn*. Under the entry for the poet Māyilī Nīrīzī, Mīrzā Aḥmad Kafrānī Iṣfahānī is described as a tyrannical and cruel government official in charge of Safavid crown lands (*khāṣṣa*) in Fārs province. Apparently, such was his cruelty and oppression that the people of Fārs rose against him and complained to Ṭahmāsp. Māyilī Nīrīzī composed a panegyric poem (*qaṣīda*) of thirty-one *bayts* rhyming in the Arabic letter *lām* (*lāmiyya*) on behalf of the people of Fārs, in which he expressed his own and their grievances. The *qaṣīda* was well received by Ṭahmāsp, who ordered Mīrzā Aḥmad Kufrānī to pay thirty *tūmāns* to Māyilī and to return the money he had taken by force back to the people of Fārs.[11]

Muṣliḥ al-Dīn Mahdawī, in his *Aʿlām Iṣfahān*, also mentions a Mīrzā Aḥmad b. Sulṭān Muḥammad Kafrānī Rūydashtī as a scholar who composed a Qurʾān *tafsīr* for a certain Mīrzā Rafīʿ al-Dīn, of which a manuscript copy has survived in Isfahan.[12] If this Mīrzā Aḥmad Kafrānī is the same as the tyrannical Safavid bureaucrat, it would indicate that he turned to more pious pursuits later in his life. What is certain is that Mīrzā Aḥmad Kafrānī established in Jamādī I 988/June 1580 a family *waqf* in favour of his lineal male descendants. The *waqf* was validated among others by the *shaykh al-islām* of Isfahan, Bahāʾ al-Dīn al-ʿĀmilī (953–1030/1546–1621).[13] According to the text of the *waqf-nāma*, the following lands in the region of Isfahan were constituted as *waqf*:

1. 6 *dāng*[14] of the village (*qarya*) of Jayshī in the district *(bulūk)* of Rūydashtīn,[15] one of the *bulūks*[16] of Isfahan.
2. 5 *dāng* of the village of Saryān, in the *bulūk* of Rūydashtīn, one of the *bulūks* of Isfahan.

---

11 See Nāṣirābādī 1388 sh./2010, 45–53.

12 Mahdawī 1386 sh./2007, I, 416.

13 Document no. 1. For the biography of Bahāʾ al-Dīn al-ʿĀmilī, also known as Shaykh Bahāʾī, an eminent jurist and polymath at the court of Shāh ʿAbbās I (r. 996–1038/1588–1629), see for example E. Kohlberg, "Bahāʾ-al-Dīn ʿĀmelī," *Encyclopaedia Iranica*, Vol. III, Fasc. 4, 429–430 (Accessed online 1 April 2023) and Stewart 1991, 1998.

14 One-sixth part of any real estate, see Lambton 1969, 426.

15 Near present-day Harand, Isfahan province, Iran.

16 Administrative division for an area consisting of villages and hamlets.

3. 9 out of 72 *ḥabba*[17] of the field (*mazraʿa*) of Isḥāqābād in the *bulūk* of Rūydashtīn, one of the *bulūks* of Isfahan.

The administration of the *waqf* was in the hands of the founder (*wāqif*) during his lifetime, and upon his death it would pass on to his male descendants (*awlād-i dhukūr*) in the following manner:

> The administration (*tawliyat*) of the entire endowment is with the founder while he is alive and for as long as he lives, and after him [it is to pass] in equal share and without preference to his sons, and after sons from his own issue, to their sons in equal share, in such a way that each of the sons of the sons has a share in the administration with his paternal uncles and so on even if they have a lower lineage of descent.[18]

A comparison of this administration clause in Mīrzā Aḥmad Kafrānī's *waqf* in Isfahan can be made with another *waqf* established in the Safavid period, the *Ẓahīrīyya* in Tabriz, which was also the object of dispute during the Qajar period. The two demonstrate both similarities and differences. According to the *waqf-nāma* of the *Ẓahīrīyya* endowments, the administration of the endowment was also with the founder during his lifetime. After this, the office of *mutawallī* would be occupied by the most righteous, learned, and pious person among his descendants. In the case of several suitable candidates, a higher lineage of descent would precede a lower lineage (*baṭn-i aʿlā bar baṭn-i asfal muqaddam bāshad*).[19] This differs, however, from Mīrzā Aḥmad Kafrānī's *waqf*, where the founder insists on control being assigned to multiple *mutawallīs* in each successive generation, even if this ends up being among descent groups of a lower lineage (*wa-in kānū fī l-baṭni l-asfal*). Not surprisingly, both ways of assigning control had the potential to and did cause a large number of disputes. For the *Ẓahīrīyya*, the problem was

17 Word meaning seed, a small amount.

18 Document no. 1: *"tawliyat-i kull-i mawqūfāt-i madhkūra-rā bi nafs-i nafīs-i khud mādāma ḥayyan – lā zāla bāqiyyan bi-baqāʾi l-ayyām-wa baʿdahu bi awlād-i dhukūr-i khud mushtarikīna fīhā bi l-sawīya bi-ghayrī mazīya, wa baʿd az har yak az awlād-i ṣulbī-yi ḥadrat-i mushārun ilayhi, bi-awlād-i dhukūr-i ū bi l-sawīya, chunānchi har yak az awlād-i awlād sharīk bāshand bā aʿmām-i khud dar tawliyat-i madhkūr wa in kānū fī l-baṭni l-asfal."* The *waqf-nāma* continues by describing how, if the male line becomes extinct, control should pass on to the daughters of the sons, but then return to the sons of the daughters, and in the event that the male line becomes extinct again, should revert back to the daughters and so forth. If both male and female lines became extinct, then control was to pass on to close relatives based on who among them was deemed most worthy (*al-afḍal*), followed by most righteous (*al-aṣlaḥ*) and then oldest in age (*al-asann*). If no relatives remained, then control of the endowment was to be entrusted to a pious Ḥusaynī sayyid of Isfahan engaged in teaching the religious sciences and who was to be appointed by the shah of the time.

19 Werner 1999, 234.

that no method was specified to determine which descendant was the most qualified to take up the office of *mutawallī*, whereas for Mīrzā Aḥmad Kufrānī's *waqf*, the problem lay in trying to work out how multiple *mutawallīs* could share control of the lands and revenue.

I use the term family *waqf* to describe Mīrzā Aḥmad Kafrānī's *waqf*, because the principal beneficiaries of this *waqf* were the descendants of the founder who not only enjoyed 50% of all income as the right of the *mutawallī (ḥaqq-i tawliyat*), but were also entitled to use the remaining 50% to cover all expenses relating to the *waqf*, such as those incurred while farming the lands. In the event that any income was left over, it was to be used to cover the travel costs of pilgrims (*zuwwār*) according to the following division: 50% of the surplus income would go to pilgrims travelling to the shrine of the Prophet in Medina; 25% to pilgrims travelling to the shrine of ʿAlī in Najaf and 25% to pilgrims travelling to the shrine of al-Ḥusayn in Karbala, Iraq.

The formal constitution of the *waqf* to the shrines of the Prophet, ʿAlī, and al-Husayn, and the stipulation that leftover income was to be used to help cover the travel costs of religious pilgrims to these places was a way of giving the private family *waqf* some pious public religious sanction and to conunter possible attempts at usurpation by powerful political authorities. In comparison, the aforementioned *Ẓahīrīyya* endowments in Tabriz were a "mixed *waqf*" with 55% of the income allocated to public and charitable causes. Of the remainder, 20% was to be allocated as a stipend to the *mutawallī* (*ḥaqq al-tawliya*) and 25% as stipends to the descendants of the founder (*ḥaqq al-awlād*).

In both cases, however, potential *mutawallīs* in each generation found it expedient to settle the distribution of income from the *waqf* through a series of rental contracts (*ijāra-nāmas*) and settlement contracts (*muṣālaḥa-nāmas*) with other descendants who also had a right over the *waqf*. The ideal situation was to keep these contracts and agreements within the family in order to reduce the possibility of the *waqf* lands being usurped and lost in the long run. In practice though, even this measure, as we will see in this case study, did not prevent the *waqf* from being usurped by one member of the family and then sold to someone outside the family.[20] Almost as if he predicted this turn of events, Mīrzā Aḥmad Kafrānī made it a condition in his *waqf-nāma* that the *waqf* lands were under no circumstance to be the subject of a rental contract or a deed of settlement with anyone:

20 The first attempted sale was of 2 *dāng* of Saryān by Mīrzā Abū Ṭālib and his nephew, Mīrzā Muḥammad Hādī, to Mīrzā Muḥammad Hāshim in 1258/1842. The second attempted sale was of 4 *dāng* of Jayshī by Mīrzā Hāshim Harandī to Ḥājjī ʿAbd al-Maḥmūd Qannādī and Āqā Mīrzā Mahdī Bunakdār in 1318/1901.

> He the aforementioned founder of the endowment (*wāqif*) – may God the Exalted make him succeed in his aims and make his future better than his past - made the following condition: the comprehensive aforementioned endowment should absolutely not be rented out, neither for a long nor for a short period, and the revenue of the aforementioned endowment should in no way be the object of a settlement with anyone for any reason whatsoever.[21]

From the surviving documents relating to Mīrzā Aḥmad Kafrānī's *waqf*, however, we can see that the *mutawallīs* did in fact enter into numerous rental and settlement contracts, both with members of the family and with individuals outside the family. Neither the *mutawallīs* nor the Iṣfahānī *ʿulamāʾ* who were repeatedly called upon to draw up and authenticate these rental contracts and agreements found it problematic to blatantly disregard the *wāqif's* wishes.[22] This raises the question as to what extent *mutawallīs* were bound to follow the stipulations of the founder in the *waqf-nāma*. If one considers a shrine complex, for instance the shrine of the eighth Shīʿī Imām al-Riḍā (d. 202/818) at Mashhad, which has a continuous history of endowments from at least the Timurid period until modern times, it is practically impossible for a *mutawallī* to follow all the stipulations of the founders of former *waqfs* historically endowed to the shrine. Some *waqf-nāmas* therefore give the *mutawallī* the power to act in a way that is deemed most suitable for the prosperity of the *waqf* and thus, if necessary, to override specific stipulations. Mīrzā Aḥmad Kufrānī's *waqf-nāma*, however, grants no such powers to the *mutawallī*.[23]

3.2.2 Mīrzā Muḥammad Taqī's *Istishhād-nāma*, 1240/1825

We have no information about how Mīrza Aḥmad Kafrānī's *waqf* was administered and who was in control of it from Jamādī al-Awwal 988/June 1580 until Shawwāl 1240/June 1825. In Shawwāl 1240/June 1825, a descendant of Mīrza Aḥmad Kafrānī named Mīrzā Muḥammad Taqī found it necessary to collect witness testimony in a

---

21 Document no. 1: "*wa sharṭ farmūd ʿālī ḥaḍrat-i wāqif-i mushārun ilayhi – waffaqahu llāhu taʿālā li-marāḍīhi wa jaʿla mustaqbala ḥālihi khayran min māḍīhi – ki mawqūfāt-i mufaṣṣala-yi mazbūra-rā muṭlaqan bi-ijāra nadahand, na bi-muddat-i ṭawīl na bi-muddat-i qaṣīr wa manāfiʿ-i mawqūfāt-i madhkūra-rā bā aḥadī ṣulḥ nanamāyand bi-hīch wajh min al-wujūh*".

22 They were, however, clearly aware of this condition, see document no. 34.

23 Mīrzā Aḥmad Kafrānī specifies that the *mutawallī* was only free to use his own opinion when it was in keeping with the sacred law (*sharīʿa*) and the conditions of the founder: "The shah of the time, the *ṣadrs* and the *quḍāt* should allow whatever course of action that is necessary in the considered opinion of the *mutawallī* to be brought into practice that is in keeping with the sacred law and in accordance with the conditions of the founder" (*pādishāh-i waqt wa ṣudūr wa quḍāt . . . guzhārand ki ānchi muqtaḍā-yi raʾy-yi ṣāʾib-i mutawallī bāshad ki har āyina-yi muṭābiq-i sharʿ-i ashraf-i aqdas wa muwāfiq-i sharṭ-i wāqif khāhad būd bi ʿamal āyad*), see document no. 1.

witness statement (*istishhād-nāma*), from the *ʿulamāʾ*, sayyids (*sādāt*) and notables (*aʿyān*) of Isfahan, confirming that (1) the village of Jayshī was *waqf* land belonging to the descendants of Mīrza Aḥmad Kafrānī and (2) the possession (*taṣarruf*) of Jayshī by the recently deceased Qajar Chief Minister (*ṣadr-i aʿẓam*), Ḥajjī Muḥammad Ḥusayn Khān (d.1239/1823), was through rental contract, and (3) any attempts at sale of the *waqf* land were against the *sharīʿa*.[24] This is the earliest recorded evidence of dispute over the *waqf*.

3.2.3 The Legal Rulings of Sayyid Asadullāh Shaftī, 1262–1263/1846–1847

On 19 Shawwāl 1258/23 November 1842, two other descendants of Mīrza Aḥmad Kafrānī, namely Mīrzā Abū Ṭālib and his nephew, sold 2 *dāng* of Saryān to a certain Mīrzā Muḥammad Hāshim.[25] This unilateral move to sell off some of the *waqf* lands brought Mīrzā Abū Ṭālib into conflict with another descendant, Mīrzā ʿAlī Muḥammad. However, it appears that Mīrzā ʿAlī Muḥammad's claims to be a direct lineal male descendant of Mīrza Aḥmad Kafrānī, and therefore a *mutawallī* of the endowment, were not recognised.

Twice, on 23 Dhū al-Ḥijja 1262/12 December 1846 and again on 10 Jamādī al-Thānī 1263/26 May 1847, Mīrzā ʿAlī Muḥammad went before Ḥajjī Sayyid Asadullāh Shaftī (1227–1290/1812–1873), an important member of the *ʿulamāʾ* of Isfahan, to confirm that he was indeed a direct descendant of Mīrza Aḥmad Kafrānī and had rights as a *mutawallī* of the endowment.[26] The legal action of Mīrzā ʿAlī Muḥammad made Mīrzā Muḥammad Hāshim, who had bought 2 *dāng* of Saryān from Mīrzā Abū Ṭālib and his nephew, realise that what he had bought was in fact *waqf* property. According to his own admission, fearing the terrible retribution that awaited him on judgement day for buying land that had been made *waqf* to sacred places (*amākin-i musharrafa*), he revoked his purchase on 26 Ramaḍān 1271/12 June 1855.[27] At some point after this, Mīrzā Abū Ṭālib and Mīrzā ʿAlī Muḥammad appear to have had equal share of possession of the two villages of the endowment. Each had control over 3 *dāng* of Jayshī and two and a half *dāng* of Saryān.[28]

24 Document no. 9.
25 Document no. 21.
26 Document no. 2.
27 Document no. 21.
28 Document no. 6.

3.2.4 The Sale by Mīrzā Hāshim Harandī, 1320/1904

Before his death, Mīrzā ʿAlī Muḥammad appointed his stepbrother, Mīrzā Hāshim Harandī, in his will, to temporarily oversee the control and administration of his share of the endowment on behalf of his two children, who were minors at the time (see x and y in Figure 68).

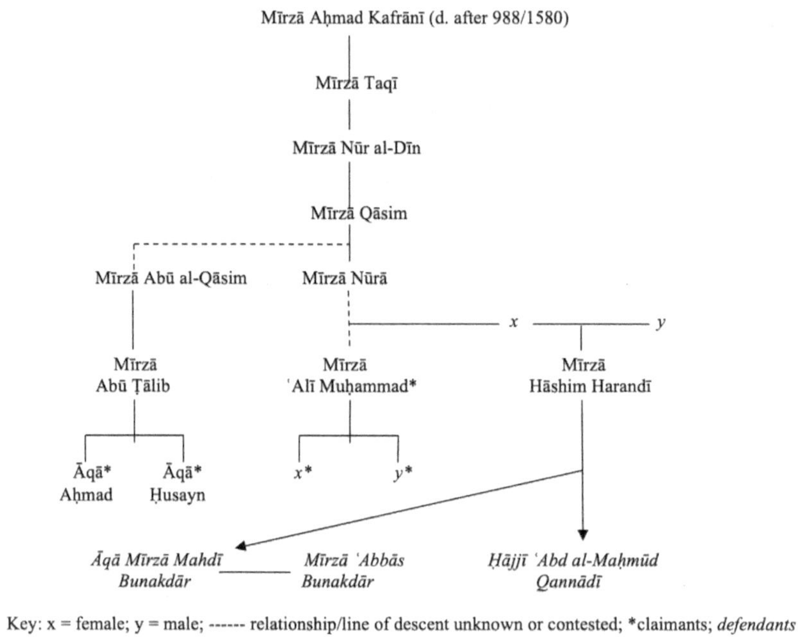

Figure 68: The descendants of Mīrzā Aḥmad Kafrānī and the claimants and defendants in the dispute.

At the same time, Mīrzā Hāshim Harandī rented Mīrzā Abū Ṭālib's share of the endowment from his sons, Āqā Aḥmad and Āqā Ḥusayn. In brief, therefore, Mīrzā Hāshim Harandī was, through bequest and rental contract, effectively in control of the entire endowment. In 1318/1901, Mīrzā Hāshim Harandī ran into trouble with the provincial administration with regard to farming the land (*giriftārī-hā-yi dīwānī dar umūr zirāʿatī*) and decided to sell 4 *dāng* of Jayshī to Ḥājjī ʿAbd al-Maḥmūd Qannādī and Āqā Mīrzā Mahdī Bunakdār in a conditional sale contract (*bayʿ-i sharṭ*), which was recorded in the register of the Masjid-i Naw in Isfahan.[29] Because Mīrzā Hāshim Harandī was unable to meet the conditions stipulated in the *bayʿ-i sharṭ* in time, the

29 Document no. 38. On the conditional sale contract in Qajar Iran, see Kondo 2021, 615–639.

matter was brought before some members of the *ʿulamāʾ*. Unaware that (1) the lands were *waqf* and (2) that Mīrzā Hāshim Harandī owed his control through bequest and rental contract, these *ʿulamāʾ* decided to confirm the sale. On 11 Dhī Qaʿda 1320/9 February 1903, they transferred 4 *dāng* of Jayshī from Mīrzā Hāshim Harandī to the property of Ḥājjī ʿAbd al-Maḥmūd Qannādī and Āqā Mīrzā Mahdī Bunakdār.[30]

Ḥājjī ʿAbd al-Maḥmūd Qannādī and Āqā Mīrzā Mahdī Bunakdār soon realised, however, that of the 4 *dāng* of Jayshī that they had purchased, one *dāng* actually belonged to Āqā Aḥmad and Āqā Ḥusayn and had only been rented out to Mīrzā Hāshim Harandī. The rental contract, which appeared in an appendix to the sale contract, had the potential to render the sale illegal. The matter was particularly urgent since Mīrzā Hāshim Harandī's rental contract with Āqā Aḥmad and Āqā Ḥusayn was coming to an end, and it would be a short time before Āqā Aḥmad and Āqā Ḥusayn would demand control over their land again. Ḥājjī ʿAbd al-Maḥmūd Qannādī and Āqā Mīrzā Mahdī Bunakdār decided to act swiftly. In 1322/1904, Āqā Mīrzā Mahdī Bunakdār called his brother, Mīrzā ʿAbbās Bunakdār, to rent out the full share of Āqā Aḥmad and Āqā Ḥusayn (that is 3 *dāng* of Jayshī and 2 and a half *dāng* of Saryān) on a new rental contract for a period of seven years. This was recorded in the register of the Masjid-i Naw in Isfahan on 19 Shaʿbān 1322/29 October 1904.[31] In the same year, Mīrzā ʿAbbās Bunakdār secretly re-rented the lands out to Ḥājjī ʿAbd al-Maḥmūd Qannādī and Āqā Mīrzā Mahdī Bunakdār for a period of seven years. When the rental contract expired, Ḥājjī ʿAbd al-Maḥmūd Qannādī and Āqā Mīrzā Mahdī Bunakdār, suppressing the fact that the property was *waqf*, filed a lawsuit over ownership (*daʿwā-yi milkiyyat*). They claimed that Mīrzā ʿAbbās Bunakdār had illegally rented the lands from Āqā Aḥmad and Āqā Ḥusayn because the lands were owned by them (Āqā Mīrzā Mahdī Bunakdār and Ḥājjī ʿAbd al-Maḥmūd Qannādī) and were in their possession (*taṣarruf*).

3.2.5 The *ʿAdliyya* Court Rulings and the Legal Opinions on the Possession of the Lands by Mīrzā Hāshim Harandī

Āqā Aḥmad and Āqā Ḥusayn, alarmed by this fight over lands that belonged to them, appointed an authorized legal proxy (*wakīl)* named Majd al-Sādāt to wrest control of the lands from ʿAbd al-Maḥmūd Qannādī, Āqā Mīrzā Mahdī Bunakdār, Mīrzā ʿAbbās Bunakdar and anyone else to whom the lands had been illegally transferred. In Dhū al-Qaʿda 1329/October 1911, the case was brought before the

30 Document no. 38.
31 Document no. 40.

recently established court of justice (*'adliyya*) in Isfahan. The *'adliyya* issued judicial rulings (*ḥukms*) to the effect that the lands were *waqf*, and control should be transferred from all usurpers to Āqā Aḥmad and Āqā Ḥusayn.[32] However Ḥājjī 'Abd al-Maḥmūd Qannādī and Āqā Mīrzā Mahdī Bunakdār took recourse to 'highly placed authorities' (*maqāmat-i 'āliyya*) and succeeded in circumventing these *'adliyya ḥukms*.[33]

Left with little choice, in Dhū al-Qa'da 1329–Jamādī I 1330/November 1911–April 1912, Āqā Aḥmad and Āqā Ḥusayn, along with Muḥammad Ḥusayn Khān, a descendant of Mīzā 'Alī Muḥammad, solicited legal opinions (*fatwā*) from three leading *'ulamā'* regarding Ḥājjī 'Abd al-Maḥmūd Qannādī and Āqā Mīrzā Mahdī Bunakdār's possession (*yad*) of the lands.[34] The question asked by the claimants to these scholars was whether the possession (*yad*) of the defendants, Ḥājjī 'Abd al-Maḥmūd Qannādī and Āqā Mīrzā Mahdī Bunakdār, was derived from Mīrzā Hāshim Harandī or not (*yad-i anhā-rā mubtanī bar yad-i marḥūm mīrzā hāshim mī-dānīd yā khayr?*). All four scholars confirmed that they considered Ḥājjī 'Abd al-Maḥmūd Qannādī and Āqā Mīrzā Mahdī Bunakdār's possession (*yad*) of the lands to be derived from Mīrzā Hāshim Harandī. This was significant because Mīrzā Hāshim Harandī's possession of the land was valid through rental contract and bequest, but not as *mutawallī* of the *waqf*. Any transfer of the lands that had occurred via him was therefore illegal.

3.2.6 The Collection of Witness Testimonies in an *Istishhād-nāma*

Having secured these legal opinions, the claimants and their associates began collecting one hundred and sixty-five witness testimonies over a period of eleven months, recorded in six separate documents, in support of their claim (see Table 2).

The documents in which these witness testimonies were collected are of two types. The first type is a simple question-and-answer format (nos. 10, 11, 12, 14, 15) and the second type is the *istishhād-nāma* (no.13). Both the question-and-answer format and the *istishhād-nāma* record the claim and request witnesses to write their testimony and affix their seal in the margins. The only difference between the two is that the request for testimonies in the *isitshhād-nāma* has, as we have seen, a distinctive opening and closing formula. The witness testimonies in support of the *waqf* claim are based on:

32 Document no. 3.
33 Document no. 6: "*bi maqāmāt-i 'āliyya multajī shudand wa nagudhārand aḥkām–i 'adliyya jārī shawad.*"
34 Document no. 3.

Table 2: Social and geographical distribution of witnesses who recorded testimonies in support of the claim of the claimants in *istishhād-nāma*.

Document no.	**Social class of witnesses (*shuhūd*)**	**Geographic distribution of witnesses**	**Number of witnesses**	**Dates of witness testimonies**
10	U	Qum	1	28 Dhū al-Qaʿda 1329/20 November 1911
11	U, N, L	Isfahan/ Rūydashtīn	40	24 Rabīʿ I 1330- Ramaḍān 1330/March 1912-August 1912
12	U, N, L	Harand, Rūydashtīn	42	Jamādī I 1330/May 1912
13	U, N, L	Isfahan/ Rūydashtīn	32	Dhū l-Qaʿda 1329-Muḥarram 1330/November 1911-January 1912
14	U, N, L	Pāy-i Qalʿa quarter, Isfahan	22	Dhū l-Ḥijja 1329-Ramaḍān 1330/December 1911-August 1912
15	U, N, L	Harand	28	Ramaḍan 1330-Shawwal 1330/August 1912-September 1912

1. Personal or hearsay knowledge of the *waqf* status of the lands.
2. Personal or hearsay knowledge of an acknowledgement (*iqrār*) made by Mīrzā Hāshim Harandī regarding the *waqf* status of the lands.
3. Personal or hearsay knowledge of receipt of rental income by the claimants from Mīrzā Hāshim Harandī and later from the defendants, Ḥājjī ʿAbd al-Maḥmūd Qannādī and Āqā Mīrzā Mahdī Bunakdār.
4. Reference to the existence of written documentary evidence on *waqf* status such as the *waqf* deed (*waqf-nāma)* and legal rulings of scholars *(ḥukms*).

Type 1 statements are quite rare:

> [Witness 22]: Āqā-yi Nadīmbāshī: I know five *dāng* of Saryān and six *dāng* of Jayshī in Rūydashtīn and 9 *ḥabba* of Isḥāqābād to be *waqf.* 9 Dhī al-Qaʿda 1329. Place of seal.[35]

> [Witness 9] Āqā Sayyid Abū al-Qāsim Ṭabīb says: "For a long time now I have heard that Jashyī and Saryān are *waqf.* Today I am certain that Jayshī and Saryān are *waqf.* When I

35 Document no. 13.

> was young, I used to go to those places, and I heard from the old men and the peasants there that these two villages were *waqf*." Place of seal.[36]

More frequent are statements which refer to 2, 3, and 4 in different combinations and sometimes with all three in a single statement. In Islamic law, the acknowledgement of rights (in court or outside) known as *iqrār* was one of the three forms of acceptable evidence (the other two being witness testimony and oath-taking). The fact that some witnesses heard Mīrzā Hāshim Harandī acknowledge the *waqf* status of the lands is significant because it constituted an acknowledgement of the rights of the claimants which was based on their claim to be *mutawallīs* of the *waqf*. Moreoever, as we saw in the earlier theoretical discussion, Imāmī Shīʿī jurists considered an *iqrār* by the possessor of the land on its *waqf* status proof the land was *waqf*.

> [Witness 28]: Āqā Mīrzā Murtaḍā Mustawfī Quhpāya: "5 *dāng* of Saryān and 6 *dāng* of Jayshī are *waqf*. Āqā Mīrzā Ḥāshim himself acknowledged (*iqrār kardand*) in my house that they are *waqf* and that he had rented them from Mīrzā Ḥusayn and Mīrzā Aḥmad. Sometimes when I used to go to Āqā Mīrzā Hāshim's house, they [Mīrzā Ḥusayn and Mīrzā Aḥmad, the claimants] were there demanding rental income."[37]

Reference to the receipt of rental income by the claimants first from Mīrzā Ḥāshim Harandī and then from the defendants, Ḥājjī ʿAbd al-Maḥmūd Qannādī and Āqā Mīrza Mahdī Bunakdār, was seen as compelling evidence of the claimant's ownership of the lands.

> [Witness 20]: Āqā Sayyid Ibrāhīm: "3 *dāng* of Jayshī and 3 *dāng* of Saryān are *waqf*. They had been rented out to the late Āqā Mīrzā Hāshim and after that they were rented out to Āqā Mīrzā ʿAbbās Bunakdār. The rental contract has now expired. Āqā Mīrzā Mahdī and Ḥājjī ʿAbd al-Maḥmūd's possession (*yad*) is through rental contract." Place of seal.[38]

Many witnesses also felt that the existence of the *waqf* deed and other legal rulings (see the testimony of witness 1 below) was something that mattered and was worth reporting about in support of the claim. One witness, for example, reports that Mīrzā Hāshim Harandī was himself in possession of several *waqf* deeds, some of which presumably related to Jayshī and Saryān:

> [Witness 24]: Āqā Muḥammad Ḥusayn Harandī: "When Āqā Mīrzā Hāshim Harandī passed away, I asked Ḥājjī Muḥammad Bāqir: 'What did you do as Āqā Mīrzā Hāshim's executor?'

36 Document no. 11.
37 Document no. 11.
38 Document no. 14.

He replied: 'I searched a great deal among his documents and discovered several *waqf-nāmas* which I gave to his heirs." Place of seal.[39]

Nevertheless, the existence of the *waqf* deed, at least in this case, was not in and of itself sufficient in proving the *waqf* status of Jayshī and Saryān. Although the original *waqf* deed and earlier legal rulings (*ḥukms*) to the effect that Jayshī and Saryān were *waqf* had survived, the claimants still found it necessary to collect widespread reported testimony in support of their claims. These testimonies were collected from many different people over a long period of time. This suggests that much of the coercive power of the legal process was derived from the living witnesses that the claimants were able to assemble in support of their case. Only by getting a very large number of *ʿulamāʾ* and notables on their side could the claimants, Āqā Aḥmad and Āqā Ḥusayn, ever hope to put enough pressure on ʿAbd al-Maḥmūd Qannādī and Āqā Mīrzā Mahdī Bunakdār to relinquish control of the *waqf* lands. The publicity generated from the process of assembling witnesses and recording their testimonies had the potential to cause serious damage to the social standing of those known to have gone against God's law.[40] We get a sense of this from one of the witness testimonies that reports the words of Mīrzā Hāshim Harandī when he complains that a certain ʿAlī ʿAllāf will no longer give his servant barley seeds because he had turned a *waqf* into private property (*milk*):

[Witness 14]: Āqā Sayyid Muḥammad, the *mutawallī* of the grave of the two "Majlisīs" – may God have mercy upon them – says: "I used to hear Mīrzā ʿAlī Muḥammad saying: 'Jayshī and Saryān, as is recorded, are *waqf*. Half of the revenue [from the lands] belongs to the sons of Mīrzā Abū Ṭālib, that is, Aḥmad and Ḥusayn, and the other half belongs to me. Aḥmad and Ḥusayn used to come and ask for their rent from Mīrzā Hāshim and he used to give it to them. Until one day he [Mīrzā Hāshim] said to them: '[Work for your living] just suppose your father had not left these two pieces of *waqf* land for you.' I used to hear Mīrzā Hāshim say repeatedly that these two villages were *waqf*. One night his servant, Qanbar, had gone to fetch barley. He came back late, and [Mīrzā Hāshim] said: 'Where were you?' [Qanbar] said: 'I had gone to fetch barley [but] ʿAlī ʿAllāf will not give me any.' [Mīrzā Hāshim] was eating his dinner at the time and he threw the morsel of food [he was eating] to the ground and said: 'May my father burn! I have turned a *waqf* into private property (*waqf rā milk kardam*) and now I am ruined by this disaster.""[41]

39 Document no. 13.
40 Sometimes publicity of this kind was the only recourse available to claimants; especially if the defendant was a powerful and influential figure, as for instance in the case of the *Ẓahīriyya* endowments, where the *qāḍī* of Tabriz had usurped two villages belonging to the endowment. See Werner 1999, 241–242.
41 Document no. 11.

Along with the number of witnesses the claimants managed to gather, the type of witnesses was also important. High-ranking *ʿulamāʾ* and notables added considerable weight to a claim, but this was also the case for local inhabitants who may have had a connection with the case. Document no.36 is a request for witness testimony from the inhabitants of Pāy-yi Qalʿa, the same quarter of Isfahān in which the claimants resided. Document no. 38 is a request for witness testimony from the inhabitants of Harand and the district of Rūydashtīn, precisely where the *waqf* lands were located. It includes testimony from peasants of Saryān, the village headman (*kadkhudā*) of Saryān, a tax collector and many others who had direct personal connections with Āqā Mīrzā Hāshim Harandī:

> [Witness 1]: "Yes, this lowest of seminary students (*aqall al-ṭalaba*), a little while before the death of Mīrzā Hāshim Khān [Mīrzā Hāshim Harandī], when I had gone to the house of Ḥujjat al-Islām Āqā-yi Āqā Mīr Muḥammad Taqī Mudarris, may God exalt his shadow, I saw the late Mīrzā Hāshim Khān taking refuge there (*mutaḥassin ast*). I spoke to him alone several times. He complained a lot about al-Ḥājj ʿAbd al-Maḥmūd [Qannādī] and Āqā Mīrzā Mahdī Bunakdār, saying that these two fellows were in control of these lands [Jāyshī and Saryān] as usurpers, and that their possession (*yad*) was through usurpation (*ghaṣb*), and [that] some people were supporting them [*baʿḍī āqāyān taqwiyat-i ānhā-rā mīkunand*].
>
> I was in [Mīr Muḥammad Taqī Mudarris's] house until night and [at one point] I was alone with him [Mīrzā Hāshim Khān] and there was no one else besides him and me. He showed [me] some written documents (*niwishtijāt*) including a reliable *waqf-nāma* and other deeds and *ḥukms* etc. I studied the *ḥukms*, one of which was in the handwriting of Ḥujjat al-Islām Ḥājjī Sayyid Asadullāh, may God exalt his rank, and had been signed by Ḥujjat al-Islām Shaykh Muḥammad Bāqir. All of these *ḥukms* indicated that the said lands were *waqf*.
>
> I said to him: 'Why don't you show this *waqf-nāma* and *ḥukms*?'
>
> He replied: 'I have shown them. No one listens and reads [them].'
>
> I said: 'Why did you act deceitfully with regard to the *waqf* and make a conditional sale contract?'
>
> He said: 'I had no choice [. . .] they [Qannādī and Bunakdār] did not give me the money; they falsified accounts (*ḥisābsāzī kardand*) [to the effect that they had given me the money] and ruined me.'
>
> I said: 'By the way, were you the *mutawallī*?'
>
> He said: 'No, I was the executor of Mīrzā ʿAlī Muḥammad, I was in charge and used to administer the *waqf* on behalf of his child, and these lands are still *waqf*.'
>
> I said: 'Haven't you brought this matter up before Mīr Muḥammad Taqī Mudarris?'

He said: 'I have.'

This is all that I know, the wretched Ḥājjī Mullā ʿAlī," place of seal.[42]

It is no accident that the emphasis in all these witness testimonies is on the fact that Jayshī and Saryān were *waqf* lands, because this was the strongest argument for confiscating the lands from the defendants, who held possession of the lands as private property (*milk*), and handing them over to the actual *mutawallīs*, the claimants.

3.2.7 The Certification of the Authenticity of the *Waqf* Deed

The collection of witness testimonies in *istishhād-nāmas* by the claimants was only one part of the process of gathering written evidence. In Shaʿbān 1330/ July 1912, the claimants decided to judicially certify the authenticity of the original *waqf* deed of Mīrzā Aḥmad Kafrānī. This move suggests that even though the case hinged on the oral testimonies, nevertheless some attention was paid to the written *waqf* deed document. A legal document similar in form to the *istishhād-nāma* was prepared requesting members of the Iṣfahānī *ʿulamāʾ* to confirm that the original *waqf-nāma* showed no signs of having been tempered with (*āthār-i ilḥāq wa qalam-khurdagī wa ḥakk namūdan dar aṣl-i waqf-nāma*).[43] Not surprisingly, the central focus of the investigation of the materiality of the *waqf* deed was its Arabic judicial attestations (*sijills*). Among the scholars and *mujtahids* that certify the authenticity of the *waqf* deed is the very *mujtahid*, Mullā Muḥammad Ḥusayn Fishārakī, to whom the case is later submitted for a legal ruling. After examining its *sijills*, Fishārakī writes the following statement concerning the authenticity of the *waqf* deed:

[1] Āqā-yi Sharīʿatmadār Ḥujjat al-Islām Ākhund Mullā Muḥammad Ḥusayn Fishārakī, may God extend his exalted shadow: "In the name of God the Benficient the Merciful. The original *waqf-nāma* was studied in the presence of a group of pious *ʿulamāʾ*, some of whom have written in detail that in no way has there been any change, substitution, or corruption (*taghyīr, tabdīl, taḥrīf*) affecting [the *waqf-nāma*'s] credibility (*iʿtibār*). It is accurate and exact in its designation of 6 *dāng* of Jayshī, 5 *dāng* of Saryān, and 9 *ḥabba* of Isḥāqābād, and in allocating expenditure and appointing the *mutawallī*. There are no defects (*khilall*) in its judicial attestations (*sijillāt*). In particular, the *sijill* of *shaykh al-ʿulamāʾ* . . . Shaykh Bahāʾī [Bahāʾ al-Dīn al-ʿĀmilī], may his grave be fragrant, bears witness to the legal (*sharʿ*) validity of the aforementioned (deed) and to the concordance of its stipulations with the conditions of the *sharīʿa*." Place of seal.[44]

42 Document no. 13.
43 Document no. 5.
44 Document no. 5.

3.2.8 The Legal Ruling of Mullā Muḥammad Ḥusayn Fishārakī

Not long after Fishārakī was asked to confirm the authenticity of the *waqf* deed of Mīrzā Aḥmad Kafrānī, in Shawwāl 1330/September 1912, a formal question was drafted by Majd al-Sādāt, the authorized proxy of the claimants. In his question, Majd al-Sādāt outlined the litigation thus far and asked for Fishārakī's legal ruling on the case based on the evidence the claimants had gathered in support of their claim.[45] In his ruling, Fishārakī first establishes the *waqf* status of the two disputed villages based on: (1) the original authentic *waqf* deed of Mīrzā Aḥmad Kafrānī which had among its *sijill*s the *sijill* of the *shaykh al-islām* of Isfahan, Bahāʾ al-Dīn al-ʿĀmilī (1547–1621); (2) contracts showing transactions according to the stipulations of the *waqf* and (3) the large number of witness testimonies. These witness testimonies were of two types. The first consisted of testimonies of individuals who had heard the descendants of Mīrzā Aḥmad Kafrānī or Āqā Mīrzā Hāshim Harandī acknowledge that the lands were *waqf* or had witnessed transactions in accordance with *waqf* deed. The second consisted of the large number of testimonies of individuals who reported having heard that the lands were *waqf*. Regarding the latter, Fishārakī notes that the *waqf* status of the lands was established not only through the direct witness testimony of two just male witnesses in this case, but also through common report (*samāʿ/shiyāʿ/iṣtifāḍa*), which Imāmī Shīʿī jurists agreed could also establish a claim of *waqf*.[46] Fishārakī also confirms the reconstruction of possession of the lands by Majd al-Sādāt and the illegal transfer of the lands via a conditional sale to the defendants. In the final part, Fishārakī makes it clear that he is issuing a binding judicial decision and not a legal opinion on the case by ending the text with the Arabic past-tense clause: I made it binding (*wa-laqad alzamatu bi-dhālika*). The binding force of his judgement was also ratified later by eight other scholars. An administrative decree (*raqam*) dated 8 Rajab 1330/23 June 1912 from the Ministry of Foreign Affairs prohibiting the sale of 6 *dāng* of Jayshī to a certain Faḍlullāh Khān as it was *waqf* land suggests that the claimants did succeed in revivving Mīrzā Aḥmad Kafrānī's *waqf* using Fishārakī's ruling. The ruling did not, however, prevent subsequent attempts to possess the lands illegally.[47]

---

45 Document no. 6. For a translation of this document, see Bhalloo 2023b.
46 On the proofs of *waqf*, see for example Khūmaynī 1390/1970, II, 85.
47 Document no. 45.

Conclusion

As in the two previous case studies examined, the dispute over Mīrzā Aḥmad Kafrānī's *waqf* highlights the significant role that scholars recognised as *mujtahid*s had come to play as *sharīʿa* practitioners in the Qajar period. They were responsible for issuing legal opinions, judicially certifying legal claims, and evaluating evidence such as oral witness testimonies and the original *waqf* deed, according to *sharīʿa* norms. In this case, the main legal ruling of Fishārakī was issued in the question-and-answer format, while the earlier rulings of Sayyid Asadullāh Shaftī were issued in the "deed" style. Neither ruling, however, gives us any indication of the counter-evidence of the defendants in the dispute. This makes it difficult to reconstruct the litigation of the defendants. The focus of our reconstruction is therefore almost exclusively based on the perspective of the paperwork of the claimants. What emerges from these documents is the crucial role played by oral witness testimony in proving the *waqf* status of Jayshī and Saryān. Though the actual *waqf* deed of Mīrzā Aḥmad Kafrānī and earlier legal rulings are referred to as evidence, it is ultimately the sheer number of witness testimonies collected by the claimants in several *istishhād-nāma*s which proves their claim that the disputed lands were *waqf*. In theoretical terms, the fact that so many people testified that Jayshī and Saryān were *waqf* was precisely what gave the claim its authoritativeness. This is because the *waqf* claim was seen as *al-mashhūr al-mutawātir*, that is, generally accepted by the community and transmitted in uninterrupted multiple lines of transmission.[48] This meant that even when it was impossible to obtain the testimony of the original witnesses who had witnessed the founding of a *waqf*, let us say in the Safavid period, the *waqf* could still, without necessary reference to the original *waqf* deed or any other legal documentation for that matter, still be revived in later periods, based uniquely on the transmitted "living" memory of its *waqf* status among a sufficiently large group of people. This type of revival of former *waqf* property and land through witness testimonies collected in *istishhād-nāma*s continues in Iran today.

48 Johansen 1997, 339–341.

Conclusion: Assessing Judicial Decentralisation

The six chapters of this book have sought to investigate the practice of Islamic law in Iran in the early modern period after the conversion of Iran to Imāmī or Twelver Shīʿīsm under the Safavids. They have brought together two inter-related strands of research concerning *sharīʿa* courts in early modern Iran. The first strand was concerned with identifying who the practitioners of Islamic law in Iran were, how the written artefacts of Islamic law were recorded, validated, annulled, and archived, and how the practitioners intervened in dispute resolution. The second strand focused on detecting shifts in the class of practitioners and the procedures surrounding the practice of Islamic law in Iran caused by the revival of the Uṣūlī school of Imāmī Shīʿī jurispudence in the eighteenth century which reinforced the judicial authority of jurists.

By focusing on a selection of narrative and documentary sources from the Safavid period, I demonstrated in chapter one the existence of centrally appointed Safavid *sharīʿa* courts presided over by the *qāḍī*, the *shaykh al-islām*, and the *ṣadr*. These state-appointed judicial actors validated legal documents in this period by the addition of Arabic judicial attestations termed *sijill*s in Safavid model legal formularies (*shurūṭ*). The evidence of *sijill*s on Safavid legal documents also points to the overlapping roles of the *ṣadr*, the *shaykh al-islām*, and the *qāḍī* as the main *sharīʿa* practitioners of this period. Besides writing *sijill*s, these officials clearly maintained *sharīʿa* court archives. This type of archive is called *jarīdat al-maḥkama* in the registration notes and registration seals that appear on Safavid legal deeds. Based on later evidence from the Qajar era *shaykh al-islām* Tammāmī *sharīʿa* court court, it is likely that the *jarīda* archive used small pieces of paper known as *fard* to register summaries of deeds. The registration notes and seals on Safavid legal deeds also mention the names of specific *sharīʿa* courts presided over by various judicial actors in towns such as Qazvin (*maḥkama-yi injuwiyya*) and Yazd (*maḥkama-yi imāmiyya*). This naming practice known as *taʿrīf-i maḥkama* is also confirmed by Safavid legal formularies.

Based on the study of *sijill*s in legal documents from the Afghan, Afshar, and Zand period of transition, I demonstrated that while the *qāḍī* and *shaykh al-islām* continued to play a significant role in validating legal documents before the rise of the Qajars, the *ṣadr* was replaced by the *mullā-bāshī*. At the same time, we see legal documents validated by the *sijill*s of independent scholars who had no clear state judicial appointment. This practice is already confirmed by the French traveller Chardin in the seventeenth century.

In chapters two and three, I compared the scribal and archival practice of two *sharīʿa* courts in nineteenth-century Iran under Qajar rule. The Tammāmī clerical

https://doi.org/10.1515/9783111239736-008

lineage presiding over the first *sharīʿa* court derived its judicial authority mainly from state appointment to the post of *shaykh al-islām*. In contrast, the second *sharīʿa* court was presided over by a scholar whose judicial authority derived from his percieved ability to carry out *ijtihād* as a *mujtahid*. The emergence of this new type of *sharīʿa* court presided over by *mujtahids*, I suggest, marks a significant shift from earlier *sharīʿa* courts associated with scholars appointed to official judicial posts. The fact that a scholar could open a *sharīʿa* court in his house and issue legal rulings, as well as authenticate, annul, and archive legal documents, simply on the basis of his perceived legal knowledge, suggests a close convergence in this period with the Imāmī Shīʿī Uṣūlī doctrinal ideal. According to Uṣūlī doctrine, valid judicial activity during the occultation (*ghayba*) of the Twelfth Shīʿī Imām was the prerogative of Imāmī scholars able to carry out *ijtihād*.

It is, however, in the domain of dispute resolution according to the *sharīʿa* that this Imāmī Shīʿī Uṣūlī theoretical position had its most noticeable effects. The three *waqf* dispute case studies presented in chapters three, four, and five demonstrate the central role *mujtahids* had come to play in Iran by acting as both *muftīs* and *qāḍīs* in such disputes. A decentralised judicial system had emerged in the nineteenth century which allowed *mujtahids* to intervene at various stages in legal disputes. This judicial decentralisation, however, was not without its problems. It meant that the *mujtahid*'s non-binding legal opinion could potentially anticipate his binding judicial certification of a claim in a case, thus increasing the probative force of non-binding opinions. As we saw in chapter four, Shaftī's opinion on the case preceded his own judicial certification of the claim. It is thus no accident that most of the dispute was focused on conflicting legal opinions. To make matters more complicated, the term *fatwā* was increasingly replaced by the generic *ḥukm-i sharʿ*, or *ḥukm* in short, to refer to the *mujtahid*'s ruling in a case. In other words, only knowledge of the circumstances of issuance (*kayfiyyat-i ṣudūr*) and textual clues in the way the ruling was recorded could help distinguish whether the *mujtahid* had acted as a *muftī* or a *qāḍī* when he wrote the ruling.

It was precisely this problem that emerged in the next dispute, examined in chapter five, between the Dirāzgīsū sayyids and the Qajar khāns of Astarābād. The micro-historical reconstruction of litigation in the case, based on the archive of the Dīrāzgīsu, sheds light on the extent to which the Uṣūlī doctrinal model of the judicial authority of the jurist (*mujtahid-i nāfidh al-ḥukm*) had come to affect day to day *sharīʿa* court practice in Iran. Powerful defendants who were part of the political elite, such as ʿAbbās Khān Qājār, were able to circumvent the enforcement of legal rulings by claiming that they did not recognise the scholars that issued them to be *mujtahids*. This in turn forced the claimants in the dispute to repeatedly certify the *ijtihād* and binding force of the legal rulings of the scholars they had approached to judicially certify their claim. Legal rulings issued by scholars based on the evidence of one side were technically known as *ḥukm bar ghā'ib* (ruling against an absent side). They could not bring about closure of the dispute based on the legal maxim *al-ghā'ib ʿalā ḥujjatihi idhā aḥḍara* (the absent party has the right to present its evidence when it appears in court). This maxim was sometimes recorded in the text of the ruling itself.[1] Only judicial certifications of claims issued as the outcome of arbitration in which the jurist had reviewed the evidence of both sides could bring about closure. In the absence of centralised recording procedures, however, it was not always clear whether the text of a given ruling had been issued to one party in the absence of one side or was the outcome of arbitration. Meticulous *mujtahid*s like Sangalajī clearly noted when the ruling was issued to one side.[2] This was significant when a dispute dragged on for several generations, something which happened in the Astarābād land dispute.

The lack of clearly defined territorial jurisdiction for judges and centralised registration procedures relating to legal rulings also meant that litigants were often able to obtain a new ruling from a *mujtahid* living in a different town, or even in the shrine cities of Iraq, on a case which had already been the subject of a prior ruling by a local cleric in their hometown. They could, therefore, almost always try to initiate a new round of litigation (*tajdīd-i murāfaʿa*) and attempt to confiscate the disputed object. This was what happened when Sayyid Faḍlullāh attempted to establish his claim over the villages of Chūplānī and Mīr-Maḥalla by seeking a ruling against ʿAbbās Khān outside Astarābād from Isfahan. The coercive power of the resolution process remained dependent on the one hand, on the publicity generated through the documentation of a claim. This involved obtaining paperwork containing witness testimonies, legal rulings, and administrative decrees. On the other hand, it relied heavily on the personal charisma and influence of the individual *ʿulamā'* and political authorities to whom the litigants sought redress. Unlike in the Astarābād case, the less influential defendants in the dispute over Mīrzā Aḥmad Kafrānī's endowment, examined in chapter six, were unable to circumvent Fishārakī's ruling. Moreover, enforcement was swiftest if there was a conjunction of interests of the clerical and political elite, as the case of Lutf ʿAlī Khān Turshīzī's *waqf* demonstrates.

What emerges from these case studies is that legal rulings issued by Imāmī scholars, or deeds bearing their attestations (*sijills*) and seals, were routinely admitted as evidence in Iran by the political authorities who used them as the basis of their own decrees and orders of enforcement. The practical exigencies of the state thus contributed to the creation of an archival consciousness and the maintenance

1 See for example S1: 611, a register copy of a *ḥukm-i sharʿ* issued by Sangalajī on 26 Shawwāl 1285/9 February 1869 with the remark *al-ghā'ib ʿalā ḥujjatihi idhā aḥḍara.*

2 S1: 611. Compare the decentralised recording procedures in Iran in this period to more centralised Ottoman practice, see for example Agmon 2004.

of different kinds of administrative and decentralised private legal documentary repositories.[3] In terms of the *sharīʿa* practitioners themselves, legal rulings and deeds, whether originals, certified copies, or archival re-issues, were only admitted as evidence in *waqf* lawsuits when accompanied by oral witness testimony. In chapter five, we saw how the issuance of the legal ruling of Ḥājjī Mullā Riḍā Astarābādī was certified through oral witness testimonies collected in an *istishhād-nāma*. Similarly, in chapters five and six, though the original Safavid *waqf* deeds of Mīr Rūḥullāh and Mīrzā Aḥmad Kafrānī had survived, the *waqf* deeds alone were not sufficient in establishing the *waqf* claim. The claimants in both cases had to resort to oral witness testimonies collected in *istishhād-nāma* documents. Correct formulae, *sijill*s, seals, and the witness clauses in *waqf* deeds gave credence to the written artefacts of the *sharīʿa*. They ensured such documents were legally valid and ready for for use vis-à-vis the administrative authorities thus guaranteeing in practice the rights of individuals. It is not surprising therefore that such documents were copied and preserved in the *fard* archive of the *shaykh al-islām* Tammāmī court or in the registers kept by Sangalajī. If, however, a lawsuit was brought to a *sharīʿa* court, written evidence such as a judicially certified *waqf* deed alone was still not able to triumph oral testimony in terms of probative force.[4]

Nevertheless, legal deeds such as sale and rental contracts were taken into consideration as evidence of possession (*taṣarruf*) in both the dispute over Mīr Rūhullāh and Mīrzā Aḥmad Kafrānī's endowment. Since we do not have access to the archive of the defendant, ʿAbbās Khān, in the former dispute, it is not clear whether the deeds of possession of the Qajar khans formed the basis of legal rulings certifying their claim without any further oral witness testimony required. Similarly, we do not know on what basis Āqā Muḥammad Mahdī certified the Dīrāzgīsu *waqf* claim relating to lands in Astarābād in Isfahan. It is possible that Sayyid Faḍlullāh Astarābādī sent the *istishhād-nāma* of Mīr Mūsā and Mīr Taqī, to him to prove the *waqf* claim. The portable *istishhād-nāma* with its recorded oral testimonies thus became a crucial written instrument in certifying legal claims in a decentralised judicial context.

To conclude, the case studies presented in this book are by no means intended as an exhaustive account of Islamic legal practice in early modern Iran. More research is required based on a different set of sources before we can draw definitive conclusions on the impact of the Imāmī Shīʿī Uṣūlī ideal on the class of

---

3 For an Ottoman perspective see Burak 2019.

4 On the long standing debate on the probative status of written documents in Islamic legal practice in light of the emphasis on oral witness testimony as evidence in Islamic legal theory, see Tyan 1959, Wakin 1972, and the recent studies and relavant literature cited in Müller 2010, Oberauer 2021 and Rustow 2021. For an anthropological approach to this question see Messick 2002.

sharīʿa practictioners in Iran and on the procedures surrounding the written artefacts of the *sharīʿa* and the probative force of such instruments beyond the example of *waqf*. What is certain is that the conversion of Iran to Imāmī Shīʿism under the Safavids opened the door to a new dialectic between Imāmī judicial theory and practice. The subsequent revival of the Uṣūlī school of Imāmī Shīʿī jurisprudence in eighteenth-century Iraq paved the way for Imāmī Shīʿī jurists or *mujtahids* to exercise, by the end of the nineteenth century, a monopoly over valid *sharīʿa* court practice in Iran without the requirement of formal state appointment. This convergence of Uṣūlī doctrine and practice in the judicial sphere in turn would help to lay the ideological and practical foundations for Ayatollah Khumaynī's extension of the Imāmī Shīʿī jurist's role over political affairs (*wilāyat al-faqīh*) during the Iranian revolution.

Appendix

Translation of Selected Documents from Chapter 4

Document no. 1 – Part 1

The question (*suʾāl*) to Mullā Aḥmad Narāqī (d.1245/1829) as recorded by his student Muḥammad b. Muḥammad Yūsuf al-Mīmaʾī al-Jūshqānī
Text: Ustādī 1380 sh./2001, 222–225.
Translation

a. [The question to Narāqī]:

The deceased Luṭf ʿAlī Khān Turshīzī owned several estates (*amlāk*) and fields (*mazāriʿ*) in the province of Ardistān. During his lifetime he rented out the said estates and fields for a period of seven years. Before the expiry of the rental contract for the said lands, he constituted them as a *waqf* for a madrasa for which he himself laid the foundation stone in the town of sayyids: Zavārih. He appointed himself administrator while he was alive and after him Mawlāna ʿAbd al-ʿAzīm Bīdgulī, an inhabitant of Zavārih and after him, Bīdgulī's children. After arranging these matters according to the sacred law, the founder died while the rental contract made when the [lands] were private property had not yet come to an end. As a result, a dispute arose between the descendants of the founder and the second administrator [Mullā ʿAbd al-ʿAzīm Bīdgulī] regarding the validity and irrevocability of the said *waqf* and its annulment and return to the heirs [of the founder]. The rulings and opinions (*aḥkām wa fatāwī*) issued by the jurists of the age on this matter were different and contradictory and caused an increase in the strife and conflict. The *ʿulamāʾ* (*arbāb-i ḥall wa ʿaqd*) of the region have decided to put the circumstances of the case before you, also including copies of some of the rulings that have been issued for you to examine. Whatever is your honourable opinion (*raʾy-i sharīf*) on this case is, it will be acted upon (*bi- ān ʿamal namūda*) to settle the dispute.

b. [Copy of the ruling of Mīrzā-yi Qummī (d.1231/1816)]:

The first *muftī* was the deceased Mīrzā Abū al-Qāsim Qummī, may God be pleased with him. These are his exact words (*wa hādha lafẓuhu*):

The *waqf* of the substance (*ʿayn*) of a property that has been leased is invalid and revocable unless it occurs in this way: the beneficiaries or the administrator take

https://doi.org/10.1515/9783111239736-009

possession (*qabḍ*) with the permission of the lessee, however, in the hypothetical situation we are in (*dar mā naḥnu fīhi*), the owner of the land [when he made it *waqf*] had no right to transfer its possession (*iqbāḍ*) to an administrator or a beneficiary [since the lands were leased out]. Because an immediate transfer of possession is not a requirement, if after the period of expiry of the lease, a transfer to the beneficiaries or administrator had occurred, the *waqf* would have still been valid. However, it is supposed (*mafrūḍ*) [in the hypothetical circumstances described] that the founder of the endowment died before a transfer of possession occurred, for this reason, the basis (*aṣl*) of the *waqf* was void [and the *waqf* therefore is invalid]. End (*intahā*).

c. [Copy of the ruling of Shaykh Muḥammad Ḥusayn Ḥāʾirī Iṣfahānī Ṣāḥib Fuṣūl (d. 1254/1838–39)]:

The second *muftī* is the deceased [sic] Mīr Muḥammad Ḥusayn Iṣfahānī. These are his exact words:

In the hypothetical situation described (*dar ṣūrat-i mafrūḍa*), the basis (*aṣl*) of the *waqf* is valid. A rental contract does not prevent it [the lands] being *waqf* and the *waqf* does not become void [as a result]. One cannot remove lands constituted as *waqf* from the possession of the lessee before the expiry of the rental contract. The permission (*idhn*) given by the founder to the lessee that the rental income be used for the aforementioned madrasa, the leasing out of the lands by the second administrator (*mutawallī*) after the death of the founder, the spending of the rental income on the *waqf*, and the endorsement (*imḍā*) of the descendants of the founder of its *waqf* status, in this case are equivalent to *qabḍ* occurring (*dar īn maqām ʿibārat az qabḍ ast*). The prior rental contract is not an obstacle to *qabḍ* occurring. End.

d. [Copy of the new ruling of Sayyid Muḥammad Bāqir Shaftī (d.1260/1844)]:

The third *muftī* was Sayyid Muḥammad Bāqir Rashtī [Shaftī], may God exalt him. These are his exact words:

What has been understood by this deficient mind is as follows: whenever an owner of land constitutes that land as *waqf* for a specific purpose (*milkī rā mālik-i ān waqf nāmāyad bar jihat-i makhṣūṣa*) and appoints himself administrator of the *waqf* for as long as he lives (*wa tawliyat-i ān bi jihat-i nafs-i khud qarār dahad mādāma l-ḥayāt*) the validity (*ṣiḥḥat*) or irrevocability (*luzūm*) of such a *waqf* is not contingent upon *qabḍ*, because of: (1) the general premise (*ʿumūm*) of *awfū bi l-ʿuqūd* and (2) and the specific meaning of the general premise (*khuṣūṣ-i ʿumūm*) of the authentic report (*ṣaḥīḥa*) of Muḥammad b. al-Ḥasan al-Ṣaffār *al-wuqūf ʿalā ḥasbi mā yūqifuhā ahluhā*, [based on which] the nessecity of acting upon the *waqf* occurs as soons as it [the *waqf*] is declared (*luzūm-i ʿamal bi muqtaḍā-yi waqf ast bi maḥḍ-i taḥaqquq-i ān*).

There exists no evidence that can be taken as a general premise to suggest that the validity or irrevocability of each and every *waqf* is contingent upon *qabḍ*, rather the examples that are commonly cited are mostly sayings dealing with children who have reached the age of maturity (*kibār-i awlād*). For instance: when a founder gives property to be constituted as *waqf* to the possession of the beneficiaries, the *waqf* becomes irrevocable, and he has no right to take it back or that he can take it back, or, if he has not yet transferred possession and he dies, the property belongs to his heirs as inheritance.

In brief, all of these [sayings] do not describe a situation where the property to be constituted as *waqf* is not in the possession of the administrator, therefore what is necessary is to distinguish between these general premises from the texts, however, this is not the subject of the debate here, what is in dispute here is whether a waqf may be considered irrevocable upon the realization of its contract. We are going to submit the following hypothetical condition [to constitute a valid *waqf*] as a general premise: It suffices as a condition [to constitute a valid waqf], that the property to be constituted as *waqf* is in the possession of the *mutawallī* after the constitution of the *waqf*, and this was realized [in the case at hand]. Given that what is intended, that the founder himself is the *mutawallī*, and the fact that the lands are leased out to someone else is not incompatible with the owner being in possession, therefore it is permissible for him to enjoy various kinds of rights of possession in this condition, for example giving a gift to someone else, sale, settlement contract etc.

This much is sufficient evidence in issuing a ruling on irrevocability, as is obtained from (3) the authentic report (*ṣaḥīḥ*) in *al-Kāfī* and *al-Tahdhīb* from Muḥammad b. Muslim from Abū Jaʿfar (peace be upon him). He said regarding a man who gives charity to a child and is not aware the child belongs to him, it is valid, because the father is the one who has authority over him, the meaning of *ṣadaqa* here, based on the understanding of the *ʿulamāʾ* is *waqf*, and the meaning of *idrāk*, being aware or not aware here, is the maturity or lack thereof of the child, and the combined meaning therefore is as follows:

If we assume hypothetically, the beneficiary, that is the child was a minor, then the *waqf* would be irrevocable, and its reason based on the saying of Abū Jaʿfar peace be upon him is that the father is the one who has authority over him, and what is useful from this, is that the ruling on the irrevocability of the *waqf* here, is from the fact of the property to be constituted as *waqf* being in the possession of the one who has authority over the beneficiary, and this is what occurred in the hypothetical case we are dealing with at present. In brief, the said *waqf*, based on the belief of this sinner, is valid and irrevocable and after the death of the founder, it is binding upon the new administrator to act upon the stipulations of the *waqf* contract.

e. [Jūshqānī's additional question on the case to Narāqī]:

I [the writer, Jūshqānī,] have a difficulty with a case like this and all other cases where conflicting opinions (*fatāwī*) are issued by jurists, the problem is as follows:

Based on the irrefutable proposition (*qaḍiyya-yi musallama*) applicable to all those who imitate a jurist (*muqallidīn*), 'whatever the *muftī* rules for me is the verdict of God (*ḥukmullāh*)': the heirs of the founder of the *waqf* were followers (*muqallids*) of the first *muftī* [Mīrzā-yi Qummī] and [therefore] their possession of the lands and its income as private property was according to the verdict of God. Similarly, the support of their supporters was [as a result] based on devoutness and piety (*bar birr wa taqwā*). The administrator and the students of the madrasa are followers of the third *muftī* [Shaftī] [and based] on his ruling on the mentioned case their possession is also according to the verdict of God and likewise [the support of] the administrator's supporters. Thus, one private object, according to the verdict of God is the property of the heirs and preventing the possession of others in it and repelling the administrator and his supporters, who were obstructing the heirs [from gaining possession], becomes obligatory for the heirs and [on the other hand] the same [requirement] applies for the side of the administrator. Consequently, all the strife, sedition, legal action, defense, and fighting was caused by the verdict of God the Exalted – this surely is the most abhorrent thing imaginable. It is requested that after issuing the requested legal ruling (*ḥukm-i sharʿī*) [on the case], please kindly settle my doubt. Your order will be obeyed.

Document no. 1 – Part 2

The reply (*jawāb*) by Mullā Aḥmad Narāqī (d.1245/1829) to the question of his student Muḥammad b. Muḥammad Yūsuf al-Mīmaʾī al-Jūshqānī

f. [The reply – Narāqī's rebuttal].

g. [Narāqī's reply to Jūshqānī's additional question]:

As for the doubt the writer [Jushqānī] has raised, well its reply is clear, and its explanation as follows:

The rulings of God the Exalted are of two kinds: actual (*wāqiʿī*) and apparent (*ẓāhirī*). What is meant here by actual (*wāqiʿī*) are those rulings in relation to which the Divine Lawgiver decreed and which were deposited in those who it was intended for (*makhzūn dar nazd-i ahlash*). This type of ruling never changes, and in practice, it is always the same and there is no multiplicity in it, but because there is no access to these rulings by way of knowledge, apparent rulings (*aḥkām-*

i ẓāhirīyya) stand in their place. Apparent rulings are those rulings which are the object of the opinions and reflection of the representatives of the masses during the period of the closure of the gate of knowledge (*dar zamān-i sadd-i bāb al-ʿilm*), and these [rulings] depending on the person involved can be different. That is to say: every *mujtahid* (jurist) is bound (*mukallaf*) to follow his opinion and every *muqallid* (follower) is bound to follow the opinion of his own *mujtahid*, and every pair of litigants [claimant and defendant] is bound to follow the ruling of the judge (*ḥākim*) between them.

Therefore, with regard to the *mujtahid* there is absolutely no problem, since he cannot follow the opinion of anyone other than himself and likewise with regard to the *muqallid*, in personal problems which relate to him only and where there is no dispute involved, since he [the *muqallid*] is free, in a situation where there are two equal *mujtahids*, to choose whichever *mujtahid* he wants to imitate in practice. Before he makes this choice, the apparent *ḥukm* has not yet become fixed for him, just like a *mujtahid* whose opinion on an issue has not yet been decided [lit: gone completely towards one side]. After he [the *muqallid*] chooses a *mujtahid*, the apparent ruling for him (*ḥukm-i ẓāhiri-i ū*) will be the opinion (*fatwā*) of that *mujtahid* and there is absolutely no disputing or refuting [it]. If there are differences in the level of knowledge between two *mujtahids*, and we accept that giving precedence to the more knowledgeable *mujtahid* is obligatory, then the *muqallid* must choose that *mujtahid* [the more knowledge one], and if not he will be in the same situation as when choosing between two equal *mujtahids*. However, with regard to those problems (*masāʾil*) which come up between two people or more and between them there is an argument (*takhāṣum*) and a dispute (*tanāzuʿ*), mere imitation (*taqlīd*) and opinion (*fatwā*) does not suffice. Instead, it requires legal proceedings (*tarāfuʿ*) before a *mujtahid* and the issuance of his ruling (*ḥukm*). After the issuance of the ruling, acting in accordance with it will be the apparent ruling of God for them.

Therefore, if two litigants mutually agree to lodge a matter before a judge (*raf-i maṭlab rā bi-khidmat-i ḥākimī*) and appear before him or present the matter via an intermediary and he issues a ruling, disobeying the ruling is not permitted, and it [the ruling he issues] will be the apparent ruling for them. If each of them wants to choose a judge, the choice of the claimant has precedence if the two judges are equal in terms of knowledge and action, in fact, even if they are not equal [in terms of knowledge of action] this is preferred (*ʿalā l-aqwā*). And what is intended here by claimant (*muddaʿī*) is someone who is at the origin of the dispute (*maṣdar-i nizāʿ*), such that if he did not take the initiative to make a claim (*mubādarat bi-iddiʿā*), no one would have a dispute with him.

There are some situations where the relation [of both the litigants] to the case is the same, and neither of them can be called a claimant and the other a defendant. For example if Zayd makes a bequest for a tribe or constitutes property as *waqf* for a tribe, and he himself by virtue of being the administrator takes possession of the endowed property (*qabḍ kunad*) and in the specification of the tribe there occurs a difference between two *mujtahids*; for instance one says: 'as I understand it, this bequest is for the paternal relatives' and the other says 'it is for the maternal relatives' and neither of them have taken possession as yet and the guardian or the heirs are waiting for the issuance of a ruling. In such a situation, it is evident that either one can take the lead in going before a judge to initiate legal proceedings and when he [the judge] rules, his ruling will be binding (*lāzim al-ittibāʿ*), it will not be merely [a ruling] issued as a reply to the request for an opinion (*istiftāʾ*), but rather a ruling on the specific details of a case (*ḥukm dar khuṣūṣ-i wāqiʿa*). God is the Knower [of the true nature of affairs].

Document no. 2

The request for an opinion (*istftāʾ*) addressed to Sayyid Muḥammad Bāqir Shaftī (d.1260/1844) as recorded in the theoretical defense of his ruling: *Risāla fī ʿadam luzūm al-qabḍ idhā jaʿala al-wāqif al-tawliya li-nafsihi*

Text: Shaftī 1379 sh./2001, 65–65.
Translation

A person (*shakhṣī*) with pious intentions gave instructions for a madrasa to be built in a certain place (*dar baʿḍ-i bilād*) so that the religious students (*ṭalaba*) living there could study the religious sciences. This person owned several estates (*amlāk-i chandī*) in that region which he had given out on rent. He gave the following instructions: that all his lands were to be constituted as a *waqf* and that the income derived [from the said lands] was to be spent on building the madrasa and for its repairs and for furnishing its student rooms (*ḥujarāt*) and [for buying] the oil for the lamps in these rooms and for all other requirements.

He laid the foundation stone of the madrasa (*qarār-i binā-yi madrasa rā guzāsht*) and instructed the lessee [of his lands] to spend the rental income due on the expenses of the said madrasa. The lessee did this as follows: based on the instructions of the founder he gave on a regular basis a portion of the rental income to the builder and construction workers engaged in building the madrasa; in addition the lessee also spent the rental income on other costs incurred while building the madrasa, and in this manner [the founder] made the *waqf* of those lands which had been designated for this specific purpose [the building of a madrasa and its expenses] operational (*wa dar ān ḥāl ṣīgha-yi waqf-i ān amlāk rā bi īn jihat-i makhṣūṣa jārī namūd*).

Before the expiry of the rental contract with the lessee the founder appointed himself in the *waqf* deed the administrator [of the endowment] for as long as he lived (*wa dar ḍimn-i ʿaqd-i waqf tawliyat-i waqf rā mā dāma ḥayātuhu bi-jihat-i nafs-i khud qarār dād*) and after him someone else and so on and so forth. After a short period of time had passed, when the madrasa had still not been properly finnished, and before the rental contract had come to an end, the founder died. Are the said lands *waqf* and acting according to the *waqf* deed binding or are the lands private property that belong to the [founder's] heirs (*māl-i wāritha*), given that a transfer of possession of the endowed property [to the administrator or the beneficiaries] did not occur? (*naẓar bi ʿadam-i taḥaqquq- i iqbāḍ wa qabḍ*)?

Document no. 3

Copy of the legal ruling of Sayyid Muḥammad Bāqir Shaftī (d.1260/1844) dated 19 Rajab 1240/9 March 1825 transcribed on the *waqf* deed of Luṭf ʿAlī Khān Turshīzī

Text: Mihrābādī, III, 1336 sh./1957, 638–640
Translation

A copy of the details written by Ḥujjat al-Islām Rashtī [Sayyid Muḥammad Bāqir Shaftī:

He is the Everlasting over the souls of his servants.

The issuance of the said properties and lands from the deceased founder has been established and acting in accordance with the conditions of the deed [of endowment] compulsory and the heirs of the deceased founder have no share, interest or control over the said properties. Thus, if any of the heirs of the deceased makes a claim in this case, their claim is invalid and against the sacred law and the victorious religion [Islam] and avoiding and abstaining [from making such a claim] obligatory. Thereafter, all believing brothers afraid of the punishment from the reckoning [of their deeds], religious scholars, descendants of the Prophet, village chiefs, peasants and all the faithful inhabitants of Ardistān and Zavārih and other places are informed that in accordance with the illuminated law it is binding upon all of you to obey the administrator (*mutawallī*) in this matter so that the revenues and income of the said properties be used for the purposes stipulated in the deed of the founder. And in accordance with the irrevocable ruling of God the Exalted, it is binding upon those who hold possession [of the said lands] in a manner other than *waqf* to vacate and deliver their possession to the administrator, and [thus] avoid and abstain from certain retribution [of God], and send the revenues in arrears for the duration of their possession to the administrator.

Written by the servant of the *sharīʿa* on 19 Rajab 1240/9 March 1825.

Place of the seal of Ḥujjat al-Islām Rashtī [Sayyid Muḥammad Bāqir Shaftī].

A Checklist of Documents from Chapter 5

Relating to the Dirāzgīsū Sayyids

I. Legal Rulings, *Waqf* Deeds and Witness Statements

Document no.[1]	Date	Type of Document	Edition Sutūda and Dhabīḥī 1354 sh./1975
1	25 Muḥarram 1251/23 May 1835	"Deed" style legal ruling of Āqā Muḥammad Mahdī b. Muḥammad Ibrāhīm Kalbāsī (d.1278/1861–2).	VI, 213–214
2*	1260/1844	Certification of the authenticity of the transcript of the ruling of Āqā Muḥammad Mahdī and the ratification issued on 16 Rajab 1260/1 August 1844 by Ḥājjī Muḥammad Ibrāhīm Kalbāsī (d.1261/1844–5).	VI, 215–218
3*	Undated	Certifications by Astarābādī *ʿulamāʾ* regarding the authenticity of the text of the ruling of Ḥājjī Mullā Riḍāʾ Astarābādī, whether he was a *mujtahid-i nāfidh al-ḥukm* and his rulings recognised as binding by the governor of Astarābād, ʿAbbās Khān.	VII, 248–249
4*	20 Jamādī II 1264/24 May 1848	Question-and-answer ruling by Mullā Muḥammad Taqī (d.1272/1855) regarding whether Ḥājjī Mullā Riḍāʾ Astarābādī was a *mujtahid-i nāfidh al-ḥukm* and his ruling was binding.	VI, 219–220
5*	1267/1850–1	Ratification issued by Mullā Muḥammad Taqī (d.1272/1855) of Ḥājjī Mullā Riḍāʾ Astarābādī's ruling certifying he was a *mujtahid-i nāfidh al-ḥukm*. 20 Jamādī II 1264/24 May 1848.	VI, 179
6	Rabīʿ I 1280/August–September 1863	Question-and answer ruling by Sharīʿatmadār Ḥājjī Mullā Muḥammad Ashrafī (1215–1305/1801–1888) and his ratification of the ruling of Ḥājjī Mullā Riḍāʾ Astarābādī.	VI, 221–223

1 Documents marked with an asterisk are originals otherwise they are certified transcripts.

(continued)

Document no.	Date	Type of Document	Edition Sutūda and Dhabīḥī 1354 sh./1975
7*	26 Rabīʿ I 1280/10 September 1863	Ratification issued by Naṣrullāh al-Ḥusaynī of the ruling of Ḥājjī Mullā Riḍāʾ Astarābādī.	VI, 220–221
8*	Rabī II 1280/October 1863	Question-and-answer rulings by Astarābādī *ʿulamāʾ* regarding the nature of the ruling of Ḥājjī Mullā Riḍāʾ Astarābādī and whether further litigation in the dispute was permissible.	VI, 224–225
9*	Undated	Question-and-answer ruling by *ufawwiḍu amrī ilā allāh* regarding the nature of the ruling of Ḥājjī Mullā Riḍāʾ Astarābādī.	VII, 560–561
10*	Rabīʿ II 1280/August–September 1863	Ratification issued by Muḥammad Ṣādiq al-ʿAqīlī of the ruling of Ḥājjī Mullā Riḍāʾ Astarābādī and the ruling of Āqā Muḥammad Mahdī Kalbāsī.	VI, 226
11	Muḥarram 952/April 1545	*Waqf-nāma* of Mīr Rūḥullāh al-Ḥusaynī al-Astarābādī endowing five *dāng* of the village of Mīr-Maḥalla and six *dāng* of the village of Chūpalānī in the countryside of Astarābād and a house in the quarter of Pāy-i Sarw in the town of Astarābād with its adjoining room decorated in glazed tiles (*uṭāq-i sifāl-pūsh*) and a large and small garden as a *waqf* for his lineal male descendants.	VI, 317–322
12	Muḥarram 1052/April 1642	A second copy of the above *waqf* deed.	VI, 344–349
13	Undated	*Istishhad-nama* (witness statement) of Mīr Mūsā and Mīr Taqī	VII, 262–268
14	Undated	*Istishhād-nāma*	VI, 255–256

II. Administrative Decrees

15*	Dhū al-Qaʿda 1240/June 1825	Royal decree (*farman*) of Fatḥ ʿAlī Shāh	VI, 124
16*	Rabīʿ II 1251/ August 1835	*farmān* of Muḥammad Shāh	VI, 142–143
17*	Jamādī II 1251/September 1835	*farmān* of Muḥammad Shāh	VI, 143–144
18	Rabīʿ II 1255/June 1839	*farmān* of Muḥammad Shāh	VI, 136–137
19	25 Rajab 1256/September 1840	*farmān* of Muḥammad Shāh	VI, 164–165
20	Jamādī II 1263/May 1847	*farmān* of Muḥammad Shāh	VI, 165–166
21	Undated.	*farmān* of Muḥammad Shāh	VI, 166–168
22	Jamādī II 1264/May 1848	*farmān* of Muḥammad Shāh	VI, 171–172
23	Rajab 1276/January 1860	*farmān* of Nāṣir al-Dīn Shāḥ	VI, 183–184
24	1282/1865–1866	*tūyūl* (assignment of tax revenues) of the village of Mīr-Maḥalla granted by Nāṣir al-Dīn Shāh to Malik ʿAbbās Yūzbāshī	VI, 553–556
25*	Rabīʿ II 1255/June 1839	Provincial administrative decree by Muḥammad Nāṣir Khān Develū Qājār, governor of Astarābād.	VI, 158
26*	Ramadan 1256/October 1840	Provincial administrative decree by Muḥammad Nāṣir Khān Develū Qājār, governor of Astarābād.	VI, 162
27*	Shawwāl 1256/December 1840	Provincial administrative decree by Muḥammad Nāṣir Khān Develū Qājār, governor of Astarābād.	VI, 164
28*	Rabīʿ II 1264/March 1848	Provincial administrative decree by Sulaymān Khān Qūyūnlū Qājār, governor of Astarābād.	VI, 168
29*	Rabīʿ II 1264/March 1848	Provincial administrative decree by Sulaymān Khān Qūyūnlū Qājār, governor of Astarābād.	VI, 169–170
30	Jamādī I 1264/April 1848	Provincial decree by Sulaymān Khān Qūyūnlū Qājār, governor of Astarābād.	VI, 170–171

(continued)

31	Jamādī II 1276/December 1859	Provincial administrative decree of Nawwāb Ḥājjī Kīyūmars Mīrzā Qājār Īlkhānī (Mulk- Ārā), governor of Astarābād	VI, 181–182
32	18 Jamādī I 1288/5 August 1871	Provincial administrative decree by Sulaymān Khān Yūzbāshī.	VI, 185

III. Petitions to the Royal Court and Correspondence

33	Undated	Petition of Sayyid Faḍlullāh to the royal court with list of pensions due to the Dirāzgīsū sayyids	VI, 156–158
34	Undated	Petition of ʿAbbās Khān addressed to the royal court	VII, 584–585
35	Jamādī II 1264/May 1848	Petition of the Dirāzgīsū sayyids to the royal court and its reply	VI, 173–174
36	Dhū al-Ḥijja 1260/December 1844	Letter to Shāhrukh Khān, *ṣāḥib-ikhtiyār* of Astarābād.	VII, 446–667
37	Rabīʿ II 1264/March 1848	Letter from the royal court to Ibrāhīm Bēg Tufangdār in Astarābād	VII, 432–433
38	Undated	Letter from Astarābād to the royal court	VII, 399
39	Undated	Letter from the Mustawfī al-Mamālīk probably addressed to ʿAbbās Khān.	VII, 402–403
40	Undated	Letter from the royal court to the local government in Astarābād	VII, 413–414
41	Undated	Letter by the Dirāzgīsū sayyids to the royal court	VII, 423–424
42	Undated	Letter by Sayyid Faḍlullāh's agent, Mullā Muḥammad Ismāʿīl.	VII, 429–431
43	Undated	Letter by a supporter of the Dirāzgīsū addressed to ʿAbbās Khān stressing the divine requirement to respect the right of the sayyids.	VII, 434–439
44	Undated	Letter by a supporter of the Dirāzgīsū to the royal court stressing the divine requirement to respect the right of the sayyids.	VII, 439–442
45	Undated	Letter addressed to the provincial governor of Astarabad.	VII, 451
46	Undated	Letter addressed to Iʿtiḍād al-Dawla, governor of Astarābād.	VII, 452–453

(continued)

47	Undated	Letter A by a jurist opposed to a settlement between the Dirāzgīsū sayyids and the children of ʿAbbās Khān.	VII, 400–402
48	27 Dhū al-Ḥijja 1284/April	Letter B by a jurist in favour of a settlement between the Dirāzgīsū sayyids and the children of ʿAbbās Khān.	VI, 228–230
49	Undated	Letter C by a jurist in favour of a settlement between the Dirāzgīsū sayyids and the children of ʿAbbās Khān addressed to Āqā Sayyid Mufīd Astarābādī	VII, 425–426
50	Undated	Letter D by a jurist opposed to a settlement between the Dirāzgīsū sayyids and the children of ʿAbbās Khān	VII, 442–445
51	Undated	Letter by a jurist named Sayyid Muḥammad Bāqir [Shaftī?] addressed to ʿAbbās Khān stressing that the land dispute between him and Sayyid Faḍlullāh must be brought to arbitration before a jurist	VII, 395–396

IV. Legal Agreements and Settlements Relating to Chūplānī and Mīr-Maḥalla

52	Rabīʿ I 1257/May 1841	Legal agreement (*qarār-dād-i sharʿī*) between Malik Kāẓim and his son Āqā Ḥusayn and the *mujtahid* Sayyid Faḍlullāh	VI, 342–343
53*	Jamādī I 1263/April 1847	Legal agreement between Qulī Khān Yūzbāshī and the *mujtahid* Sayyid Faḍlullāh.	VI, 344–345
54	12 Shaʿbān 1263/26 July 1847	Binding agreement (*iltizām-nāmcha*) signed between the agent of Sayyid Faḍlullāh, Mullā Muḥammad Ismāʿīl and the agent of ʿAbbās Khān, Ḥājjī Mīrzā Khānjān.	VI, 346–348
55	Shaʿbān 1276/October 1860	*muṣālaḥa-nāma* settlement contract between the Dirāzgīsū sayyids and Āqā Mīrzā Aḥmad, *wazīr* of Astarābād.	VII, 98–99
56*	11 Jamādī I 1288/29 July 1871	*ṣūlḥ-nāma* settlement between the Dirāzgīsū sayyids and the Qajar khans dividing the village of Chūplānī.	VII, 122–123

A Checklist of Documents from Chapter 6

Relating to the Waqf of Mīrzā Aḥmad Kafrānī

I. *Waqf* Deed and Legal Rulings

Document no.[2]	Date	Type of Document	Edition Ishkawarī 1388 sh./2009, III,
1	Jamādī al-Awwal 988/June 1580	*Waqf-nāma* of Mīrzā Aḥmad Kafrānī	269–282
2	23 Dhū al-Ḥijja 1262/12 Dec 1846 and 10 Jamādī II 1263/26 May 1847	"Deed" style legal rulings of Ḥājjī Sayyid Asadullāh Shaftī about the rights of Mīrzā ʿAlī Muḥammad	404–406
3	2 Dhī al-Qaʿda 1329/25 October 1911	Legal rulings and report issued by the *ʿAdliyya* court of Isfahan	367–374
4	Dhī al-Qaʿda 1329/November 1911	Question-and-answer ruling by three *ʿulamā* with regard to the possession of Āqā Mīrzā Mahdī Bunakdār and Ḥājjī ʿAbd al-Maḥmūd Qannādī	342–343
5	Various dates: Shaʿbān 1330–Ramaḍān 1330/July–August 1912	Certification of *ʿulamāʾ* regarding the authenticity of the *waqf-nāma*	283–285
6	Autumn (*pāyīz*) 1330/1912–25 Shawwāl 1330/7 October 1912	Copy of the question of Majd al-Sādāt and the answer (legal ruling) of Mullā Muḥammad Ḥusayn Fishārakī and ratifications of other *ʿulamāʾ*	286–294
7	22 Jamādī I 1331/29 April 1913–26 Jamādī I 1331/May 3 1913	Question-and-answer ruling of Ākhund Mullā ʿAbd al-Karīm Jizī	296–297
8	19 Muḥarram 1332/18 December 1913–19 Muḥarram 1332/18 December 1913	Question by Mīrzā ʿAbd al-Ḥusayn Khān to Muhammad Ḥusayn Fishārakī and his answer	294–296

2 All documents are certified transcripts.

II. Witness Statements

9	Shawwāl 1240/May 1825	*Istishhād-nāma* of Mīrzā Muḥammad Taqī (34 witness testimonies)	407–416
10	28 Dhū al-Qaʿda/20 November 1911	Witness testimony requested from Ḥājjī Shaykh Muḥammad ʿAlī Harandī in Qum and his reply (1 witness deposition)	346–347
11	24 Rabīʿ I 1330–Ramaḍān 1330/13 March 1912–August 1912	Witness testimonies (40) collected by Āqā Mīrzā Ḥusayn and Āqā Mīrzā Aḥmad and Āqā Mīrzā ʿAlī Riḍā Sarrishtadār-i Ardistān on behalf of the heirs of Mīrzā ʿAlī Muḥammad	298–309
12	Jamādī I 1330/May 1912	Witness testimonies (42) collected by Mirzā Aḥmad and Mīrzā Ḥusayn from the *ʿulamā, sayyids*, *rīsh-sifīdan wa kad-khudāyān* (village elders and chiefs) and inhabitants of the village of Harand and Rūydashtīn	351–363
13	Dhū al-Qaʿda 1329–Muḥarram 1330/November 1911–January 1912	*Istishhād-nāma* from *ʿulamāʾ*, notables and elders (*aʿyān wa ashrāf wa rīsh-sifīdān*) of Isfahan and Rūydashtīn. (32 witness testimonies)	330–341
14	Dhū al-Ḥijja 1329–Ramaḍān 1330/December 1911–August 1912	Witness testimonies (22) of Āqā Ḥusayn and Āqā Aḥmad from the *ʿulamāʾ*, notables and inhabitants of Pāy-i Qalʿa quarter, Isfahan	321–329
15	Ramaḍan 1330–Shawwal 1330/August 1912–September 1912	Witness testimonies (28) of Mīrzā ʿAbd al-Ḥusayn Khān from the notables, merchants, peasants and *ʿulamāʾ* of Harand.	395–403

III. Contracts and Settlements Relating to Jayshī and Saryān

16	13 Rabīʿ II 1245/12 October 1829	*Muṣālaḥa-nāma* of 3 years of revenues (*manāfiʿ wa madākhil*) of 3 *dāng* Jayshī between Mīrzā ʿAlī Muḥammad and Mīrza Muḥammad Muḥsin	381–385
17	Shaʿbān 1245/Febuary 1830	Document relating to sowing of seeds in Jayshī	386
18	13 Rabīʿ II 1246/1 October 1830	*Muzāraʿa-nāma* of 3 years of 3 *dāng* Jayshī between Mīrzā Abū al-Qāsim and Āqā Muḥammad Taqī	455–457
19	Ramaḍān 1246/Febuary 1831	*Ijāra-nāma* of 10 years of 3 *dāng* of Jayshī between Mīrzā Abū al-Qāsim and ʿAlī Akbar Khān	451–454

(continued)

20	Ramaḍān 1246/Febuary 1831	*Ijāra-nāma* of 10 years of 3 *dāng* of Jayshī between Mīrzā Abū al-Qāsim and ʿAlī Akbar Khān	429–431
21	19 Shawwāl 1258/23 November 1842 and 26 Ramaḍān 1271/12 June 1855	*Bayʿ-nāma* of 2 *dāng* of water and land of the field of Saryān between Mīrzā Muḥammad Hādī and Mīrzā Abū Ṭālib to Mīrzā Muḥammad Hāshim + annexe revoking the sale	387–391
22	3 Dhū al-Ḥijja 1271/17 August 1855	*Muṣālaḥa-nāma* of 5 years 5 *dāng* of Jayshī between Mīrzā Abū Ṭālib and Mīrzā Muḥammad Hādī	417–419
23	3 Dhū al-Ḥijja 1271/17 August 1855	*Muṣālaḥa-nāma* of 3 *dāng* of Saryān between Mīrzā Abū Ṭālib and Mīrzā Muḥammad Hādī	420–421
24	3 Rabīʿ II 1272/13 December 1855	*Muṣālaḥa-nāma* between Mīrzā ʿAlī Muḥammad and Mīrzā Muḥammad Hādī before Ḥājjī Sayyid Asadullāh of 3 *dāng* of Jayshī and cancellation (*faskh*) of a previous rental contract	392–394
26	27 Rabīʿ II 1273/10 December 1856	*Muzāraʿa-nāma* of 3 *dāng* of Jayshī and 3 *dāng* of Saryān between Mīrzā Muḥammad Hāshim and Mīrzā Abū Ṭālib	432–434
27	22 Dhū al-Qaʿda 1274/4 July 1858	*Muṣālaḥa-nāma* of 5 years of 3 *dāng* of Jayshī and 3 *dāng* of Saryān between Mīrzā Abū Ṭālib and Mīrzā Faḍl ʿAlī Anṣārī	436–437
28	Shaʿbān 1276/Febuary 1860	*Muzāraʿa-nāma* of 3 *dāng* of Jayshī between Mīrzā Abū Ṭālib and Mīrzā Faḍl ʿAlī Anṣārī + cancellation of *muzāraʿa-nāma*	425–428
29	7 Rabīʿ I 1279/ 2 September 1862	*Muzāraʿa-nāma* of 3 *dāng* of Jayshī between Mīrzā Muḥammad Hāshim and Mīrzā Abū Ṭālib	438–439
30	Muḥarram 1280/June 1863	*Muzāraʿa-nāma* of 3 *dāng* of Jayshī between Mīrzā Muḥammad Hāshim and Mīrzā Abū Ṭālib	440–442
31	Muḥarram 1280/June 1863	*Muzāraʿa-nāma* of 10 years of the other 3 *dāng* of Jayshī between Mīrzā Muḥammad Hāshim and Mīrzā Abū Ṭālib	441–445
32	Rabīʿ I 1284/July 1867	*Muzāraʿa* + *muṣālaḥa-nāma* of 3 *dāng* of Jayshī and 3 *dāng* of Saryān between Mīrzā Muḥammad Hāshim and Mīrzā Abū Ṭālib	446–448
33	Jamādī I 1286/August 1869	Renewal of the *Muṣālaḥa-nāma* 3 *dāng* of Saryān between Mīrzā Abū Ṭālib and Āqā Mīrzā Hāshim	449–450

(continued)

34	Jamādī II 1286/September 1869	*Muzāraʿa-nāma* of of five years of 3 *dāng* of Saryān between Mīrzā Abū Ṭālib and Mīrza ʿAlī Muḥammad *(refers to the *wāqif's* wishes)	422–434
35	3 Rabīʿ I 1299/23 January 1882	*Ijāra-nāma* between Āqā Mīrzā Hāshim and Āqā Aḥmad and Āqā Ḥusayn of 3 *dāng* of Jayshī	310–311
36	Rabīʿ II 1302/January 1885	*Ijāra-nāma* between Āqā Mīrzā Hāshim and Āqā Aḥmad and Āqā Ḥusayn of 3 *dāng* of Jayshī	312–313
37	18 Rabīʿ II 1311/29 October 1893	*Ijāra-nāma* between Āqā Mīrzā Hāshim and Āqā Aḥmad and Āqā Ḥusayn of 3 *dāng* of Jayshī	314–315
38	11 Dhī Qaʿda 1320/9 Febuary 1903	Transfer of *waqf* land from Āqā Mīrzā Hāshim to Āqā Mīrzā Mahdī Bunakdār and Ḥājjī ʿAbd al-Maḥmūd Qannādī	344–345
39	8 Rabīʿ I 1322/23 May 1904	*Ijāra-nāma* of Āqā Mīrzā ʿAbbās Bunakdār b. Ḥājjī Mīrzā Abū l-Ḥasan Bunakdār of 3 *dāng* of Jayshī and 3 *dāng* of Saryān from Mīrza Ḥusayn and Mīrzā Aḥmad	316–318
40	19 Shaʿbān 1322/29 October 1904	*Muṣālaḥa-nāma* between Āqā Mīrzā ʿAbbās Bunkdār and Āqā Mīrzā Mahdī Bunakdār and Ḥājjī ʿAbd al-Maḥmūd Qannādī as recorded in the register of Masjid-i Naw, Isfahan	319–320
41	22 Shawwāl 1329/16 October 1911	*Muṣālaḥa-nāma* of the revenues of 7 years of 3 *dāng* of Jayshī and 2 *dāng* of Saryan between Āqā Aḥmad and Āqā Ḥusayn and Mīrzā ʿAbd al-Ḥusayn Khān	348–350
42	15 Dhū al-Qaʿda 1329/7 November 1911	*Ijāra-nāma* of 2 *dāng* of Saryān between Mīrzā ʿAbd al-Ḥusayn Khān and the *kad-khudā* of Saryān, Ḥājjī Maḥmūd b. Karabalāyī Ramaḍān	364–365
43	16 Dhū al-Qaʿda 1329/8 November 1911	Copy of a *ḥawwāla* document of wheat and barley seeds	366
44	Muḥarram 1330/December 1911	List of seeds received and sown by cultivators of Jayshī and Saryān including witness testimonies presented before Muḥammad Ḥusayn Fishārakī	376–382

IV. Administrative Documents

45	8 Rajab 1330/23 June 1912	*Raqam* administrative decree from the Ministry of Foreign Affairs prohibiting the sale of 6 *dāng* of Jayshī to Faḍlullāh Khān as it was *waqf* land	375

Editions of Selected Documents from Chapters 2, 3, and 6

Chapter 2

The conditional sale contract (*bayʿ-i sharṭ*) of Ḥajjī Imām Qulī b. ʿAlī Muḥammad Bēg Nūrī dated 15 Jamādī II 1276/9 January 1860 produced and registered in the Tammāmī *shaykh al-islām sharīʿa* court of Shiraz

Text: Madrasaʿ-yi Imām-i ʿAṣr collection, Shiraz, Document no. 69, digital archive, Majmaʿ-yi Dhakhāʾir-i Islāmī, Qum.

[A] [سجل شيخ أبو القاسم التمامي:]
[a] حسبی اللّه
[b] أقرّ الحاج امامقلی البایع الشارط المعروف
بجمیع ما نمی إلیه حسبما زبر و رقم فیه
متناً لديّ [c] و کتبه الداعي في الثالث و العشرین من شهر جمادی الأخر
من شهور عربیة مطابق سنة ۱۲۷۶ [d] اصلاح ابراهیم در سطر سیم [...]
و والد مشتریان حاجی محمد ابراهیم علاف شیرازی [...]
شرح حاشیه بسطر نهم [...] [e] در محکمه اسلامیه امامیه ثبت و ضبط نمایند و [...]
[B] [f][سجع مهر چهارگوش:] لاشه شد

[حاشیه راست:]
[C] [یادداشت ثبتدار محکمه:] ثبت مَحکمهٔ مُحکمهٔ اسلامیه شد، ثبت شد
[سجع مهر مربع:] دارد شرف بر أنبیاء محمد ۱۲۵۰

[E] [سجع مهر چهارگوش:] «لا إله الّا اللّه الملک الحقّ المبین عبده عبدالجواد»
[F] أقرّ المعروف بما رقم فیه متناً و هامشاً لدی [سجع مهر چهارگوش:] «لا إله إلّا اللّه الملک الحقّ المبین عبده محمدعلی بن اسداللّه»
[G] [سجع مهر بیضوی:] «عبده الراجی محمدرضا الحسینی».
[H] [سجع مهر چهارگوش:] «لا إله إلّا اللّه الملک الحقّ المبین عبده محمد الحسینی».
[I] [سجع مهر چهارگوش:] «محمدعلی ابن محمد مهدی التمامی»؛

1[D] خلاصهٔ مفاد این کتاب صواب آنکه در محضر شریعت‌گستر حضرات اهالی شرع شریف حاضر گردید عالیجاه معلی جایگاه، خیرالحاج و العمّار حاجی امامقلی، خلف مرحوم علی‌محمد بیک نوری

2 و به اشدّ رضا و رغبت تمام، بلا مظنّهٔ اکراه و اجبار متصدی معد [؟] و فروخت به عقد مبایعهٔ خیاریهٔ شرعیه به عالی‌شان معلی نشان میرزا محمدعلی، ولد علیاجناب فرح سلطان، صبیّهٔ

3 مرحوم حاجی محمدابراهیم علّاف شیرازی بطریق ارث تمامی و جملگی موازی دو فرد و سدس فرد دیگر
از جمله ده فرد و دو ثلث فرد اختصاصی خود من جمله چهل فرد
4 افراد کل شش دانگ مزرعهٔ دودج زرقان معیّنهٔ معلومه واقعه در حومهٔ شیراز با جمیع متعلقات و منضمات
مشتمله بر اراضی شتوی‌کار و صیفی کار و کشتخوانات شحنه و تحسیر [؟] و مراتع
5 و معالف و بساتین و طاحونهٔ جدید البناء محدثات در مزرعهٔ مزبوره و جی و جُدران و مجاری و مشارب
از قنوات اربعهٔ مختصات مشهورات به قنات دودج
6 و آب باریک ده زیاب بیک و دم آس و سایر ملحقات داشته [...] و قلعه و دهکده و غیره، دایراً بایراً بدون
استثنائی از آن به انضمام ممرّ آب، سیصد من غلّه بالمناصفه
7 به ورثهٔ ایشان که از بابت بذر مبلغ از مال مشتریان بر ذمهٔ بایع مزبور قرار یافت که در ختم زمان خیار
سیذکر مؤدی نماید در مزرعهٔ موصوفهٔ [...] کافهٔ قاطبهٔ دو مزرعه موصوفه [...]
8 به طاحونه، هریک در محل وقوع عند اهالیها و سگّانها مستغنی الحد و الوصف است، ملکی اربابی خود را
به ثمن معیّن مبلغ یکصد و بیست و چهار تومان تبریزی [...] سی و هشت نخودی
9 یک‌هزار دینار مقبوض بایع مزبور در مجلس عقد دفعهٔ واحدهٔ مبایعتی شرعی و بایع مزبور اسقاط جمیع
خیارات شرعیه در مبایعهٔ مزبوره سوای خیار شرط نموده و ضامن
10 دَرَک تمامی مبلغ موصوف گردید که عند ظهور الفساد کلاً أو بعضاً، عیناً أو منفعةً از عهده برآید و ضمن
العقد شرط شد که چنانچه بایع مزبور مثل کلّ ثمن معهودهٔ [؟] موصوف را
11 در ظرف مدت دو سال[3] تمام عددی از تاریخ تحریر را به سوی مشتریان مزبوران أو من قام مقامهما
بقدرالحصه نماید، مسلط شود بر فسخ مبایعهٔ مزبوره، والّا فلا
12 و منفعهٔ زمان خیار ضمن العقد به جهت بایع مزبور شرط شد که از عهدهٔ اخراجات و خدمات ملکی و مُلکی
مبلغ موصوف در ظرف خیار إلی پنجاه تومان وجه نقد
13 برآید و مشتریان مزبوران قبول مبایعه را به جهت خود به طریق ارث نموده و صیغهٔ شرعیه عرفیه جاری
عربی و فارسی شد فی پانزدهم شهر جمادی الأخر سنه ۱۲۷۶ [J] [سجع مهر چهارگوش:] لاشه شد
15 [حاشیهٔ راست:]
شرح حاشیه آنکه مبلغ متن سیزده سهم مشاع از جمله دویست و چهل سهم سهام شش دانگ مزرعهٔ دودج
مزبور و بساتین و طاحونه و قنوات مفصلهٔ متن بقدر الحصه و سایر متعلقات به انضمام مقدار سیصد من
غلّه بالمناصفه به ورثهٔ ایشان به نحو متن میباشد که به نحو متن مبایعه نموده و صیغه جاری شد.

[L] شهد علی ذلك:
- عالیشان رفیع مکان اشرف الحاج و العمار حاجی محمدکاظم، کدخدای محله درب السلطنه.
[M] [سجع مهر مربع:] «محمد کاظم ..».
- عالیشان رفیع مکان کهف الحاج حاجی رئیس علی رشتادرانی.
[N] [سجع مهر بیضوی:] «علیّ مع الحقّ».
عالیشان رفیع مکان کربلائی محمدرحیم صراف مرادی.

Chapter 3

A legal ruling (*ḥukm-i sharʿ*) of Āqā Sayyid Ṣādiq Ṭabāṭabāʾī Sangalajī issued in the question-and-answer format dated 2 Dhū l-Ḥijja 1290/21 January 1874

Text: Document no. 1258A17, WWQI, Tehran Notary 25 Museum, ʿAbd al-ʿAlī Sulṭānī Muṭlaq collection.

3 All amounts are also expressed in *siyāq* in the inter-linear text.

[حکم شرعی:]

[A]1 بسمه تعالی

2 بلی این اعتراف بلا شبهه واقع شده است

3 اقرار را و احتمال نمیشود حمل بر رسم القباله

4 نمود شرعا باری گذشتن ابرام موقوف

5 بر ترافع نزد حاکم شرع جایز الحکومه

6 و السلام حرره فی۲ ذی الحجه الحرام

7 ۱۲۹۰

[B] [مهر سجع بیضوی:] « محمد صادق بن محمد مهدي الحسيني الطباطبائي »

1 [C] حجة الاسلاما قبلة الأناما [D] در باب قریهٔ «دِه نو» واقعه در بلوک غار، سؤالی از جناب حجة الاسلام نمودهاند

2 که این دِه، در اصل مال نوّاب اکبر میرزا بوده، بعد از آن به مرحومهٔ مغفورهٔ فخرالدوله منتقل شده، بعد از آن

3 در ثبت جنابعالی چنین بروز کرده و مرقوم فرمودهاید: در ۳ جمٰدی الأولی ۱۲۸۳ مرحومه فخرالدوله به علیاجاه

4 خورشیدخانم منتقل نموده است بر جنابعالی معلوم و مبرهن است که اقرار رسم القباله زیاد اتفاق میافتد،

5 بعد بهم میخورد و زیاد از این مبایعات و معاملات اتفاق افتاده، بعد، هریک به یک جهة صورت نگرفته است

6 و آن قبالهٔ وکاله مانده، یا پاره مینمایند و دوباره به ثبت رجوع نمیکنند و ثبت آن را اخراج نمینمایند؛

7 ثبت در دفتر میماند، مایهٔ زحمت مردم میشود دویّم آنکه سند مالک، تصرف است تحقیق بفرمایید

8 از سنهٔ ۱۲۸۳ الی الآن و قبل از آن تاریخ هیچ وقت یک روز و یک ساعت علیاجاه خورشید خانم

9 [E] در آن ملک متصرّف نبوده و هیچ کس ندیده و نشنیده که در آنجا،

10 مشارإلیها تصرف نموده باشد، مدتهاست الی الآن مالک و متصرّف، کبری است

11 در این صورت حکم جناب آقای حجة الاسلام چیست؟ آنچه حکم خداوندی است

12 مرقوم فرموده که از آن قرار عمل شود

A legal ruling of Ḥājj Mullā Muḥammad Kazim dated Shaʿbān 1296/August 1879 issued as a deed/certificate, ratified by Āqā Sayyid Ṣādiq Ṭabāṭabāʾī Sangalajī in Dhū l-Ḥijja 1296/November 1879

Text: Document no. 14126A14, WWQI digital archive; no. 3613, Āstān-i Quds Collection, Mashhad.

[حکم شرعی:]

1 [A] بسم الله خیر الاسماء

[F][امضای حکم ۱:]
بسمه تعالی، حکم صادر از جناب فخر المجتهدین عمدة العلماء و قدوة الفقهاء سرکار شریعتمدار حاج ملا کاظم سلّمه اللہ تعالی مطاع و متبّع و ممضی است حرره الأقل في غرة ذي الحجة الحرام سنة ۱۲۹۶
[سجع مهر بیضوی:] « محمد صادق بن محمد مهدي الحسيني الطباطبائي »

[G] [امضای حکم ۲:]
حکم صادر از سرکار عمدة العلماء الاعلام زبدة الفقهاء الکرام الحاج ملا محمد کاظم مجتهد سلّمه اللہ تعالی ممضی و متبّع است یجب اتباعه و لا یجوز ردّه
[سجع مهر بیضوی:] « العبد محمدرحیم ۱۲۶۰»

2 [B] مخفی و مستور نماند نظر به اقرار و اعتراف مرحوم مبرور جنّت آشیان، حاجی محمدرضا تاجر خراسانی شهیر به حکّاک
3 نزد این خادم شریعت مطهّره و داعی دوام دولت قاهره بر تصالح و انتقال: همگی و تمامی حصّه و سهم ملکی و متصرّفی خود را از کلّ مزرعهٔ موسومه
4 به زرکش با کافهٔ ملحقات شرعیه و منضمّات عرفیه؛ و تمامی یک ثلث شایع کامل از کلّ یک باب جوّالی ملکی خود، مشاعی بین ورثهٔ
5 مرحوم حاجی محمد حسن؛ و تمامی یک باب جوّالی کوچک خود، شهیر به جوّالی کربلائی حسن، مع کلّما یتعلّق بها که هریک فی محلّه غنیّ [عن] التحریر و التوصیف است؛
6 به حلیلهٔ جلیلهٔ خود مرحومهٔ المغفوره بی‌بی کوچک خانم، صبیّهٔ مرضیّهٔ مرحمت‌پناه آقا کربلائی محمد زرگر و مصالحه نمودن مرحومهٔ مصالحٌ لهای مزبوره به صیغهٔ شرعیه
7 حین حیاتها تمامی مایملک خود را در محضر داعی و جمعی از ملک و جوّالی و نقد و جنسش از منقول و غیر منقول به دخترزادهٔ خود، عالیجناب
8 مستطاب وصایت‌مآب آقا شیخ محمدحسن ـ زید فضله ـ به‌علاوه بر شهادت کتبیهٔ جناب مستطاب شریعت‌مآب الفاضل الکامل، افتخار الحاج حاجی ملّا نوروزعلی
9 شهیر به فاضل بسطامی زید فضله بناءً علی‌هذا؛ تمامی اعیان مزبوره محکوم به ملکیّت عالیجناب مصالح له مزبور است و چون
10 مبنای تصرف ورثهٔ مرحوم حاج مصالح مزبور من حیث الإرث است، تصرف آنها محض غصب و عدوان است؛
11 حسب الشرع الأنور بر ورثه و متصرّفین املاک مزبوره واجب و لازم است که بعد حلفی (؟) للاستظهار، تمامی املاک و اشیاء مسطورهٔ فوق
12 را تخلیهٔ ید خود نموده و به تصرّف مالکانهٔ عالیجناب موصی إلیه واگذار نمایند که عالیجناب موصی إلیه استفاده و تصرف مالکانه نماید.
13 این چند کلمه حسب الحکم الشرعی قلمی و تحریر شد. و کان ذلک تحریراً فی سلخ شهر شعبان المعظّم من شهور ستّة وتسعون ومأتین بعد الألف 1296.

[D] [حاشیهٔ ذیل:]
نعم؛ قد حکمت بذلك كذلك والحكم للّه العليّ الأعلى
[سجع مهر مستطیل:] «المتوکّل علی اللّه عبده محمّد کاظم».

[E] [حاشیهٔ راست:]
و چون جناب نور چشمی، آقا شیخ حسن ـ زید قدسه ـ در تاریخ ذیل/ وارد قصبهٔ خبوشان شد و اظهار اتمام و انجاح مهم دریافت املاک/ مسطوره و اجرت سنوات و سایر اشیاء محکوم بها له به اجراء/ صیغهٔ قسم در هردو فقره نمود؛ لهذا این خادم شریعهٔ مطهّره در هیک/ از دو فقره او را قسم داده و انجاح مهمّ ایشان شد؛ لهذا/ بر محکوم علیهم لازم است ایصال و تأدیهٔ املاک مسفوره/ و اجرت سنوات تصرفی و سایر غرامات و لوازم/ شرعیهٔ ایشان بلا اهمال نمایند./
فی نوزدهم شهر شوال المحرم 1296.
[سجع مهر مستطیل:] «المتوکّل علی اللّه عبده محمّد کاظم».

[H] [سند ظهریه:] شد ثبت. [سجع مهر:] ۱۲۸۳ سنه حسین محمد

Seq. 65 from Register 1 of Āqā Sayyid Ṣādiq Ṭabāṭabāʾī Sangalajī, Tehran

Text: S1: 65, Scribe A, Ms. No. 67032/692, NLAI, Tehran

يوم ۱۳ ذی الحجّه الحرام ۱۲۸۴

[1]

مصالح آقا میرزا بزرگ خلفمرحوم حاجی عبدالله. مصالح له آقا میرزا محمّد برادر مرحومه مذکوره . تمامی اعیان سه دانگ خانه مفروز مشتمل بر یك اطاق و ضروفخانه (ظروفخانه) و بالاخانه و سیّال مخصوص و ممرّ و مدخل از جمله ششدانگ خانه واقعه در اراضی چهارده معصوم در کوچه شاهسونها محدود بحدود اربعه ذیل با کافّه ملحقات

________ ________ ________ ________

شرعیّه آن از ممر و مدخل و عمارات و فضا و اطاقها و دروب و پنجره و غیره بدون وضع شیئی از آن سه دانگ مال المصالحه هشتاد تومان روپیه ۲۶ نخود وزن یکهزار دینار رواج که بعد از اجرای صیغه شرعیّه قبض و اخذ نموده و اسقاط جمیع خیارات خود را بهر جهت از جهات شرعیّه ولو کان فاحشاً بل افحش نموده و صیغه مصالحه لازمه بر مراتب مسطوره جاری شد توضیح آنکه اعیانی این سه دانگ از مرحومه ساره خواتون بنت مرحوم آقا میرزا جانی کاشانی موافق صلحنامه جداگانه معتبره ممهوره بمهر علمای اعلام منتقل شده بود به پسر عموی خودش آقا میرزا حسین کاشانی و نیز موافق مصالحه نامه جداگانه آقا میرزا حسین منتقل نموده بود به آقا میرزا بزرگ مصالح مزبور و ایشان نیز منتقل نمودند موافق این قباله به آقا میرزا محمّد برادر مرحومه ساره خاتون و حال ملك اوست ، وکان تحریراً فی ۳ شهر شوّال ۱۲۸۴

---

[2] **اعترف البایع الشارط المکرم بما سطر من المبایعة وقبض الثمن وقبول الاجارة والالتزام لديّ فی ۳ ذي الحجّة الحرام ۱۲۸۴**

بایع آقا میرزا بزرگ خلفمرحوم حاجی میرزا محمّد فراهانی. مشتریه کیمیا خانم زوجه مکرمه خود که صبیه مرحمت پناه حاجی محمّد ولی میرزا مباشد تمامی نیم دانگ از یك دانگ نیم سهم مختصّ خود از کلّ ششدانگ قریه اسنجران واقعه در بلوك سادات من بلوکات فرهان را که از غایت شهرت مستغنی از تحدید است با جمیع منضمّات شرعیّه آن از اراضی و صحاری و مزارع و مراتع و مجری المیاه و دهکده کلّا و طُرّا بقدر الحصّة المشاعیّه ثمن دویست تومان ریال ۲۶ نخودی مأخوذی خیار در ظرف ده روز بعد از یکسال از این تاریخ مال الاجاره چهل و هشت تومان موصوف که در آخر مدّت رساند. و در ضمن عقد خارج بایع ملتزم شد که در صورتی که قبل از لزوم یا بعد از لزوم الی پنجاه سال دیگر مبیع مزبور مستحق للغیر برآید کلّا او بعضا اینکه بعلاوه ثمن مزبور مجّاناً سیصد تومان دیگر بمشتریه دادنی باشد .و صیغتان جاری شد و التزام واقع شد فی دهم ذی الحجّه ۱۲۸۴

---

[3] **اعترفت البایعة الشارطة المکرّمه بما سطر من المبایعة وقبض الثمن وقبول الاجارة والالتزام لديّ فی ۱۳ ذي الحجّة الحرام ۱۲۸۴**

بایعه کیمیا خانم صبیه مرحمت پناه شاهزاده محمّد ولی میرزا که بالفعل زوجه آقامیرزا آقابزرگ خلفمرحوم حاجی میرزا محمد فراهانی میباشد. مشتری جناب آقا میرزا ابوالقاسم الملقّب بمعین الملك تمامی نیمدانگ که عبارتست از هشت شعیر از نه شعیر مختصّ بمسمّاة مسطوره از بابت صداق خود از کلّ ششدانگ قریه اسنجران از بلوك سادات من بلوك عراق که قریه مزبوره از غایت شهرة مستغنی از تحدید است با جمیع منضمّات شرعیّه آن از اراضی و صحاری و مزارع و مراتع و مجری المیاه و باغات و قنوات و ده کده کلّا و طُرّاً بقدرالحصّة المشاعیّه ثمن دویست تومان ریال ۲۶ نخودی مأخوذی خیار در ظرف ده روز بعد از یکسال مال المصالحه منافع چهل و هشت تومان وجه موصوف که در آخر مدّت رساند و در ضمن عقد خارج لازم بایعه ملتزمه شد که در صورتی که مبیع مزبور قبل از لزوم یا بعد از لزوم الی پنجاه سال دیگر مستحق للغیر برآید اینکه بعلاوه ثمن مجّاناً سیصد تومان بجناب معظم الیه دادنی باشد و صیغتان جاری فی نهم شهر ذی الحجّه ۱۲۸۴

[4] **اعترف المصالح المزبور بما سطر من الصلح وقبض العوض وسقوط الخيارات والالتزام لديّ فی ۱۴ ذي الحجّة الحرام**
مصالح له حبيب اله خلفمرحوم آقا محمّد باقر بيك. مصالحه لها قمر حاج خانم ملقبه بخانم شاهزاده صبيه مرحمت پناه سهراب خان شعری؟ که بالفعل زوجه عبدالحسين خان پيشخدمت ميباشد بر تمامی کلّ ششدانگ عمارت ملکی متصرفی خود که مشتمل است بر حياط اندرونی و خلوت متصلحه بآن وطويله بهاربند و حياط بيرونی متصله بآنها که واقع مباشند در اراضی باغ دراز از محلّه سنگلج من محلات طهران که تماما محدود است بحدود مفصله:

بشارع عام	بخانه آراد خان	بعمارات آقا ميرزا هدايت مستوفی	بباغ سرکار معظم اليه

با جميع منضمّات شرعيه آنها از عرصه و اعيان و ابنيه و عمارات تحتانی و فوقانی و ممر و مدخل و کرمايی و سردر و فضای آنها کلّا و طُرّا که تمامی عمارات حسب الصلح ملك طلق آنمخدّره بوده باشد در عوض يکهزار و دويست و شصت پنجتومان ريال ۲۶ نخودی مأخوذی با اسقاط خيارات محتمله از طرفين از غبن و غير غبن با التزام در ضمن عقد خارج لازم که درصورتی که بعد اليوم فسادی در مصالحه ظاهر شود و عمارات مسطوره کلّا ام بعضاً مستحق للغير برآيد [4]از حال الی پنجاه سال ديگر اينکه بعلاوه مال المصالحه از عهده اجرت المثل وغرامات و خسارات وارده بر آنمخدّره جميعا الی زمان بروز الفساد برآيد.و صيغه مصالحه جاری شد و التزام واقع شد، و اسقاط خيارات واقع گرديد فی شهر ذي الحجّه ۱۲۸۴

Seq. 682 from Register 2 of Āqā Sayyid Ṣādiq Ṭabāṭabāʾī Sangalajī, Tehran

Text: S2: 682, Scribe F, Ms. No. 67032/692, NLAI, Tehran

[1]

بلی، ملتزم با اينکه مدّعی فساد شرعی باشد از عهده الزام هزار تومان بايست که شرعا برآيد حرّر فی ۲۳ شعبان المعظّم ۱۲۹۴

حجة الاسلاما تعالی بموجب معاملات مصالحهجاتيکه در حضور بندهگان عالی مقامان وکيل داعيان و وکيل مشهدی حسين در حضور خود مشهدی حسين وهو ميرزا حسن خان منشی اوّل سفارت عثمانی در يازدهم سال ۱۲۹۴ در قريه کرکن؟ واقع شد آقا مشهدی حسين الی الآن و بالفعل مديون و مشغول الذمّه داعيان بمبلغ يکهزار تومان رائج که عبارت از ده هزار ريال ۲۶ نخودی ناصر الدين شاهی باشد مدانيد يا خير مستدعی است آنچه معلوم و محقّق خيريت؟ بندهگان عالی است بطريق حکومت مرقوم و محتوم فرمائيد که عند کافه حجة بوده باشد فی تاريخ فوق ۱۲۹۴

[2] بلی صلح مزبور بوکالة ثابتة از اشخاص مزبورين با جنابان شما و قاضی حاج ميرزا عبد الصمد بمبلغ مزبور و وجه اسانيد مزبوره و شرط اينکه در صورتيکه وجه اسانيد ظاهر شود که بشماها رسيده است يا اسقاط از اشخاصيکه سند برايشان است معلوم شود شماها از عهده براييد و رجوع بسوی شماها بشود و الا فلا در حضور اين اقل خدّام شريعت مطهره واقع گرديد و خود عاليجاه مجدت همراه آقا ميرزا حسن وکيل ثابت الوکاله حضرات شرط مزبور را بتفصيل مزبور که شما بيان نموديد در ضمن اجراء صيغه قبول نمود و ميگفت که مراد ازعبارت هرچند ابهام دارد همين است و توضيح را بايستکه محرّ ر بخط خود بنويسد والسلام حرّر فی 63 شعبان المعظّم ۱۲۹۶

4 This text appears on the the left-hand margin.

حجة الاسلاما! بتاریخ یازدهم شعبان میرزاحسن خان شوکت منشی اوّل سفارت دولت عثمانی بوکالہ ثابتہ محققه از جانب فاطمه سلطان خانم صبیه کریم عزّت و مشهدی حسین و یوسف و عبد المحمد در محضر جنابعالی و تمامی حضرات را مصالحه لازمه نمود با داعیان در عوض دویست تومان ریال ۲۶ نخودی و [...؟] متعارف مأخوذ و وجه هفت طغرا سند و شرط شد هفت طغرا سند معیّن در مصالحه نامه را بعالیجاه مزبور رد نمایم که بحضرات مفصله رد نماید، و بهیچ وجه ضمانی در ایصال و وصول وجه اسانید از برای داعیان نباشد مگر آنکه نوشته حضرات مسطور در اسانید ابراز نمایند که شرعاً معلوم بود که وجه اسانید را داعیان دریافت یا بمصالحه اسقاط نمودهئیم و اینفقره در مصالحه نامه مجمل و خالی از بیان و مطلب گنگ بود، در حین اجرای صیغه مکرّر ذکر شد و بعالیجاه مزبور اظهار شد که توضیح نماید قبول کرد و اظهار نمود که نوشته را درست مبکنم بعد از... نوشته بهمان حال ماند و به سفارت برده شد. استدعا آنکه مراتب مفروضه را که در محضر واقع شد در صدر عریضه مرقوم مرقوم فرمائید.

---

[3] **اعترف بما سطر من المبايعة الشرطيّة والقبض لديّ في ليلة ٧ شهر رمضان المبارك ١٢٩۴**

بایع آقا میرزا ابوطالب خلفمرحمت پناه آقا میرزا داود میری خلف الله خان [...] مع مقدار یك خروار نون[؟] همدان روغن زرد خالص مأخوذ از گاو و گوسفند بالمناصفه خبره پسند را به مبلغ بیست تومان ریال 62 نخودی مأخوذی که روغن مزبور را [5]در ظرف پنجروز بعد از چهل روز از تاریخ ذیل در همدان تسلیم مشتری نماید. و در ضمن العقد شرط شد خارج مصالحه از برای بایع مزبور از[...] مثل ثمن به سوی مشتری یا قائم مقام شرعی او و لو احدی از حکّام شرع جایز الحکومه همدان و در صورت نبودن و امتناع میرزا از اخذ ثمن در ظرف مدّ ت چهل روز از تاریخ ذیل که هر قدر از ثمن را به مرور رد نمود بالنسبه بهمان قدر از مبیع فسخ نماید، صیغه جاری شد فی غرّه رمضان ١٢٩۴

---

[4] **الامر كما سطر و زبر وحكمت بعزل السابقين ونصب اللّاحقين حرّر في ٢٢ رجب المرجّب ١٢٩۴**

---

[5]

با فرض مسطور حکم منشأ اثر نیست شرعاً و تقاص در غیر محل است و مالیکه برده است از او استرداد مشود شرعاً با اینکه حقّ یّ ه خود را بحسب شرع ثابت نماید والله العالم .حرّر فی لیلة ١٣ شهر رمضان المبارك ١٢٩۴

حجة الاسلاما! زید فوت شده مالی دارد صغار و کبار چندی هم وارث هستند. شخصی مدعی شده است که طلبی دارم لا علی التعیین بدون سند شرعی و بدون اطلاع و حضور وصی و قیّم صغار و خود کبار رفته حکم عرفی صادر نموده و تقاص کرده ملك و مالی را که از زید متوفی مانده است بدون تقویم اهل خبره برده است آیا چنین تقاص صحیح است یا خیر؟ دو کلمه در صدر ورقه مرقوم و مزین فرمایید، والسلام.

Chapter 6

A Qajar era *istishhād-nāma* dated Shaʿbān 1280/February 1864, relating to the *waqf* lands belonging to the *imām-zāda* ʿAlī b. Muḥammad b. Zayd b. Mūsā al-Kāẓim shrine in the village of Jundān near Isfahan

Text: File no. 490, digital archive, Majmaʿ-yi Dhakhāʾir-i Islāmī, Qum.

5 This text appears on the bottom right-hand margin.

استشهاد و استخبار و استعلام می رود از عامه و قاطبه اهالی و سکنه قراء رودنشین از عالیجنابان علماء و سادات و طلاب و مؤمنین و صلحاء و متدینین دامت برکاتهم که هر کس علم قطع و خبرت تمام داشته باشد در باب وقف بودن بر امام زاده علیه السلام مقدار دوازده حبه ملک از جمله هفتاد دو حبه املاک قریه جندان که مجهول الحال و خالصه است، شهادة خود را در حواشی ثبت نموده که به مضمون هداية مشحون آیه کریمه «ومن یکتم شهادته فإنه آثم قلبه»[6] مورد سخط و غضب حضرت قهار عل الاطلاق تعالی واقع نشود و عندالله مأجور و عند الرسول صلی الله علیه و آله معرّی؟ و مثاب بوده باشد و در ثانی شهادة خود را در باب مخروبه بودن و لم یزرع شدن این ملک موقوف مزبور از اوان غلبه افغان تاکنون نیز ادا نموده باشند که شاید – انشاء الله تعالی – برخلاف سابق به یمن دولت و خلوص عقیده ملازمان دولت علّیه – امّرالله عمارهم و کرم الله وجوههم فی الدارین – منافع و نماء املاک وقف به مصارف خیرات از تعمیر عمارات و مخارج خدّام و قاریان قرآن و افروختن مصابیح که فی الحقیـ[قـ]ـة صدقات جاریه است که اعظم مثوبات است عاید بر ارواح و احوال بانیان این امر شریف شود به مضمون حدیث «وصوی الدالّ علی الخیر کفاعله». فمن بدّله بعدما سمعه فإنما اثمه علی الذین یبدّلونه؛ تحریراً فی شهر شعبان المعظم سنه ۱۲۸۰.

[حاشیه چپ:]

شهود قریه قورطان

1- اقل خلق الله زارعین قریه قورطان ابراهیم ولد مرحوم رحمن قریه مزبوره، آنچه از آبا و اجداد و ریش سفیدان استماع نمودم مذکور داشتند که دوازده حبه املاک قریه جندان وقف امام زاده واجب التعظیم قریه مزبوره است و از قرار متن صحیح است.

[سجع مهر بیضوی:] ابراهیم ابن محمد رحمن[؟]

2- اقل عباد الله زارع قریه قورطان آقا اسمعیل ولد مرحوم رحیم آنچه از آبا و اجداد خود شنیدم مذکور ساختند که دوازده حبه املاک قریه جندان وقف امام زاده است و از زمان افغان تاکنون مخروبه است، ۱۲۸۰.

[سجع مهر بیضوی:] عبده الراجی محمداسمعیل.

3- اقل خلق الله زارع قریه قورطان رمضان ولد مرحوم آقا حسین آنچه از آبا و اجداد خود استماع نمودم و علم قطع دارم دوازده حبه املاک قریه جندان وقف امام زاده واجب التعظیم است و از زمان افغان تاکنون مخروبه است، ۱۲۸۰.

[سجع مهر بیضوی:] پیرو دین نبی رمضان.

4- اقل عباد الله زارع قریه قورطان آقاعلی ابن مرحوم رحیم چنین علم دارم که از اجداد خود استماع که دوازده حبه املاک قریه جندان وقف است.

[سجع مهر بیضوی:] یا علی ادرکنی ۱۲۲۷.

5- اقل عباد الله و زارعین قریه قورطان کربلائی محمدحسین علم و قطع دارم بر وقف مذکور در متن و در زمان افغان تا حال مخروبه است؛ ۱۲۸۰.

[سجع مهر بیضوی:] یا امام حسین.

6- عالیشان احمد کدخدا قریه قورطان آنچه از پدران و ریش سفیدان قریه مزبوره شنیدم دوازده حبه املاک قریه جندان وقف امام زاده واجب التعظیم است و از زمان افغان تاکنون مخروبه است؛ ۱۲۸۰.

[سجع مهر بیضوی:] عبده احمد.

6 Q 2:283.

7- اقل الساداة الحسینی میرمحمد[؟] زارع قریه قورطان آنچه از اجداد خود استماع نمودم مذکور ساختند که دوازده حبه املاک قریه جندان وقف امام زاده قریه مزبوره است و از زمان افغان تاکنون مخروبه است.
[سجع مهر بیضوی:] محمد؟ الحسینی.
8- اقل الساداة الحسینی میرمحمدزمان قورطانی چنین علم دارم آنچه از آبا و اجداد خود استماع نمودم مذکور داشتند دوازده حبه املاک قریه جندان وقف است و از زمان افغان تاکنون مخروبه است؛ ۱۲۸۰.
[سجع مهر بیضوی:] محمدزمان الحسینی.
9- عالیشان آقا اسمعیل کدخدا اهالی قریه کفرود علیم و خبیر هستیم بر وقف بودن مساحة دوازده حبه ملک مرقوم در متن و از زمان افغان تا حال مخروبه و لم یزرع است؛ ۱۲۸۰.
[سجع مهر بیضوی:] عبده الراجی محمداسمعیل.
10- عالیشان کربلائی هادی کدخدا [خالصه؟] قریه کفرود علیم و خبیر هستیم بر وقف دوازده حبه ملک از قریه مزبوره بر امام زاده واجب التعظیم(ع) و مخروبه است؛ ۱۲۸۰.
[سجع مهر بیضوی:] پیرو دین محمد هادی.
11- عالیشان آقامحمد ولد مرحوم جعفر علیم و خبیر هستیم بر وقف بودن دوارده حبه ملک بر امام زاده مرقوم به طریق متن و مذکور در حواشی و حال نیز مخروبه است؛ ۱۲۸۰.
[سجع مهر بیضوی:] یا محمد أدرکنی.
[B] 12- اقل السادات الحسینی میرزین العابدین ساکن قریه کفرود رودشتین علیم و خبیرم بر وقف در متن و حواشی و صحیح است؛ ۱۲۸۰.
[سجع مهر مربع:] یا امام زین العابدین أدرکني
13- اقل عباد الله ابوطالب ولد مرحوم مغفور جنت مکان آقابابا ساکن قریه ورزنه علم قطع و خبرت تام دارم بر وقف بودن دوازده حبه ملک من جمله املاک قریه مزبوره و از زمان افغان تا امروز؟ مخروبه و لم یزرع است؛ ۱۲۸۰.
[سجع مهر بیضوی:] عبده ابوطالب[؟]
14- اقل عباد الله تعالی حاج حاجی علی اکبر ولد مرحوم مغفور حاجی عزیزالله ورزنه علیم و خبیر هستم بر وقف بودن دوازده حبه ملک مرقوم در متن و از زمان افغان تا حال مخروبه و لم یزرع است؛ ۱۲۸۰.
[سجع مهر بیضوی:] العبد المذنب علی اکبر.
15- اقل خلق الله ابن مرحمت پناه جنت آرامگاه آخوند ملا محمد [...] از مراتب مسطور در متن مطلع و مستحضر می باشم و آنچه از هذه الصحیفه تحریر شده بیان واقع است [...] از متن در او نمی باشد... سنه ۱۲۸۰.
[سجع مهر بیضوی:] المتوکل علی الله عبده عبدالله.
16- اقل عباد الله ملا مهدی خلف جنت مکان حاجی صادق ورزنه عالم و خبیر هستم بر صحت مراتب مرقومه در متن [...]
17- اقل عباد الله [...]

شهود قریه کریت[؟]
18- اقل عباد الله کربلائی علی ساکن و زارع قریه کریت قهپایه علیم و خبیر هستم و از آباء و اجداد خود یداً بید شنیده ام و مشهور است که مساحة و مقدار دوازده حبه ملک قریه جندان وقف بر امام زاده –علیه السلام- است از زمان افغان تا حال مخروبه است.
[سجع مهر بیضوی:] پیرو دین محمد علی.
19- اقل عباد کمترین زارعین قریه کریت نادعلی علیم و خبیر هستم چنانچه از [آ]باء و معمرین نیز شنیده ام و مشهور و معروف است که دوازده حبه ملک قریه جندان وقف امام زاده قریه مزبوره است و مخروبه و لم یزرع است؛ ۱۲۹۰.
[سجع مهر بیضوی:] [...] محمد علی.
20- اقل بندگان یوسف ساکن و زارع کریت علم دارم بر وقف بودن دوازده حبه ملک قریه مذکور در متن و مخروبه بودن همین ملک والله [...]؛ ۱۲۸۰.
پیرو دین محمد یوسف.
21- اقل عباد الله غلامعلی کبریتی قهپایه آنچه از [آ]باء و اجداد خود استماع نموده ام دوازده حبه ملک قریه جندان وقف امام زاده واجب التعظیم است و حال مخروبه است؛ ۱۲۸۰.

22- کمترین عباد الله ملاحسین ساکن قریه کریت قهپایه علم قطعی دارم بر وقف نمودن دوازده حبه ملک قریه جندان بر امام زاده واجب التعظیم و از زمان افغان تا حال مخروبه است؛ ۱۲۸۰.
[سجع مهر بیضوی:] پیرو دین محمد حسین
23- اقل عباد الله احمد ولد آقا اسمعیل کفرودی زارع اربابی[؟] علیم و خبیر هستم بر وقف ملک مزبور در متن و مخروبه است.
[سجع مهر مربع:] یا احمد.
24- عباس ولد جعفر، زارع کفرود علم دارم به طریق متن و حواشی.
[سجع مهر بیضوی:] پیرو دین نبی عباس.
25- اقل زارعین قریه کفرود آقا اسمعیل ولد مرحوم محمدعلی امیر علم قطعی دارم بر وقف بودن دوازده حبه ملک و خرابه بوده از زمان افغان تا حال.
[سجع مهر بیضوی:] عبده الراجی محمد اسمعیل.
26- اقل عباد الله و زارعین قریه کفرود آقا قاسم ولد مرحوم علی اکبر علم دارم بر وقف مذکور و از زمان افغان تا حال مخروبه است؛ ۱۲۸۰.
[سجع مهر بیضوی:] عبده محمد قاسم [؟].
27- اقل زارعین و عباد الله آقا محمد ولد مرحوم استاد قاسم علیم و خبیر هستم که دوازده حبه ملک از املاک قریه جندان وقف است و خرابه است؛ ۱۲۸۰.
[سجع مهر مستطیل:] ادرکنی یا مهدی.
28- اقل عباد الله و زارعین قریه کفرود اسمعیل ولد مرحوم کرمعلی علیم و خبیر هستم بر وقف مذکور در متن و مخروبه است تا حال؛ ۱۲۸۰.
[سجع مهر بیضوی:] عبده اسمعیل.
29- اقل عباد الله تعالی و کمترین زارعین و سکنه قریه کفرود رودشتین علم و قطع دارم بر وقف مذکور در متن و از زمان افغان تا حال مخروبه است؛ والله العالم. حسین ولد مرحوم علی اکبر؛ ۱۲۸۰.
[سجع مهر بیضوی:] پیرو دین محمد حسین.

[حاشیه راست:]
30-[...]علی اکبر سید محمدزمان فورکانی [...] مزبوره در متن [...] سنه ۱۲۹۰[...]
31- احقر انام احمد ابن مرحمت پناه حاجی عبدالغفور ورزنه... اخلاق؟ علم دارم.
[سجع مهر بیضوی:] یا احمد.
32- تراب اقدام مؤمنین عزیزالله خلف الحاجی الحرمین حاجی علی اکبر ورزنه علم بهم رسانیدم برآنکه املاک مزبوره در متن بطریق مذکور وقف است و مخروبه و لم یزرع است؛ ۱۲۸۰.
[سجع مهر بیضوی:] یا عزیز الله.
33- اقل بندگان درگاه الله تعالی عابد ولد مرحوم مغفور مشهدی حسن علیم و خبیر هستم بر وقف بودن دوازده حبه ملک مزبور بطریق مذکور در متن و خرابه است تا حال؛ ۱۲۸۰.
[سجع مهر بیضوی:] پیرو دین محمد عابد.
34- عالیجناب [...] ملا محمدعلی ابن مرحوم مغفور مبرور جنت و رضوان آرامگاه آخوند ملا عبدالله جندانی علیم و خبیر هستم که دوازده حبه ملک وقف است و مخروبه است؛ ۱۲۸۰.
[سجع مهر بیضوی:] الله محمد علی المتوکل[؟] المؤمن[؟] عبده [...]
35- کمترین دعاگویان و زارعین قریه جندان قاسم مشهور آنجا را علیم و خبیر هستم بر وقف مذکور در متن که الحال خرابه است، چنان مسموع بود قبل از این زمان نیز خرابه و لم یزرع است؛ ۱۲۸۰.
[سجع مهر بیضوی: المعتصم بالله العالم عبده محمد قاسم].
36- وقف بودن دوازده حبه املاک مضبوطه؟ معلوم است و مخروبه بودن آن [...] والله اعلم.
اقل طلبه محمد حسین.. الحال؛ ۱۲۹۰.
[سجع مهر مربع ناخوانا]
37- اقل طلبه محمد ابن الحسن الورزنه علیم و خبیر هستم بر وقف بودن دوازده حبه ملک در متن. خلافی ندارد؛ ۱۲۸۰.
[سجع مهر بیضوی:] یا محمد ۱۲۲۷.
38- عالیجناب آقا ملا محمدقاسم ولد غفران پناه جنت آرامگاه آخوند ملا محمدحسین مسکنانی؟ من محال

قهپایه از آباء و اجداد علیم و خبیر هستم بر وقف مذکور در متن و از زمان افغان تا حال مخروبه است.
[سجع مهر:] افوض امری الی الله عبده محمدقاسم.
39- عالیشان آقا کریم کدخدا قریه جندان علیم و خبیر هستم بر وقف مذکور در متن و مخروبه بودن ملک مزبور؛ ۱۲۸۰.
[سجع مهر بیضوی:] انه لقرآن کریم [؟]
40- آقا محمدولی علیم قطع دارم بر وقف و خرابی و لم یزرع بودن ملک مرقوم کما ذکر فی المتن؛ ۱۲۸۰.
[:سجع مهر بیضوی:] پیرو دین نبی محمد
41- کمترین عباد الله و زارعین قریه جندان علم قطع دارم بر وقفیت ملک مزبور بطریق مذکور در متن بلا ریب.
مشهدی علی ولد مرحوم قاسم.
[سجع مهر مربع:] پیرو دین محمد علی ۱۲۲۲[؟]
42- اقل زارعین و بندگان درگاه اله، اسمعیل ولد مرحوم آقا علی علیم و خبیر هستم بر وقف مذکور و مخروبه بودن بطریق مذکور در متن؛ ۱۲۸۰.
[سجع مهر بیضوی:] پیرو دین نبی اسمعیل ۱۲۳۱

شهود قریه سهران
43- و من الشاهدین علی هذا عالیشان عزت نشان آخوند کدخدای قریه سهران، ولد مرحوم آقا حسن کدخدا.
[سجع مهر مربع:] عبده احمد.
44- و من الشاهدین علی هذا آقا قاسم اخوه.
45- اقل عباد الله ابراهیم ولد مرحوم آقا حسن نهرانی علیم و خبیر هستم بر وقف بودن تمام دوازده حبه ملک بر امام زاده واجب التعظیم قریه جندان و مخروبه بودن؛ ۱۲۸۰.
[سجع مهر مربع:] سلام علی ابراهیم ۱۲۰۰[؟]
46- کمترین زارعین ملا کدخدا؟ قاسم سهرانی آنچه از پدران خود استماع نموده ام و علم قطعی دارم برآنکه دوازده حبه ملک جندان وقف است و از زمان افغان تا حال مخروبه افتاده است والله عالم؛ ۱۲۸۰.
[سجع مهر بیضوی:] یا قاسم الارزاق.
47- کمترین زارعین قریه سهران آقا محمد ابوالحسن از آباء و پدران و ریش سفیدان [ننوشته؟] شنیده ام که املاک بر وقف امام زاده در جندان دوازده حبه است از زمان افغان تا حال مخروبه افتاده است. والله العالم؛ ۱۲۸۰.
[سجع مهر مربع:] پیرو دین نبی محمد ۱۲۷۱[؟].
48- کمترین بندگان درگاه اله محمد جندانی ساکن و زارع قریه سهران علیم و خبیر هستم بر وقف بودن دوازده حبه ملک مرقوم در متن و از زمان دولت افغان تا حال مخروبه است؛ ۱۲۸۰.
[سجع مهر مربع:] پیرو دین نبی محمد.
49- و من الشاهدین علی ذلک که دوازده حبه ملک وقف است. ابن محمد سلیم، یوسف.
[سجع مهر بیضوی:] پیرو دین نبی یوسف.
50- علی ولد مرحوم اسماعیل آقایار علم دارم بر وقف مذکور و مخروبه است؛ ۱۲۸۰.
[سجع مهر مربع: ناخوانا].
51- و من الشاهدین علی وقفیت مذکور کمترین قاسم ولد مرحوم حسن حلال.
[سجع مهر مربع:] پیرو دین نبی قاسم.
52- اقل زارعین و عباد الله عبدالرحیم ابن آقا عزیز الله علم قطع دارم بر وقف مذکور در متن و مخروبه است؛ ۱۲۸۰.
53- کمترین عباد الله و زارعین آقا محمد ولد مرحوم حسن علیم و خبیرم بر وقفیت ملک مزبور یعنی دوازده حبه ملک بر امام زاده و از زمان افغان تا حال مخروبه است.
[سجع مهر مربع:] منتظر لطف الهی محمد.
54 – و من الشاهدین علی هذا شمس الدین ابن حسن علم قطع دارم بطریق مذکور.
[سجع مهر مربع:] پیرو دین نبی شمسعلی.
55 – اقل عباد الله تعالی شانه حسن ولد مرحوم مغفور آقا اسمعیل علم قطع دارم بر وقف بودن همین ملک و خرابه بودن او که در متن است.

[سجع مهر بیضوی:] یا امام حسین ادرکنی.

56- عباد الله و زارعین قریه جندان محمد ولد مرحوم آقا ابراهیم علیم و خبیر هستم بر وقفیت مذکور در متن و مخروبه بودن ملک وقف از زمان افغان.

[سجع مهر مستطیل:] عبده محمد [...].

57- عباد الله و زارعین حسن اخوه؟ علیم و خبیر هستم به نهج مذکور در متن و مخروبه بودن ملک وقف تا حال.

[سجع مهر بیضوی:] یا امام حسین ادرکنی.

58- اقل عباد الله تعالی محمدحسن ولد مرحوم مغفور جنت مکان ملا آقا کدخدا علیم و خبیر بر وقفیت ملک مزبور در متن هستم؛ ۱۲۸۰.

[سجع مهر بیضوی: ناخوانا].

59- کمترین عباد الله ملا عباس ولد مرحوم آقا محمدمهدی علیم و خبیر هستم بر وقف بودن دوازده حبه ملک بطریق مذکور در متن؛ ۱۲۸۰.

[سجع مهر مربع:] پیرو دین نبی عباس[؟].

60- کمترین زارعین قریه سهران آقا رحیم ولد مرحوم مغفور آقا اسمعیل بوداق کدخدای سهران، علیم و خبیر هستم بر وقفیت و مخروبه بودن ملک مزبور بطریق مسطور. فمن بدله انما اثمه علی الذین یبدلونه؛ ۱۲۸۰.

[سجع مهر مربع:] منتظر لطف الهی رحیم.

61- اقل زارعین قریه سهران ابراهیم ولد مرحوم مغفور بوداق علیم و خبیر هستم بر وقفیت دوازده حبه من جمله هفتاد و دو حبه املاک قریه جندان و دائم الاوقات مخروبه و لم یزرع است تا حال تحریر؛ ۱۲۸۰.

[سجع مهر مربع:] سلام علی ابراهیم.

62- اقل رعایا قریه خالصه سهران، حسن ولد مرحوم آقا باقر نهرانی دائماً از پدران و سایرین استماع می نمودم و علم و خبرت قطعی بر وقفیت مقدار دوازده حبه ملک مزبور بر امام زاده؛ ۱۲۸۰.

[سجع مهر بیضوی:] پیرو دین نبی حسین.

63- اقل عباد الله اسمعیل ولد آقا حسن علیم و خبیر هستم بر وقف بودن بر همین نهج مذکور و از زمان افغان تا حال مخروبه است؛ ۱۲۸۰.

[سجع مهر بیضوی:] پیرو دین نبی اسمعیل.

64 – این اقل زارعین قریه سهران رجبعلی آنچه از آباء و ریش سفیدان استماع کرده ام و علم قطعی بهم رسانیده ام بطریق متن است که دوازده حبه ملک قریه جندان وقف امام زاده است و مخروبه است؛ ۱۲۸۰. [A]

[سجع مهر بیضوی:] پیرو دین نبی اسمعیل.

Bibliography

1 Archival Sources

Islamic Museum, al-Ḥaram al-Sharīf, Jerusalem.
Document no. 868.
Kitab-khāna-yi Markazī wa Markaz-i Asnād-i Dānishgāh-i Tihrān (Central Library and Documentation Centre, University of Tehran), Tehran.
Document no. 4042f.
Kitāb-khāna wa Mūza-yi Millī-yi Malik (Malek National Library and Museum), Tehran.
Document no. 1393.310–2292.
Document. no. 1393.21.02294.
Madrasa-yi Imām-i ʿAsr collection, Shiraz.
Document no. 69.
Markaz-i Asnād wa Maṭbūʿāt-i Āstān-i Quds-i Raḍawī, Mashhad.
Document no. 146370/1.
Document no. 146370/2.
Mīrzā Muḥammad Kāẓimaynī collection, Yazd.
Document no. 002/6.
Document no. 002/390.
Sāzmān-i Asnād wa Kitāb-khāna-yi Millī-yi Jumhūrī-yi Islāmī-yi Īrān (National Library and Archive of Iran, NLAI), Tehran.
File no. 91.
Document no. 997/49.
Sāzman-i Awqāf wa Umūr-i Khayriyya (Central Waqf Archive), Tehran.
File no. 15, Fārs province.
File no. 18, Fārs province.
File no. 90, Fārs province.
File no. 119, Fārs province.
File no. 164, Fārs province.
Sāzmān-i Awqāf wa Umūr-i Khayriyya, Isfahan.
File no. 612/3 G-9.
Majmaʿ-yi Dhakhāʾir-i Islāmī, Qum.
File no. 490, digital archive.
Women's World in Qajar Iran (WWQI) Digital Archive, Harvard University, Massachusetts URL: http://www.qajarwomen.org/en/index.html (Accessed 1 April 2023).
Document no. 14142A81, Amir Hossein Nikpour Collection.
Document no. 15161A110, Meisam Ahmadi Kafshani Collection.
Document no. 14130A3, Banu Badr al-Shari'ah 'Alavi (Imami) Collection.
Document no. 1258A17, Tehran Notary 25 Museum, 'Abd al-'Ali Sultani Mutlaq Collection, Tehran.
Document no. 1258A4, Tehran Notary 25 Museum, 'Abd al-'Ali Sultani Mutlaq Collection, Tehran.
Document no. 14126A14, no. 3613, Āstān-i Quds Collection, Mashhad.
Document nos. 902A2 (Sangalajī I) and 902A3 (Sangalajī II), National Library and Archive of Iran (NLAI).

https://doi.org/10.1515/9783111239736-010

2 Unpublished Manuscripts

Sāzmān-i Asnād wa Kitāb-khāna-yi Millī-yi Jumhūrī-yi Islāmī-yi Īrān, Tehran, MS no. 296/23845 (Sangalaji I and Sangalaji II).

Kitab-khāna-yi Markazī wa Markaz-i Asnād-i Dānishgāh-i Tihrān, Tehran, MS no. 7486.

MS Kitāb-khāna-yi Shūrā-yi Majlis, Tehran, MS no. 11548. *Majmūʿa-yi ijāzāt-i ḥujjat al-islām sayyid muḥmmad bāqir bi-ʿidda-ī az ʿulamā'.*

Kitāb-khāna-yi ʿĀyatullāh Marʿashī Najafī, Qum, MS no. 3132. *Ṣafwat al-maqāl.*

Kitāb-khāna-yi ʿĀyatullāh Marʿashī Najafī, Qum MS no. 3136. *Mulakhkhas al-maqāl fī dafʿ al-qīl wa-al-qāl.*

3 Edited Primary Sources

Arends, K.A., A.B. Khalidov, and O.D. Chekhovich, eds., (1979), *Bukharskii vakf XIIIogo veka*, Moscow: Nauka.

(al-) Baḥrānī, Yūsuf (1966), *Lu'lu'at Baḥrayn fī al-ijāzāt wa-tarājim rijāl al-ḥadīth*, edited by Muḥammad Ṣādiq Baḥr al-ʿUlūm, Najaf: Maktabat al-Nuʿmān.

Bīgdilī, Ghulām Ḥusayn Muḥammad Riḍā ed., (1367 sh./1988), *Tārīkh-i Bīgdilī: Madārik wa Asnād*, Tehran: Bū ʿAlī.

Busse, Heribert ed., (1959), *Untersuchungen zum islamischen Kanzleiwesen an Hand turkmenischer und safawidischer Urkunden*, Cairo: Kommissionsverlag Sirović Bookshop, 1959.

Chardin, Jean (1711), *Voyages de Monsieur le chevalier Chardin en Perse et autres lieux de l'Orient*, Amsterdam: Jean Louis de Lorme.

Chekhovich, Olga Dmitrieva (1974), *Samarkandskie dokumenty 15–16 vv.: O vladeniiakh Khodzhi Akhrara v Srednei Azii u Afganistane*, Moscow: Izdatel'stvo Nauka.

Dhabīḥī, Masīḥ ed., (1348 sh./1969), *Astarābād-nāma*, Tihrān: Ibn Sīnā.

Dunbulī, ʿAbd al-Razzāq Beg (1349 sh./1970), *Tajriba al-aḥrār wa tasliya al-abrār, bakhsh-i nakhust, silsila-yi mutūn-i fārsi, shumāra-yi 14*, edited by Ḥasan Qāḍī Ṭabātabā'ī, Tehran: Intishārāt-i Mu'assasa-yi Tārīkh wa Farhang-i Īrān.

Fasā'ī, Ḥasan Ḥusaynī (1367 sh./1988), *Fārs-nāma-yi Nāṣirī*, edited by Manṣūr Rastgār Fasā'ī, 2 vols., Tehran: Mu'assisa-yi Intishārāt-i Āmir Kabīr.

Floor, Willem transl., (2008) Mīrzā Naqī Nāṣirī, *Alqāb wa mawājib-i dawra-yi salāṭīn-i ṣafawiyya*, Washington DC: Mage Publishers.

Hidāyatī, Muḥammad ʿAlī ed., (1344 sh./1965), *Āstāna-yi Ray: majmūʿa-yi asnād wa farāmīn*, Tehran: Shirkat-i sahāmī-yi ufsit.

Iʿtimād al-Saltana, Muḥammad Ḥasan Khān (1363–1367sh/1984–1988), *Tārīkh-i Muntaẓam-i Nāṣirī*, edited by Muḥammad Ismāʿīl Riḍwānī, 3 vols., Tehran: Dunyā-yi Kitāb.

Ittiḥādiyya, Manṣūra and Saʿīd Rūḥī eds., (1385 sh./2006), *Dar maḥḍar-i shaykh faḍlullāh nūrī: asnād-i ḥuqūqī-yi ʿaṣr-i nāṣirī*, Tehran: Nashr-i Tārīkh-i Īran.

Ishkawarī, Sayyid Ṣādiq Ḥusaynī ed., (1388 sh./2009), *Asnād-i Mawqūfāt-Iṣfahān*, 12 vols., Qum: Majmaʿ-yi Dhakhā'ir-i Islāmī.

Ishkawarī, Sayyid Jafar Ḥusaynī (1382 sh./2003), "Ijāzāt-i shaykh ṣāliḥ al-baḥrānī (1098 q.)", *Mīrāth-i ḥadīth-i shīʿa* 10, 479–518.

Iṣfahānī, Muḥammad b. Sabz ʿAlī (d. after 1259/1843–1844), *Wajīzat al-taḥrīr. Dar chigūnagī-yi tanẓīm-i asnād-i sharʿī, millī wa ḥuqūqī dar dawra-yi ṣafawī wa qājār*, edited by Rasūl Jaʿfariyān, Qum: Nashr-i Muʾarrikh.
(al-) Jūshqānī, Muḥammad b. Muḥammad Yūsuf al-Mīmaʾī (1380 sh./2001), *Rasāʾil wa Masāʾīl: shāmil-i hashtṣad wa pānzdah suʾāl wa jawāb wa dawāzdah risāla-yi fiqhī wa ghayra taʾlīf-i ʿallāma-yi buzurgwār Mullā Aḥmad Narāqī (1185–1245q)*, edited by Riḍā Ustādī, 2 vols., Qum: Chāp-i Salmān-i Fārsī.
Kāshānī, Muḥammad Kāẓim Shaybānī, (1395 sh./2016), *Qawānīn al-siyāq*, edited by ʿAlī Riḍā Nīk-Nijād, Tehran: Anjuman-i Āthār wa Mafākhir-i Farhangī.
Khūmaynī Rūḥullāh (1390 sh./1970), *Taḥrīr al-Waṣīla*, 2 vols., Najaf: Maṭbaʿa al-Ādāb.
Khwānsārī Muḥammad Bāqir (1987), *Rawḍat al-Jannāt fī aḥwāl al-ʿUlamā wa-al-Sādāt*, Qum: Maktabat Ismāʿiliyān.
Kirmānī, Isḥāq Ghiyāth al-Dīn Muḥammad (1398 sh./2019), *Risāla-ī dar siyāq*, ed. ʿAlī Riḍā Nīk-Nijād, Tehran: Nigāristān-i Andīsha.
Kondo, Nobuaki, ed., (2018), *Mīrzā Muḥammad Rafīʿ Anṣārī, Dastūr al-mulūk, matn-i kāmil bar asās-i nuskha-yi ḥaydarābād-i hind*, Tokyo: Research Institute for Languages and Cultures of Asia and Africa (ILCAA).
Mihrābādī, Abū al-Qāsim Rafīʿī (1336 sh./1957), *Ātashkda-yi Ardistān: Mushtamal bar Jugrāfiyā wa Tārīkh-i Ardistān wa taḥqīq dar ansāb-i sādāt-i Ṭabāṭabāʾī-yi Īrān*, 3 vols., Tehran: Chāp-i Ātishkada.
Minorsky, Vladimir ed., (1943), *Tadhkirat al-Mulūk: A manual of Ṣafavid administration (circa 1137/1725) Persian text in facsimile (B. M. Or. 9496)*, London: Luzac & Co.
Miura, Toru and Kentaro Sato, eds., (2015), *The Vellum Contract Documents in Morocco in the Sixteenth to Nineteenth Centuries, Part 1 (Toyo Bunko Research Library 15)*, Tokyo: The Toyo Bunko.
——. (2020), *The Vellum Contract Documents in Morocco in the Sixteenth to Nineteenth Centuries, Part 2 (Toyo Bunko Research Library 22)*, Tokyo: The Toyo Bunko.
(al-) Muḥaqqiq al-Ḥillī (1409/1989), *Sharāʾiʿ al-islām*, edited by Sayyid Ṣādiq al-Ḥusaynī al-Shīrazī, 4 vols., Tehran: Istiqlāl.
Musavi, T.M., (1977), *Orta Asr Azarbaijan tarikhina dair farsdilli sanadlar (XVI-XVIII)*, Baky: Elm nashriiiaty.
Nāṣirābādī, Muḥsin Nājī ed., (1388 sh./2010),*ʿArafāt al-ʿĀshiqīn wa ʿAraṣāt al-ʿĀrifīn*, 5 vols., Tehran: Asāṭīr.
Papazian, Akop Davidovich (1968), *Persidskie dokumenty Matenadarana: II Kupchie (14–16 vv.)*, Erevan: Izdatel'stvo Akademii Nauk Armianskoi SSR.
Qāʾim-Maqāmī, Jahāngīr ed., (1348sh./1969), *Yak-ṣad wa panjāh sanad-i tārīkhī: az jalāyiriyān tā pahlawī*, Tehran: Chāp-khāna-yi Artish-i Shāhanshāhī-yi Īrān.
Rajabzāda Hashim and Koichi Haneda eds., (1997), *Fifty Five Persian Documents of the Qajar Period. Persian documents series no. 1*, Tokyo: Institute for the Study of Languages and Cultures of Asia and Africa.
Rajabzāda and Kinji Eura eds., (1999) *Sixty Six Persian Documents of the Qajar Period, Persian documents series no. 2*, Tokyo: Institute for the Study of Languages and Cultures of Asia and Africa.
——. eds., (2016), *Religious and Judicial Documents from Qajar Iran. Persian Documents Series no.3*, Tokyo: Institute for Advanced Studies on Asia.
——. eds., (2017), *Legal Deeds, Judicial Documents and Religious Documents from Qajar Iran. Persian Documents Series no.4*, Tokyo: Institute for Advanced Studies on Asia.
——. eds., (2018), *Social and Judicial Documents from Qajar Iran. Persian Documents Series no.5*, Tokyo: Institute for Advanced Studies on Asia.

——. eds., (2019), *Eighty-Eight Documents on Irrigation from Qajar Iran. Persian Documents Series no.6*, Tokyo: Institute for Advanced Studies on Asia.

——. (2020) *Seasons of Persian Gardens in the Documents from the Qajar Period, Persian Documents Series no.7*, Tokyo: Institute for Advanced Studies on Asia.

——. (2021) *Bazaars, Stores, and Caravenserais in the Documents from Qajar Iran, Persian Documents Series no.8*, Tokyo: Institute for Advanced Studies on Asia.

Riḍā'ī, Umīd, ed., (1383 sh./2005), *Panjāh wa yak ʿarīḍa wa ḥukm-i sharī.ʿ Majmūʿa-yī az pursish-hā wa pāsukh-hā-yi ʿulamā-yi barjasta-yi dawra-yi qājār dar mawḍūʿ-i waqf 1253q-1346q*, Tehran: Muʿāwinat-i Farhangī-yi Sāzmān-i Awqāf wa Umūr-i Khayriyya.

——. ed., (2008), *Dar-āmadī bar asnād-i sharʿī-yi dawra-yi Qājār (Introduction to Shariʿa Documents from Qājār Iran)*, Studia Culturae Islamica n°92, MEIS Series n°9, Tokyo: Research Institute for Languages and Cultures of Asia and Africa (ILCAA).

——. ed., (2021), *Risāla-yi dastūr-i Mīr Qawām al-Dīn Shīrāzī (10 h.q.)*, Studia Culturae Islamica n°113, MEIS Series n°27, Tokyo: Research Institute for Languages and Cultures of Asia and Africa (ILCAA).

(al-) Shaftī al-Mūsawī, Muḥammad Bāqir b. Muḥammad Naqī, (1385 sh./2007), *Maqāla fī taḥqīq iqāmat al-ḥudūd fī hādhihi l-aʿṣār*, edited by ʿAlī Awsaṭ Nāṭiqī and Laṭīf Farādī, Qum: Muʾassasa-yi Bustān-i Kitāb.

Shaftī, Sayyid Muḥammad Bāqir (1379 sh./2001), *Risāla-yi Waqf: Az muʾallifāt-i ʿālim-i bāriʿ wa faqīh wa muḥaqqiq Sayyid Muḥammad Bāqir Shaftī Iṣfahānī maʿrūf bi Ḥujjāt al-Islām, mutawaffā-yi 1260 hijrī qamarī*, edited by Sayyid Aḥmad Tawisirkānī, Tehran: Muʿāwinat-i Farhangī-yi Sāzmān-i Awqāf wa Umūr-i Khayriyya.

Sutūda, Manūchihir and Masīḥ Dhabiḥī (1354 sh./1975), *Az Āstarā tā Astarābād shāmil-i asnād-i tārīkhī-yi Gurgān*, vols. 6 and 7, Tehran: Anjuman-i Āthār-i Millī.

Ṭabāṭabā'ī, Ḥusayn Mudarrisī, ed., (1361 sh./1982) *Bargī az tārīkh-i Qazvīn: Tārīkhcha-yi Āstāna-yi Shāhzāda Ḥusayn wa dūdmān-i sādāt-i Marʿashī-yi qazvīn*, Qum: Kitāb-khāna-yi ʿumūmī-yi Ḥaḍrat-i Āyatullāh al-ʿUẓamā Najafī Marʿashī.

Tunikābūnī, Muḥammd b. Sulaymān (1396 sh./1976), *Qiṣaṣ al-ʿUlamāʾ*, edited by Muḥammad Hādī Aminī, Tehran.

Tunikābūnī, Muḥammd b. Sulaymān (1372 sh./1994), *Tadhkira al-ʿUlamāʾ*, edited by Muḥammad Riḍā Azharī and Ghulām Riḍā Paranda, Mashhad: Bunyād-i Pazhuhish-hā-yi Islāmī.

(al-) Zanjānī, Mullā ʿAlī al-Qazwīnī (1372 sh./1993), *Ṣiyagh al-ʿuqūd wa-l-īqāʿāt*, edited by Bayāt, Jawād, Qum: Instihārāt-i Shukūrī.

Zawārihī, Mīrzā Muḥammad ʿAlī Wafā (1385 sh./2007), *Tadhkira-yi Maʾāthir al-Bāqiriyya bi inḍimām-i risāla-yi ashʿār-i masjidiyya-yi Mīrzā Muḥammad ʿAlī Wafā Zawārihī*, edited by Ḥusayn Masjidī, Isfahan: Markaz-i Iṣfahān-shināsī wa khāna-yi milal.

4 Dictionaries, Catalogues and Facsimiles

Aljoumani, Said, Zahir Bhalloo and Konrad Hirschler (2023), *Catalogue of the New Corpus of Islamic Documents from the Ḥaram al-Sharīf in Jerusalem*, Berlin: De Gruyter.

Ishkawarī, Sayyid Jaʿfar Ḥusaynī (1383 sh./2005), *Majmūʿa-yi asnād-i kitāb-khāna-yi mīrzā-muḥammad kāẓimaynī (yazd-iran), daftar-i awwal*, Qum: Majmaʿ-i Dhakhāir-i Islāmī.

——. (1387 sh./2007), *Asnād-i sharʿī dar kitāb-khāna-yi mīrzā muḥammad Kāẓimaynī –Yazd-Īrān*, Qum: Majmaʿ-i Dhakhāʾir-i Islāmī.

Ishkawarī, Sayyid Aḥmad Ḥusaynī (1380 sh./2001) *Fihrist-i nuskha-ha-yi khaṭṭī-yi Markaz-i iḥyā᾽ al-turāth al-islāmī*, vol.2, Qum: Chāp-i Sarwar.
Little, Donald (1984), A Catalogue of the Islamic Documents from al-Ḥaram aš-Šarīf in Jerusalem, (Beiruter Texte und Studien 29.), Wiesbaden: Franz Steiner Verlag.
Riḍā᾽ī, Umīd (1387 sh./2008), *Hizār-nāma: Fihrist-i qabālajāt-i dawra-yi qājāriyya 1212q-1399q: ihdā᾽ī-yi Mīrzā Muḥammad Kāẓimaynī bi-Imāmzāda Jaʿfar (Yazd-Īrān)*, Qum: Majmaʿ-i Dhakhā᾽ir-i Islāmī.
——. (1398 sh./2019), *Fihrist-i majmūʿa-yi qābāla-hā-yi asnād-i maḥākim-i sharʿ-i fārs wa zanjān dar kitāb-khāna-yi majlis-i shūrā-yi islamī*, Kitāb-khāna, Mūza wa Markaz-i Asnād-i Majlis-i Shūra-yi Islāmī, Tehran.
Shahristānī Ḥasan (1381 sh./2002), *Jilwa-hā-yi hunar-i īrānī dar asnād-i millī*. Tehran: Sāzmān-i Asnād-i Millī.
Tihrānī, Āqā Buzurg (1403/1982–3), *Al-Dharīʿa ilā taṣānīf al-shīʿa*, vol. 22, Beirut: Dār al-Aḍwā᾽.
Tihrānī, Āqā Buzurg and ʿAlī Naqī Munzawī (1372 sh./1993), *Ṭabaqāt aʿlām al-shīʿa*, vol. 6, Qum: Ismāʿīlīyān.

5 Secondary Sources

Abe, Naofumi (2016), "The Ambivalent Position of the Landlord: A Dispute over Ownership of an Iranian Village in the 19th Century", *Islamic Law and Society* 23, 1/2, 52–88.
Abisaab, Rula J. (1994), "The Ulama of Jabal Amil in Safavid Iran, 1501–1736: Marginality, Migration and Social Change", *Iranian Studies* 27, 103–122.
——. (2018), "Delivering Justice: The Monarch's ʿUrfi Courts and the in Safavid Iran", in: Anver M. Emon and Rumee Ahmed, eds., *The Oxford Hanbook of Islamic Law*, Oxford: Oxford University Press, 511–536.
Aljoumani, Said and Konrad Hirschler (2023), *Owning Books and Preserving Documents in Medieval Jerusalem: The Library of Burhan al-Din*, Edinburgh: Edinburgh University Press.
Agmon, Iris (2004), "Recording Procedures and Legal Culture in the Late Ottoman Shari'a Court of Jaffa, 1865–1890", *Islamic Law and Society* 11/3, 333–377.
Arjomand, Said Amir (1983), "The Office of Mullā-bāshī in Shiʿite Iran", *Studia Islamica* 57, 135–46.
——. (1988), "The Mujtahid of the Age and the Mullā-bāshi: An Intermediate Stage in the Institutionalization of Religious Authority in Shiʿite Iran", in: Said Amir Arjomand, ed., *Authority and Political Culture in Shiism*, Albany: State University of New York Press, 80–97.
Algar, Hamid, "Moḥammad Bāqer Behbahānī", *Encyclopedia Iranica*, vol. IV, Fasc. 1, 98–99.
Asili, Susan (2023), "From Home to Notary: Women's Economic Life in the Late Qajar Period", unpublished paper presented on March 6, 2023 at The Institute for Advanced Studies on Asia, University of Tokyo, Tokyo.
Āshtiyānī, ʿAbbās Iqbāl (1325 sh./1946), "Sharḥ-i ḥāl-i Ḥujjat al-Islām Ḥājjī Sayyid Muḥammad Bāqir Shaftī", *Yādgār* 10, 24–35.
Aykan, Yavuz (2016), *Rendre la justice à Amid. Procédures, acteurs et doctrines dans le contexte ottoman du XVIIIème siècle*, Leiden: Brill.
Barkat, Muḥammad (1397 sh./2019), "Nukātī pīramūn-i zindagī-yi muḥammad mu᾽mīn jazā᾽irī shīrazī", *Rāhyaft-i farhang-i dīnī* year 1 no.3, 11–19.
Bhalloo, Zahir (2014), "Judging the Judge: Judicial Competence in 19th Century Iran", *Bulletin d'etudes orientales* 63, 277–294.
Bhalloo, Zahir and Omid Reza'i (2017), "A *Sharīʿa* Court Document from Neyrīz, Fārs (1303/1886)", *Studia Iranica* 46/1, 77–106.

——. (2019), “Inscribing Authority: Scribal and Archival Practices of a Safavid Decree”, *Journal of the Economic and Social History of the Orient* 62, 824–855.

Bhalloo, Zahir (2023a), “A pre-Mongol New Persian legal document from Islamic Khurāsān dated AH 608/1212 CE”, *Bulletin of the School of Oriental and African Studies* (forthcoming).

Bhalloo, Zahir (2023b), “A *Sharīʿa* Court Judgement of Muḥammad Ḥusayn Fishārakī (d. 1353/1935) reviving the Safavid *Waqf* of Mīrzā Aḥmad Kafrānī (d. after 988/1580)”, in: Omar Anchassi and Robert Gleave, eds., *Islamic Law in Context: A Primary Source Reader*, Cambridge: Cambridge University Press, (forthcoming).

Bhalloo, Zahir and Sayyid Sadiq Husayni Ishkawari (2024a) “Writing and Preserving Islamic Legal Documents: Bukharan Fatwas inside a Central Asian *Jung* Manuscript”, in: Olly Akkerman, ed., *Social Codicology: The Multiple Lives of Texts in Muslim Societies, Leiden Studies in Islam and Society*, Leiden: Brill, (forthcoming).

Bhalloo, Zahir (2024b) “From Document to Written Formula: The *Qāḍī*’s *Sijill* in Early Modern Iran”, in: Toru Miura, ed., *Contracts, Litigation and their Norms Compared: Asian and Islamic Regions*, Tokyo: The Toyo Bunko (forthcoming).

Bhalloo, Zahir and Ryoko Watabe (2024c), “A Fourteenth-Century Persian Archival List from al-Ḥaram al-Sharīf in Jerusalem” *Der Islam* (forthcoming).

Burak, Guy, (2016), “Evidentiary truth claims, imperial registers, and the Ottoman archive: contending legal views of archival and record-keeping practices in Ottoman Greater Syria (seventeenth–nineteenth centuries)”, *Bulletin of the School of Oriental and African Studies* 79/2, 233–254.

Burak, Guy, (2019), “In Compliance with the Old Register”: on Ottoman Documentary Depositories and Archival Consciousness”, *Journal of the Social and Economic History of the Orient* 62, 799–823.

Buskens, Léon (2008), “Tales according to the Book: Professional Witnesses (ʿudul) as Cultural Brokers in Morocco”, in: Baoudin Dupret, Barbara Drieskens and Annelies Moors, eds., *Narratives of Truth in Islamic Law*, London: IB Tauris, 143–160.

Busse, Heribert et al., “Fārs-nāma-ye Nāserī”, *Enyclopeadia Iranica*, vol. IX, Fasc. 4: 374–378.

Calder, Norman (1979), “Judicial Authority in Imāmī Shīʿī Jurispudence”, *Bulletin of the British Society for Middle Eastern Studies* 6, 104–108.

——. (1980), “The Structure of Authority in Imāmī Shīʿī Jurisprudence”, Unpublished PhD thesis, University of London.

——. (1982), “Accomodation and revolution in Imāmī Shīʿī Jurispudence: Khumaynī and the classical tradition”, *Middle Eastern Studies* 18/1, 3–20.

——. (1987), “Legitimacy and Accommodation in Safavid Iran: The Juristic Theory of Muḥammad Baqir al-Sabzavari (d. 1090/1679)”, *Iran* 25, 91–105.

——. (1989), “Doubt and Prerogative: The Emergence of an Imāmī Shīʿī Theory of Ijtihād”, *Studia Islamica* 70, 59–60.

Cole, Juan R.I. (1988), *Roots of North Indian Shi’ism in Iran and Iraq. Religion and State in Awadh, 1722–1859*, Berkley and Los Angeles: University of California Press.

Farīmānī Maḥbūb, Elāhe and Hūshang Khusrawbēgī (1395 sh./2016), “Dafātir-i mālī dar dīwān-sālārī-yi ʿaṣr-i ṣafawī”, *Dū faṣl-nāma-yi ʿilmī pazhūhishī-yi tārīkh-nāma-yi Īrān baʿd az Islām*, year 6, no. 12, 221–251.

Farmayan, Hafez (1974), “Observation on Sources for the Study of Nineteenth- and Twentieth-Century Iranian History”, *International Journal of Middle Eastern Studies* 5/1, 32–49.

Fīrūzbakhsh, Pejmān (1400sh./2022), “Muṣālaḥa-nāma-ī bi-zabān-i fārsī az sāl-i 473 q.” in: Jawād Basharī (ed.) *Bi-yād-i Īraj Afshār*, vol. 1, Tihrān: Bunyād-i mawqūfāt-i Duktur Maḥmūd Afshār, 439–448.

Floor, Willem (2000a), “The Secular Judicial System in Safavid Persia”, *Studia Iranica* 29, 9–60.

——. (2000b) "The ṣadr or head of the Safavid religious administration, judiciary and endowments and other members of the religious institution", *Zeitschrift der Deutschen Morgenländischen Gesellschaft* 150/2, 461–500.
——. (2008), "Weights and Measures in Qajar Iran", *Studia Iranica* 37, 57–115.
Gaubert Christian and Jean-Michel Mouton (2014), *Hommes et villages du Fayyoum dans la documentation papyrologique arabe (Xe-Xie siècles), Hautes études orientales – Moyen et Proche Orient 6*, Geneva: Droz.
Gleave, Robert, (2000), "Two classical Shiʿi theories of qaḍāʾ", in G.R. Hawting, J.A. Mojaddedi and A. Samely, eds., *Islamic and Middle Eastern Texts and Traditions in memory of Norman Calder*, Oxford, Oxford University Press, 105–120.
——. (2007), "The Qāḍī and the Muftī in Akhbari Shiʿi jurisprudence", in: P. Bearman et al., eds., *The Law Applied: Contextualising the Islamic Shariʿa*, New York, IB Tauris, 237–238.
——. (2007), *Scripturalist Islam: The History and Doctrines of the Akhbārī Shīʿī School*, Leiden: Brill.
——.(2013), "Muḥammad Bāqir al-Bihabahānī (d. 1205/1791)", in: Oussama Arabi, David Powers and Susan A. Spectorsky, eds., *Islamic Legal Thought: A Compendium of Muslim Jurists*, Leiden: Brill, 415–434.
Gronke, Monika (1982), *Arabische und persische Privaturkunden des 12. Und 13. Jahrhunderts aus Ardabil (Aserbeidschan)*, Berlin: Klaus Schwarz.
——. (1986), "The Arabic Yarkand Documents", *Bulletin of the School of Oriental and African Studies* 49, 454–507.
Haim, Ofir (2019a), "What is the "Afghan Geniza" A short guide to the collection of the Afghan Manuscripts in the National Library of Israel, with the edition of two documents", *Afghanistan* 2/1, 70–90.
——. (2019b), "Acknowledgement deeds (iqrārs) in Early New Persian from the Area of Bamiyān (395–430 AH/1005–1039 CE)", Journal of the Royal Asiatic Society 29/3, 415–446.
Hallaq, Wael B. (1995), "Model Shurut Works and the Dialectic of Doctrine and Practice", *Islamic Law and Society* 2/2, 109–134.
——. (1998), "The qāḍī's *dīwān* (*sijill*) before the Ottomans", *Bulletin of the School of Oriental and African Studies* 61, 415–436.
Hambly, Gavin R. G. (1991), "Āgā Muḥammad Khān and the Establishment of the Qājār Dynasty", in: Peter Avery, Gavin R.G. Hambly and Charles Melville, eds., *Cambridge History of Iran: From Nadir Shah to the Islamic Republic*, Cambridge: Cambridge University Press, vol. 7, 104–143.
Heern, Zachary M. (2011), "Usuli Shi'ism: the emergence of an Islamic reform movement in early modern Iraq and Iran", Unpublished Ph.D. dissertation, University of Utah.
Hermann, Denis and Omid Rezaʾi (2007), "Le rôle du vaqf dans la formation de la communauté shaykhī kermanī à l'époque Qājār (1259–1354/1843–1906)", *Studia Iranica* 36/1, 87–131.
——. (2008), "Constitution en Vaqf d'une 'Mosquée Sanctuaire' Niʿmatullāhī à Téhéran à l'Époque Pahlavī", *Iran* 46/1, 293–306.
Hermann, Denis (2016), "Dispositions testamentaires et financement de la transmission religieuse: le recours au *waqf* par un gouverneur qajar de la région de Takāb dans la deuxième moitié du XIXᵉ siècle", *Studia Iranica* 45, 275–301.
Herrmann, Gottfried (2004), *Persische Urkunden der Mongolenzeit, Documenta Iranica et Islamica 2*, Harrassowitz Verlag: Wiesbaden.
Herrmann, Gottfried and Gerhard Doerfer (1975),"Ein persisch-mongolischer Erlass aus dem Jahr 725/1325," *Zeitschrift der Deutschen Morgenländischen Gesellschaft* 125, 317–346.
Heyd, Uriel (1969), "Some Aspects of the Ottoman Fetvā", *Bulletin of the School of Oriental and African Studies* (BSOAS) 32/1 (1969), 35–56.

Hoffmann, Birgitt (2000), *Waqf im mongolischen Iran: Rašīduddīns Sorge um Nachruhm und Seelenheil, Freiburger Islamstudien XX*, Franz Steiner Verlag: Stuttgart.

Horst, Heribert (1961), "Zwei Erlasse Šāh Ṭahmāsps I.", *Zeitschrift der Deutschen Morgenländischen Gesellschaft* 110 (1961): 301–09.

——. (1964), *Die Staatsverwaltung der Grosselǧūqen und Ḫōrazmšāhs, 1038–1231: eine Untersuchung nach Urkundenformularen der Zeit, Veröffentlichungen der Orientalischen Kommission, Akademie der Wissenschaften und der Literatur 18*, Verlag Franz Steiner: Wiesbaden.

Hovden, Eirik (2018), *Waqf in Zaydī Yemen: Legal Theory, Codification, and Local Practice*, Leiden: Brill.

(al-) Ḥukamāʾī, ʿImād al-Dīn Shaykh (1387 sh./2008), "Fard-hā-yi Astāna-yi Shaykh Safī Ardabīlī", *Guzārish-i Mīrāth* 25–26, 1–17.

Humāʾī, Jalāl al-Dīn (1327 sh./1948), "Surūsh Iṣfahānī", *Yaghmā* no. 3, 133–140.

İpşirli, Mehmet (1988), "İlmiye mensublarının imza ve tasdik formülleri", in: Mübahat S. Kütükoğlu ed., *Tarih Boyunca Paleografya ve Diplomatik Semineri*, Istanbul, 177–200.

Ishrāqī, Iḥsān (1376 sh./1997), "Muʿarrifī-yi yak sanad az dawrān-i ṣafawī", *Faṣl-nāma-yi ganjīna-yi asnād* 27–28, 4–9.

Isogai, Ken'ichi (2003), "A Commentary on the Closing Formula found in Central Asian Waqf Documents", in: Nobuaki Kondo, ed., *Persian Documents: Social history of Iran and Turan in the fifteenth to nineteenth centuries*, London: Routledge, 3–12.

——. (2011), "Seven Fatwa Documents from Early 20th Century Samarqand: The Function of the Muftī in the Judicial Proceedings Adopted at Central Asian Islamic Court", *Annals of Japan Association of Middle East Studies (AJAMES)* 27/1, 259–282.

Jackson, Peter, "Beglerbegī", *Encyclopaedia Iranica*, vol.IV, Fasc. 1, 84.

Jackson, Sherman (1996), *Islamic Law and the State: The Constitutional Jurispudence of Shihāb al-Dīn al-Qarafī*, Leiden: Brill.

Jaʿfariyān, Rasūl (1382 sh./2003), "Dar-āmadī bar mushārikat-i ʿulamā dar sākhtar-i dawlat-i ṣafawī: taʿāmul-i khāndān-i karakī wa dawlat-i ṣafawī", *Ḥukūmat-i Islāmī*, year 18, no. 2, 122–194.

Jahānpur, Farhang (1348/1969), "Farāmīn-i pādshāhān-i Ṣafawī dar mūza-yi Brītāniyā", *Barrasī-hā-yi tarīkhī* 4, 221–264.

Johansen, Baber (1997), "Formes de langage et fonctions publiques: stéréotypes, témoins et offices dans la preuve par l'écrit en droit musulman", *Arabica* 44/3, 333–376.

Khadr, Mohamed (1967), "Deux actes de waqf d'un Qarāḫanide d'Asie Centrale [avec une introduction par Claude Cahen]", *Journal Asiatique* 255/3–4, 305–334.

Khan, Geoffrey, *Bills, Letters and Deeds Arabic Papyri of the 7th-11th Centuries*, Oxford: Oxford University Press, 1993.

Khusrawī, Muḥammad ʿAlī (1384 sh./2005), *Haft waqf-nāma. Namūna-ī az yakṣad va haftād sāl-i waqf-nāma dar dawra-yi ṣafawiyya*, Tehran: Ṣāʾin.

Khusrawbēgī, Hūshang and Elāhe Maḥbūb (1394 sh./2016), "Barrasī-yi sākhtār wa ajzā-yi daftar-i tawjīhāt dar ʿaṣr-i ṣafawī", *Pazhūhishī-hā-yi īrān-shināsī* 5/2, 33–50.

Knost, Stefan (2006), "The Waqf in Court: Lawsuits over Religious Endowments in Ottoman Aleppo", in: Muḥammad Khalid Masud, Rudolph Peters and David S. Powers, eds., *Dispensing Justice in Islam: Qāḍī s and their Judgements*, Leiden: Brill, 427–450.

Kohlberg, Etan, "Bahāʾ-al-Dīn ʿĀmelī," *Encyclopaedia Iranica*, Vol. III, Fasc. 4, 429–430. URL: http://www.iranicaonline.org/articles/baha-al-din-ameli-shaikh-mohammad-b (accessed online 1 April 2023).

Kohlberg, Etan (2014), "Introduction: Shi'i Hadīth", in: *The Study of Shi'i Islam: History, Theology and Law. Papers Originally Delivered at the First International Colloquium Dedicated Exclusively to Shi'i*

Studies, Held in 2010 at The Institute of Ismaili Studies, London, eds. Farhad Daftary and Gurdofarid Miskinzoda, The Institute of Ismaili Studies, London-I.B. Tauris, 165–179.
Kondo, Nobuaki. (2003), "The Waqf of Ustad Abbas: Rewrites of the Deeds in Qājār Tehran", in: Nobuaki Kondo, ed., *Persian Documents: Social History of Iran and Turan in the Fifteenth to Nineteenth Centuries*, London: Routledge, 106–128.
——. (2009), "Shi'i 'Ulamā' and Ijāza during the Nineteenth Century", *Orient* XLIV, 55–76.
——. (2014), "The Lives of Qabalahs: Annotation, Transcription and Registration of Documents in Early Modern Iran", in: N. Balbir and M. Szuppe, eds., *Lecteurs et copistes dans les traditions manuscrites iraniennes, indiennes et centrasiatiques, Eurasian Studies 12*, 561–575.
——. (2017), *Islamic Law and Society in Iran: A Social History of Qājār Tehran*, London: Routledge.
——. (2021) "Conditional Sales and other Types of Loans in Qajar Iran", *Journal of the Economic and Social History of the Orient* 64, 5–6, 615–639.
Kotzageorgis, Phokion P. (2014), "The Multiple Certifications in Ottoman Judicial Documents (Hüccets) from Monastic Archives", *Archivum Ottomanicum* 31, 117–127.
Kütükoğlu, Mübahat S. (1998), *Osmanlı Belgelerinin Dili*, Istanbul, 1998, 350–359.
Lambton, Ann K. S. (1967), "The Case of Ḥājjī Nūr al-Dīn, 1823–47: A Study in Land Tenure", *Bulletin of the School of Oriental and African Studies* 30, 54–72.
——. (1969), *Landlord and Peasant in Persia: A Study of Land Tenure and Land Revenue Administration*, Oxford: Oxford University Press.
Livingston, Daisy, (2018), "Managing Paperwork in Mamluk Egypt (c. 1250–1517): A Documentary Approach to Mamluk Archival Practices", Unpublished Ph.D. dissertation, University of London, School of Oriental and African Studies (SOAS).
Mahdavi, Asghar (1983), "The Significance of Private Archives for the Study of the Economic and Social History of Iran in the Late Qajar Period", *Iranian Studies* 16/3–4, 243–278.
Mahdawī, Muṣliḥ al-Dīn (1371 sh./1992), *Khāndān-i shaykh al-islām-i iṣfahān*, Gulbahār: Iṣfahān.
——. (1386 sh./2007), *A'lām Iṣfahan*, vol.1, Iṣfahān: Markaz-i Iṣfahān-shināsī wa khāna-yi milal.
Martin, Vanessa (2008), "'Murder in Bushehr in 1844: The Case of Bibi Asilu", *Iran* 46, 285–292.
Masjidī, Ḥusayn (1381 sh./2003), "Sayf al-Dawla Sulṭān Muḥammad Mīrzā", *Majalla- yi pazhūhishī-yi dānishgāh-i iṣfahān* 13–1, 67–90.
Messick, Brinkley (1996), *The Calligraphic State: Textual Domination and History in a Muslim Society*, Berkley: University of California Press.
——. (2001), "Indexing the Self: Intent and Expression in Islamic Legal Acts", *Islamic Law and Society* 8, 151–178.
——. (2002), "Evidence: From Memory to Archive", *Islamic Law and Society* 9/2, 231–270.
——. (2018), *Shari'a Scripts: A Historical Anthropology*, New York: Columbia University Press.
Milad, Salwa Ibrahim (1975), "Registres judiciaires du tribunal de la Ṣāliḥiyya Nağmiyya. Étude des archives [avec 11 planches]", *Annales Islamologiques* 12 (1974), 161–243.
Müller, Christian (2010), "Écrire pour établir la preuve orale en Islam. La pratique d'un tribunal à Jérusalem au xive siècle", in: Akira Saito and Yusuke Nakamura, eds., *Les outils de la pensée. Étude historique et comparative des « textes »*, Paris: Éditions de la Maison des sciences de l'homme, 63–97.
——. (2011), "The Ḥaram al-Šarīf collection of Arabic legal documents in Jerusalem: a Mamlūk court archive?", *Al-Qanṭara* 32, 435–459.
——. (2013), *Der Kadi und seine Zeugen: Studie der mamlukischen Haram-Dokumente aus Jerusalem (Abhandlungen für die Kunde des Morgenlandes, Band 85)*, Wiesbaden: Harrassowitz Verlag.
——. (2018), "The Power of the Pen: Cadis and their Archives from Writings to registering Proof of a previous action taken", in: Alessandro Bausi, Christian Brockmann, Michael Friedrich, Sabine

Kienitz, eds., *Manuscripts and Archives: Comparative Views on Record-Keeping*, Berlin: De Gruyter, 361–385.

Newman, Andrew, J. (1992a), "The Nature of the Akhbārī/Uṣūlī Dispute in Late Ṣafawid Iran. Part 1: 'Abdallāh al-Samāhijī's *'Munyat al-Mumārisīn'*", *Bulletin of the School of Oriental and African Studies*, 55/1, 22–51.

Newman, Andrew, J. (1992b), "The Nature of the Akhbārī/Uṣūlī Dispute in Late Ṣafawid Iran, Part 2: The Conflict Reassessed", 55/2, 250–261.

Neyestani, Jawād, "Gorgān, vii. From the Safavids to the End of the Pahlavi Era", *Encyclopeadia Iranica*, vol.11, Fasc. 2, 154–162.

Nezam-Mafi Mansoureh Ettehadieh (1989), "The Council for the Investigation of Grievances: A Case Study of Nineteenth Century Iranian Social History", *Iranian Studies* 22/1, 51–61.

Oberauer, Norbert, (2021), "The Function of Documents in Islamic Court Procedure: a Multi-Dimensional Approach", *Islamic Law and Society* 28/3, 156–233.

Peters, Rudolph et al. (2000), "Wakf", *Enyclopeadia of Islam*, 2nd edition, vol.11, 59–63.

Powers, David S. (1990), "A Court Case from Fourteenth-Century North Africa", *Journal of the American Oriental Society* 110, 229–254.

Rāġib, Yūsuf (1997), "La parole, le geste et l'écrit dans l'acte de vente", *Arabica* 44/3, 407–422.

Rajani, Kumail (2021), "Between Qum and Qayrawān: Unearthing early Shii *ḥadīth* sources", *Bulletin of the School of Oriental and African Studies* 84/3, 419–422.

Reza'i, Omid (2022), "Ṣarīḥ'ol-Melk va'l-Vaqf by Mīrzā Ḥabīb'ollāh Sharīfī dated 1519", *Journal of Asian and African Studies* 103, 55–92.

Riḍā'ī, Umīd (1382 sh./2004), "Khaṭṭ wa muhr-i umanā-yi sharʿ-i tihrān dar dawra-yi qajar", *Mīrāth-i Jāwidān* 43–44, 60–91.

——. (1383 sh./2004), "Barrasī-yi ʿillal wa tiʿdād-i nisbī-yi tahiyya-yi nuskha-hā-yi hamsang-i yak sanad bar asās-i waqf-nāma-hā-yi tihrān dar dawra-yi qājār", *Mīrāth-i Jāwīdān* 46, 76–83.

——. (1385 sh./2006), "Silsila-yi shaykh al-islāmiyya-yi Tammāmī-yi shīrāz: pīshgām dar thabt-i niwishtijāt-i sharʿiyya-yi dawra-yi qājār", *Mīrāth-i jāwīdān* 54, 77–94.

——. (1385 sh./2007), "Āqā Sayyid Ṣādiq Mujtahid-i Sangalajī wa thabt-i niwishtijāt-i sharʿiyya-yi dawra-yi qājār", *Mīrāth-i Jāwīdān* 56, 57–68.

——. (1386 sh./2007), "Jāygāh-i khāndān-i bihbahānī dar tawlīd wa thabt-i niwishtijāt-i sharʿiyya", *Mīrāth-i Jāwīdān*, 44–55.

——. (1386 sh./2008), "Barrasī wa taḥlīl-i muhr-hā-yi bī-yāddāsht dar qabāla-hā-yi dār al-ʿilm-i shīrāz, *Mīrāth-i Jāwīdān* 60, 26–38.

——. (1388 sh./2009), "Naẓariyya-yī bar sabk-i mubāyaʿa-nāma-nigārī-yi fuqahā-yi shāfiʿi-yi Kurdistān az dawra-yi afshāriyya tā qājāriyya", *Mīrath-i Jāwīdān* 66, 28–47.

——. (1388 sh./2009), *Qabāla-hā-yi Pārsī: pardāzish-i ṣūrī wa muhtawā'ī*, Tehran: Intishārāt-i Uswa.

——. (1390 sh./2011), "Pishīna wa nahw-i thabt-i asnād-i sharʿī dar bandar-i būshahr", *Faṣl-nāma-yi asnād-i bahāristān:* 79–94.

——. (1390 sh./2012) "Kārkard wa jāygāh-i khāndan-i tammāmī dar manṣab-i shaykh al-islamī-yi shīrāz dar dawra-yi qājār", Unpublished M.A. thesis, Dānishgāh-i Āzād-i Islāmī, Tehran.

——. (1391 sh./2012), "Digital kardan-i arshīw-hā wa ḍarūrat-i tawajjuh bi-furm dar ṭūmār-hā-yi chand sanadī (namūna-yi mawrid-i muṭālaʿa, ṭūmārī az shīrāz-i dawra-yi afshār)", *Asnād-i Baharistān* 5, 391–408.

——. (1392–1393 sh./2014), "Mithāl-i intiṣāb-i muḥtasib-i qazwīn dar sāl-i 1058 qamarī", *Tārīkh-i Irān* 73/5, 43–52.

——. (1394 sh./2015), "Arzish-i mubādala-i-yi kutub-i ṣafā-yi shīrāzī dar sāl-i 1337 q./1297 sh.: rawish-i taʿsīr-i nirkh-i mabālīgh-i qadīm bi-arzish-i fiʿlī-yi ān-ha", *Awrāq-i ʿatīq* 4, 815–822.

——. (1397 sh./2018), "Thabt-i qabāla-hā-yi qarn-i dahum-i hijrī qamarī dar jarīda-yi maḥkama-yi sharʿ", *Pazhūhish-hā-yi nuskha-shināsi* 2, 213–220.
——. (1397 sh./2018), "Istifāda az naqsh-i muhr-hā-yi shakhsī dar bāz-shināsī-yi dawbāra-yi shaykh al-islām-hā-yi shīrāz dar dawra-yi qājār", *Faṣl-nāma-yi arshīw-i millī* 15, 102–103.
——. (1401 sh./2022), "Pārcha-niwishta-hā-yi ḥuqūqī dar īrān-i dawra-yi mudarn", in: Sayyid Muḥammad Ḥusayn Ḥakīm ed. *Awrāq-i ʿatīq, majmūʿa-yi muṭālaʿāt-i matn-pazhūhī, nuskha-shināsī wa fihrist-nigārī, daftar-i panjum*, vol.5, Tehran: Kitāb-khāna, Mūza wa Markaz-i Asnād-i Majlis-i Shūrā-yi Islāmī, 937–956.
Rizvi, Sajjad H. (2010), "Sayyid Niʿmat Allāh al-Jazāʾirī and his Anthologies: Anti-Sufism, Shiism and Jokes in the Safavid World", *Die Welt des Islams* 50, 224–242.
Rustow, Marina (2020), *The Lost Archive: Traces of a Caliphate in a Cairo Synagogue*, New Jersey: Princeton University Press.
Rustow Marina (2021), "New Approaches to Islamic Law and the Documentary Record before 1500", *Journal of Islamic Law at Harvard Law School*, URL: https://journalofislamiclaw.com/current/article/view/rustow (accessed online 16 April 2023).
Sartori, Paolo (2017), *Visions of Justice: Sharīʿa and Cultural Change in Russian Central Asia*, Leiden: Brill.
——. and James Pickett (2019), "From the Archetypical Archive to Cultures of Documentation", *Journal of the Economic and Social History of the Orient* 62, 773–798.
Sarwān Muḥammad Kashmīrī (undated), ed., *Nabard-hā-yi Āq Qalaʿa*, *Barrasī-hā-yi Tārīkh* no. 4, year 5, 75–97.
Schneider, Irene (2002), "Muḥammad Bāqir Šaftī (1180–1260/1766–1844) und die Isfahaner Gerichtsbarkeit", *Der Islam* 79, 240–273.
——. (2006), *The Petitioning System in Iran. State, Society and Power Relations in the Late 19th Century*, Harrassowitz: Wiesbaden.
Sepis, A. (1844), "Quelques mots sur l'état religieux actuel de la Perse", *Revue de l'Orient* 3/9–12, 97–114.
Shahīdī, Hamīda (1397 sh./2019), *Farmān-hā-yi āstān-i quds-i raḍawī dar dawra-yi ṣafawiyya, parwāncha-hā, arqām wa taʿlīqcha-hā*, Mashhad: Bunyād-i Pazhūhish-hā-yi Islāmī-yi Āstān-i Quds-i Raḍawī.
Sheikh al-Hokamaee, Emad al-Din (2013), "La vision religieuse des Safavides, la conservation des archives pré-safavides et l altération des documents", in: Anne Regourd, ed., *Documents et histoire. Islam*, VIIe-XVIe siècle, Geneva: Droz, 137–154.
Stern, Samuel Miklós (1964), *Fatimid Decrees: Original Documents from the Fatimid Chancery*, London: Faber and Faber.
Stewart, Devin J. (1996), "The First Shaykh al-Islām of the Safavid Capital Qazvin", *Journal of the American Oriental Society* 116/3, 387–405.
——. (1991), "A Biographical Notice on Bahāʾ al-Dīn al-ʿĀmilī (d. 1030/1621)", *Journal of the American Oriental Society* 111, 563–571.
——. (1998). "The Lost Biography of Bahāʾ al-Dīn al-ʿĀmilī and the Reign of Shāh Ismāʿīl II in Safavid Historiography", *Iranian Studies* 31/2, 177–205.
Ṭabāṭabāʾī, Ḥusayn Mudarrisī (1352 sh./1973), "Yak sanad az qarn-i dahum", *Wahīd* 121, 991–996.
Ṭabāṭabāʾī, Muḥīt (1344 sh./ 1965), "Shiʿrī az Vafā dar dīwān-i Yaghmā", *Yaghmā* 4– 204, 182–184.
——. (1354 sh./1975), "Madrasa-yi Luṭf ʿAlī Khān Turshīzī dar Zavārih", *Kānūn-i Sardaftarān* 9, 11–17.
——. (1354sh/1975), "Yak āthār-i arzanda-yi chāp nāshuda az yak marjaʿ-i taqlīd", *Kānūn-i Sardaftarān* 7, 15–22.
Tak, Ekram (2019), *16–17. Yüzyıl Üsküdar Şer'iyye Sicilleri Diplomatik Bilimi Bakımından Bir İnceleme*, Ankara: Neyir Matbaacılık.

Tawīsrkānī, Sayyid Aḥmad (1376 sh./1998), "Ikhtilāf-i naẓar-i dū faqīh-i ham ʿasr dar yak masʾala-yi waqfī", *Mīrāth-i Jāvīdān* 19–20, 25–33.
——. (1379 sh./2000) "Pazhūhishī dar masʾala-yi qabḍ wa qabūl dar ʿaqd-i waqf", *Mīrāth-i Jāvīdān* 31–32, 25–33.
Tyan, Émile (1943), *Histoire de l'organisation judiciaire en pays d'Islam, Tome II*, Annales de l'Université de Lyon, Troisième Série, Harissa, Lebanon: Imprimerie de Saint-Paul.
——. (1959), *Le notariat et le régime de la preuve par écrit dans la pratique du droit musulman*, Harissa, Lebanon: Imprimerie de Saint Paul.
Teh Gallop, Annabel and Venetia Porter (2012), *Lating Impressions: Seals from the Islamic World*, Kuala Lumpur: Islamic Arts Museum Malaysia.
Velkov, Asparouh (1992), "Signatures-formules des agents judiciaires dans les documents ottomans à caractère financier et juridique", *Turcica* xxiv, 193–240.
Wakin, Jeanette A. *The Function of Documents in Islamic Law: The Chapters on Sales from Ṭaḥāwi's Kitāb al-Shurūṭ al-Kabīr*, Albany: State University of New York Press, 1972.
Warscheid, Ismail (2017), *Droit musulman et société au Sahara prémoderne. La justice islamique dans les oasis du Grand Touat (Algérie) aux XVII ^e^ -XIX ^e^ siècles*, Leiden: Brill.
Werner, Christoph (1999), "A Safavid Vaqf in Qājār Times – the Ẓahīrīya in Tabriz", in: Rika Gyselen and Maria Szuppe eds., *Matériaux pour l'Histoire économique du monde Iranien*, Paris: Peeters, 233–248.
——. (2000), *An Iranian Town in Transition: A Social and Economic History of the Elites of Tabriz, 1748–1848*, Wiesbaden: Harrasowitz.
——. (2003), "Formal Aspects of Qajar Deeds of Sale", in: Nobuaki Kondo ed., *Persian Documents: Social History of Iran and Turan in the Fifteenth- Nineteenth Centuries*, London: Routledge, 13–49.
——. (2005), "Urf oder Gewohnheitsrecht in Iran: Quellen, Praxis und Begrifflichkeit", in: Michael Kemper and Maurus Reinkowski eds., *Rechtspluralismus in der Islamischen Welt: Gewohnheitsrecht zwischen Staat und Gesellschaft*, Berlin-New York: Walter de Gruyter: 153–175.
—— Daniel Zakrweski and Hans-Thomas Tillschneider (2013), *Die Kuǧuǧī-Stiftungen in Tabrīz. Ein Beitrag zur Geschichte der Ǧalayiriden (Edition, Übersetzung, Kommentar)* Weisbaden: Reichert Verlag.
——. (2021), "Flexible Forms of Contracts: Transactions through Fictitious Settlements (*ṣulḥ/muṣālaḥa*) in Iran", *Journal of the Social and Economic History of the Orient* 64, 5–6, 864–893.
Yaycioğlu, ʿAlī (1997), "Ottoman Fatwa: An Essay on Legal Consultation in the Ottoman Empire", Unpublished M.A. dissertation., Bilkent University.

Index of Places

https://doi.org/10.1515/9783111239736-011

Index of People

https://doi.org/10.1515/9783111239736-012

Index of Technical Terms

https://doi.org/10.1515/9783111239736-013